D1572336

EASTERN EUROPE ...

CENTRAL EUROPE ...

EUROPE

EASTERN EUROPE ...

CENTRAL EUROPE ...

EUROPE

edited by
Stephen R. Graubard

Westview Press
BOULDER • SAN FRANCISCO • OXFORD

Copyright © 1991 by Westview Press, Inc.

Published in 1991 in the United States of America by Westview Press, Inc., 5500 Central Avenue, Boulder, Colorado 80301, and in the United Kingdom by Westview Press, 36 Lonsdale Road, Summertown, Oxford OX2 7EW

Library of Congress Cataloging-in-Publication Data
Eastern Europe . . . Central Europe . . . Europe / edited by Stephen R. Graubard.
    p. cm.
  Includes index.
  ISBN 0-8133-1189-6 (hc). ISBN 0-8133-8150-9 (pb).
  1. Europe, Eastern—Politics and government—1989– 2. Central Europe—Politics and government. I. Graubard, Stephen Richards.
DJK51.E26 1991
940.5—dc20   90-24995
                                                                  CIP

Printed and bound in the United States of America

The paper used in this publication meets the requirements of the American National Standard for Permanence of Paper for Printed Library Materials Z39.48-1984.

10   9   8   7   6   5   4   3   2   1

Contents

v

vi   *Contents*

Introduction

Nineteen eighty-nine will almost certainly figure as one of the seminal years in twentieth-century European history, perhaps in world history. Although it is not certain to achieve the universal, almost instantaneous recognition that is connected to certain other dates, including 1789, 1815, 1848, 1870, 1917, 1933, 1939, and 1945, there are few other years in the post–World War II era that compare with it. Many other years have seemed crucial in their time, and one thinks immediately of 1953, the year of Stalin's death and the East Berlin uprising; 1956, the year of the Hungarian revolution and the aborted efforts by Great Britain and France to keep Nasser from seizing control of the Suez Canal; 1968, the year of the Soviet crackdown on Czechoslovakia and of growing student rebellions in Western Europe, particularly in France, where de Gaulle's Fifth Republic seemed on the verge of collapse; 1973, the year of the first of the oil crises and the rise of a new international force in OPEC; and several other years since that might be considered important because of the elections of Margaret Thatcher in Great Britain and Ronald Reagan in the United States and the rise to power of Mikhail Gorbachev in the Soviet Union. However, it is not likely that any of these years will seem as monumental from the perspective of the twenty-first century as 1989—because of the events in Eastern Europe and the Soviet Union.

Military and political conditions largely created by the events of World War II, in part ratified by the Yalta agreements, and left essentially intact despite the continuing international discord and disagreements—conspicuous features of the whole of the Cold War period—were accepted by much of the world as seemingly inevitable. They were the price that others were

vii

required to pay for the astonishing Soviet victory in World War II. Even though that price included such obviously glaring institutional aberrations as the construction of the Berlin Wall, dividing a city and a nation, few imagined that such malign inventions would soon disappear.

Indeed, when the group responsible for this book first assembled in Cambridge at the House of the American Academy of Arts and Sciences, in April 1987, there were many reasons for believing that the situation in Eastern Europe—Central Europe was the phrase preferred by some—although clearly and obviously changing, would not soon be wholly and radically transformed. Yet, a review of the transcribed discussions of that informal and closed conference suggests that the anticipations of change were real, though the timetable remained uncertain. Although no one explicitly said, "This cannot last; this will not last," compelling arguments were advanced for believing that Europe east of the Elbe was then in a state of transformation, that greater changes were almost certainly in the offing, and that Stalin's Cold War vision of the world evolving into some sort of Communist monolith was never really possible. (That vision was even less accurate in 1987 than it might have been some two or three decades previously.)

Acutely aware of the intellectual and political stirrings in large parts of the European Communist world, those who helped plan this study began by doubting that continued control by repressive Communist regimes was likely and questioning whether the efforts to create something like the "civil societies" of the West would be permanently defeated. After the meeting, I sought to give something of the flavor of the occasion to contributors to this volume who had not participated.

> We start with a number of simple propositions: that history mattered enormously in the ways these individual societies developed after the Second World War; that today, politically, socially, economically, and culturally, there are substantial differences among them; that their individual populations, geographic locations, resources, and traditions need constantly to be taken into account. We are not interested in dwelling simply on the uniformities among them, though these, where they exist, will be given considerable attention.

I alluded to recent efforts of certain Communist systems to relate to their indigenous cultures and mentioned particularly the interest evoked, "in the instances of resistance to old-fashioned totalitarian controls, or at least certain kinds of Party domination." Again, reporting on the discussions held in Cambridge, I wrote with a certain calculated imprecision: "We think we know what the Soviet interest in the region is. Do we? What is the American interest, the British interest, the Japanese interest? Who, in short, is paying heed to this region, and why?"

In late 1987 and early 1988 invitations went to scholars and others who knew the problems of the region intimately; the majority lived either in Western Europe or in the area we were increasingly defining as Central or Eastern Europe. Given all that has happened since 1988, it is important to recall how events stood even as late as the winter months of that year. It was a time when it was impossible to ask for anything but anonymous contributions from individuals in certain countries. Men and women who were open and known dissidents felt free to write under their own names, having already done so frequently at some risk to themselves in both European and American publications. There were others, however, who chose to be more careful, who risked a great deal by writing, who were best reached not through invitations sent by open mail but by much more discreet means, generally involving individuals who would act as trusted intermediaries. In certain countries, the controls were so exacting, the penalties so severe, that one did not even consider asking for a contribution. As the project on Eastern Europe proceeded, it became increasingly clear that those countries included, obviously, Romania and Albania, but also certain others that were still governed by people whose sympathies for the more orthodox Stalinist policies were as conspicuous in 1988 as they had been in 1953.

Because relations between the United States and many of these countries had improved markedly by the late 1980s, because official diplomatic ties and scholarly exchanges made possible the kinds of informal discussions that would not have occurred earlier, conversations took place in New York and Washington, D.C., that would have been wholly unthinkable even in the late 1970s. It was possible to meet openly with a major East German scholar, for example, who might be unusually frank in his comments about his own country, the Soviet Union, the Federal Republic, Poland, or the United States. Such candor, however, was generally limited to oral and private communications; it did not translate into a willingness to become involved in what could be seen as an American intellectual publishing enterprise. Men and women of the most diverse views were ready to voice their opinions over coffee, but they were not prepared to say the same things in print or indeed, to write at all. Invitations to contribute to the *Dædalus* volume had to be sent through appropriate channels; one knew better than to imagine that a letter sent to a private home address in the German Democratic Republic would be responded to affirmatively, even when the request was intentionally open— essentially an invitation to write on anything that the individual cared to treat. In short, if one was serious in searching for contributions from authors still living in many of Europe's "people's democracies," one had to accept the fact that in all but a few countries individuals would not be prepared to pay the penalties for candor, which might be high—often prohibitive.

Still, even such an account does not tell the whole story of a time that from the perspective of autumn 1990 seems extraordinarily remote. In 1987 in Poland, for example, although martial law had been lifted, Solidarity remained an outlawed organization. It may have been possible to ask for a contribution from Bronisław Geremek, one of Europe's leading medieval historians and one of Solidarity's major intellectual figures, expelled from the Polish Academy of Sciences in April 1985; but one could not expect the Polish government to grant Geremek an exit permit to join the other authors in conferences abroad. From the first Geremek intended to write. The fact that there is a contribution from him in this volume is testimony to his insistence that his own changed situation and that of Solidarity, and his new position in the Sejm, had not precluded his stealing hours from his many duties to complete the essay.

There have been so many remarkable reversals of fortune and so many unanticipated events that one can only look with sympathy and understanding on those studies of the region published in 1987 and 1988 that seem so antiquated in the context of more recent events. Indeed, even some works that appeared in 1989 seem to have an element of quaintness about them, as if written before a great flood, before the summer and autumn storms that wholly transformed the landscape. Looking at a catalogue of an exhibition of the works of twelve artists from the German Democratic Republic, at Harvard in the autumn of 1989, one has a sense of how dramatic the changes have been. To secure the paintings—to arrange the exhibition at all—required great diplomatic patience and tact. It is therefore not at all strange that the Editor's Introduction to the catalogue, although not explicitly intending to flatter the East Germans, should include what must at the time have seemed an innocuous statement: "the G.D.R. celebrates its 40th anniversary on October 7, 1989, and this has certainly focused attention on the country, its achievements, and its increasingly prominent role on the world stage." Who could have dreamed of the events that occurred in East Berlin on October 7, with the cries of "Gorby, Gorby" echoing in the streets and nightly demonstrations in many of the principal cities of the country? Who could have imagined the events of the next year, culminating in the unification of Germany on October 3, 1990?

To recall these incidents is to express the good fortune of those who planned this volume, who saw it appear at a most propitious time, in January 1990, initially in *Dædalus*, the Journal of the American Academy of Arts and Sciences. It is a comment on what they wrote in the autumn of 1989 that they were obliged to change so little in the revolutionary days that immediately preceded the actual publication of the *Dædalus* issue. Though some used the fax machine to incorporate certain last-minute changes and a few have added addenda for this edition, the greatest part of the study remains essentially as it was when originally conceived and executed. I regard this as a tribute to what the authors were able to do in the first instance, at a moment when it would have been easy to become wildly euphoric, unprofessional, to make egregious blunders.

The book was planned at a time when it was already apparent that the old concept of a frozen and immobile East European society, subject wholly to the dictates and whims of Moscow, sclerotic and uniform, required substantial revision. It is no accident that a number of the authors have made such ample use of historical materials. From the beginning, the importance of the pre–World War II period was recognized; there was concern also with the long period when these states were not independent, when they formed parts of multinational empires largely destroyed as a consequence of World War I. There was never any nostalgia in the planning of the original edition for the world theoretically "lost" either in 1914 or in 1918, though there was never any denial of its importance.

Indeed, one of the more remarkable features of these essays— what makes them different from many others—is that they avoid all attempt at prophecy (on the grand scale) while insisting, implicitly and explicitly, that we think again in quite new ways of all that has happened to Europe and the world since the Russian Revolution. There is a real possibility that much of what was once thought to be permanent and immutable will be shown to be quite as ephemeral as the European monarchies that disappeared in the second decade of the twentieth century. The transformations that have occurred since the publication of these essays only confirm a very simple proposition: The twentieth century is not ending as some imagined it would— with two great world powers confronting each other and with a good part of Europe essentially dormant, subordinate to the great nuclear power of the East.

The transition from the seemingly permanent conditions that obtained for decades, particularly in the Soviet bloc, is now only beginning. What will happen in the next months (and years) in these disparate societies is of course preoccupying; still, certain larger questions must also be confronted. Are the recent events harbingers of something that has been too rarely considered, almost never uttered: that neither in the East nor in the West is post–World War II society moving toward those ends considered by so many experts, so recently and so confidently, as inevitable? If the events of 1989 have been surprising—if they have outdistanced and exceeded all expectations—have they not also suggested that even the most authoritarian regimes are less capable of transforming societies than is sometimes imagined?

This fact, for some, is an additional reason for jubilation, for seeing 1989 as a veritable *annus mirabilis*. Without questioning or minimizing the possibilities of further and even more significant change, we might find it useful to exercise some caution. Such caution, it seems to me, is implicitly recommended by many who know the region, accept its complexity, have a sense of history, and are unwilling at this juncture to make new grand generalizations of the kind that were common when so many prated about "Eastern Europe."

The title of the *Dædalus* issue and of this edition, *Eastern Europe . . . Central Europe . . . Europe,* suggests a progression that is important. The first phrase, coined to express the realities of the Cold War, seems almost obsolete; the second, preferred by certain individuals and groups in the 1960s, 1970s, and 1980s, retains much of its earlier ambiguity; the third, the term of the moment, may come to be increasingly used in the 1990s. Whether that progression will lead many in the West to reflect on why or how they came to settle for so much less—whether it was really ever necessary for them to do so—will be more than a debate about mistakes made at Yalta, decisions taken by NATO, and policies pursued by the Soviet Union and the United States. The debate will have to do with the nature of war and revolution in the twentieth century—the tragedies and follies, promises and foibles, both political and intellectual, that have done so much to shape this violent age.

The final essay in this volume by Z (Professor Martin Malia of the University of California, Berkeley) caused a great stir at the time of its publication. Excerpted segments, published originally in the *New York Times,* and then widely disseminated abroad, led some to be overwhelmingly concerned with Z's identity. Only gradually did they come to recognize the significance of his argument and begin to show interest in debating its merits; that discussion goes on to this day. The reasons for the anonymity, on which the author insisted, were compelling. Given the conditions at the time that Malia wrote his essay, a signed essay would have endangered his sources—overwhelmingly younger men and women known to the KGB who had not yet emerged as active critics of the Gorbachev regime.

The euphoria of 1989 is now a thing of the past, but so much has changed in just one year. In these circumstances, it is well to look at the new governments in Eastern Europe, and indeed at the new Germany, with tolerance and understanding. The other obligation, no less serious, may be to study closely what is happening in the rest of Europe and in the United States in order to gauge how both are reacting to the new political map of Europe. A postwar era appears to have ended in 1989, but it is not at all clear what the new age is likely to bring. The principal merit of this volume is that it is a work of history, not of prophecy; and a knowledge of history may be more helpful in the present circumstances than any number of imaginative projections, essentially utopian, without any firm grounding in the traditions and memories of the region.

Thanks are due to Timothy Garton Ash, who helped in innumerable ways, often under great pressure, and who set aside other obligations and commitments.

Stephen R. Graubard

Mitteleuropa?

Timothy Garton Ash

One *of the greatest questions of the moment is whether German hopes for a new Central Europe can be reconciled with those of their immediate neighbors to the east. Of course there are many German visions of Central Europe, just as there are many Czech, Polish, and Hungarian ones. But there is also a hard reality of West German policy in this region:* Ostpolitik. *Now more than ever we need to look carefully at both the visions and the reality.*

Central Europe is "a great territory of unanswered questions and unresolved contradictions, a region of half-demands which until now have enjoyed as little realization as proposals counter to them, and which seem products of visionary caprice because they aim at something whole, something new and enormous." Thus wrote Bruno Bauer in 1854.[1] Plus ça change, plus c'est la même chose!

One of the major unresolved tensions in the contemporary debate about "Central Europe" is the strain between the visions, proposals, and half-demands of Hungarian, Czech, and to a lesser extent, Polish intellectuals and political activists, on the one hand, and those of West German intellectuals and politicians on the other. Of course there is no single East European or West German concept of Central Europe. The discussion is far too diffuse and inchoate for that. A few generalizations may be ventured nonetheless.

The East European debate, as initiated by Milan Kundera and carried forward by György Konrád, Václav Havel, Czeslaw Milosz,

Timothy Garton Ash is a Fellow at St. Antony's College, Oxford University. This article was completed before the dramatic events of late autumn 1989 in East Germany.

1

Danilo Kiš, Mihály Vajda, and Milan Šimečka, to name but a few
leading intellectual participants,[2] is generally remarkable for its
omission of Germany and "the German question." Historically, it
looks back toward Austria-Hungary and forward "beyond Yalta."
Politically, it looks away from Soviet Russia, toward an idealistically
defined "West." The Eastern spiritual-political frontier is an object of
fierce controversy: how does Russia stand in relation to Europe?[3]
The Western spiritual-political frontier, in contrast, has been curi-
ously uncontroversial. To be sure, independent East European intellectuals have made serious attempts to look afresh at the German
question.[4] The perhaps rather obvious—but emotionally difficult—
conclusion has been reached that it is hard to overcome the Yalta
division of Europe without overcoming the division of Germany. Yet
this intellectual-political argument has not been integrated into any
common definition of the goal of restoring Central Europe.

The West German debate, however, is remarkable for the relatively
small part played by these East European visions and aspirations. It
is to some extent true that the concept of *Mitteleuropa* was reintroduced into German intellectual discourse via Paris (through Kundera), Budapest (through Konrád), and Prague (through Havel).[5] But
once reintroduced from these sources it rapidly took on a life of its
own, picking up themes of the so-called "Historians' debate," the
unceasing discussion about German identity and the German question, the future of Berlin, German-German relations, *Ostpolitik* more
generally, security policy, and the Federal Republic of Germany's
relationship with the United States.

In fact, if one looks more closely, the concept of Mitteleuropa had
already resurfaced, very cautiously, in German *political* discourse,
before what one might call the Kundera shock (by analogy with the
"Solzhenitsyn shock" in France in the 1970s) catapulted it to the
center (or center left) of the fashionable intellectual stage. Of course,
German intellectuals could hardly pick up where the author of
Mitteleuropa (1915), Friedrich Naumann, left off, as, in a sense,
Czech intellectuals could pick up where Támas Garrigue Masaryk
left off, or even British intellectuals where the historian R.W. Seton-
Watson left off. Hitler got in the way. As the American scholar Henry
Cord Meyer amply demonstrated, the concept popularized by Nau-
mann in his book of 1915 was, by 1945, thoroughly poisoned
through Nazi usage.[6] Yet there was not a complete hiatus between, as

it were, Hitler and Kundera. This author has written that the concept survived only as a ghostly "Mitropa" on the dining cars of the Deutsche Reichsbahn. The German essayist Karl Markus Michel observes that it lived on only as the M in MEZ *(Mitteleuropäische Zeit)*. These observations capture a general truth but at the price of obscuring a particular one.[7]

The term *Mitteleuropa* can be found in Social Democratic (SPD) documents even in the late 1950s: and notably in the Deutschlandplan of 1959.[8] And it was precisely in the brilliant circle of Berlin Social Democrats around Willy Brandt, with such figures as Heinrich Albertz and Egon Bahr, that some concept of the thing—if not a positive usage of the word—reemerged in the early 1960s.[9] It reemerged in the context of the first fearful, tentative attempts to develop a distinctive German approach to overcoming or at least reducing the division of Europe, Germany only recently and shockingly having been cut in half by the Wall. These ideas went with Brandt and Bahr to Bonn in 1966, when Brandt became foreign minister and Bahr head of his planning staff. There Bahr tentatively, and with all due realistic caveats, looked forward to the day when a central European security system would replace the existing alliances of NATO and the Warsaw Pact.[10]

It was then in the context of presenting and defending his new Ostpolitik, after he became chancellor, that Brandt himself used the word in public, albeit in a cautious and relatively neutral way. "It is sensible and high time," he declared to the Bundestag in January 1973, "to create more confidence through more good sense in *Mitteleuropa*." Significantly, the immediately preceding passage concerned arms reductions.[11] Two years later, it was Chancellor Schmidt who observed to the Bundestag that "the GDR as a Central European *(mitteleuropäischer)* state, must face up to its responsibility for détente in Europe."[12] By January 1988, Egon Bahr would publicly observe that a letter from the East German leader Erich Honecker to the West German chancellor Helmut Kohl pressing for further arms reduction was "an expression of [a] common interest in *Mitteleuropa*. . . ."[13]

Arguably, this particular, and so to speak native, strain of thinking about Mitteleuropa is the most important one in the West German discussion. But it is by no means the only one. In the West German intellectual-political debate of the late 1980s one might tentatively distinguish four intersecting circles of Central European discussion. The first is that of cultural-historical rediscovery. It is best represented in a slim volume by the Berlin historian Karl Schlögel, published in 1986 and entitled *Die Mitte liegt ostwärts: Die Deutschen, der verlorene Osten und Mitteleuropa* (The Center Lies Eastward: The Germans, the Lost East, and Central Europe). This stimulating, discursive essay is essentially an invitation to West German intellectuals and citizens to rediscover their lost cultural and social ties with the East. Schlögel is a scholar and an enthusiast, not a politician. In a subsequent lecture to a conference organized by the Social Democrats' Friedrich Ebert Foundation, he specifically disavowed the political instrumentalization of the concept, the "proclamation of Mitteleuropa as a goal."[14]

Instead, he has a vision of restoring the web of human and cultural exchange, rather as the Alpen-Adria and Pannonia groups have attempted to do for the formerly Habsburg-ruled Kuk territories, but with Berlin taking its proper place next to Vienna, Prague, and Budapest. Berlin, he says, could be "a classical site for antipolitics and antipolitical diplomacy."[15] He thus takes up the notion of "antipolitics," which, as I have suggested elsewhere, plays a significant part in the East European debate about Central Europe.[16] In Schlögel's conception, the rediscovery of Mitteleuropa would be carried forward in the realm of ideas, culture, nonpolitical exchange, and, to put it in Marxist terms, consciousness. That this change in consciousness might, in time, affect the being of politics is possible, even desirable, but the cultural-historical rediscovery is a good in itself.

The second and third circles might be described as historical-geopolitical, right-national and historical-geopolitical, left-national. The former takes as its starting point not the concept of Mitteleuropa as such but, rather, a view of German history as being primarily determined by that country's geopolitical position in or even *as* "the European center" *(die europäische Mitte)*. Germany, in this view, is the classical land of the center *(Land der Mitte)*. Both its expansion and its final defeat and amputation are explicable in terms of the unavoidable dilemmas of this geopolitical position in an age of power politics and imperialism.[17] This is, in the first place, a scholars' argument, advanced by such influential conservative historians as Andreas Hillgruber, Klaus Hildebrand, and Michael Stürmer.

In another slim volume, which was one of the prize exhibits in the rancorous West German historians' debate, Andreas Hillgruber reprinted revised versions of two lectures: one about the Eastern front in 1944–1945 and one about the Holocaust. The book was entitled *Zweierlei Untergang: Die Zerschlagung des Deutschen Reiches und das Ende des europaischen Judentums* (roughly, Two Sorts of Ruin: The Smashing of the German Reich and the End of European Jewry), and it was the title, with its apparent equation of German and Jewish loss, that caused most controversy. For this, the creative and forceful Berlin publisher Wolf Jobst Siedler (who also published Schlögel and Bahr) rather than the author may have been mainly responsible. Yet the author, a careful and respected diplomatic historian, writes in his preface that what is at issue is "not just a Jewish or a German catastrophe, but that the whole of Europe, *but above all the European centre broken in the war,* became the victim [of the event or 'events', 'das Geschehen']." And in his essay on the German part of the double catastrophe, he writes of the event(s) "that would bring to an end the German Reich *and therewith the European centre* [my italics]."[18]

This notion of the European center and the land of the center passed, partly through the personal mediation of the historian Michael Stürmer, into the early rhetoric of the Kohl government. Yet it was linked, both in the case of Stürmer and, more importantly, in the case of Chancellor Kohl, with an emphatic rejection of any notion of recreating Mitteleuropa. "We are . . . opposed to any fashionable thought-experiment about a special position for Mitteleuropa," the chancellor said in his 1987 state-of-the-nation address to the Bundestag. "With all that binds together the peoples of the central European region in history and culture, this concept must not become—as Joseph Rovan well put it—'a dangerous explosive charge against the political integration of a Europe of freedom.' "[19]

The explosive charge that the chancellor had in mind lay most obviously in the circle I have described as historical-geopolitical, left-nationalist. This is a position captured once again in a book title: *Neutralität für Mitteleuropa* (Neutrality for Central Europe).[20] One of its more interesting exponents is Willy Brandt's son, Peter Brandt. This position, or elements of this position, find support among the Greens, in the peace movement, and well into the left of the SPD. It reaches back, indeed, to the position of the SPD in the late 1940s and early 1950s, when its leaders attacked Konrad Adenauer for allegedly closing the door to national reunification by opening the door to Western integration, and specifically to NATO. History plays a part here too: in particular, reference to the supposed missed opportunity of Stalin's March 1952 offer of reunification in return for neutrality.[21]

The fourth, and arguably most important, circle of intellectual-political Mitteleuropa debate is a mainstream Social Democratic discussion that is an attempt to integrate the concept of Mitteleuropa into a second phase of Ostpolitik. The central themes of this second phase are multilateral disarmament and East-West cooperation, or as its exponents say, "peace." Mitteleuropa is a goal of détente. This argument thus builds directly on the ideas developed by Bahr, Brandt, and others first in Berlin and then in Bonn. While Bahr is characteristically cautious in using the term, it has been taken up—in a positive sense—by one of the more influential "thinkers" of Ostpolitik since the early 1960s—Peter Bender. Europe, writes Bender, "was divided from the margins in; if it is to grow together again then, then from the centre out."[22] *Mitteleuropa* is an acceptable term of art, or motto, for that ever closer web of common interests and mutual dependencies between the states of Eastern and Western Europe that the circle of Berlin Social Democrats set out to create more than a quarter of a century ago.

Even more explicit, and uninhibited, is the former general secretary of the SPD, Peter Glotz, himself a Sudeten German, or as he puts it, a German "from Bohemia."[23] "We must win back Mitteleuropa," he writes, "first ás a concept, then as reality."[24] "Let us use the concept of Mitteleuropa as an instrument in a second phase of détente policy *(Entspannunspolitik),*" he argued elsewhere. And, going into detail, he suggested a chemical-weapon-free zone embracing the GDR, Czechoslovakia, and the Federal Republic; a nuclear-weapon-free corridor in the two German states; energy arrangements among Austria, Czechoslovakia, and others; new kinds of tourist agreements; a more intensive *Wandel durch Handel* (change through trade), hindered as little as possible, he added, "by Dick Perle's COCOM-ideology," and even a small, modest central European UNESCO for the systematic preservation of churches, marketplaces, and houses and for the restoration of communications inside this "family of small nations."[25] Although thrown down somewhat at random, this short list gives, in its priorities, in what it mentions and what it does not mention, a rather vivid and representative picture of what might be the Mitteleuropa agenda of the SPD in its putative second phase of Ostpolitik.

Plainly, these four circles of intellectual-political interest are loosely defined, and intersecting. The debate is, I repeat, inchoate and fragmented. Yet as the West German historian Arnulf Baring has argued, there is a strong case for suggesting that even marginal movements of intellectual opinion are more important pointers for the political future in the Federal Republic than, for example, public opinion polls.[26] German scholars usefully distinguish between public opinion *(die öffentliche Meinung)* and published opinion *(die veröffentlichte Meinung)*. In published as opposed to public opinion, Mitteleuropa is once again a significant theme. Moreover, the case of the SPD concerns the real foreign policy platform of the main opposition party. In a year or two it might actually be policy.

Nonetheless, at the time of writing (in fall 1989), there remains a wide gulf between the high-spirited and colorful intellectual debate, on the one hand, and, on the other hand, the sober, quotidian reality of the actual relations between the Federal Republic and the countries of Eastern Europe. What basis does this reality offer for any idealistic projections of Mitteleuropa? How, to put it in Marxian terms, does the ideological superstructure relate to the material base?

In 1961 the Polish writer Juliusz Mieroszewski published a collection of essays in German under the pregnant title *Kehrt Deutschland in den Osten zuruck?* (Is Germany Returning to the East?). More than a quarter of a century later the answer to Mieroszewski's question is plain: yes. Germany is once again a major power and presence in East Central Europe. To be sure, this statement begs the question: which Germany? After all, even in 1961 parts of Germany were in the East, in the geopolitical sense of lying within the Soviet bloc. Virtually all observers would have agreed that the German Democratic Republic was (a) part of Germany and (b) politically and economically in the East. Hence the Western shorthand usage "East Germany" for what is, in terms of historical geography, Central Germany *(Mitteldeutschland)*. In addition, everyone would have agreed that the city of Berlin was part of Germany, dramatically divided between East and West. In 1961, most West Germans would also have maintained that the former territories of the German *Reich* now incorporated into the Soviet Union and the Polish People's Republic were in some sense parts of Germany, as well as being obviously in the East. They would further have included in their notion of Germany the few million ethnic Germans still living in Poland, Romania, the Soviet Union, and Hungary.

The Germany that was not already in the East was thus, in the first place, the Federal Republic of Germany, or "West Germany" in post-1949 Western parlance. In the second place, there was some notion of the German presence that had been so important (alongside the Jewish presence) in the pre-1939, and indeed pre-1914, Central Europe but that, as a result of the war, Allied decisions (Yalta, Potsdam), the flight or deportation of perhaps thirteen million Germans, and the nonrecognition of East European states by the Federal Republic (following the Hallstein Doctrine), was notable precisely because of its absence. When we say that Germany has returned to the East, we mean, therefore, that West Germany has become a presence in East Central Europe in a way that it was not in 1961.

Yet one should also note that East Germany is more of a presence in East Central Europe than it was in 1961. Until the building of the Berlin Wall in August 1961 it was a very weak state, hemorrhaging skilled labor to the West and contemptuously referred to as "the disappearing satellite." Only when the Wall sealed in that skilled labor force was the GDR able to embark on the consolidation that brought it to the top place among the economies of Eastern Europe. And with that political consolidation and economic growth so also has grown its weight in East Central Europe. This too is part of "Germany in the East."

In what follows I shall, however, confine myself to "West Germany in the East," and chiefly to the Ostpolitik whose conceptual origins are also to be found in Berlin after August 1961 but whose dramatic realization had to await the transformation of Berlin's then governing mayor, Willy Brandt, into the federal chancellor of 1969 to 1974. The term *Ostpolitik* is used here to cover the complex of *Deutschlandpolitik* (that is, policy toward East Germany, Berlin, and Germany as a whole), *Osteuropapolitik* (policy toward the rest of Eastern Europe), and policy toward the Soviet Union (formerly *Russlandpolitik*). It is, in theory at least, a consistent and coherent approach that combines all these aspects of policy in a strategy for long-term, peaceful, evolutionary change: overcoming the division of

Germany and Europe in a "European peace order." To draw up anything like a comprehensive balance sheet of that Ostpolitik over the last quarter century would be far beyond the scope of this essay. What follows is a set of highly selective observations (although they are based on a more comprehensive survey).

The first hallmark of this Ostpolitik, the element which above all earned it the description "new" in the 1960s, was its recognition of the existing East European states, and therewith its acknowledgment that the territories east of the Oder-Neisse line could not—for as far ahead as any reasonable statesman could foresee—be any more considered as parts of Germany in the East. The renunciation of Germany in the East, in this sense, was thus the sine qua non of the return of Germany (West) to the East. Moreover, one of the plainest results of this Ostpolitik has thus far been to diminish still further the permanent German presence in the East. For Bonn lists among its achievements the securing (generally with the aid of substantial hard currency transfers to the state in question) of the right to emigrate of more than a million ethnic Germans from the Soviet Union, Eastern Europe, and of course the GDR.[27] Although both social-liberal and liberal-conservative coalition governments in Bonn have declared it their goal to secure conditions in which ethnic Germans can stay and live—as Germans—in Eastern Europe, this has thus far proved possible only with Hungary. (I leave aside, for the moment, the question of how far people feel they can continue to live as Germans in the GDR). There is thus a certain irony in this "return." It is the return of Germany but as a plainly external, foreign presence, where for many hundreds of years Germany and the Germans had been a domestic presence.

The second hallmark of this new German presence is economic. Trade relations were the first kind of relations that the Federal Republic restored with East Central Europe in the 1950s. In the early 1960s the opening of trade missions was a deliberate prelude to the restoration of diplomatic relations. Trade preceded the flag. Eastern trade *(Osthandel)* and Eastern policy (Ostpolitik) were thus intimately linked from the outset. What precisely the links are, how Osthandel helps the goals of Ostpolitik, is a matter of some dispute. The Nestor of postwar Osthandel, Otto Wolff von Amerongen, has spoken rather dismissively of the "romantics of Osthandel," who believe that it can bring peace on earth, goodwill to all men, and a transformation of the communist system to boot. Those, like Otto Wolff von Amerongen, who actually practice Eastern trade, often have a more sober assessment of its possibilities and impact than those who merely write about it.[28]

The mainstream West German view might be summarized thus: Osthandel is good in itself; Germans have always traded with and in East Central Europe; it would be most unnatural for them not to do so today. Trade has a stabilizing effect on East-West relations, and in this sense it is also a contribution to securing peace. It forms ties of interdependence, and these too are good in themselves. It may also have a beneficial effect on the internal affairs of the East European country concerned—raising the standard of living (of some at least) and perhaps encouraging reform. As noted above, the slogan "change through trade" is still occasionally heard.

However, the only direct linkage that is made between economic relations and politics or human rights concerns the position of Germans in these countries (and, of course, in the GDR). Pierre Hassner has wittily observed that, in Eastern policy, the Americans believe in sticks, the Germans in carrots, and the French in words. Yet stronger than any belief in the beneficent effect of carrots is the emphatic rejection of sticks—that is, of economic sanctions and negative linkage. The difference between the American and the German approaches was starkly apparent in the gas pipeline dispute and the argument about economic sanctions after the imposition of martial law in Poland in December 1981. More recently, and mildly, it has been clear in discussions about reducing the COCOM restrictions on technology transfer to the East.[29]

West German politicians like to point out that the Federal Republic's total Eastern trade is less than its trade with Switzerland. This is true, although the dependency of particular sectors of German industry on Eastern trade (iron and steel, machine tools) is much greater than the overall statistics suggest. But far more significant than any dependency of West Germany on trade with Eastern Europe is the dependency of Eastern Europe on trade with West Germany. This is self-evidently the case for the GDR: more than half of its Western trade is with the Federal Republic. But it is also true elsewhere. West Germany is Hungary's second largest trading partner, second only to the Soviet Union. Exchange with West Germany also makes up some 30 to 35 percent of Western trade for Poland and

Czechoslovakia, compared with just 5 to 8 percent with the United States, Britain, or France.[30]

This new-old dependency is, moreover, apparent in individual or household economies as well as in national economies. Hard currency transfers from friends or relatives in the West are a significant part of individual and household economies in the GDR. Going to the West for a time to earn hard currency is the only way many Poles can make ends meet. And "the West" in this context means, in the first place, West Germany: a reality reflected in the revival of *na saksy,* the old phrase for going to work abroad. According to some estimates, as many as a million Poles will be staying in the Federal Republic at any one time, and most of them will be earning some hard currency, whether legally or not. According to an official Polish estimate, in 1986 and 1987 private hard currency transfers from Poles abroad almost equaled the total hard currency surplus of the state sector![31] German firms lead the way in establishing joint ventures and exploiting what is, by Western standards, the extraordinarily cheap labor on offer in Poland and Hungary.[32] German tourists are by far the most numerous single group of Western visitors.

In sum, West Germany's economic and commercial ties with East Central Europe are unrivaled by any other Western power. Increasingly, they recall the traditional relationship of East Central Europe to Germany, which is one of unequal dependency. Economically, Mitteleuropa is already more than just an idea. West German policymakers are, however, at pains to stress that these economic relations are only one thread in a whole fabric of ties that the Federal Republic hopes to make with Eastern Europe so as to weave a divided Europe back together again. Policymakers mention cultural and academic exchange, young people's visits, scientific and environmental cooperation, town twinning, and political dialogue. In comparison with the Eastern policies of the United States, France, and Britain, West German policy over the past two decades has had more emphasis on cooperation than contestation, on stability rather than political change. The West Germans have sought an all-round, long-term improvement of relations, in whatever area progress has seemed possible, albeit only in environmental protection or cultural exchange. The United States, however, has pursued a policy of "differentiation" linked closely to the short-term domestic or foreign political performance of particular states.

The West German approach is rooted in a perception of national interest (an all-European détente being seen as the necessary condition for the further progress of intra-German détente)[33] but also in a more general argument about the best way to promote peaceful change in Eastern Europe, and, not least, in an (historically understandable) emotional predilection for security, stability, predictability, and harmony.[34] A further analysis of these ingredients and their changing mix in West German policy would require another article.

Yet it should be noted that West Germany's relations are in practice "differentiated," although according to other criteria. Relations with the GDR are in a category of their own: their unique quality exemplified bureaucratically in the direct subordination of Deutschlandpolitik to the federal chanchellery (Bundeskanzleramt) rather than to the foreign office (Auswärtiges Amt). Between the other three East Central European countries there is what one might call a dual differentiation. On the one hand, like the United States, France, and Britain, the Federal Republic has found it easier to develop closer relations with states that are more "reformist" or "liberal," to use two very inadequate terms. On the other hand, the Federal Republic has a special form of differentiation, which consists in rewarding (or not rewarding) states on the basis of their attitude toward their German minorities, and specific (West) German interests, such as the establishment of a Goethe Institute to represent free German culture in contradiction to the existing cultural representation of the GDR.

Thus the 1975-1976 "jumbo credit" for Poland negotiated by Helmut Schmidt was directly linked to arrangements for increased German emigration. And when the Bonn government guaranteed a billion Deutschemark credit for Hungary in autumn 1987, this credit was as much for the state's exemplary treatment of the country's small German minority, and for the agreement to open a West German cultural institute, as it was for any general purpose of supporting reform. Indeed, Hungarian reform economists at the time suggested that such a large, untied loan would hinder rather than help arguments for radical economic reform. For its part, the Bonn government said that its relations with Hungary were "model" in character, thus clearly implying that if Poland and Czechoslovakia treated these German concerns in the same understanding way, they too might reap similar rewards. Of course, the general political developments in these countries, as constantly assessed through the mechanisms of Western and especially West European political cooperation, were by no means irrelevant to Bonn's policy. But these special, national interests still played a very large part—in hindering the improvement of relations with Poland as much as in facilitating the improvement of relations with Hungary.

It cannot be said that the Federal Republic has so far played a leading role in directly encouraging the process of liberalization in Hungary. In terms of contacts with opposition groups and movements, or an explicit high priority for human rights and democratization, the United States and the United Kingdom have been bolder. Yet in terms of encouraging overall human contacts (in the original sense of the "third basket" of the Helsinki Final Act), in the movement of goods and people, and in attempting to keep the West European Community open to Hungarians, the Federal Republic has been in the front line. The actual development of Hungarian–West German relations since 1973 may not suggest that the Federal Republic has thus far succeeded in giving the reality of Mitteleuropa, in practice, a sense with which other Western democrats or European liberals might be entirely happy. But it is certainly much closer to such a Western and European sense than it is to the pre-1945 Mitteleuropa of brutal German hegemony. That is, however, to measure by a rather low historical standard. Moreover, Hungary, a historical ally, is easy. The really difficult test cases are Poland and Czechoslovakia.

It is not, however, the Hungarian model which is at the heart of the discussion about German Ostpolitik and the potential future shape of a new Mitteleuropa. At the heart of this discussion is Germany in relation to itself, or Deutschlandpolitik. Increasingly, it is suggested that West–East German relations might be, to some extent, a model for West–East European relations, or even for East-West relations. This suggestion refers both to the way in which West Germany has attempted to reduce the division of the nation by a policy of cooperation and reassociation, and to the responsible conduct of both states in the general business of East-West relations, specifically on the issue of peace. The emphasis here is on the "common interests" of the two German states, and more generally the common interests of the states and (it is said) of the peoples of Central Europe. There is still a considerable gulf between what is said in this regard by an SPD intellectual like Peter Bender and what is actually done in this regard by the Kohl government. However, this is the point at which, as it were, the theory and practice of Mitteleuropa are least far apart. Moreover, given the central role of the security dialogue with the ruling Communist party (SED) in the SPD's second Ostpolitik, it is reasonable to assume that practice would come somewhat closer to theory were the SPD to return to power.

Now anyone who knows the recent history of Germany must recognize the achievement of Deutschlandpolitik. If one compares the condition of divided Germany in August 1989 with what it was in August 1961 after the building of the Berlin Wall, one can see that there are far more contacts of all sorts between the Germans in East and West, that successive Bonn governments have gone a long way toward achieving their goals of alleviating human suffering and holding the nation together. The figures for trips to the West by East Germans under pensionable age—rising from almost nothing in 1971 to more than one and a half million in 1988—are just the most remarkable testimony to this. There are many other indices of reassociation—telephone contacts, mailing of parcels, and so on—all exhaustively recorded by official West German sources. In addition there is the perpetual, but on the whole successful, struggle to maintain the viability of West Berlin and its ties with the Federal Republic. In terms of recent German history, and the state and national agendas of the Bonn government, the balance sheet is strong.

What is less clear, however, is what lessons this record might have for developing close ties between other states and nations in Central Europe. The salient feature of German-German relations is precisely their uniqueness. Much of Deutschlandpolitik consists in the solution of problems that do not even exist for other countries. One thinks of the position of Berlin, for example, and the uniquely draconian restrictions on the freedom of movement of GDR citizens. Secondly, there is the problem of political change in the GDR, or rather (at the time of writing) the lack of it. In the years 1983–1984, the GDR manifested its new self-confidence and limited autonomy as a state by partially defying the confrontational line in Soviet foreign policy. But since Gorbachev has come to power, in 1985, the GDR has manifested these qualities by an almost total refusal of the Soviet example of *glasnost* and *perestroika*—memorably dismissed by the country's chief ideologist as mere new wallpapering. The GDR remains the closest thing that Eastern Europe can offer to a working model of the Leninist Party-state and centrally planned economy. It probably has (at the time of writing) some three thousand prisoners who may be classified as political, although many of them are waiting to be "bought free" by the West German government. The contrast with Poland and Hungary, with the blooming pluralization of their political life and the marketization of their economies, is very stark.

How much West Germany has contributed to political change—or the lack of it—in East Germany is, of course, a very complex question. One has to distinguish between the passive and the active influence of the Federal Republic: that which it exerts by virtue of its mere existence, freedom, prosperity, and that which it exerts by virtue of deliberate policy (that is, Deutschlandpolitik). The former is arguably larger in influence than the latter. The existence of the Federal Republic is per se a permanent challenge to the rulers of the GDR. It may be said to encourage them to try to make their own system more competitive—if only with the images of West German life that most East Germans see on their television screens every evening. East Germany's rulers are, as they themselves put it, "building socialism under world-open conditions." On the other hand, they must always fear that if they grant the first inch of liberalization, their own people will want to take the full mile of reunification in freedom. This is arguably one major reason that the GDR has always lagged far behind Poland and Hungary in respect of economic and political reform.[35]

Nonetheless, there is also an argument that the Federal Republic's deliberate policy has contributed to slowing down rather than speeding up the process of desirable change in the GDR. It is suggested, for example, that the various forms of economic advantage granted to the GDR—ranging from direct state-to-state hard currency transfers, through government-guaranteed credits, to special arrangements for "inner-German trade"—have actually helped that state to postpone necessary economic reforms. These advantages may have also helped to take the edge off popular discontent—or, in other words, to reduce that pressure from below that has been the social motor of reform in Poland and Hungary. A small, but significant example of a very direct intervention by the Federal Republic in the politics of the GDR is the buying free of some one to two-and-a-half thousand political prisoners a year. Clearly, there is a strong human-itarian case for this practice. But if one considers the impact that just a few hundred members of the democratic oppositions had in Poland, Hungary, and Czechoslovakia in the 1970s, then it seems reasonable to suggest that Erich Honecker's unique facility of exporting his dissidents for hard currency has had a not necessarily positive impact on the domestic politics of the GDR.

Yet developments in the years 1988 and 1989 might lead one to qualify this critique, for the dramatic increase in travel to the West by East Germans under pensionable age—an increase for which the Federal Republic has patiently pressed over two decades—has, it appears, had the effect of increasing the domestic pressure for change (in combination, of course, with "the Gorbachev effect"). This pressure is expressed collectively, through demands and programs for change articulated most clearly at the synods of the Protestant churches. It is also expressed individually, through a growing number of applications to emigrate. Plainly, this was not the result the GDR leadership desired when it liberalized travel to the West as "a safety valve." The safety valve has proved rather to be a steam piston. Whether it was the result desired, intended, or expected by the West German government is a more difficult question, but the answer is probably, on balance, no.

A third question mark over the German model of putting central Europe back together again concerns the tension between the Ger-man and the East Central European paths. The test case here was the Polish revolution of 1980–1981 and the imposition of martial law. West German reactions in general, and those of the Schmidt govern-ment in particular, gave rise to the suspicion and the fear—in Eastern Europe as well as the West—that West Germany was putting its own interests in the continuation of the intra-German détente (and the overarching international détente as a necessary condition for that intranational détente) before the interests of the Polish people. Chancellor Schmidt was actually meeting with Erich Honecker, for their long-awaited summit in the GDR, on the day martial law was imposed. Asked about his first reaction, he delivered himself of the unfortunate judgment that "Herr Honecker was as dismayed as I was, that *this has now proved necessary*" (my italics). The image (albeit momentary) of two German leaders proclaiming "l'ordre règne à Varsovie" was a little chilling to their neighbors, especially to those in Poland just thrown into prison. Such fears and suspicions were hardly allayed by statements like that of Egon Bahr—"world peace is more important than Poland"—and by the German Social Democrats' apparent support for Polish colonels against Polish Social Democrats.

This experience provoked some extreme reactions, such as the essay "A New Rapallo," by the Hungarian intellectuals Ferenc Fehér and Agnes Heller. It also provoked a spirited and pained discussion in West Germany.[36] Probably the least important aspect of this debate was the disagreement with the United States over the range and desirability of economic sanctions. That was a separate and older argument, in which German and American interests had clashed before. It was quite possible for Germany's European neighbors (East and West) to be opposed to some or all of the range of sanctions proposed by the Reagan administration and yet to be equally worried by the West German reaction.

The worry concerned not only West Germany's apparent desire to maintain good relations with the Soviet Union, as it were "over the head" of the East Central Europeans, but also what one might call the exclusivity and "unfalsifiability" of the claim to be working in the best long-term interests of Europe and of peace. ("World peace is more important than Poland.") The memory of this debate sounds through the reaction of at least one distinguished French scholar to the revival of the Mitteleuropa concept on the West German Left in the late 1980s. "I want," wrote Joseph Rovan, "to live in Europe with Walęsa, not in Mitteleuropa with General Jaruzelski."[37]

This brings one to a fourth and final question mark. Early in the Mitteleuropa debate François Bondy pointed out that, whereas the revived concept of Central Europe implied, in Czech and Hungarian usage, a distancing from the East, the concept of Mitteleuropa had, in German usage, usually implied some distancing from the West. In criticizing the revival of the concept, quoting Joseph Rovan, Chancellor Kohl implied that he, at least, believed this to be a danger again. More neutral critics have also seen, in the building of the idea of Mitteleuropa into the second Ostpolitik of the SPD, and, in particular, in the joint documents prepared by the SPD with the ruling Communist parties of Eastern Europe, a dangerous distancing, not just from the consensus security policies of the Western alliance but, more importantly, from the common values of the West. It is independent East European observers, in particular, who detect in the language of the SPD a relativization of precisely those Western values which are at the center of *their* idea of Central Europe.

To speculate about how the debate, or the policies, might evolve in future is far beyond the scope of this essay, as is any policy prescription. Two observations on the intellectual instruments of the West German debate must serve in place of a conclusion. The first observation is that much of this debate is conducted at a level of abstract, vague, idealistic generalization that makes rational, empirically based criticism impossible. The second observation, eloquently expressed by the Tübingen historian Dietrich Geyer, is that the debate continues to be remarkably Germanocentric or Russocentric.[38] Independent Polish, Hungarian, Czech, and, for that matter, French and Italian voices are little heard. This situation may be changing somewhat.[39] But in a field of such ambiguity and subjectivity, yet also of such importance for the future of all Europe, the least one can hope for is that those involved will listen to each other. That they should understand each other may still be to ask too much. But to listen with real attention and mutual respect: that must be possible. Even in Central Europe.

ENDNOTES

[1]Fritz T. Epstein, *Germany and the East* (Bloomington, Ind.: 1973), 67.

[2]A useful introduction to that debate is George Schöpflin and Nancy Wood, eds., *In Search of Central Europe* (London: Polity Press, 1989).

[3]See the contributions by Vajda et al. in Schöpflin and Wood.

[4]See, for example, the Polish discussion usefully collected in Waldemar Kuwaczka, *Entspannung von Unten, Möglichkeiten und Grenzen des deutsch-polnischen Dialogs* (Stuttgart: Burg Verlag, 1988), and, particularly for references to the Czech and Slovak discussion, Jacques Rupnik's article "La problème Allemand vu de l'Europe du centre-est" in *Revue Française de Science Politique* 37 (June 1987). See also the articles by Jiri Dienstbier in *Listý* (6) (1984), and *Komentáře* 10 (1987); the latter was reprinted in *Neue Gesellschaft/Frankfurter Hefte* 4 (1988).

[5]See the useful review article by Rudolf Jaworski, "Die aktuelle Mitteleuropadiskussion in historischer Perspektive," in *Historische Zeitschrift* 247 (1987). The fact that the prestigious *Historische Zeitschrift* chose to run this as its first article is itself a small sign of the times. See also the chapter by Karl Schlögel, in Dietrich

Spangenberg, ed., *Die blockierte Vergangenheit, Nachdenken über Mitteleuropa* (Berlin: Argon, 1987).

[6]Henry Cord Meyer, *Mitteleuropa in German Thought and Action* (The Hague: 1955).

[7]See my essay "Does Central Europe Exist?" *New York Review of Books,* 9 October 1986, reprinted in Timothy Garton Ash, *The Uses of Adversity, Essays on the Fate of Central Europe* (New York: Random House, 1989), and Karl Markus Michel, "Landkarte des Vergessens," in *Neue Gesellschaft/Frankfurter Hefte* 8 (1988).

[8]For the text of the "Deutschlandplan" see Helga Haftendorn et al., *Die Aussenpolitik der Bundesrepublik Deutschland* (Berlin: Wissenchaftlicher Autcren-Verlag, 1982): 250–54.

[9]For the Berlin circle see Peter Bender, *Neue Ostpolitik* (Munich: Deutscher Taschenbuch Verlag, 1986): 123–29.

[10]For a lucid and sober discussion of the Bahr plans see Werner Link's contribution to Karl Dietrich Bracher et al., *Republik im Wandel, 1969–74* (Stuttgart: Deutsche Verlags-Anstalt, 1986); *Geschichte der Bundesrepublik Deutschland 5,* 169–79.

[11]*Verhandlungen des deutschen Bundestages, Plenarprotokolle,* 7th Wahlperiode, 7th Sitzung (18 January 1973), 123.

[12]*Verhandlungen des deutschen Bundestages, Plenarprotokolle,* 7th Wahlperiode, 146th Sitzung (30 January 1975), 10035.

[13]*Parlamentarisch-Politischer Pressedienst* (PPP), 5 January 1988.

[14]Spangenberg, 31–32.

[15]*Ibid.,* 33. For Pannonia and Alpen-Adria see the review article by Jaworski cited in endnote 5 above.

[16]See my essay "Does Central Europe Exist?"

[17]Of course one finds exactly the same leitmotif in the historiography of Poland, Hungary, and Czechoslovakia. "Geography" thus seems to dictate that Germany must inevitably invade and that Poland must inevitably be invaded.

[18]Andreas Hillgruber, *Zweierlei Untergang, Die Zerschlagung des Deutschen Reiches und das Ende des europaischen Judentums* (Berlin: Siedler, 1986), 10 and 25.

[19]*Verhandlungen des deutschen Bundestages, Plenarprotokolle,* 11th Wahlperiode, 33d Sitzung (15 October 1987), 2160. It is interesting to note that Rovan subsequently crossed swords with a close aide to President Richard von Weizsacker, Friedbert Pfluger, who had taken up the Mitteleuropa idea in a positive, indeed almost a Social Democratic, sense. See his article in the *Frankfurter Allgemeine Zeitung* (21 May 1988), and Rovan's letter to the same paper (27 June 1988).

[20]Jochen Löser and Ulrike Schilling, *Neutralität für Mitteleuropa* (Munich: Bertelsmann, 1984). The title is the most interesting thing about this work.

[21]For a statement of the "missed opportunity" thesis see Rolf Steininger, *Eine vertane Chance, Die Stalin-Note vom 10. Marz 1952 und die Wiedervereinigung* (Bonn: Dietz, 1985).

[22]In Spangenberg, 103. Of course one could argue that Europe was *divided* from the center out: that is, starting with Hitler in Berlin.

[23]See his interview in *Marxism Today* (August 1987): 14 and passim.

[24]*Neue Gesellschaft/Frankfurter Hefte* (7) (1986): 585.

[25]Quoted from *Niemandsland* 2 (1987): 126. The Paris-based Coordinating Committee on the export of Western technology includes Japan and all the NATO countries except Iceland.

[26]Arnulf Baring, *Unser neuer Grössenwahn* (Stuttgart: Deutsche Verlags-Anstalt, 1988): 77 ff.

[27]This rough total, which includes various categories of emigrants, is based on Interior Ministry figures for the years 1970–1987.

[28]See Michael Kreile, *Osthandel und Ostpolitik* (Baden-Baden: Nomos, 1978), 138 and passim.

[29]See, most recently, Angela Stent, "Technology Transfer to Eastern Europe," in William E. Griffith, ed., *Central and Eastern Europe: The Opening Curtain?* (Boulder, San Francisco: Westview Press, 1989), esp. 97–99.

[30]See Table A-12 in the statistical appendix to Lincoln Gordon, ed., *Eroding Empire: Western Relations with Eastern Europe* (Washington, D.C.: Brookings Institution, 1987).

[31]Jacek Rostowski, "The Decay of Socialism and the Growth of Private Enterprise in Poland," quoting an article by A. Rajkiewicz in *Zycie Gospodarcze* 34 (1987).

[32]The point about cheap labor was made, with a clear invitation to West German capital, by the Polish industry minister Mieczysław Wilczek in an interview with *Der Spiegel;* see "Arbeitskraft ist in Polen besonders billig," in *Der Spiegel,* 3 (1989). The word *exploitation* was used, to me, in sorrow, by a West German diplomat who has worked in this field.

[33]A powerful statement of this argument is Josef Joffe's chapter in Gordon.

[34]See Hans-Peter Schwarz, *Die gezähmten Deutschen* (Stuttgart: Deutsche Verlags-Anstalt, 1985) and Gebhard Schweigler, *Grunglagen der aussenpolitischen Orientierung der Bundesrepublik Deutschland* (Baden-Baden: Nomos, 1985).

[35]Interestingly, precisely this point was made by Egon Bahr in his seminal "Tutzing speech" of 1963.

[36]For Fehér and Heller's essay and some German responses see *New German Critique* (37), (Winter 1986). See also Heinrich Böll et al., eds., *Verantwortlich für Polen?* (Reinbek bei Hamburg: Ro Ro Ro, 1982).

[37]Letter to the *Frankfurter Allgemeine Zeitung,* 27 June 1988.

[38]Dietrich Geyer, "Ostpolitik und Geschichtsbewusstsein in Deutschland," in *Vierteljahrshefte fur Zeitgeschichte* 34 (2) (1986): 147–59.

[39]Witness, for example, the emergence of a German-language edition of the journal *Lettre Internationale;* the planned biennial journal of the Institut für die Wissenschaften vom Menschen in Vienna, with this as a significant part of its brief; and the tentative broadening of debate by the SPD's Friedrich-Ebert-Stiftung, to include, for the first time, a few genuinely independent East European voices.

July 1989

POSTSCRIPT

The extraordinary events from the East German "October Revolution" of 1989 to German unification on October 3, 1990—Germany's *annus mirabilis*—have self-evidently overtaken much of my argument, although not half so much as they have overtaken the arguments of some of the German advocates of "Mitteleuropa" discussed in this article! The historical sketch of German Ostpolitik in the 1970s and 1980s, in practice and theory, does not require major revision, merely completion. Now there are answers where before there were just questions. Whether the German vision of Mitteleuropa—or for that matter the reality that will now develop—is any closer to the East Central European dream of Central Europe remains, however, very much an open question.

October 1990

The Rediscovery of Central Europe

Tony Judt

What Central Europe *means has shifted with shifting borders and rule. Western imagination mapped its cultures with Germany through the first half of this century, and with the Soviet Union more recently. Now as political change sweeps the continent, the West is "rediscovering" the region. No longer the displaced persons of some imaginary landscape, for the present at least, Central Europeans themselves are projecting their cultural geography to the watching world.*

Leontes: Where is Bohemia? Speak!
—Act V, Scene ii

Bohemia. A desert country near the sea.
—Stage direction, Act III, Scene iii

From William Shakespeare, *A Winter's Tale*

In the cultural baggage of the West, Central Europe has long been an optional extra. This is especially so in the case of the English-speaking world, but the French have been little better. For the opinion makers and political leaders from William Shakespeare to Neville Chamber-

Tony Judt is Professor of History in the Institute of French Studies at New York University.

lain, the frontiers of civilization did not extend beyond the territorial aspirations of the more timorous Carolingian monarchs. And what was already a restricted vision in 1938 became positively myopic after 1945.

In large measure this was the consequence of the Soviet conquest of half the European continent. East of Vienna, peoples and lands of which little had been known now disappeared from sight altogether. But in cultural terms, what mattered perhaps even more was the disappearance of Germany, for it was the Germans, and their language, that had served as the vital conduit in Europe between East and West, at once unifying and dividing the identity of the landmass between Russia and the Atlantic.

Until 1945, the term *Central Europe* had a peculiarly Germanic ring to it, reflecting the hitherto dominant German place in the region. From Metternich, who first developed the theme, to Friedrich Naumann (whose 1915 work *Mitteleuropa* codified its modern usage), the very concept of an area of Europe called central was parasitic on the problem of German unification. In its mid-nineteenth-century usage (in the work of Friedrich List, for example), *Central Europe* referred to a broadly conceived economic union based in Prussia and the Austrian lands but extending from Copenhagen to Trieste. So long as the form and territorial extent of a united Germany remained unclear, and with no other nation-states established in the region, the future of Europe's geographical center could be imagined in many different ways.[1]

All such dreams were scotched by Prussia's defeat of the Austrian army at Sadowa in 1866, the outcome of the Franco-Prussian war of 1870, and Bismarck's establishment of a Prussian-centered empire. Europe's military and political center of gravity shifted eastward, and the unresolved conflicts of empires and nations moved in concordance, with *Central Europe* now describing the lands between Germany and the Russian empire, focused on Vienna. Naumann's own conception reflected this development. His Mitteleuropa still included Germany (the book was published at a moment of close German-Austrian military and diplomatic collaboration, during World War I) but moved the frontiers eastward to the Vistula, proposing Central Europe as a candidate for an economic union that would simultaneously incorporate and resolve the national tensions that had arisen since the establishment of the German Empire to its west.

As a result of the war, however, Naumann's vision was rendered obsolete. The reemergence of Poland, the creation of Czechoslovakia and Yugoslavia, together with the reduction of Austria and Hungary to small states, all combined to give the prewar idea of a unified Central Europe a quite new meaning. In the face of ethnic and national pride and the territorial claims and insecurities of the new countries, Mitteleuropa was at best an anachronistic utopia, at worst a stalking horse for the military and economic hegemony of Germany. Even the term itself had become imprecise. The disappearance of the Austro-Hungarian Empire (a truly momentous event in European history) left a huge gap in the conceptual geography of the continent. Of what did Central Europe now consist? What was East, what West in a landmass whose political divisions had been utterly and unrecognizably remade within a single lifetime?

In one important French study of 1931, the countries taken to comprise Central Europe were Austria, Hungary, Czechoslovakia, Poland, Romania, Yugoslavia, and Italy.[2] Such a list ignored the newly established Baltic states of Estonia, Latvia, and Lithuania (whose capital Vilna is the birthplace of some of today's best-known Central European intellectuals), but more immediately it left out Weimar Germany. This exclusion may well reflect the interwar French wish to forget the very existence of their German neighbor, but it hardly corresponded to the view of many contemporary Germans, for whom the new and vulnerable countries to their southeast were open terrain for dreams of German economic revival, territorial expansion, and geopolitical influence. Nor was such a perspective confined to Germans. Until the military implications of treating Central and Southeastern Europe as Germany's natural backyard became inescapable, Western diplomats and scholars of the interwar generation were not averse to such a future for the region. Many of them saw German domination there as the key to containing the Soviet Union, and most would probably have agreed with the contemporary Hungarian economist Elemér Hantos that the Versailles settlement was radically unstable in that part of the world (*mutatis mutandis,* Western readiness to accept the status quo in modern Central Europe, even at the price of Soviet control there, is a response to similar fears of instability in the area between what had historically been nation-states).[3]

With the defeat of Hitler, all such German-centered perspectives ceased to be credible. Moreover, as a result of Nazism, they also lost their historical legitimacy. And thus, from 1945 until quite recently, "Central Europe" became invisible to the West. Obviously, this proposition taken literally is a trifle tendentious. Politicians and diplomats in the United States, Britain, and France took note of events in the area of Europe that fell under Soviet domination in the years 1945–1949 and watched closely for signs of rebellion, if only as a card to play in the great diplomatic game with the Soviet Union itself. But in the domestic politics of the Western allies, and in the world of the "thinking classes," the notion of an entity called Central Europe disappeared from consideration. In the Western intellectual and political imagination, reconstructing Europe after 1945 became synonymous with creating economic and diplomatic cohesion among the Western allies and the reconstructed countries of Western Europe. At best, Europe became the dream of Jean Monnet and his followers, a sort of reduced Naumannism, supranational economic union but confined to the beneficiaries of the Marshall Plan and consecrated in the Treaty of Rome. The "lands between" entered into cultural limbo and Russian political tutelage.[4]

There was certainly nothing overdetermined about this process. Western public opinion and Western writers and scholars had a long history of concern about the rest of Europe, dating at least as far back as the outcry over the tsars' treatment of Polish uprisings in the first half of the nineteenth century. British liberals and their electors had a long and honorable involvement in the revolutions and revolts of the years 1848–1918, and Hungarians, Czechs, Serbs, and Poles had all at some point looked to London or Paris for support and encouragement. The mass emigration from this region to the United States around the turn of the century had produced a small but well-organized electorate in cities like Cleveland, Chicago, and New York, and American support for the creation of independent states in Central and Eastern Europe owed something to their presence. Serbian losses during the First World War and the abandonment of Czechoslovakia at Munich in 1938 did not pass unnoticed in the Western press, and the rise of fascism had helped mobilize a generation of Western intellectuals in defense of democracy and political freedoms in East and West alike. Not everyone was shocked into collaboration at the prospect of dying for Danzig.

The disappearance of this part of Europe from the consciousness of the Western intelligentsia after 1945 thus represents an astonishing act of collective cultural amnesia, matched only by the delight with which the other half of the continent was rediscovered in the late 1970s. This rediscovery has itself been accompanied by an embarrassing degree of intellectual hubris, a sense that Central Europe indeed exists only in those moments when Western thinkers happen to imagine it into being. This sort of solipsistic geographical nominalism is rampant, for example, in a speech by Susan Sontag, at the International Writers' Conference in Lisbon, in May 1988. "Central Europe," she declared, "was an American [*sic*] metaphor, an anti-Russian concept to explain that the countries of the Soviet bloc were not appendages of the Soviet Union but some even preceded it . . . . It was a very useful concept for non-Russians."[5]

The context for such breathtaking ignorance is the peculiar political circumstances of the postwar years. In France, Italy, Britain, and the United States (the countries with which I am concerned in this essay), the only people who consistently spoke of and for the lands from Vienna to Vilna were the political emigrés of the Cold War era. The latter ranged across the political spectrum from embittered social democrats to nostalgic monarchists but were united in their anti-communism. In the decade following the end of the war, this stand rendered them virtually inaudible to the intelligentsia of the Left who dominated public discussion of politics in France and Italy and also exercised a determining influence in literary and academic circles in Britain and (to a lesser extent) the United States. But even writers and thinkers of the political Center and Right were less interested in the fate of the region as such than in the role it played in the strengthening of the Soviet Union as a global power. When exiles from the Eastern bloc spoke or wrote of the enslavement of Poland, the 1948 coup in Prague, the political persecutions, and the popular protests, they certainly got a hearing in right-wing circles and the conservative press. But they deluded themselves (as some of them came to appreciate) if they supposed that their audience cared deeply about the condition of their homelands. For anti-Communist intellectuals, what was happening in Budapest or Prague was just the logical extension of what had already happened years before in Moscow and Kiev. Events in Poland and Romania might further strengthen the case for Western vigilance and military superiority, but eyes remained firmly fixed on the Kremlin. It was part of the tragedy of the postwar emigrés that they could never fully grasp the marginality to which such geopolitical concern consigned all their efforts to enlighten the free world.

Intellectuals of the Left, on the other hand, sought only to think well of the Soviet Union. Communists and non-Communists alike, they projected onto Stalin and his heirs the Socialist dreams frustrated and unfulfilled in the industrial and American-dominated West. Between the glory attaching to the "victor of Stalingrad" and the heartfelt desire to find in the East the future of a utopian project stalled in the lands of its birth, the Western intellectuals of the postwar years had little time for news from the laboratory in which the experiment was being conducted. That Central and Eastern Europe should be the industrial frontline of Soviet advance so soon after providing the agricultural resource base for Nazi conquest was a matter of small consequence. For the Western Left from 1945 until the early 1960s, the Sovietization of Eastern Europe was both good in itself and the best guarantee of the survival of the Russian revolutionary state.

After Stalin's death, and more especially following the crushing of the Hungarian Revolution in 1956, there were signs of change. In Italy, the increasingly independent attitude of the Communist party itself, nuancing its identification with the Soviet Union in a variety of ways, made it easier for "right-thinking" intellectuals of the Left to distance themselves from the Soviet bloc without rendering themselves vulnerable to charges of having sold out to the Americans. In Britain and the United States, the Manichaean habits of the Cold War declined, making it possible for socialists and liberals to criticize their own governments without offering an accompanying apologia for the order of things in Prague or Moscow. Only in France, where the cultural hegemony of the Communist party had not yet diminished, was criticism of the Soviet invasion of Hungary (by Sartre, for example) still ritually followed by a reaffirmation of faith in the possibilities of communism.[6]

Notwithstanding these developments, and the momentary outburst of anger at the events of 1956, Central Europe remained essentially invisible to Western thinkers. For with the diminished credibility of the Soviet utopia (notably as a by-product of Khruschev's revelations at the Twentieth Congress), the intelligentsia of the Left in the West turned away from the region altogether and began instead to project their hopes onto the non-European world. As a consequence, with attention centered on Algeria, Ghana, Cuba, and (eventually) the Far East, the Soviet satellites closer to home became an embarrassing irrelevance—irrelevant because for all but the most hard-bitten of Communists they no longer served as prototypes of postrevolutionary societies, embarrassing because they offered disconcertingly proximate reminders of the achievements of real socialism in its European homelands.

If anything, the gap between East and West that had opened up in 1945 became wider still after 1956. In the immediate postwar years, some intellectuals in the Soviet bloc (notably in Hungary and Czechoslovakia) still spoke the same language as their Western colleagues, criticizing their own governments in the name of a socialist ideal. But after 1956, intellectuals in Poland and elsewhere turned increasingly critical of the Marxist regimes they had helped create, offering revisionist critiques of the political and economic impasse of the peoples' democracies and becoming even less inclined to accept the terms of debate and description officially approved. Similar distaste for mainstream Communist practice produced the New Left in France and Italy during the 1960s, but there the parallel ends, for the anti-Communist Left in Paris or Rome had nothing but scorn for the "bourgeois" concerns of the reformist critics in Prague or Warsaw. It was this fear that the East European revisionists had abandoned Stalinism only to embrace liberalism that accounts for the lukewarm response in many radical circles in the West to the Prague Spring. The appearance of Soviet tanks in August 1968 met of course with near-universal condemnation, but Western intellectuals, absorbed in their domestic conflicts and mobilized against the war in Vietnam, had been far from enthused by the moderate aspirations of a Dubček.[7] As for the student protests of March 1968 in Warsaw, they were drowned out by the debates in the Sorbonne, while the subsequent anti-Semitic repression in Poland aroused hardly an echo in opinion-making circles in the West.

It is thus not absurdly counterintuitive to suggest that whereas 1956 and 1968 in Central Europe marked staging points in the revival of cultural and political self-consciousness in these lands, these years had a depressingly contrasting effect in the West. In effect, they served further to remove Central Europe from the attention of

Western intellectuals by rendering it progressively less relevant to their concerns. Just as in 1950 the other half of Europe had been treated simply as a reflection of the Soviet Union, so the latter's fall from grace (in part as a result of its actions in the region) dragged Central Europe itself away from the focus of attention. By the early 1970s, following the emergence of Gierek in Poland and Husák in Czechoslovakia, and with the "independent" policies of Kádár and Ceauşescu, Central and Eastern Europe appeared once again to be stable; the events of the 1960s had been followed by "normalization," and interest, such as it was, had dissipated.

It is thus all the more remarkable that in the space of less than a generation, Central Europe is once again on the agenda of the West. Editorials in the major dailies of Britain, France, Italy, the United States, and of course West Germany are devoted to the theme. Significant journals of opinion assign whole issues to the subject. Colloquia are held from Berkeley to Berlin on the geography, history, culture, politics, and meaning of the very term. Emigrés from all the lands of Eastern and Central Europe are called upon to offer their views, and prominent literati expatiate confidently upon the works of authors whose names and countries they could not have pronounced a few years before. There has been a spate of studies on *fin-de-siècle* Vienna, with similar books on their way for pre-1914 Budapest and Prague (anticipatory echoes, perhaps, of our own nearly completed century). Exhibitions on the art, architecture, and society of early twentieth-century Central Europe have traveled halfway around the world. Today, we are all Central Europeans. What happened?

One answer might simply consist of a list of events from the 1970s. Between the publication of Solzhenitsyn's *Gulag Archipelago* in 1973 and the declaration of martial law in Poland in 1981, there intervened the Helsinki Conference and Agreement of 1975, the strikes in Poland in 1976 followed by the creation of KOR (Workers' Defense Committee), the announcement the following year of the birth of Charter 77 in Czechoslovakia, and of course the remarkable emergence of Solidarity in Poland in the summer of 1980. In the local context, these might be seen as part of a cumulative series of catalytic moments, starting with the uprising in East Berlin in 1953. But for the West the developments of the 1970s and 1980s came as if from nowhere, with correspondingly dramatic effects.

Nonetheless, such a litany of significant news items from abroad cannot in itself account for the reception accorded them at home. One reason for the response of Western intellectuals in recent years is the shift in the domestic political balance. During the 1950s and 1960s, anticommunism was most marked among scholars and writers of the northern countries of the West—notably West Germany. In the south (e.g., Italy, France), where strong local Communist parties flourished, the dominant left-leaning intelligentsia was largely undiluted by critical voices from the Center, much less the Right (witness the fate of Raymond Aron, ignored in Paris for most of his career but lionized in the Federal Republic and the United States). Since most postwar Western intellectuals took their cues from Paris, the pattern of intellectual response to events in the Soviet bloc was much as described above. But from the mid-1970s on, the Communists have been in decline in Latin Europe (precipitate in France and Spain, steady in Italy), with moderate Social Democratic parties replacing them on the left of the domestic political spectrum. If anything, it is the left intelligentsia of northern Europe that is now more sympathetic toward Soviet policies and actions. The peace initiative of 1979, coinciding as it did with the coming of Cruise and Pershing missiles, received a friendly hearing in political and academic circles in Scandinavia, West Germany, the Benelux countries, and Britain. By way of contrast, the increasingly anti-Communist intelligentsia of France in particular turned a deaf ear to Moscow but listened with growing interest to news and views from the Soviet satellites.

If this explanation helps us see why men and women in Paris or Rome are once again interested in developments to their east, it does not in itself account for the positively modish taste for talking about Central Europe in particular. To account for this fashion, which has now spread to the United States as well, we should perhaps begin with Milan Kundera. In articles that appeared between 1981 and 1985 in American, French, and British journals, he decried the impending disappearance of Central Europe, the deleterious effect of Russian domination of the region, and Western ignorance of the vital significance of the central lands for the survival of Europe as a whole.[8] In Kundera's wake came a veritable baggage train of Central European writers. In many cases they had been around before Kundera and had even been saying much the same sort of thing. But now they were noticed in the West for the first time by something more than a minority of specialists and fellow nationals. Important works by historians and philosophers from Poland, Hungary, and Czechoslovakia were translated into English (translations into French and Italian had come a little earlier in most cases, and into German earlier still), while accessible writings hitherto published only in emigré journals like *Zeszyty Literackie, Listy,* and *Svědectví* received rapid translation and recognition in Italy, France, Britain, the United States, and Canada.

Kundera's is a peculiarly Czech vision of Central Europe—gloomy, skeptical, suspicious, self-critical, and insecure, and the way in which it colors his polemics has undoubtedly in turn affected the Anglo-American understanding of the concept. But his own work is also the culmination of a process. Periodicals concerned with Central Europe (such as *Alternative* in France and *Cross Currents* in the United States) existed before Kundera's work accelerated interest in them, although the writings of 1984 in particular certainly provided a stimulus for other publications (*Autre Europe,* begun in 1984, *Micro-Mega,*[9] and *East European Reporter,* established in 1986). In general, the reception accorded in the West to emigré and dissident writers appears to have been a process of accumulation. Those who left Czechoslovakia or Poland in 1968–1969 took nearly a decade to receive a hearing (except in Germany, and Austria, where Vienna and Munich proved hospitable to exiles of the Left in particular). Even in the rare instance to the contrary, interest was not always of the most welcome kind. Leszek Kołakowski, the Polish philosopher and leading revisionist thinker of the 1950s, aroused interest among Western intellectuals more for his magnum opus on Marxist thought than for his many writings on theology and ethics, a preference that is indirect confirmation of the very different concerns of radical intellectuals in the two halves of Europe.

By the time Solidarity appeared, however, the ground was a little more fertile and intellectual celebrities like Adam Michnik could get published and read almost as rapidly in the West as in the underground press at home in Poland.[10] Sympathy with Lech Wałesa and his movement (during, but especially after, its public successes) was notably marked in political and labor circles in France and Italy (and significantly tepid in Britain or West Germany). As a result, Polish emigrés and exiles of the 1981 vintage integrated almost immediately into the inner circles of the Parisian intelligentsia. Even though their initial welcome and the enthusiasm for their cause subsided, they have never been consigned to the sort of marginal and near-pariah status accorded their predecessors.

Another factor in opening the way to a more sympathetic reception by the early 1980s was the increase in academic exchange in recent years—notably to the benefit of Hungarian scholars, who came to teach and lecture in all the Western countries, reestablishing the link with an older generation of Hungarians from 1956 and after, many of whom now hold senior positions in American universities in particular. Prominent figures like Györgi Ranki, the late Hungarian historian, organized exchanges between their own academies and Western institutions (Oxford University, the University of Indiana) and were accompanied in their endeavors by numerous Hungarian economists who debated with their Western counterparts the virtues and otherwise of the Hungarian economic model. This Eastern involvement in Western academic discussions inevitably produced at least some reciprocal Western concern for affairs in the socialist lands, a concern both real and critical, in contrast with the abstract and somewhat abstracted gaze of sympathetic leftist scholars of an earlier generation.

The reference to academic exchanges suggests that some role in the raising of Western consciousness has been played by events in the Soviet bloc itself—more communications, eased restrictions on certain categories of professional travel, new lines of official thinking on economic policy, a new generation of nonideological dissidents (but not Gorbachev, who appeared only late in the process). There is of course some truth in this, but at best it accounts for the ease with which the renewed interest in Central Europe can now be converted into knowledge. Its significance as an account of the interest itself should not be exaggerated. There have been détentes before. Indeed, almost everything that was on offer from Central Europe in the 1970s and 1980s had come around before. Kundera's own writings had been anticipated, for example, by the Romanian Mircea Eliade, writing in *Preuves*, in Paris, in 1952: "These cultures [that is, those of Central Europe] . . . are on the eve of their disappearance. . . . Does not Europe feel the amputation of a very part of its flesh? Because, in the end, all these countries are in Europe, all these peoples belong to the European community."[11]

Yet when Eliade wrote those words, the master thinkers of Western culture looked past him. Neither neo-Marxists like Sartre nor Christian moralists like Emmanuel Mounier ignored the contemporary imprisonment of the eastern half of Europe. Indeed, they acknowledged and disapproved of it. But they and their contemporaries on the Left (with certain honorable exceptions like Elio Vittorini and Ignazio Silone) looked beyond Budapest and Bucharest, their eyes firmly fixed on the metahistorical justifications for present Soviet misdemeanors. Moral appeals to common European sensibilities received little echo anywhere (Raymond Aron stands out as an exception in France, but then he too was only rediscovered in Paris in the early 1980s!).[12]

The salient factor, then, was not altered circumstances in the East but changed sensibilities in the West. When Solzhenitsyn's *Gulag Archipelago* was published, it offered nothing except rich detail that was not already known about the Soviet system of forced labor camps (down to the very term *gulag*, used by Kravchenko in 1946). Any number of memoirs and essays had been published during the late 1940s and thereafter, and the fact of the camps' existence was no longer disputed, as it had once been.[13] It was the timing that counted. When the *Gulag Archipelago* arrived in the West, it encountered an intellectual community in profound flux. It would be pleasing to be able to say, with the Yugoslav writer Danilo Kis, that the sympathetic reception accorded to Central Europe has arisen from the Western discovery "that it had lost a part of its own heritage and that it had been thereby impoverished."[14] But this is naive. Czechs, Poles, and Hungarians have long looked West in search of confirmation of their European identity (Hungarians and Poles with some ambiguity perhaps). That they should now, beginning in the late 1970s, have met with a response is gratifying, but that is little owing to any collective Western sense of loss.

What had been lost, notably in France and Italy, was the faith in Marxism (it is a matter of some curiosity that Marxism still survives and occasionally thrives among intellectuals and academics in the English-speaking world, where it has never acquired any political purchase; for this reason among others, Central Europeans feel more at home in Latin Europe). The spell cast over the radical intelligentsia of Western Europe by Marxism from 1945–1975 was not of course dissipated overnight. The trajectory of French intellectuals is paradigmatic (the more so in that during these years theirs was the example most commonly followed). First, in 1956, there came the double blow of Khrushchev's speech and the attack on Hungary, ending the consubstantiality of Marxism-Party-proletariat. Then, Marxism was exported, with spontaneous peasantries ostensibly replacing organized workers in the driving seat of history. Only when this myth in turn lost its credibility (somewhere between the Cultural Revolution and Pol Pot) did intellectuals return their gaze to Europe, a continent where the Soviet Union had once again, in 1968, contributed to the further undermining of its own foundation myth. By the time Solzhenitsyn appeared in French translation, the former epigones of Stalin and Mao had adjusted their critical fire, first on Marx, then on Hegel, and finally on all forms of utopian or system-building theories, deemed collectively responsible for their totalitarian progeny.[15]

In other words, it was only when French intellectuals had found their own reasons (highly idealistic and abstract) for reclassifying Marxism as a failed and faulted fantasy of nineteenth-century master thinkers that they could look afresh at the Soviet Union (or *a fortiori* Eastern Europe) and recognize more earthbound reasons for weighing ideological anchor. And even then, the mirage of Eurocommunism (a brief moment from 1975 to 1978 when there was hope that the Communists of France, Italy, and Spain would forge a renewed, democratic Communist movement) slowed down the process. But the coincidence of domestic political decline (for all Western Communist parties), continued ideological etiolation, the invasion of Afghanistan, and the rise and fall of Solidarity helped complete the picture. By 1982, Marxism in its former Western strongholds was almost as dead as it is in the lands of its enthronement and a channel of communication had opened up. Once they stopped sounding like Party bureaucrats and began to speak the same language as their Central European counterparts, Western intellectuals could begin to hear what the latter were saying.

The reference here to language is not entirely gratuitous. Another element in the pan-European convergence was the reemergence of rights in Western political theory. For most of this century, philosophers and political theorists have disdained "rights talk," either on the grounds that rights cannot be logically grounded (Bentham's "nonsense on stilts") or else because they are historically circumscribed, the product of circumstance and legal practice, rather than timeless and essential. And for Marxists, of course, the term was usually preceded by a pejorative qualifying adjective (e.g., "bourgeois"). But a number of seminal English-language works of political thought published during the 1970s began the task of replacing rights at the center of ethically based political argument, supported in this by numerous special-interest groups seeking to appropriate the language of rights in support of their claims ("women's rights," etc.). Although these writings have only recently begun to be translated into French and Italian, the growing local interest in analytical political philosophy as a substitute for discredited continental metaphysics is unmistakable.

It does not always follow from this that the language of rights now in vogue in the West corresponds tidily to the sort of rights that dissident intellectuals in Central Europe have been claiming for many years. When Central European dissidents talk about rights, they often mean something both larger and more precise than the sense contained in the more restricted philosophical discourse of Western theorists (though here the Italians and French serve as something of a bridge). Nonetheless, it does not seem unreasonable to see in these developments the emergence of a common language of political claims and duties.[16]

One effect of the new Western enthusiasm for rights talk (an enthusiasm which, in Paris at least, is on occasion demagogic and in inverse proportion to previous interest in the subject) has been to offer a way of undermining the cultural relativism so fashionable in Western writings of the 1960s and early 1970s, that very particular refusal to criticize the ways of others (however abhorrent) in the name of one's own political culture. The revival of a variety of neo-Kantianism offers the possibility of condemning the ethical shortcomings of others and has enabled Western writers to deal directly with the experience of Central Europeans, instead of denying them the very evidence of their own senses, as in the past. This observation is not universally applicable, however. There are still writers and teachers in the West who cling to the philosophies of suspicion, heirs to Heidegger and Sartre where they are not also the followers of Derrida. But it is significant that Western intellectuals today form less of a bloc than at any time since the war; there are to be found, scattered from Milan to Michigan, followers of Marx,

Gramsci, Foucault, Nietszche, Popper, Proudhon, and Jesus as well as those who follow none of the above. Or, to take just one important contemporary figure, it would have been unthinkable for Jürgen Habermas and his communitarian liberalism to attract widespread respect among the mainstream intellectual Left until very recently indeed.[17]

If the death of Marxism constitutes the fundamental reference point in the new Western empathy for Central Europe, and if the fashion for rights has provided at least the illusion of a common political language, other factors have also played their part. For most of the period 1948–1973, the cultural identity of Western Europe was heavily colored by anti-Americanism. Beginning in Britain during the war itself, resentment at the privileged American ("over-paid, oversexed, and over here") took off during the 1950s, a combination of economic jealousy and political opposition fueled by the frustration born of that same European decline that had propelled the United States into its position of privilege. In France and Italy matters were exacerbated by the presence of an aggressively anti-American Communist party and by memories (especially strong in France) of the ambivalent mood during the Liberation, when resentment toward U.S. presence and policies came to outweigh appreciation of the American role in the freeing of these countries.[18]

Although opposition to the American alliance and the U.S. presence in Europe declined following the end of the Korean war, it was refueled by the conflict in Vietnam, which coincided with a growing sense of the reemergence of Europe as a world power. Defending the claims and the actions of the Soviet Union more as a counterweight to American power than on ideological grounds, many Europeans in the 1960s were sympathetic to de Gaulle's vision of a Europe stretching from the Atlantic to the Urals. But a Europe so described, including Russia and its western territories, paradoxically diminished the significance of the Slav and other lands on Russia's western borders by treating them simply as extensions of the mother country. Having no comparable relation to any West European nation (except Britain, in the eyes of de Gaulle), the United States was in these years regarded as both an outsider and an intruder, in Europe no less than in Southeast Asia.

In more recent times, anti-American sentiment in Europe has taken cultural rather than political form. Just as Western Europe during the

1970s was becoming more superficially Americanized (in clothing, music, and commerce), so resentment toward this process surfaced. Although the French Socialists today fall over themselves to "modernize" France on the Californian model, as recently as 1981 the minister of culture, Jack Lang, spoke out aggressively against the nefarious mediocrity of American popular culture. Spanish leftists sought the closing of American bases, partly in belated retaliation for U.S. support of Franco. And in northern Europe especially, nuclear disarmament movements have urged their governments to pursue what amounts to neutralism in international affairs. But what is common to these demonstrations of irritation toward the United States is the way in which they have increasingly been couched in the vocabulary of *Europe*. This is particularly the case in West Germany, where talk of Europe, not all of it confined to intellectuals of the Left, is effectively synonymous with the desire to create a nuclear-free neutral zone between the superpowers.

Here, and for the first time, West European dislike of the United States is at least potentially compatible with the perspective and interests of the other Europeans. Although the relatively mild anti-American sentiments of Italians and French still sit more comfortably with the experience and instincts of intellectuals in the Soviet bloc, the aggressive neutralism of the British, Dutch, and German activists in END (European Nuclear Disarmament) has found some favorable response, especially in East Germany, where a parallel peace movement has significant support in dissident and church circles. Initially there were difficulties, since to the ears of a Pole or a Czech, the writings of someone like Edward Thompson carry disturbing echoes from the past. Calling down a plague on the houses of Washington and Moscow alike carries little conviction to those for whom the Soviet army and its local quislings are the only reality that counts. Only when the emphasis on peace (i.e. Western disarmament) had been matched by demands for rights and the restoration of liberties to unofficial peace activists in the East was some sort of fragile dialogue established.[19]

It remains a slim basis for mutual understanding. What the more radical of the Western peace movements and their supporters in the Green movements have always sought is the removal of the United States from any military role in Europe. The presence of Russia in such a Europe, the exclusion of the United States, and the disarmament of the Western allies strikes Socialist bloc dissidents, however sympathetic, as being monumentally naive (an opinion tacitly shared by many on the Left in France and Italy as well, further evidence of the growing importance of the north-south division in Europe today). A common opposition to militarism (expressed in some parts of Eastern Europe by a refusal to undertake military service), shared fears of nuclear and ecological catastrophe, and a certain puritan antimaterialism among writers and political activists in Czechoslovakia and West Germany, for example, point to a possible convergence of concerns but not much more.[20]

In a sense, what we are seeing here is once again a projection of a Western radical vision onto an imaginary Central European landscape. Where once it was the fantasy of socialism, now it is the dream of "a united, independent Europe." If it cannot be achieved in the West because of the presence and interests of the United States, then let it be enacted further east, in some loosely defined Central Europe miraculously released from all historical and geographical constraints. Indeed, the dissidents in the region, eagerly sought out by Western theorists as interlocutors and as living evidence of the plausibility of their own projects, are also something of a projection. They are ascribed a place in the Western radical's scheme of things, serving to legitimate the anti-American bent of the West European plan for the Continent by virtue of their own symmetrical anti-Soviet radical demands. It is a role that few dissident intellectuals in Central Europe are equipped for or care to fill.

A final, circumstantial factor tending to favor interest in Central Europe has been the steady decline in the polarities and tensions of Western European political life itself. It is only a very few years since France, Italy, and Spain were gripped in the embrace of Left-Right divisions with deep historical roots, Communists and Socialists on one side, Liberals and Catholics on the other. Now, all is in flux. The most important aspect, already alluded to, is the internal transformation of the old Left, although the ending of the romance with Marxism has also opened opportunities for dialogue across the ancient divide. Socialist parties in Portugal, Spain, France, and Italy have all governed or been part of a governing coalition in the course of the past decade, and are now closer in most respects to liberals and moderates of the Center than to the Communists to whom they were once linked.

This reduced importance of the terms *left* and *right* in Western European parlance (reflected in interminable debates in France especially about the "end" of the Left and so forth) has removed the sting from debates over Central Europe. There is a remarkable level of agreement across the Western political spectrum, at least so far as it concerns the more superficial dimensions of the meaning of European identity. Milan Kundera and Václav Havel are as much admired within one political family as they are in the camp of its opponents. This is an odd situation, and it is probably destined to crumble in the face of serious political choices about the future of Central Europe. But for the present there is agreement on the essentials: Central Europe is part of Europe, it should be free, its writers and thinkers are interesting.

One explanation for this receptivity lies in the current fashion for "Euro-chat," the obsession with plans for the big bang of 1992, when the twelve-member European Community is due to remove all barriers, tariff and human, between its constituent parts. Beyond the predictable focus on taxes, customs levies, pricing policies, and the like, there lie matters of real significance for the Continent as a whole. Over the last two decades, the European Community has moved a long way toward the creation of a federal system. In the smaller nations, but also in Italy, France, and the Federal Republic, it is no longer mere cant to speak of Europeans or a European outlook. There are of course internal distinctions; in one recent poll the British and the Danes showed little enthusiasm for the idea of a European parliament with true legislative powers. But the same poll showed the French (and especially the Italians) very much in favor of just such a federal political arrangement.[21] And in general the southern half of the community has responded positively to the reduction of national distinctions—after the Italians and the French, it is the Spanish who have come around most readily to the idea (the Communist parties of France and Portugal have dragged their feet on this issue, but like the anti-Europeans within the British Labor party, their views no longer count for much with anyone).

However, the uncertainties of 1992, no less than its opportunities, have helped focus attention on "the other Europeans." When the European Community expands still further, as it surely must, whom will it include? Austria and Yugoslavia? And after that? Such questions received little attention in earlier years, if only because all such visions were politically unrealistic. No longer cut off from Western Europe, with their economies already linked to the West by loans, trade, and gifts (in the case of the two Germanies), the countries of East Central Europe have every reason to press for closer links, at a time when the Soviet Union is no longer actively discouraging such moves. West Europeans, already accustomed to talking about the prospects for a wider, transnational Europe, can hardly avoid acknowledging these developments. The two Europes are still very far apart (and not just because of the East-West divide), and much of the conversation between them is at cross-purposes. But there is a conversation taking place, and the coming transformation of the one-time Common Market will only intensify such exchanges.

In offering suggestions to account for the renewed Western interest in Central Europe, I have proceeded on the fiction of a common Western experience, a vision of Central Europe informing Western reaction as a whole. This is a necessary fiction, if we are to grasp the global significance of the "rediscovery." But on the ground and in detail there are some telling distinctions. One of these has already been noted. In the last few years there has been quite a remarkable revival of Germany (or the Germanies, all three of them, if we include Austria in this context). Without some such reemergence of the German-speaking lands onto the center of the European stage, any rediscovery of the idea of Central Europe would have been incomplete (and perhaps impossible). But because of the peculiarities of the German and Austrian situations, *Central Europe* again has more than one meaning, a multiple resonance.

The German perspective on this question will be discussed at length in another essay in this issue. (See "Central Europe or Mitteleuropa?" by Jacques Rupnik.) Here I want simply to draw attention to the way in which this perspective differs from that of the Western nations. When German writers look at Central Europe, they see a region in which there lived, in addition to Germans living in what are now West Germany, East Germany, and Austria, some 11 million ethnic Germans. After the last war, some 9 million to 10 million of these left or were deported, some to the German Democratic Republic, most to the Federal Republic of Germany. For a long time they formed a phalanx of conservative voters, preventing West German governments from recognizing the postwar settlement or engaging directly with the satellite governments of the Soviet bloc.

The impact of that experience is now all but absorbed, but it has been replaced by an equally important concern with the past on the part of a new generation of Germans who are coming to terms with the history of the present divisions.

Here, as in the nineteenth century, Central Europe as a theme has become inextricably intertwined with debates over German identity. Left-wing intellectuals and activists look eastward for a solution to the dilemma of a divided nation, the nationalism of the Greens and of some Social Democrats feeding off a political neutralism and the anti-Americanism already noted.[22] On the Right, the German presence in Europe's center is part of another debate, the revisionist controversy raised by the historians Andreas Hillgruber and Ernst Nolte. For these writers, the "legitimate" fear of annihilation by the Soviets explains (and helps justify) the military actions of the Nazis, which thus become defensible even though they had the incidental effect of buying Hitler time with which to kill more Jews. As part of an updated strategy in the continuing German struggle to survive the Soviet challenge, Hillgruber especially favors the "reconstruction" of a lost Central Europe, and he is not alone.[23]

There are other considerations, too. The renewed contacts with the GDR, and the anticipation of an expansion of the Federal Republic's role in the economic life of the region date back to Willy Brandt and the Ostpolitik of the 1960s. With the coming of Gorbachev and the increased Soviet enthusiasm for Western links, the West Germans see themselves as the natural interlocutors in the region. Discussion of these matters and of a place for Germans in some sort of Central European community have occupied much space in the German press in recent years. But such prospects as these are far from uncontentious, domestically. For the Germans are themselves Central Europeans in this sense, that their own identity is part of the problem. Is the Rhineland in Central Europe? Is Hamburg? Certainly not in the way that would be true of Bavaria or Saxony. It is only by historical accident (or, put differently, as part of the vagaries of German history) that the Germans can be said to be actors in the rediscovery of Central Europe. What has really been disinterred is the German problem (for Germans and non-Germans alike), and that is why this subject sounds so utterly different when discussed by Germans.

The same applies to the theme in its Austrian context. Here, too, things look different. Austria might well have gone the way of

Czechoslovakia in 1945. That it did not was its good fortune, but it left the country (as in 1920) with no natural center of gravity. Now, with expanding contact across the Hungarian frontier in particular (and with Mariahilfestrasse the main shopping artery for Budapest), Austrians have once again begun to look East for an economic and a cultural constituency (in some sense they never lost it—Vienna is still a terribly important city for Eastern Europeans, their stepping-stone to the West and a vital source of news as well as commodities). It is surely significant that it is a figure in the conservative People's party, Erhard Busek, who has raised afresh the idea of an Austro-centered Mitteleuropa, more geographically restrained than Naumann's but with remarkable similarities to the thinking of an earlier generation of Austrians, the "Austromarxists" Otto Bauer and Rudolf Hilferding.[24] To the extent that the Austrian vision of Central Europe has something in common with ideas circulating in Prague and Budapest, it is more truly in keeping with the indigenous understanding of the term than are those French or American writers who enthuse over a more abstracted Erewhon-like cultural continent.

Austria is different for another reason. The rediscovery of Central Europe, as seen from Vienna, includes a region almost wholly neglected in Western debates. For Austria is a neighbor of Yugoslavia, and there, too, the term *Central Europe* has a special local resonance. Whereas for Czechs it means seeking to rejoin the West, and in West Germany it is a movement away from the (American-dominated) West, so in Yugoslavia it is about regional autonomy. The republics of Croatia and Slovenia (the latter especially) have always felt uncomfortable as part of a multinational federation dominated by Serbs and including poorer, southern national groups who were never part of a European empire and whose failing economies are subsidized by the more prosperous north (echoes of similar resentments in Italy). Here, then, discussions about Central Europe are a way of expressing anti-Serb opinions and are also part of a longer, larger debate between unity and particularism. For many Slovene and Croat intellectuals it is a question of peripheries. Of which center are Zagreb and Ljubljana the fringes—Serbian-dominated Yugoslavia or the Central Europe to which they once belonged in the old Dual Monarchy? The link to Austria is obvious: the Austrian region of Carinthia has a significant Slav minority, and Slovenes in particular are at least as much a part of any Austro-centered European heartland as, say, Slovakia.

That Yugoslavia should until very recently have been left out of Western discussions is of course an ironic tribute to Tito's success in separating the experience of his country from that of the rest of Central and Southeastern Europe. Only in Italy has there been some attention to this matter, and that for a very special reason: in Italy, too, Central Europe is in part a domestic matter. In this respect Italy stands aside from the rest of the West as commonly defined. Much of northern Italy was until fairly recently part of the Austrian Empire. Lombardy was only liberated in the war of 1859–1860, and the region of Friuli–Venezia Giulia was Austrian until 1866 and even today contains significant German and Slav minorities. Like other Italian regions in recent years, it has sought to expand its regional autonomy and assert a local identity. But unlike other such regions of the country, the northeast has sought to secure its distance from Rome through the formation of a transnational region for mutual cultural collaboration, comprising Friuli–Venezia Giulia, Austrian Carinthia, Slovenia, and Croatia. The political and economic significance of this collaboration, known as Alpen-Adria, is necessarily limited, but it has colored perception of the Central Europe debate in the country.

Italy is in any case different in other ways as well. Like the Federal Republic, it has welcomed dissidents from the Soviet bloc for many years. Czechs especially, but Hungarians and Poles as well, have taken up posts in the universities, held elected and appointed offices, and been prominent in the print and other media. When Alexander Dubček came to accept an honorary degree from the University of Bologna in November 1988, his presence and his speech were matters of national prominence. The role of the Italian Communists is relevant here. For a long time the Italian Communist party (PCI) functioned as a conduit for negotiations between discontented Western Communist reformers and the Moscow center to which they still owed formal allegiance. In 1981, however, the popular leader of the party, the late Enrico Berlinguer, condemned the declaration of martial law in Poland, just as he had openly split with Brezhnev over the invasion of Afghanistan. Ever since then, the PCI and its national daily paper *L'Unita* have served as privileged outlets for dissident and opposition thought within the Soviet bloc as well as in the West. As a result, the left-leaning Italian political community has been kept unusually well informed about ideas and events in Poland, Czechoslovakia, and Hungary in particular, and Central Europe is a place and a theme with which Italian readers are well acquainted.

Finally, and in marked contrast with the French, Italian intellectuals have less reason for guilt and embarrassment over their writings and actions during the Stalinist and post-Stalinist years. They have thus spent rather less time atoning for past sins and have been less extreme in their abandonment of all past affiliations. They are thus not quite so apt to have flights of pessimistic fancy as their Parisian colleagues, and they may have a better-informed view of what is and is not realistic in the future of Central Europe. At the same time, theirs is a closer and probably more enduring concern with the region than that of British or American writers.

Nonetheless, it is precisely along the Atlantic seaboard of both continents that the rediscovery of Central Europe has been most touted. Is it a passing fashion, the vacuum left by Marxism and filled by nostalgia and fantasy, by cost-free demands for the recognition of human rights and an expanded cultural tourism? What future is there for "Central Europe" (as distinct from the prospects for the place itself)?

To begin with, it should be acknowledged that if there is indeed a wider Western acquaintance with Central Europe, it has not so far led to a deeper understanding (in this respect Kundera's plea, addressed to Western intellectuals, has fallen on ground little more fertile than that worked by Miłosz[25] and Eliade in an earlier generation). Take the case of the universities. The academic study of the history, politics, or literature of the region between Germany and the Soviet Union remains a minority taste. Very few universities in Western Europe or North America teach the languages of Central, Eastern, or Southeastern Europe. Where courses on the region exist, they normally treat it as a subordinate field in the wider category of Soviet studies (or Soviet history or Russian and Slavonic literature). Few students take such courses, fewer still learn any of the relevant languages, and only an infinitesimal minority give serious thought to specializing in the region.

One reason for this is the generally poor quality of the instruction they are likely to receive. A disturbingly high proportion of the knowledgeable teachers are exiled nationals of the countries of the region. The older ones came in the 1950s, a middle generation dates from the Polish and Czech exodus of 1968–1969, and a smaller number left and came West after the suppression of Solidarity. If the situation in the Soviet bloc does not suddenly deteriorate, this supply is likely to dry up. The education of the West in the history and culture of half of Europe will come to depend on professors trained in other areas, with at best only a secondary interest in Central Europe itself.

This situation is superficially alleviated in France and Italy by the presence in universities and institutes of professional experts, men and women with a genuine interest in the subject of Central Europe but often with no firsthand knowledge of it and trained in something else (even linguistic competence is often an optional extra). In Britain, where interest in the subject is lower than on the Continent, the history and politics of at least eight separate Central or Southeastern European states are commonly taught by experts in Soviet affairs, who unabashedly treat Eastern Europe as an adjunct to the study of the Soviet Union (echoing an earlier generation who saw the same region as a mere footnote to the study of another "historical" nation, in that case Germany).[26] In Oxford and Cambridge, for example, the study of Central Europe can only be pursued as a minor option in courses devoted to the Soviet Union. Things are better in the United States and Canada, but not by very much. And it is an open secret that in recent years it has not proved easy to recruit into East European studies the very best graduate students.

If I am correct in my earlier characterization of the reasons for the rediscovery of Central Europe, this lack of any concerted academic focus is not surprising, for most of the factors leading to the renewed receptivity of Western intellectuals are negative—the end of Marxism, loss of faith in the Soviet Union, suspicion of the United States, neutralism. It is not, after all, as though there had been some seminal work on Central Europe in recent years that captures and transforms the Western consciousness. And I think, too, that this situation helps explain something else, the particularly sympathetic reception accorded what we might call the cultural reading of Central Europe offered by Kundera and by the Hungarian novelist György Konrád—Central Europe as an idea, a state of mind, a worldview.

Kundera in particular was addressing himself to the West, and his vision of a disappearing Central Europe accords most closely with the revived interest in the general European fin-de-siècle. But whereas nostalgia for Proust's Paris or the London of Edward VII is compatible with an acknowledgment of present realities (Paris and London are still with us), an enthusiasm for the Vienna of Freud, or Kafka's Prague, cannot help but be bound up in a sense of regret and loss. Hence the understandably fonder memories of the Habsburg Empire, once so reviled by most of its subjects. Milan Kundera is not of course proposing a revival of Kakania, the Austria-Hungary of Robert Musil which has somehow entered Western mismemory as a fantasy kindgom conflated from Johann Strauss and Graham Greene. But it is the Czechs, more than most, who have opened up for debate the original wisdom of destroying the multinational state, and their sense certainly is that it is Czechoslovakia, as the most western of the lost lands of Europe, that has suffered the most from events since 1918.[27] Between this and the often-noted analogy with the Jewish experience (the Czechs frequently detecting an affinity in the situation and a precariousness about the two peoples), it is not surprising that the Czech understanding of what is at stake in Central Europe, and what has been lost, has been most influential in forming Western opinion.

As a consequence, few of the newly minted Western enthusiasts for Central Europe care to learn too much about the deep historical rifts within the region. Not many Western writers now pay much attention, for example, to Hungary's losses in the settlements that followed both world wars. Yet these losses of people and territory were to the advantage of Czechoslovakia, Romania, and Yugoslavia and comprised some 25 percent of the ethnic population of Hungary. To take another example, the rather better understanding of Polish suffering and the prominence of certain Polish writers and thinkers does not in itself increase Western appreciation of the difference between the Polish and the Czech understanding of what is meant by *Central Europe*. Many of Poland's poets and writers look East rather than West for their roots, to Vilna rather than Vienna. If they have looked to the West, to Paris in particular, it has been in a search for understanding and contact, not because they harbor any doubts about the centrality and legitimacy of their own national culture. To take a final example, there is Bucharest (or what now remains of it), a city whose intelligentsia long saw themselves having a privileged relationship with Paris, a relationship still echoed, albeit dimly, by the uniquely French interest in Romanian matters. Yet for many Central Europeans (and not just Hungarians justifiably bitter over Ceauşescu's treatment of ethnic Hungarians in Transylvania), Romania is not even part of the region, but is eastern, perhaps Balkan. Is Romania, then (with or without its present dictator), a part of Central Europe? How many Westerners, even today, know or care? More to the point, do they know how much their own lack of concern is shared in Central Europe itself?

There is a Central European fantasy of a never-never Europe of tolerance, freedom, and cultural pluralism. It is held to be all the more firmly implanted in the consciousness of Czechs and Hungarians, for example, for want of the reality. But whereas for Central Europeans this fantasy has served perhaps as a necessary myth, it is odd to see it reflected in Western fantasies about Central Europe, the geographical expression. To suppose that this part of the Continent was once a near-paradise of cultural, ethnic, and linguistic multiplicity and compatibility, producing untold cultural and intellectual riches, has been part of the Western image in recent years. Yet such imaginings take us back to Kakania again, when in truth Central Europe, from the Battle of the White Mountain down to the present, is a region of enduring ethnic and religious intolerance, marked by bitter quarrels, murderous wars, and frequent slaughter on a scale ranging from pogrom to genocide. Western Europe was not always much better, of course, but on the whole it has been luckier, which is almost as good. And it is surely reasonable for Central Europeans, in the light of their history, to dream a little of Sweden. But it is just as surely inappropriate for the West to make of Central Europe a fantasy, past or present. Indeed, it smacks of bad taste, and is not so very different from the other sorts of political fantasies projected eastward in the 1950s.

The problem seems to be that Central Europe is always at risk of being the product of someone's imagination. For many years it was an ideological projection of Western radical thought. With ideology currently being sold very short, Central Europe has become the idealized Europe of our cultural nostalgia. Because this has something in common with the way certain prominent dissidents have chosen to articulate their opposition to Soviet domination, a dialogue has been struck up. But down on the ground, Central Europe remains a very opaque sort of proposition. Is some sort of Central European federation a future possibility? Is it sensible to envisage an expansion of the present European Community to include, say, Hungary and Czechoslovakia? It does seem improbable. Commentary 98 of the current Czech criminal code explicitly forbids any propagation of the idea of a Central European federation, and starting with its veto of a Balkan federation in 1948, the Soviet Union has always frowned upon that sort of bilateral relationship between its allies, much less multinational federal linkages. As to whether the European Community could absorb even more peripheral members, serious doubts have already been expressed in certain quarters. Taking in Portugal, Spain, and Greece has already created many difficulties—much expense and some local resentment.

The concentration on Central Europe as a cultural entity shorn of its immediate geopolitical constraints has entailed ignoring one of the most salient features of its recent history. The fact is that the future of Europe still rests on extra-European considerations, notably the intentions of the Soviet Union (which is why some West Europeans have taken to including Russia in the European equation, resolving the difficulty by redefining it). Central Europe's future is still very largely dependent on the outcome of events in Moscow. And here a curious paradox begins to emerge. As the Gorbachev reforms proceed in the Soviet Union, the Western attitude toward his country grows distinctly more favorable. Whereas just nine or ten years ago the Soviet Union was seen by most observers in Europe and the United States as the brutal headquarters of an imprisoned continent, so now it is seen by many as Central Europe's best hope. If only, the argument runs, the rulers in Prague or Berlin or Bucharest would follow Moscow's lead.

But as a result of this shift in perspective, interest in the West has already begun to move away from Central Europe toward the Soviet Union. In this sense, it sometimes seems as though intellectuals in the West have a limited tolerance for news and opinion from the East. Appreciation of the importance of Moscow is gained only at the price of diminished interest in the space between, just as the recent enthusiasm for Central Europe was secured at the price of a refusal to acknowledge the continuing Soviet presence there. How many writers in Britain or the United States have responded comprehendingly to the opinion of certain Hungarian critics, who warn that if *perestroika* amounts at best to nothing more than imitation of the new economic model as implemented by Kádár, then things look pretty bleak? This is not something that most people want to hear just now. It becomes possible to imagine a scenario in which

Gorbachev offers Central Europe de facto autonomy, thereby so raising the stock of the Soviet Union in the eyes of Western thinkers that they will lose all interest in listening to the views of the Central Europeans themselves.

Of course, no such hypothesis applies in the case of the West Germans. Although the present West German government, like its predecessors, cares little for the interests of the successor states as such, and has always preferred to deal directly with the puppet master, the debate that has opened up in Germany on that nation's recent past and its future prospects will not soon subside. And to the extent that it is of necessity about the division of Europe, its causes and meaning, it is also a debate that will always be about Central Europe. But here a further consideration intrudes. Any serious resolution of the German question as it concerns a divided country, any long-term role for Austria in some newly constructed Mitteleuropa, would require the dismantling of the postwar settlements.

Such a prospect is not necessarily one that all would favor. That the Soviet Union would oppose any undoing of Yalta is obvious. The whole point of Helsinki and the human-rights concessions it entailed was to secure international confirmation of the permanence of the postwar arrangements. But Western governments, from Rome to Paris, not to speak of London and Washington, also have an abiding interest in the present stability—always assuming things do remain stable and on the condition of a reasonably benevolent Soviet leadership. Even Poles and Czechs might not look too kindly on serious revisions. An opening up of the map of Europe for diplomatic reconsideration would raise too many ghosts. Accordingly, it seems fair to expect the present dispensation to remain in place, nibbled away only at the margins, and in no case in the name of some reestablished Central European independence.

This, above all, is why the whole subject remains in the hands of the *Zivilisationsliterati,* of East and West alike. This is not such a terrible thing, and it by no means consigns Central Europe to insignificance. After all, the fashion will pass, but it will at the very least leave in paperback translations a library full of works by authors, living and dead, of whom the Western reader was hitherto ignorant. It has increased Western travel to Central and Eastern Europe (which is probably just about a net benefit to all parties), and in Italy and France it has certainly enriched local cultural and intellectual life through the presence of a host of exiled and emigré writers, actors, artists, philosophers, and politicians.

On the other hand, it is likely that interest in Central Europe will fade fastest where it is indeed only an interest in the literary output of the region and where firsthand acquaintance with Central Europeans and their culture and history is slim or nonexistent.[28] But where the discussion of Central Europe forms part of other debates of enduring local significance, as in Italy, or where, for whatever reason, there is a significant Central European presence (as in Toronto), there it may be expected to last. What this suggests is that, as so often in the checkered history of that part of the world, its fate (or, in this case, the Western echo of that fate) lies only partially in its own hands.

This is no doubt particularly galling when it takes the form of being reinvented by those who until only recently ignored one's very existence, although Central European writers may draw some ironic satisfaction from the role they have inadvertently played in the remaking of our own Western intelligentsia. But what Western enthusiasts for Central Europe so often miss is the beam of weariness in the eyes of Polish or Czech writers as they explain themselves to their new audience. There is a sort of asymmetrical exploitation at work here. Dissident writers and thinkers from Budapest and Warsaw look West by habit and necessity, for support (practical if not moral). But this does not mean that they for one second accept the audience's view of them or that they define their own identity and existence via that audience's acknowledgment or appreciation. Similarly, the Western intellectual has in recent years used the concept and example of Central Europe to renew and recast cultural and political debates at home, in Paris or New York, conducting a kind of domestic housecleaning with imported equipment. It will take time to overcome this historically conditioned state of semicommunication. Meanwhile, Central Europeans may take comfort from the thought that they were there long before they were so fortuitously rediscovered. Should they again be misplaced, they will doubtless survive.

ENDNOTES

[1] Friedrich Naumann, *Mitteleuropa* (Berlin: Reimer, 1915). On List, see "Frédéric List et l'idée de Mitteleuropa," in Jacques Droz, *l'Europe Centrale, Evolution historique de l'idée de "Mitteleuropa"* (Paris: Payot, 1960).

52   Tony Judt

[2]Ernest Lémonon, *La nouvelle Europe centrale et son bilan économique* (Paris: Alcan, 1931).

[3]See Elemér Hantos, *Mémorandum sur la crise économique des pays danubins* (Vienna: St. Norbertus, 1933), and *Der Weg zum neuen Mitteleuropa* (Berlin: Mitteleuropaverlag, 1933).

[4]See Jean Monnet, *Mémoires* (Paris: Fayard, 1976).

[5]See report in "Soviet Bloc Writers Clash at International Forum," *New York Times,* 9 May 1988.

[6]See Jean-Paul Sartre, "Le fantôme de Staline," *Les Temps Modernes* (129–31) (January-March 1957).

[7]In 1969, certain prominent intellectuals in the French Parti Socialiste Unifié, the home of much New Left thought at the time, condemned their party's leaders (Michel Rocard and Pierre Mendès-France) for supporting the Czech reformers. The latter, they declared, were "victimes consentantes des idéologies petites-bourgeoises (humanisme, liberté, justice, progrès, suffrage universel secret, etc. . . .)." Quoted by Pierre Grémion in *Paris-Prague* (Paris: Julliard, 1985), 79.

[8]See Milan Kundera, "Quelque part là-derrière," *Le Débat* (January 1981): 50–62; "Un occident kidnappé, ou la tragédie de l'Europe centrale," *Le Débat* (27) (November 1983): 2–24; "A Kidnapped West or Culture Bows Out," *Granta* (11) (1984): 93–123; "The Tragedy of Central Europe," *New York Review of Books,* 26 April 1984.

[9]*Micro-Mega* does not confine its attention exclusively to Central Europe—far from it. But the many articles in this review by Central Europeans, notably those translated from the Hungarian, suggest a particular interest in the subject within the nonparty Left in Italy. *Alternative,* founded in Paris in 1979, went under in 1984 but has since resurfaced as *La Nouvelle Alternative,* devoted exclusively to Central and Eastern Europe. Its first issue appeared in 1986.

[10]See, for example, Adam Michnik, *Penser la Pologne* (Paris: La Découverte-Maspero, 1983) and *Letters from Prison and Other Essays* (Berkeley: University of California Press, 1985).

[11]Mircea Eliade, "Examen Leprosum," *Preuves* 14 (April 1952): 29.

[12]Raymond Aron's *Mémoires* were published in Paris in 1983 (by Julliard) to a fanfare of enthusiasm, in instructive contrast to the silence that greeted his writings over the previous thirty years. For Vittorini, who crossed swords with the Communist leader Togliatti before leaving the Party, see *Diario in Pubblico* (Milan: Bompiani, 1957), notably the entries for January 1947. Among many writings by Ignazio Silone, see his speech to the International Conference of the PEN Club on 5 June 1947, "Sur la dignité de l'intelligence et l'indignité des intellectuels," reprinted in *Les Temps Modernes* (23–24) (August-September 1947): 405–12.

[13]For a representative example of the available evidence, see Viktor Kravchenko, *I Chose Freedom* (New York: Scribner's, 1946); and David Dallin and Boris Nicolaevsky, *Forced Labor in the Soviet Union* (New Haven: Yale University Press, 1948). In the late 1940s in Paris, David Rousset sued two Communist journalists for libel. They had accused him of inventing the existence of camps in

the Soviet Union. See David Rousset, *Le Procès concentrationnaire pour la vérité sur les camps* (Paris: Editions du Pavois, 1951).

[14]Danilo Kis, "Thèmes d'Europe Centrale," *La Nouvelle Alternative* 8 (December 1987): 6.

[15]For a detailed account of this process, see Tony Judt, *Marxism and the French Left* (New York: Oxford University Press, 1986), chap. 4, passim. The process of precipitate retreat from social theory can be seen in the works of the Parisian "new philosophers" of the 1970s, notably Bernard-Henri Lévy, *La Barbarie à visage humain* (Paris: Grasset, 1977) and André Glucksmann, *Les Maîtres Penseurs* (Paris: Grasset, 1977). Although published after the appearance of the *Gulag Archipelago*, these books were of course the product of intellectual shifts predating Solzhenitsyn's Western publication.

[16]See, in this context, John Rawls, *A Theory of Justice* (Cambridge: Harvard University Press, 1971), Robert Nozick, *Anarchy, State and Utopia* (New York: Basic Books, 1974), and Ronald Dworkin, *Taking Rights Seriously* (Cambridge: Harvard University Press, 1977). Although not published in translation until some years later (Rawls was the first to secure a European audience), these works of moral and legal philosophy have become well known in academic circles in Western Europe. They are taken to be about rights in a broader sense, which is more important for many of their readers than the philosophical debates to which they were in fact contributing. More directly concerned with human rights as such were the essays of Joel Feinberg. See his *Rights, Justice and the Bounds of Liberty* (Princeton: Princeton University Press, 1980).

[17]In this context, the most representative of Habermas's recent work is *Autonomy and Solidarity* (London: Verso, 1986).

[18]See H. Footitt and J. Simmonds, *France 1943–1945, The Politics of Liberation* (New York: Holmes and Meier, 1988), and G. Madjarian, *Conflits, Pouvoirs et Société à la Libération* (Paris: Union générale d'editions, 1980).

[19]See the comments of Václav Havel, who, frequently visited by Western peace activists, for a long time saw the disarmament movement as a vehicle for the diversion and neutralizing of the Western intelligentsia, in *"Politika a svedomi,"* *Svědectví* 18 (1984): 631.

[20]For a more extended discussion of the nature of contemporary intellectual opposition in Central Europe, see Tony Judt, "The Dilemmas of Dissidence: The Politics of Opposition in East-Central Europe," *Eastern European Politics and Societies* 2 (2) (1988): 185–240.

[21]See the opinion poll taken by "Eurobaromètre" and published in *Bulletin Européen* (Rome) 39 (2) (February 1988): 6.

[22]See, for example, Jochen Löser and Ulrike Schilling, *Neutralität für Mitteleuropa: Das Ende der Blöcke* (Munich: Bertelsmann, 1984), where Poland, Czechoslovakia, and Hungary receive a total of ten pages, while Germany and its anomalous situation take up most of the book. The real interest lies in the perceived threat of Central Europe as a nuclear war zone. See also the slim volume by Karl Schlögel, *Die Mitte liegt ostwärts: Die Deutschen, der verlorene Osten und Mitteleuropa* (Berlin: Siedler, 1986).

²³For details of this debate, which has deeply divided the German historical profession and been widely debated in the press, see the material collected in *Der Historikerstreit, Chronologisch Geordenete Quellensamlung 1986–1987* (Augsburg: Fachschaft Geschichte der Universität Augsburg, May 1987). Nolte pleads his case in *Das Vergehen der Vergangenheit, Antwort an meine Kritiker in sogenannten Historikstreit* (Frankfurt: Ullstein, 1987), especially 13–68, 171–79.

²⁴Erhard Busek and Emil Brix, *Projekt Mitteleuropa* (Vienna: Überreuter, 1986). Despite the heavy Austro-centered focus, this book has the virtue of acknowledging the many meanings of *Central Europe,* including the important role once played in the region by Jews.

²⁵See Czesław Miłosz's book, *The Captive Mind* (New York: Vintage Books, 1981).

²⁶The notable and only exception being of course London University's School of Slavonic and East European Studies.

²⁷The debate among Czech historians, which has ranged from the wisdom of advocating national independence to the ethical impropriety of the expulsion of the Sudeten Germans in 1947, has gone much further in the direction of national self-examination than has been the case in Hungary or Poland, where the nation-state goes largely unquestioned. It should be noted that in Czechoslovakia such debate is usually conducted within the dissident community, official history being in a supine and depressed condition since the purge of the academy in 1969–1970. See H. Gordon Skilling, "The Muse of History—1984," *Cross Currents* 3 (1984): 30–42; Charter 77, document no. 11, 1984; "Právo na dějiny," *Listy* 14 (5) (October 1984): 11–76; Petr Pithart, "Let Us Be Gentle to Our History," *Kosmas* 3 (2–4) (Winter 1984–Summer 1985): 7–22.

²⁸Even where an interest in "the other Europe" persists, it is often merely pro forma. Thus, in a recent collection of essays, published in Paris under the title of *Lettres d'Europe* (Paris: Albin Michel, 1988), the introduction by Jean-Pierre Angremy (pseudonym for a highly placed French Foreign Ministry official) speaks with rotund enthusiasm of the European ideal, "from Edinburgh to Sofia, from Lisbon to Leningrad." Having acquitted himself of this ritual bow in the direction of Central and Eastern Europe, Angremy then confines his attention exclusively to an area delimited by the European Community (minus Portugal!). No further reference is made to the other Europe.

It is not uncommon to find this sort of cavalier inclusion or dismissal, in writings from France especially, and such an approach is quite often (and not perhaps accidentally) accompanied by the assumption that Central Europe stretches to the Volga. As a rule, the larger the geographical area covered by the term, the shorter the span of attention paid to it.

January 1989

POSTSCRIPT

All contemporary political commentary is at risk of being overtaken by events. Commentators on Central Europe were for a long time less exposed than most, since the material in which they specialized had altered depressingly little over the years. The European revolutions of 1989 changed all that. Few if any of us can claim to have had any inkling of the speed with which developments in the Soviet Union would be echoed and overtaken in its erstwhile Western imperium. In this respect, it is a real pleasure to have been overtaken by events. The internal history of Europe's eastern half switched gears dramatically in the course of a few crowded months, and the terms in which this region has hitherto been discussed have undergone wholesale revision.

Conversely, *Western* reactions to the European revolutions of 1989 seem oddly consistent with the earlier patterns suggested in my article. The collapse of the papier-mâché Communist regimes in Czechoslovakia and Poland, the steady shift to a parliamentary democracy in Hungary, and the upheavals in Bulgaria and Yugoslavia have all been interpreted along preexisting battle lines drawn up within the political and intellectual communities of the West. In its crudest form, these developments amount to the claim that "we" won the Cold War, that the mirage of Marxism-Leninism has been defeated by the verifiably superior claims of democracy and the free market. It would be a mistake to imagine that this reading of events is confined to Washington and Downing Street. In a more sophisticated form it can be found not only in the newly liberal circles of French and Spanish intellectuals but *also* in the writings of what remains of the true believers of the Marxist Left (in Italy and the United States, *inter alia*). For the latter, Late Stalinist state-socialism has collapsed under the weight of its own contradictions, defeated by the liberal-capitalism to which it was never more than a false alternative.

Both sides in this odd partnership, an eerie shadow dance of nineteenth-century dogmas trapped in the last years of a century they never understood, share with their less ideological bedfellows a common reading of events in Central Europe: In place of the dictatorial, centralized state systems of the postwar years there will now be parliamentary democracies, more or less stable, committed to free-market economies (more or less effective). Socialism is dead. The only point left to debate is just how good, or bad, this news really is.

This response is almost as remote from reality as the fantasies described in my original article. The former cold warriors are probably in tune with the emotions of Poles or Hungarians, but their projections of a new capitalist frontier are sadly at odds with local realities (as those same Poles and Hungarians could all-too-readily demonstrate). But what of the legions of Western scholars now to be found bemoaning the loss of socialist institutions (child care, women's rights, secure employment, free medicine, etc.)? Most of these benefits existed only on paper or were applied and distributed in arbitrary, corrupt, or self-defeating ways. The residents of the erstwhile people's democracies were the heirs to the promise—however empty—of socialism, a promise and a dream once shared as widely in Eastern Europe as they are in the West. The promise and the dream had long since been broken and abandoned—Western regret today resembles the sensation experienced by those drawn to the fading light cast by a long extinct star.

What has been only sporadically remarked upon in the West is the emergence of the altogether sharper light cast by the presocialist history of this region from behind a forty-year cloud. In every instance, from the unresolved violence of Romania to the unsavory splits in Solidarity, there are resurfacing echoes of an earlier Central Europe, the one that "flourished" briefly between Versailles and Munich. After fifty years of dictatorship, the only political and cultural models available to these nations are those they managed to cast for themselves in their brief era of independence.

Thus in Poland and Hungary, for example, the nuances of political language, the role of the intelligentsia, the ethnic resentments, and social divisions are redolent of interwar history not because circumstances are similar (they aren't) or because the protagonists cannot do better (they can, and maybe they will), but because after being placed in a deep-freeze for two generations, the societies of East-Central Europe lack a political vocabulary with which to negotiate new domestic relationships. Hence the initial ease with which new politicians evoked old sentiments: the better to secure a hearing among the electorate.

Western observers, initially disposed to think only well of the new leaderships, began catching a whiff of the revived language of narrow nationalism, anti-intellectualism, anti-Semitism, and ethnic chauvinism from the early spring of 1990. Although some on the Left immediately asserted that this development was the price to pay for abandoning socialism, the more common reaction was a retreat from concern, as though in the matter of Central Europe a nuanced response was not an option—one either adored and idealized these people, or else one wrote them off as hopeless. Havel, the idol of the Western intelligentsia in December 1989, blotted his copybook by meeting Waldheim; and Walesa in his neo-Pilsudski mode is not nice to contemplate. There is a point in both cases: The sanctimonious, witness-bearing moral arbiter always dwelt somewhere within the imprisoned playwright, and Walesa the populist was often a little bit nastier than Michnik and others wanted to believe. But each man is well within the heritage bequeathed him by the peculiar traditions of his own nation and its experience and possibilities. Why should we expect less of them . . . or more?

The problem, *pace* my own original concluding paragraphs, is that the *real* Central Europe has reemerged, effacing all the previous ones invented for it by East and West alike. It is undoubtedly an integral part of the continent's identity, but only a part of it. Always peripheral to someone else (at least in the last two hundred years), it is *still* rent by linguistic, ethnic, religious, and historical divisions, still insecure and defined more by its culture and the peculiar intensity of its misfortunes than by secure boundaries, firmly established states, and rationally exploited and distributed resources. Periodically reentering the European historical mainstream at moments not of its own choosing, it finds identity and continuity only in its past. This might change now, but it has not changed yet, as any recent traveler in Yugoslavia or Slovakia will confirm.

The West would do well to bear in mind its own recent history before withdrawing in offended distaste at the bad linguistic habits of Polish demagogues and Hungarian nationalists. With the desecration of a Jewish cemetery in Carpentras fresh in their minds and Vichy an unpleasant family skeleton, the French are ill-placed to condemn too rapidly the shadow cast by the past upon Central Europe's present. And if Italy and Spain emerged from dictatorships rather more successfully than Romania or Bulgaria, it should be kept in mind that fascism, clerical or otherwise, lacked the socially disintegrative capacities of communism. All in all, the "lands between," the heirs to the Austro-Hungarian and Turkish empires, started out with few cards and lost most of them *en route*. What they need just now is practical help and critical sympathy rather than oscillating sentiments of adulation and disapproval. What they will probably get is German investment. But that is another story.

September 1990

The Political Traditions
of Eastern Europe

George Schöpflin

T*he Western political tradition always empha-sized pluralism and the fragmentation of power. In Eastern Europe, which was politically back-ward, the state played a much more dominant role as the principal agent of change. This re-sulted in a politically preeminent bureaucracy and a weak society. The independent states of the interwar period were fragmented socially and ethnically and were unable to make much progress toward democracy. However, their record did allow for some political pluralism, which was then destroyed by the Communists after the war.*

Hamlet: Do you see yonder cloud that's almost in the shape
of a camel?
Polonius: By the mass, and 'tis like a camel indeed.
Hamlet: Methinks it is like a weasel.
Polonius: It is backed like a weasel.
Hamlet: Or like a whale?
Polonius: Very like a whale.

—William Shakespeare,
Hamlet, Act III, Scene ii

The political traditions with which Eastern Europe entered the contemporary period can be generally characterized as backward. This backwardness manifested itself notably in the significantly

George Schöpflin is Lecturer in East European Politics at the London School of Economics and at the School of Slavonic and East European Studies.

different relationship between state and society to what had evolved in Western Europe, in attitudes toward modernity and the definitions of modernity, as well as the demands that modernization makes on any society. Modernity in the context of an emergent Eastern Europe, that is in the nineteenth century, comprised the aspiration for greater prosperity embodied in the visible symbols of the West at that time—industrialization in a word—and the growing complexity of social, economic, and political transactions. In the political realm, modernity also implied a measure of participation by society in the determination of political strategies in the broadest sense. With its prosperity, the West also acquired power, something which in Eastern Europe was comparatively scarce. The scarcity existed at two levels: the ruling political systems, the empires of Prussia, Austria, Russia, and Ottoman Turkey, were weak in relation to the West; while at the same time, East European societies were weak toward the empires.

The set of political values and institutions developed on the basis of preexisting habits to meet the challenge of modernity were, therefore, aimed at catching up with the West and paradoxically this produced a set of polities which differed markedly from the original model. These differences, which were intensified by the further differences existing between individual East European polities and societies, have persisted to the present day and have done so quite independently of the Soviet-type systems introduced into the area after 1948. In this article, I am basically concerned to trace both the "East European-ness" of Eastern Europe and to explore what changes have been effected by the Communist revolutions, as well as to look at the workings of the system itself. In other words, it will look at both the political cultural and the systemic factors involved.

STATE AND SOCIETY IN THE WEST

The Western political tradition that eventually produced the European variant of modernity differed from that of Eastern Europe in a number of ways, albeit Eastern Europe did share in some of the Western cultural and political tradition, however fitfully. The distinction here is between the Western tradition and the one that evolved in Russia, for in this regard Eastern Europe forms a transitional zone culturally, just as it does geographically. The salient factors of the

Western political tradition in the context of this analysis—others are possible—are concerned with the conception, generation, legitimation, and exercise of power. From the earliest period onwards, the West gradually evolved toward a position that power should be divided, that the different areas of power should be separated and the ruler should not be absolute either in his power or in his legitimation.[1] The peculiarity of the Western pattern of development lay in the separation of religious and secular legitimation. The ruler claimed to rule in the name of a divine right to do so, but this did not absolve him from a certain duty to God. To this extent, this feature of the Western political tradition was paralleled in other systems, but the radical distinction lay in the autonomy of the religious sphere and the power of the Church to enforce its claim to be the sole arbiter of religious legitimation.

The symbolic drama of Canossa illustrated this vividly. In no other historical tradition was it conceivable that a powerful secular ruler like Emperor Henry IV would undertake a penitent's pilgrimage, in a hair shirt and with a rope around his neck, to expiate his politico-religious sins or, in power terms, to recognize the religious authority of Pope Gregory VII, whom he had unsuccessfully challenged.[2] The idea of the tsar of Muscovy or the Byzantine emperor or the Ottoman sultan performing an analogous penance is an inherent absurdity.[3]

The particular point to be stressed is the fragmentation of power, both at the level of thought and of practice. Over the centuries in Western Europe, institutions evolved roughly in accordance with this tradition, despite repeated breaches and derogations. But the fact that they were viewed as breaches indicates the strength of the underlying tradition; no ruler ever succeeded in capturing the high ground of absolutism in this respect, apart from limited periods of time. Thus feudalism reinforced the concepts of reciprocity and accountability. The feudal superior, however grand he might be, had certain obligations to his vassals, notably those of protection, which he was expected to discharge. If he failed in this, he could be held accountable according to a set of recognized rules, thereby permitting the emergence of legality—a set of autonomously enforceable rules not within the hands of the ruler.

The concept of a contract, which was embodied in the oath of fealty or in the commercial codes serving the growing urban trading centers of the Middle Ages, constituted a crucial element in underpinning reciprocity in this system of values. A further feature of the feudal contract deserves notice. The contracting parties took on certain obligations in consideration of some duty to be performed in the future, that is to say, the privileges of feudal power were conditional on performance and could, in theory at least, be challenged for nonfeasance. The existence of these mutually recognized rights and duties would not in itself have been enough to sustain the set of values encapsulated in it. To achieve this, it was necessary to create autonomous organs of enforcement, a mutually respected tribunal, which regulated disputes without undue intervention from either involved party. Here again, the role of the Church and the canon law courts was essential, albeit secular courts were also of significance. The grudging acceptance by the ruler of the autonomy of the law and of the broader interest in a regular, predictable, and relatively transparent system of legal administration came to constitute a further feature and a factor on which the Western tradition was based.

An equally important development was that the rivalry of the ruler and the Church made it possible for third parties to emerge with their own sources of power. Three of these spheres—commercial, scientific, and urban—had very far-reaching consequences. The emergence of the commercial sphere took place in the teeth of Church opposition, given the Christian ban on usury (and thereby on interest) and at times of secular rulers as well, who disliked the growing strength of money over which they had no control but on which they depended. Centrally, the growth of networks of trading centers allowed a Europe-wide system to withstand repeated assaults by both secular and religious power holders.[4]

Of equal, if not greater, significance was the emancipation of a scientific sphere from the tutelage of the Church. This took longer. The Church was unquestionably the custodian of classical and other learning and its role in safeguarding these during the Dark Ages cannot be overestimated, but it regarded this as being within its own religious sphere, to be used for its own purposes. However, by the thirteenth century, this had begun to change. The founding of universities, originally as institutions for cultivating learning in the religious sphere, was decisive. Although for a long time, universities remained within the ambit of the Church and were closely associated with religious learning, a shift took place through the rise of universities with a degree of their own autonomy. The pivot of this was the movement away from rote learning. It came to be accepted that knowledge was more than a set of facts to be safeguarded, but—however uncomfortable this might have been—it involved speculative thought. Thus, in the universities which were founded in several European centers (Bologna, Montpellier, Paris, Oxford) at much about the same time, the norm became the investigation of phenomena and the exploration of the underlying causation, instead of the repetition of previously amassed information, by whatever criteria seemed appropriate, rather than those acceptable to the Church. This development was crucial, inasmuch as it legitimated the idea of change and innovation. The shift from rote to conceptualism gradually resulted in the claim to an autonomous scientific sphere through the secularization of learning. The implications of this were extremely serious. It eventually provided cognitive instruments for challenging all claims, all privilege, all power flows. At its heart was the secularized variant of the originally Christian concept that the present can and must always be transcended in the name of a better future. But it involved the translation of a religious eschatology into a secularized teleology. Hence, it was applicable to political situations as well.

All this points to the centrality of autonomous thought and practice from the power of the ruler in the Western tradition. The ruler was constrained to recognize that he did not exercise absolute power over his subjects, who retained politically, economically, etc. important spheres of autonomous action. Despite repeated attempts by various rulers—religious as well as secular—to extinguish or suppress these spheres of autonomy, whether in the name of order or routine or unity or rationalization, these were never completely successful. Autonomy and the separation of spheres remained a crucial feature of Western patterns and subsequently became the foundation for the extension of liberties.

However, another aspect of this tradition deserves emphasis. It follows logically from the foregoing that the Western tradition included a concept of change, a state of affairs where relationships shifted and where the various political and economic actors moved autonomously. Indeed, built deeply into this tradition was the idea of improvement through transcendence, derived ultimately, as suggested, from Christian eschatology. The contrast here with the significantly more static empires of the East is clear, not least in the recognition of complexity as something not to be rejected but as a normal feature of life. The continuity of intellectual curiosity in the West was another noteworthy facet of this tradition. The Arab world, having begun with a great burst of intellectual activity following on the rise of Islam, then settled into a static, unchanging order in which innovation was frowned on and knowledge was reiterated in an unchanging fashion.

The role of towns likewise demands special discussion. The concept of the autonomous city, one which is not necessarily directly subordinated to the ruler and which is self-regulating is, again, a Western development. The political and economic power built up by these cities, together with the particular concentration of specialized skills that only urban centers could provide and coupled with the autonomy of these skills, came to comprise an important element in this complex of contending centers of power. The idea of exchange and specialization together with the uncontrolled character of these, fostered and strengthened the reciprocal and multilateral quality of power and the framework within which it was exercised.[5]

Two crucial techniques of government were developed on the basis of this tradition as a whole. The essential powers of the ruler that had to be controlled were those of money raising and army raising. In both these areas, with greater or lesser success, the ruler was gradually prevented from exercising absolute power. In seventeenth-century England, the clash between the king and Parliament centered precisely on this issue. In Holland, too, the power of the monarch was curtailed. In France, it was precisely this conflict which finally led to the revolution of 1789. The idea that society should have a say over how the fruits of its labor should be used through representation in a popularly elected assembly had both religious and secular roots—many of the techniques of voting were developed in Church government, and the word *vote* originally meant "prayer"—but by the modern period, a politically significant section of society had come to insist that its existence, aims, and aspirations did not depend on the ruler, but on the contrary that the ruler should depend on it. Indeed, there is a strong argument to the effect that the modernizing revolution of the nineteenth century was concerned with the extension of full rights of participation in politics to all sections of society, albeit the practice of this may have been very much less than perfect.[6]

The upshot of this pattern of development in the West was to create a political ethos in which the right to participate was tacitly accepted in theory, even if it was denied in practice, which had within it the possibility of reopening the question of full participation at some later date. The French demand for the summoning of the Estates-General after well over a century of abeyance of royal absolutism illustrates this point. Equally, the intermediate institutions derived from long-established traditions of autonomy functioned reasonably effectively to represent the interests of society against the state and to provide a framework within which the growing complexity of modern life could find room for maneuver.

THE EAST EUROPEAN PATH

There was much in the history of Eastern Europe that overlapped with that of Western Europe, and, to this extent, Eastern Europe is quintessentially a part of the broad pattern of shared experiences and values in the European arena. To a greater or lesser extent, especially where Eastern Europe had adopted Western Christianity—Central Europe—these societies shared in aspects of feudalism, medieval Christian universalism, the Renaissance, the Reformation and Counter-Reformation, and the Enlightenment. Yet each one of these was shared slightly differently, less intensively, less fully, with the result that East European society's participation in the European experience was only partial. Not every East European society shared all the features sketched here or not to the same depth, but as a broad picture, the model is viable; how far any one society took part was determined by geography and politics, with the two often reinforcing each other.[7] In practice, Eastern Europe constituted a transitional zone between the Western tradition of the division of power and the Eastern tradition of concentration of power. In Eastern Europe, there were indeed elements of autonomy, but the role of the state was generally stronger than in the West. The power of the ruler was, in fact, challenged, but these challenges were on the whole rebuffed, with the result that the power of society failed to develop and could not attain the necessary critical mass.[8] Instead, the state emerged as far more dominant than in the West, whether in politics or in economics. The experience of foreign rule and the corresponding weakening or destruction of native institutions made a further contribution to the emergence of the dominant state. The degree of dependence—smaller under the Habsburgs, greater in the Ottoman Empire—thus affected both the extent of native political experience and the survival of native political traditions, usually in an attenuated and distorted form.

The central principles of reciprocity and autonomy of law, while not entirely nonexistent, were weak, sometimes to the point of invisibility. In Central Europe, some acceptance of reciprocity by rulers and ruled—the nobility as represented by the estates—ensured a fitful survival of the principle in both Bohemia and Hungary; in Poland, the ruler was maintained in a position of complete weakness and concentrations of the nobility exercised power without any regard for society. In all these cases, the imperial overlordship and experience of imperially generated industrialization, i.e. a political-military-administrative reform based on foreign models and imperial (not local) interests, ensured the continued preeminence of state power in the area. This complex constituted the origins of etatism.

Particularly noteworthy in this connection was the doctrine of the discretionary power of the state. The concept is an extension of the principle of the royal prerogative, that the ruler has the right to take action in any area of politics unless he is expressly prevented from doing so by law or custom. This principle enabled the state to retain and promote *its* autonomy in the crucial fields of taxation and military organization. Society was too weak to exercise control over these areas, whereby it could not sustain its autonomy vis-à-vis the state. Where conflict between state and society did erupt, the state proved strong enough to hold off challenges. In the long term, this precluded the emergence of parliamentary sovereignty in the nine-teenth and twentieth centuries, even when elections were held under rules of universal suffrage—as in the pre-1914 Austrian Reichsrat—because these assemblies lacked control over certain key areas of state activity. By way of illustration, in 1914 Austria declared war without any form of parliamentary sanction and throughout the 1900–1939 period, governments in Eastern Europe did not lose elections. There were only two exceptions (Hungary in 1905–1906 and Bulgaria in 1932[9]), both resulting from divisions in the ruling elite rather than having anything to do with the popular will. The state, using its control of the administrative machinery, was generally able to "make" elections in its favor; it was only when the elite was divided and state power was used ineffectively that governments could change.

The enduring features of this system included an unmistakable element of façade politics. This had two aspects. On the one hand, it involved a measure of outward and occasionally genuine respect for constitutional proprieties. The need to avoid opprobrium for some particularly outrageous action—and thus the weight of international opinion—was another factor in this complex.[10] Hence, some real autonomy could and did exist.

On many occasions, the courts delivered politically uninfluenced verdicts, the press could and did print criticism of the state, and interest protection organizations, like trade unions, could work for the benefit of their members. On the other hand, the system was equally evidently guided by the power elite, which tended to regard constitutional and legal procedures as an inconvenience and a façade, behind which it was free to defend its positions and interests unhindered by other forces. An external appearance of an institutional framework to provide for mass participation in politics existed, but in real terms political participation remained the privilege of the elite. Reciprocity of rights was largely limited to what the elite was prepared to concede. The political rights accorded to individuals in this system were few, although usage and practice could make it difficult to retract some long-established custom. In the main, these were restricted to near-ritualistic participation in elections and certain limited welfare provisions, like a few years of education. Participation by instruments of press criticism, strikes, and political opposition already presupposed a measure of group organization which the state could not suppress entirely. In all, these systems could be termed hegemonial. The state exercised a paramountcy over society that the latter could do little to modify; by the same token, the state never claimed a monopoly of power for itself. It permitted reluctantly or otherwise the continued existence of areas of political, economic, social, religious, etc. autonomy, preferably inchoate and unpoliticized. This was something else that would disappear in the postwar revolution.

The backwardness of Eastern Europe vis-à-vis Western Europe, both real and perceived, had further ramifications for political development. From the outset of the modern period, the late Enlightenment to the middle of the nineteenth century, East European elites took Western Europe as their criterion of modernity. It was immediately obvious that the task facing East European societies was to effect modernization. But the definition of this and the means to this end were not so obvious. Indeed, the East European elites tended to oversimplify the task by assuming that political and economic development to West European levels could be achieved quickly and by the practice of adopting West European political forms regardless of their local appropriateness. Often, it seemed, East European elites were content with the introduction of West European institutions into their own polities pro forma and were unable or unwilling to appreciate the generations of development in values and attitudes that lay behind particular Western political technologies.

The crux of this problem lay in the existence of comparatively strong autonomous spheres and centers of power in Western Europe on which a new "modern" political system relying on civil society could be based, whereas these were weak to nonexistent in Eastern Europe.[11] This led to the situation where the functions performed by these autonomous centers had to be performed by some other agency in Eastern Europe and there was only one—the state. Thus from the outset the East European modernizers were involved in a contradiction, that of having to construct civil society from above. In the event, this proved impossible, not surprisingly. Whenever society moved to fulfill the role that modernity assigned to it, the state proved unwilling to relinquish the power it had assumed to carry through modernization. Society, it would be argued, was not yet ready for this and would continue to need the preeminence of the state to protect it against itself or external enemies.

At the same time, the state as agent of change proved quite unable to make the far-reaching transformation needed for modernization, at least in the sense defined by the elites. Most of all, a modernizing revolution from above—for this was what the Eastern European elites were aspiring to in the second half of the nineteenth century—was by definition ill suited to provide for the ever-increasing complexity entailed by modernity. Whether in the sphere of institutions or of social groups or even of theory, state-promoted modernization tends to work toward models of simplicity and the predictability that makes for easier administration; it shuns complexity or even rejects it, as some theories of populism and nationalism did. So in this one particularly important respect, modernizing states in Eastern Europe tended to underestimate the difficulty of promoting economic growth from above and of establishing an entrepreneurial class that would act continuously to maintain expansion.

There were a number of strands in this failure. First, although some state bureaucrats did have a vision of economic modernity copied from Western Europe, their primary concern was generally the well-being of the state machinery itself and their own standard of living as compared with that of their counterparts in the West. Hence, more investment was channeled into military-strategic purposes or into consumption by the bureaucracy itself than could be supported by the local economies. This had further repercussions. A job in the bureaucracy became a coveted meal ticket in itself rather than for the ostensible goal of rational administration, and if employment by the state could provide almost permanent security, then inevitably the state attracted many of the most talented to its service. This effectively drained off not just intellectual talent, for there would hardly have been any other employer for the possessors of technical knowledge at this stage of development, but it also sucked in any potential entrepreneurial talent and ensured that such persons could avoid the dangers of risk taking, like bankruptcy.

For the members of the elite, service in the bureaucracy offered another enormous advantage—it offered a way out of the economic decline resulting from inefficient agrarian methods, while at the same time it provided them with a form of employment in which their traditional values of hierarchy could be conserved. In some instances, notably in Poland, where entry into the bureaucracy was less straightforward seeing that Poland's rulers were alien, the professions played the role of a functional equivalent.[12] Thus, the old elite did not suffer disintegration as a result of economic changes, as it generally did in the West, but survived the crisis only marginally transformed in its habits and attitudes. An anti-entrepreneurial ethos was strengthened thereby and the emergence of a social group which could have been the foundation of political autonomy was blocked. Politics, therefore, offered the vista of the glittering prizes at a lower personal cost than independent economic activity and, what is more, these were available without any serious checks on how power was acquired and whether or not it was used for personal gain. This ensured that the ethos of the elite would continue to penetrate politics, the state, the structure of institutions and attitudes toward economic activity as something not quite desirable.

In this last category a further phenomenon deserves notice—the hostility to "modern" entrepreneurial types of money making among the nobility, which viewed the handling of money with disfavor. Although the management of estates had a long tradition among the nobility, risk taking was spurned not least because of the exemption from taxation enjoyed as a feudal privilege. Particularly in the polities where the native nobility was sizable (Poland, Hungary, Croatia, Romania), a tendency arose to attract an ethnically alien group to undertake the task of economic development. This perpetuated a perception of enterprise as somehow alien and as something in which the political elite did not engage. Furthermore, the political values represented by the entrepreneurial class, including a recognition of growing complexity, a commitment to institutions reflecting greater choice and the autonomy of spheres and thus to pluralism, likewise tended to be viewed with suspicion, not least because any substantial move in this direction would have provided for wider access to political choice. Thereby the elite's control of power would have been diminished. In all, this combination of factors ensured that the state would retain its dominance over society and the political class which benefited from this arrangement would have no incentive to transform matters by introducing meaningful reform in the direction of redistributing power. On the contrary, the elite legitimated its attitudes by arguing that the state was the source of modernity and progress, whilst society was backward.

In the other polities of Eastern Europe (the South Slav lands and, for that matter, Greece), the situation was not substantially different, except for the absence of a native aristocracy. In their place had arisen a patrician-military-mercantile elite, with very similar values of regarding the state as a source of private benefit and considering it as the embodiment of modernization.[13]

Only in the Czech lands of Bohemia and Moravia did anything like a native entrepreneurial class succeed in achieving a political position commensurate with its economic strength and in creating political structures corresponding roughly to the growing complexity of social life, even though this aspiration was partly blocked by the imperial power (Austria) and ethnonational rivalry with the Germans of the area. But even with its much wider social base, politics in the Czech lands were not fully democratic in the strict sense of the word. Before 1914, the practice of politics was indelibly marked by the Habsburg experience of discretionary power and the areas of power reserved to the state. In the interwar period, Czechoslovak politics were unquestionably pluralistic and a very wide range of interests was able to participate in the political process. Parliamentary sovereignty, however, was not the reality of the system, and global strategy was determined by the various interpenetrating Czech elites (political, administrative, economic, commercial, trade union, military), as articulated through the *pětka*, the group of five parties permanently in office and guided by the presidency.[14] In all, the Czech experience suggests that even with patterns of development close to those of the West, especially industrialization and the existence of a native entrepreneurial class, these do not in themselves guarantee the evolution of a Western-style political system; they did, on the other hand, make Czechoslovakian politics substantially more open and flexible than other East European polities.

THE CITY

In West European development a key role in the evolution of autonomous organization and power was played by the existence of a fairly dense network of towns. The West European town was a unique phenomenon in a number of ways—most significantly in its ability to develop autonomously of the ruler and the Church and to create specific political techniques intended to safeguard the basis of this autonomy, namely trade. The legal sphere and the emergence of various legal codes with the function of underpinning the reciprocity of contracting parties were a crucial contribution to a relatively open tradition of politics. The practice of municipal government had a similar function. Most important, however, was the existence of the city as a forum of continuous exchanges, economic and social, in which transactions of growing complexity could be played out. The rules governing this complexity had to strike a balance between predictability and routine on the one hand and flexibility and change on the other. To these factors may be added the role played by towns in the development of political identities and concepts of citizenship.[15]

It is a matter of some controversy whether in this area of development Eastern Europe was always different from the West or whether it diverged from the Western pattern as a result of foreign conquest. For the purposes of tracing the emergence of an East European political tradition, this disagreement is less important; more significant is that by the eighteenth century the area was characterized by a dearth of urbanization. There were very few cities of any size in Eastern Europe and those that did exist lacked the economic and political autonomy, the commitment to interaction and innovation, found in the West. There were no significant trading centers or urban settlements with any serious claim to political autonomy. The urban settlements of the area were either bureau-cratic agglomerations—the seat of the administration—or garrison towns or static, introverted settlements clinging to commercial priv-ileges and basing their existence on commodities of declining value, exceptional rights demanded by conservative guilds and unable to cope with the new technologies of the West.

Vienna serves as an instance of the first type. It lost its autonomy in 1621 and thereafter it was quintessentially the seat of the Habs-burg administration and owed its position primarily to this, with the result that its citizenry was dependent on the imperial court and state for its employment to a disproportionate degree until relatively well into the nineteenth century.[16] Timişoara (Temeschwar, Temesvár) was an instance of a garrison town founded in the Banate to act as bulwark against the Ottoman Empire; nonmilitary activities tended to be subordinated to the needs of the garrison until the nineteenth century. Dubrovnik (Ragusa) or Braşov (Kronstadt, Brassó) illustrate the third category; in these towns a patrician elite clung to its liberties, remained frozen in time, and was unable to respond to the challenge of new trade patterns.

The nineteenth century saw some changes in this dispensation and towns did begin to grow, but this growth was uneven and was seldom accompanied by the rise of a conscious and confident bourgeoisie prepared to fight for equal access to political power. On the contrary, towns tended to remain dependent on the state which fostered their growth and sought to use them as instruments on their own, to extend greater discipline over the population and to infuse the people with a loyalty to the ideals of the state. Hence, the city in Eastern Europe could not act either to integrate urban and rural areas—the gap between town and country was significantly wider than in the West—or to develop new political ideas and identities. The cities that did grow up in the nineteenth century tended to acquire a certain alien quality in the minds of the bulk of the population; they were all but colonial intrusions in the countryside. Only toward the end of the imperial period did cities like Vienna, Prague, Budapest, or Lwów (Lemberg) begin to function as centers of political, economic, and social exchange, important for the integration of rural populations into a wider political consciousness, though even then, their roles as centers of autonomy were somewhat limited.

These two factors were to an extent interdependent. If Budapest had to serve as the center of ethnic integration—the melting pot in which Slavs, Germans, Romanians, and Jews turned into (cultural) Hungarians with the encouragement of the state—then it proved difficult for either old or new members of the political community to develop claims to political autonomy, as these were resisted by the elite and popular aspirations were diverted into regarding the political structure primarily in national rather than in economic or social terms. In Prague the ethnic conflict between Czechs and Germans, which resulted in a victory for the former by the end of the nineteenth century, tended to promote ethnic considerations above all others for both communities.[17]

THE BUREAUCRACY

The end of World War I saw the establishment of a network of relatively small states in Eastern Europe.[18] They were all endowed with theoretically democratic constitutions and they all based their existence on the national principle, the principle of national self-determination. Their weakness was widely recognized and fully documented in the context of international affairs. Internally they had to cope with all the problems of establishing and managing new state structures, usually on the basis of limited political experience and with socially and ethnically disparate populations. This last had one vital consequence—the failure of either social or ethnic integration of society into a single relatively homogeneous civil society also represented the failure of these new states to develop a single public opinion which could exercise control over the political sphere. The political elites had neither the instruments nor the interest to overcome this segmentation, despite a great deal of rhetoric to the contrary. Consequently the political elites retained their hegemony and remained the preeminent political class.

The makeup of the political bureaucracy varied somewhat from polity to polity and owed something of its composition and values to the emergence and previous history of that polity. Thus, in Poland, Hungary, Romania, and Croatia (Bosnia also falls into this category) the neofeudal character of the political elite, with the colonization of the state administration by a gentry class (*szlachta, boyars*) having values similar to the way in which they ran their estates, was dominant. Despite lip service to land reform—Romania instituted a very radical reform, much of which remained on paper—the power of the landed aristocracy was only marginally affected, whether it drew its power from the land or not, and it continued to use the political resources of the state for its own purposes. The landowning or formerly landowning elite was intimately connected with the military, which it controlled and supplied with senior officers; naturally, the same stratum provided many, though not all, senior officials of state and local administration. Below the landowning stratum came the gentry, which had been largely obliged to abandon its uneconomic landholdings, but was unwilling to give up its nobiliary values to the extent of participating in trade; this sizable group moved into the state administration at the middle levels and lent particularly the Polish and Hungarian administrative machinery their peculiarly neofeudal character. Although recruitment from the peasantry was not unknown, it was still rare and tended to affect the wealthiest stratum of peasants, which could afford education for its sons.

The financial elite was separate from the political elite, though not wholly so. In Hungary this elite was overwhelmingly Jewish—assimilated by this time to the Hungarian language and culture, but regarded as not quite fully fledged members of the national community; the gentry-bureaucracy had successfully imposed its concepts and political values on the commercial-financial aristocracy, despite the fact that these were very much at variance with the logic and apparent interests of this entrepreneurial class. In Romania, the financial elite was small and weak and tended to be dependent on external, Western patrons; it too was heavily Jewish and was far less assimilated than in Hungary. Its political strength was negligible, except for the international leverage it exercised through Western opinion, which then served only to underline its alienness from the Romanian majority. In Poland, the situation was similar, except that a native entrepreneurial class, based primarily on the population of former Prussian Poland, had begun to emerge and to compete with a Jewish entrepreneurial class that it regarded as alien.

In the Balkans (Yugoslavia, Bulgaria) the bureaucracy was run by an analogous group, though without the landed aristocratic antecedents—the native aristocracies had been eliminated by centuries of Ottoman rule. They had come to power in the nineteenth century and had seized control of the state machinery. Entrepreneurial activity was in any case limited, and the economy was heavily dependent on the state, founded on backward agriculture. In Albania there was no state administration to speak of, and tribal structures, based notably on the Moslem clans of the north, dominated society.

In Czechoslovakia, there existed a somewhat different constellation, with a relatively well-functioning administration and considerable autonomy. Nevertheless, there was no qualitative difference, inasmuch as there was no full integration of society and politics was mostly a Czech preserve. This greatly weakened the constitution and cohesiveness of the Czechoslovak polity, for it operated as a civil society by and large for the Czechs only. There were, of course, numerous non-Czech participants in the political process and beneficiaries of the political system, but only the Czechs were fully integrated into it. The Czech bureaucracy was recruited from and generally lived by the norms it had learned in Austria-Hungary; within the Czech national community, it functioned rationally and effectively, but for non-Czechs attitudes to the system were not so straightforward and these varied from regarding it with favor for its respect of the formal rules of democracy to deep distrust as a semicolonial regime.

What was common to all these polities was the institution of the government party operating in a pseudo-parliamentary system. The government party, which was subjected to some electoral choice, was for all practical purposes an emanation of the bureaucracy. The bureaucracy oversaw its successes at elections, regarded it as a political dependency, and exchanged its personnel at will. An illustration of this was the way in which prime ministers emerged from the political elite and then proceeded to "elect" a new parliament to serve them. It is noteworthy, on the other hand, that East European parliaments were not monolithic; the elite did not seek to control the entire electorate, only so much of it as would give it uncontested control over public politics. This accounted for the continued existence of opposition parties of both Right and Left, often quite radical, and resulted in such apparent paradoxes as the presence of Social Democrats in the Hungarian parliament in 1944, in the center of occupied Europe. In effect, the hegemonial system operated with a degree of flexibility, in that it accepted a wider range of options than its Communist successors were to do.

The instruments of control used by the bureaucracy varied from outright fraud to intimidation. In some electoral districts, opposition voters would be prevented from registering their votes; opposition parties might be suddenly banned; politicians might be temporarily arrested; phony parties might be floated to confuse a particular section of the electorate; or the franchise might be seriously restricted.[19] Open terror was rare and indeed, it was rarely needed. Electorates were either docile or prevented from voting or their votes proved irrelevant. Thus, while elections were held in Yugoslavia, the Croatian Peasant party dominated the Croatian electorate; this electoral strength could never be translated into political power.

Other aspects of elite politics also deserve notice. Political parties frequently tended to be personal coteries united by loyalty to an individual rather than a political program or ideology. This meant that clientelism was a key feature of the political order, regulated by a system of rewards and sanctions within the elite and from the elite downwards. It also meant that the makeup of parties could be labile; the composition of their personnel could change and individuals could readily transfer their ostensible political loyalties—ostensible because in reality personal links proved to be more significant than "ideological" ones. This had the consequence that political commitments could be relatively weak and that politicians appeared to be opportunistic and unscrupulous. Again, the system was devised as much for the personal benefit and security of its participants as for the polity as a whole, to put it charitably. It is worth noting that an analogous uncertainty characterized popular support as well, particularly where peasant voters were concerned, so that parties would rise and disappear with bewildering speed.

A further aspect of the personal nature of politics in Eastern Europe is the role played by tight networks of informal influence, which sometimes resembled secret societies. Groups of individuals who had undergone some particularly intense shared personal experience, especially if concentrated in time, would attribute unique significance to that experience and elevate it to a level of loyalty higher than all others. This loyalty would then cut across lines of political interest, and individuals on very different points of the political spectrum would participate in such networks. The Czech legionnaires, those who had taken part in the epic journey across Siberia, were an example of a network of this kind; in this case they ensured that the newly created Czechoslovakian army would be dominated by ex-legionnaires and that former Austro-Hungarian officers, who for whatever reason had not been members of the legion, would play a lesser role regardless of professional competence. The Hungarian Etelköz Alliance, a group of anti-Communist and anti-Semitic officers who provided the shock troops for the White Terror of 1919–1920, were another example. So was the Crna Ruka, the Serbian Black Hand. Examples of greater or lesser significance could be found in every East European country.

INTEGRATION

Reference has already been made to the failure of East European politics to effect political integration in the interwar period. Integration operates on two levels: social and national. It implies that the overwhelming majority of society accepts the constitutional and political framework, together with broad, imprecisely defined goals of political and social development within the state. Both in terms of their historical legacies and their actual problems, East European polities found integration an extremely complex and ultimately insuperable task. In the first place, national integration was virtually impossible to achieve. The new frontiers left substantial national minorities or created multinational states, in which distinctive national subcultures with clearly divergent political objectives complicated matters. It is theoretically possible that an appropriate political and institutional framework could have integrated some or all of these minorities over a period of time, but that would have required the national majorities to make greater concessions to minorities than the former found possible or prudent or desirable. The pattern is well illustrated by the fate of Czechoslovakia, which failed to retain the loyalty of the non-Czech minorities to the state in 1938. A genuinely integrated polity would not have disintegrated in this fashion, for its constituent member groups would have regarded loyalty to the state as of a higher order than any other.

After the Paris Peace Settlement, Czechoslovak spokesmen made promises to the effect that democracy would safeguard the rights of the non-Czech minorities and that the country would become a kind of "Eastern Switzerland."[20] The political implications—as distinct from the legal ones—of this promise to the minorities were that the new state would draw equally on all the national political traditions and cultures included within the new frontiers and that no one nation would enjoy preeminence. In fact, from the outset the dominant Czech elites had a different conception of the constitution of the state. It was to be a polity in which there would be legal equality for all, but politically the Czechs would have the constitutive core function, so that Czechoslovakia would primarily be a Czech state. This did not result in the exclusion of the non-Czech population from the political process but it certainly did create a political disequilibrium. The symbolic enactment of this was the failure to ensure the presence of any representatives of the large German minority at the Constitutional Assembly. The eventual consequences of this approach entailed the inability of the Czechs to effect genuine integration—to command the overriding loyalty of the non-Czechs—or to feel secure that all the citizens of the state had an equal commitment to it. Therefore, when the state came under overwhelming pressure from abroad, from Nazi Germany, the Czechs suddenly woke up to the weakness of their position and concluded that they had no alternative but to capitulate to the demands of the minorities, in spite of enjoying certain military advantages both at home and abroad. The collapse of 1938 was as much the function of the loss of Czechs' self-confidence through the sudden recognition that only they actually wanted Czechoslovakia to remain as one entity as it was Nazi German pressure.[21]

Social integration exists in analogous fashion and proved just as elusive. Here the problem was that various social strata in the East European polities might have been cohesive within themselves—though even that is a somewhat doubtful proposition—but they lacked any overall commitment to the state and any sense of participating in the same political venture. The political elite, the peasantry, the workers, the bourgeoisie and other middle strata all tended to lead politically disparate lives guided by significantly different values and to have no well-defined communication with each other. In a word, these polities had to cope with the problem of both ethnonational segmentation and social fragmentation.

Social mobility was low to very low, with the consequence of a relative weakness in the structure of the state—analogous to ethnonational segmentation—of a higher reliance on coercion or the threat of it than is compatible with political consensus, of low levels of loyalty and thus of legitimacy. At this point, ethnonational and social cleavages could coincide. It was an obvious choice for these weakly grounded semi-authoritarian or fully dictatorial regimes of the interwar period to seek to build loyalty to the state by the promotion of nationalism. To some extent this was successful, but it raised two problems. In the first place, it left open or exacerbated the issue of the national cleavage. Reliance on the national ideology of one ethnonational community frequently brought that community into conflict with another, as national ideologies tended to be incompatible and concerned with mutually exclusive goals, defined in terms of territory or people. Second, nationalism as a political doctrine provided answers to very few questions of political organization and the distribution of power. It created strong identities and a sense of belonging to the state—for members of the dominant group—but said next to nothing about political structures, the resolution of conflicts of interests, the allocation of resources and values, participation and representation, i.e. the day-to-day problems of political, economic, and social life. If anything, by stressing a transcendental vision of politics, in which implicitly all members of the nation shared a near identical view of the political elements of nationhood, nationalism came close to denying the need for intermediate institutions between the state and the individual, and state and society. The comparative vagueness of the nationalist message, together with its emotional intensity, produced a somewhat contradictory result. East European nations in the interwar period reached a fairly high state of national consciousness as to their political identities as members of a nation and as to who was to be excluded as nonmembers. At one and the same time, the implicit promise of equality and justice, encapsulated in the nationalist message, was left unfulfilled, with inevitable frustration and resentment at the social-political closures enforced against society by its rulers.[22]

SOCIAL CLASSES: THE PEASANTRY

The composition and values of the political elites of Eastern Europe have already been discussed in detail and need little further analysis at this point. Although there was considerable inequality within some East European societies, e.g. with respect to landholding, even where there were no latifundia or where they were restricted in number, no corresponding political equality ensued. In other words, the correlation between wealth and political preeminence was not direct. Bulgaria, for instance, had an egalitarian landholding structure: 63.1 percent of all landholdings were between zero and five hectares and only 0.4 percent held over thirty hectares (1934 figures).[23] In spite of this and in spite of the existence of a fairly well-organized peasant party, Bulgarian politics was controlled by a bureaucratic-military elite which did not differ significantly from its counterparts in other East European countries.[24] The explanation for this state of affairs has to be sought in the character of the elite, its sense of ruling rightfully and the benefits to be gained from membership (in the terms discussed above), as well as from the difficulties of translating peasant aspirations into political realities and sustaining them organizationally.

One of the key factors helping to explain the survival of the bureaucracy in the face of formidable mass challenges in the aftermath of the First World War—a proposition valid for the entire area, not just Bulgaria—was the political experience and skills of bureaucracy. The corresponding inexperience of its opponents complemented this. The former understood how politics and power were to be managed, how people could be manipulated and how opponents could be bought off—this last factor was of particular significance in relation to post-1918 peasant parties, the leaders of which were extremely readily co-opted into the system.

The whole of the peasantry in Eastern Europe was marked by a deeply internalized set of values deriving from centuries of tradition and from contemporary structural constraints. The peasant was characterized by living in relatively small, insular communities, with strict ascriptive value systems. This generated a suspicion of the outside world, of strangers with different and inexplicable behavior patterns. Within these communities there tended to exist clear-cut hierarchies which were perceived as unchanging and unchangeable. Overall, the peasant lived in a world marked primarily by the seasons, by a lack of functional specialization, by low levels of technology and little incentive to improve on this and by a kind of negative egalitarianism that sought to equalize downwards (thereby fettering improvement through initiative). This system was stable, within the long cycles of upward and downward movement of agricultural prices, and self-reproducing. Crucially, peasant values concerning futurity and thus the feasibility of effecting change were governed by existential security; and that, in turn, was a matter of the reliability of the harvest. In much of Eastern Europe, large numbers of peasants lived at or below subsistence level, so that their faith in the future was low. This value was inevitably carried over into the political realm and fed the sense of deference, helplessness, and suspicion with which much of the peasantry treated the outside world. Correspondingly, it continuously aggravated a quest for security, which was seen as reachable either through the acquisition of land or escape through upward mobility. Neither was a ready option. The peasant lacked the surplus capital either to buy land or to buy education for his children. This self-reproducing system, therefore, was a vicious circle, which at the same time appeared to be the norm, so that the slow encroachment of the market by the late nineteenth century—which destroyed the system—was felt to be a severe threat, especially as its dynamics were not really understood.

This raises the entire question of peasant values, aspirations, and attitudes to politics. Broadly speaking, the peasantry could be divided into three socioeconomic categories, each with its own set of attitudinal responses to politics. The first and smallest was the entrepreneurial agriculturist, who farmed a comparatively sizable landholding and responded to the market and to market conditions. In this category, attitudes to the state were relatively relaxed—there was some understanding of how politics operated, how interests could be validated, how peasant interest organizations (like cooperatives) should function, and how much could be expected from politics. Those in this category might not have had any particular love for politics, but equally they did not treat the political game as alien and undesirable. Significant sections of the peasantry in the Czech lands and Slovenia, as well as a rather smaller proportion in Poland and Hungary[25]—notably those fairly close to the urban concentrations to which they could sell their produce—fell into this category. They had begun to make the shift from patrimonial to commodity production where their output had an assured market. They responded quickly to changing circumstances and understood the importance of investment. This category was the most efficient and thus the most prosperous agricultural producer. After the Communist takeover, they bore the brunt of the antikulak campaigns.

The second category was the medium peasant, who had some knowledge of the outside world, but remained deeply suspicious of it. In this category, the market was accepted to some extent, but it was at the same time regarded as a manipulation by the state against the peasant. On occasion, those in this category took part in commodity production and at others, they withdrew into subsistence, discouraged by the tough discipline of the market and responsibility, for which they had neither the preparation nor the economic strength. The political focus of this category was the state and it sought to achieve its ends by means of peasant politics and parties. On the other hand, it continued to view the state and politics as alien and as the preserve of "them," a group which was socially and sometimes even ethnically different. Thus this category tended to look backwards towards the old village community and the values of that community, often nostalgically, as an idealized vision of society where there was order and predictability even while the community itself was disintegrating and ceasing to be effective as a social and political unit.

The third and much the largest category was the one to which the term *peasant* was customarily applied: the category that was either landless or a dwarf-holder, that was almost entirely outside commodity production, whose worldview was bounded by the village and the seasons and whose experience of the state left it suspicious and hostile. Its contact with the state was through the tax gatherer, the gendarme, and the recruiting officer, all of them regarded as agents of the alien, parasitical "city" that siphoned off the fruits of peasant labor, in consequence of which the peasant remained poor and exploited. There was a deep-level set of values in this urban-rural dichotomy. It included the honest peasant against the deceitful townee; virtue against vice; generosity against meanness; authenticity against duplicity; and so on.

The political ideas of this category were strongly influenced and reinforced by religious concepts, particularly that of "salvation." Its perception of change was heavily conditioned by its understanding of change in the religious context—its dominant experience of a world outside the village commune—viz. Christian salvation. This lent peasant politics a certain flavor of messianic expectations. Those in this category had a rather weak commitment to organization and to sustained, incremental action, as well as having a low sense of personal responsibility or expectation of being able to effect changes. Its attitude toward the outside world, the money-using economy, and everything that was seen as different was fundamentally hostile. In a word, this was the world of *Gemeinschaft*, the traditional community of status, ascription, and static life-styles, already under threat from the dynamism of the modern *Gemeinschaft* with its constant challenge of change and personal choice, but resisting with all that it could muster.

The First World War had a considerable impact on these values and wrought certain changes on peasant politics, albeit without effecting any fundamental transformation.[26] In the first place, the peasant was able to observe the importance of food production to the wartime economy and of his own role in this process, this contributing to a rise in self-confidence. In this period, the agricultural-industrial terms of exchange favored the former, again boosting self-perceptions. Then, as soldiers, very large numbers of peasants, who had previously lived in static village communities, suddenly underwent mobilization and enormously expanded their store of personal experience and thereby their criteria for judging their own status. The difference between the rigid discipline of peacetime soldiering as conscripts and of wartime combat was sufficient to explain why military service before the war had failed to make much impact on the peasant way of life.

Wartime political propaganda and the learning process undergone by the peasantry—as evidenced, for example, by the growing number of desertions during the war, which by 1918 had reached 100,000 in Croatia-Slavonia alone[27]—all helped to modify attitudes and to fuel rising expectations. In particular, stronger peasant self-confidence was unquestionably channeled into the newly emergent peasant parties, which had the welfare of the peasantry as their central objective. At the same time, the impact of these parties proved to be limited because the old political establishments had nowhere been conquered, only temporarily defeated; because the political systems had been created by the elite, which therefore knew how to operate its levers; and because peasant politicians proved not just inexperienced but also incapable of resisting cooptation through the lure of power. This inexperience, which peasant leaders to an extent recognized, resulted in peasant parties relying on a section of the intelligentsia for guidance through the maze of politics and for representation in the political game. In consequence, peasant experience of politics remained limited and, indeed, there was little in peasant values to predispose the peasantry to adapt to an alien, urban style of power dealing. Hence, peasant values remained colored by the messianism inherited from the past and reinforced by the frustrations of the present, and by hostility to sustained organization, cooperation with outsiders, all of which combined to undermine the impact of the spasmodic irruption of the peasantry into politics.

THE INTELLIGENTSIA

The intelligentsia developed in Eastern Europe as a very specific social and political group, with features which differed markedly from its counterparts in the West. In this context, the working definition of *intellectual* used here is someone involved in the generation of values, ideas, alternatives and critiques of the present, whereas the "intelligentsia," the bearers of technical knowledge, is involved in the administration of these values and ideas. The political role of the intelligentsia has generally been perceived as oppositional shading off into revolutionary—indeed, members of the intelligentsia are often regarded (and regard themselves) as the quintessence of opposition and as a substitute for it. This is particularly the picture in the context of nationhood and national consciousness. This assessment of the intelligentsia, however, is only a part of the picture and the other part, the conformist, is just as valid and significant as his nonconformist opposite number. The peculiar position of the intellectual and the intelligentsia in Eastern Europe can be derived from the general underdevelopment of the area and the continuation of the salient role played by this group is an indicator of the survival of political backwardness.[28]

Before the modern period, the size of the intelligentsia was small. Its membership was to be found overwhelmingly in the churches, the armed forces, and the bureaucracies, but with the introduction of improved education and wider access to it, the numbers increased. The problem was this: whereas in the West, the newly emergent bourgeoisie could provide a political and an economic medium for an equally autonomous and integrated intelligentsia, the absence or weakness of capitalist market development restricted the options open to budding members of the intelligentsia. What is more, the survival of premodern political traditions channeled the intelligentsia into two relatively constricted areas. Their function was either to sustain the theological and teleological legitimation of the system or to provide it with the technological support necessary for the construction of modernity, as defined by the elite. Hence, the rise of the ideologically committed, "engaged" intellectual, whose origins are readily traced back to the Counter-Reformation and who placed his talents at the service of the political elite by creating the new ideology of nationalism or serving the ruling empires and creating an ideology of dynastic loyalty. Alternatively, there arose the pariah intellectual, who failed to find employment or status within the system and was forced to look for other sources of support, often in opposition to the system. The last group became the stereotype of the intellectual revolutionary, with a vested interest in the "total" transformation of the system, and came to constitute an intellectual proletariat, not least in consequence of the overproduction of graduates toward the end of the nineteenth century.

The social origins of the intelligentsia also proved to be significant in ensuring the survival of certain political values not necessarily in tune with the pattern of development.[29] These roots varied somewhat from country to country in detail but not in essence. The churches provided a most important reservoir in training individuals and providing a channel of upward social mobility (Bohemia-Moravia, Serbia, Bulgaria). Elsewhere (Poland, Hungary, Croatia), the intelligentsia was in the first place recruited from the nobility and the socially and economically hard-pressed gentry. The latter had lost its livelihood, and to an extent its social status and function, in the nineteenth century, having proved incapable of meeting the challenge of competitive agriculture, and moved wholesale into towns, in order to look for employment in a form which it regarded as compatible with its status and values. The importance of military and legal occupations in this value system, which placed greater emphasis on birth and status than on achievement and merit, tended to bear out the validity of this conflation of old values and new careers.

At the center of this complex of the identity of the intelligentsia was the value system of power. This remained in the hands of the traditional elite, which was hostile to the ideas of the intelligentsia where these represented a challenge to its power. Hence a kind of compromise was born. The intelligentsia, dependent as it was on the state, was accorded a subsidiary position in the hierarchy of power, allowed to exercise some of its intellectual functions—independent, non-status-bound knowledge—as long as this did nothing to damage control over power by the elite. This system of cooptation, which relied heavily on the high value of traditional status deployed as an instrument of legitimation by the elite, lived on with minor modifications up to the Second World War and, arguably, was reproduced in the post-1960s compromise.

For a minority of intellectuals, however, this subsidiary status within the hierarchy of power, for all the benefits it conferred on them in the exercise of technical knowledge without serious constraints from public opinion, was insufficient. This minority was attracted by a radical vision of progress, in the name of which it sought to exercise its technical knowledge and committed itself to the service of intellectual objectives, often of a utopian or messianistic kind, rather than to immediate political goals. It lived in a utopian vision of the future and could readily subordinate its short-term technical rationality to the long-term aim. Radicalism of this kind was invariably oppositional, hostile to the existing order, attracted to power, and because it saw the future as a perfect society in which its own values would predominate, it tended to be dismissive of democratic values and the transactions of the marketplace.

There is much in this value system that resembled that of the peasantry. Many, though by no means all, of its protagonists had peasant antecedents and, arguably, there was a carryover from one value system to the other. The intellectual minority, frustrated and resentful in its sense of failure, thus went on to formulate the ideologies of left and right extremes, which were in this sense and in this sense only united by a vision of total, radical change. Finally, the political significance of the radical minority should also be seen in its role of providing alternative conceptions of the future and strategies of development. In this respect, the radical minority could contribute to establishing the limits of the debate and, to an extent, to setting the agenda for the remainder of the intellectual community. Hence, however isolated these utopian and semi-utopian groups may have been, their wider political impact was not to be underestimated.

THE BOURGEOISIE

In Eastern Europe, given the weakness of towns and the inability of the area to compete with the developed West, no sizable bourgeoisie—an entrepreneurial class—emerged. The Czech lands constituted the sole exception and even there, the bourgeoisie was to a greater extent integrated into the politically determined ethos of the bureaucratic system than in polities further West, where autonomous economic values were preeminent. The Czech bourgeoisie was subordinated to the bureaucracy in a number of ways, although it was a more equal partner and had much greater power of its own vis-à-vis the bureaucracy than its counterparts in other East European polities. The nineteenth century saw the absorption of the surviving urban merchant class in Poland, Hungary, and the Balkans and many of them gravitated toward the intelligentsia and adopted nonbourgeois values.

Hence, the relatively weak bourgeoisies that grew up with and were partly responsible for the economic expansion of the nineteenth and twentieth centuries were on the whole a new social group. Given that the traditional elite, with its anticompetitive, status-determined nobiliary values—in the maintenance of which exemption from taxation played a not insignificant role—would not assume the dangers of risk taking and the chance of losing status, wealth and power, the new bourgeoisie had to be recruited from elsewhere, in the main from low-status natives or immigrants. The ethnosocial group that assumed the largest role in this process were the Jews emigrating into Eastern Europe from the Pale of Settlement in Galicia and Russia. Other ethnically different groups included Germans, Greeks, and Armenians. Thus, whereas in the West, the entrepreneurial class tended to be well established and comparatively open, relying on agricultural prosperity for new capital and new entrepreneurs, the situation in Eastern Europe was quite different from the outset.

The central problem with entrusting economic development to an ethnically alien group was that both the group and its values tended to remain alien. Although many Jews sought to assimilate to the dominant local culture, the majority was nowhere fully accepted and, on the whole, they remained to a greater or lesser extent to one side of the national majority. While ethnosocial segmentation of this kind might have been a standard feature of many traditional, static societies, in modern societies, with a steady expansion of the number of interactions and widening of choice and experience, segmentation could not be easily reconciled with the prevailing norms.

The lasting result of this order was that the entrepreneurial value system remained the ethos of a social segment, a kind of alien element intruded into or superimposed upon these societies. The alienness, whether of the system or of its representatives, never disappeared completely and the capitalist, whether Jewish or not, was regarded as different from the majority. Even in Hungary, where Jewish immigrants were closest to integration and indeed, were most fully assimilated in language, culture, and customs, the foreignness remained. A peasant was reported as having remarked in the 1960s that there had been two Jews in his village, that both kept shops, "though one was a Jew only by his profession."[30] This illustrates vividly the merger of the alienness of the two value systems. The alienness began to break down in the interwar period, as a native entrepreneurial class began to emerge, rather fitfully in some cases, only to discover that it had to compete with a group that it continued to regard as alien.

This state of affairs contributed materially to a deep-rooted, persistent hostility to the entrepreneurial values of risk taking, the market, competition, democracy, change—an attitude that was in any event a well-entrenched hangover from the traditional *Gemeinschaft*. It is in this sense that the East European bourgeoisie constituted a "colony" of the West, not tied into the native sociopolitical fabric, in consequence of which it was incapable of performing the integrative function that it had carried out in the West. If anything, the bourgeoisie sought to assimilate to the neofeudal values of political power and to the status of the elite, in the hope of gaining acceptance and access to a share of power. The structural weakness of the East European bourgeoisie, attributable in this sense to delayed modernization, contributed significantly to a corresponding weakness in the conceptions of modernity, attitudes to change, and the institutions that would mediate between society and the state.

THE WORKING CLASS

With the exception of the Czech lands and the areas later to constitute the GDR, no East European polity had anything like a sizable and politically conscious working class by the interwar period. The bulk of the population was still on the land and the economy had not expanded sufficiently to permit industrialization. Hence, no working class could emerge, except for pockets of manufacturing and extractive industry in Poland, Hungary, and the Balkans (very limited in the last). Where one did exist, the level of technology tended to be low and relatively straightforward, e.g. food processing, textiles, or construction. Indeed, the level of industrial production was well below the level of modernity in consumption practiced by the elite. The industrial proletariat was, consequently, small and politically uninfluential. Its value system was characterized by this and also by the fact that most workers had only recently moved from peasant status, so that they tended to be quiescent in their political demands, even though they might be active in the pursuit of economic or welfare objectives. Their aspirations were articulated through trade unions and the Social Democratic parties which existed in the area.

Radicalism, especially radicalism of the Left, was confined to a few geographically or occupationally distinct sectors. Thus, in Poland, the Communist party could rely on militancy in the Dąbrowa basin, on the textile workers of Łódź and the industrial workers in Warsaw. In Hungary, the radical Left gathered support from small groups of heavy metallurgical workers in Budapest, especially Csepel, from the miners in the north and some seasonal workers.[31] In the Balkans, even this limited degree of industrialization did not exist. The occupations, as can be seen, which contributed the most strongly to left radicalism were mining, seasonal workers and some other marginal categories. As these marginal categories increased in size in the depression of the 1930s, radicalism increased correspondingly, but not automatically to the benefit of the Left. The newly impoverished workers, especially those whose links with their peasant antecedents were recent, could just as easily gravitate to right radicalism, attracted by the slogans of nationalistic communalism and the rhetoric of sudden, all-encompassing change.

Economic activism, however, was another matter. Polish workers developed the technique of the occupation strike as a response to lockouts in the 1930s and, in 1936, 675,000 strikers took part in strikes in 22,016 factories, out of a total industrial working class of 830,000.[32] In Yugoslavia, the working class was overwhelmingly peasant-worker in character, with working-class households drawing at least a part of their incomes from the land and being to some extent enmeshed in peasant values. According to the 1931 census, 1.53 million workers plus dependents drew incomes from industry, including mining, out of a total population of 13.93 million. The bulk of Yugoslav industry was based on primary technology and the availability of raw materials. Of around 1,800 factories, one-third were involved in processing food and agricultural products, another sixth in timber; had it not been for the number of workers employed in urban power plants, these proportions would have been much higher. These workers could hardly constitute a foundation for working-class politics as this had developed in the West and, indeed, left-wing parties were marginal after the initial upsurge of the post-1918 era, which had drawn its energies from peasant radicalism and war weariness.

The situation was somewhat different in the Czech lands and in what became the GDR. Here there was a sizable and politically conscious working class, sections of which had a markedly militant tradition. In Czechoslovakia after the split in social democracy, the Communists emerged stronger than the Social Democrats and remained a mass party, at least in terms of support, for the interwar period. The situation was reversed for Germany, although there was strong support for left radicalism in some areas that were brought together to form the GDR, i.e. Saxony and Saxony-Anhalt, as well as in Berlin. In these two countries, the contribution of the working class to politics was far from having been negligible.

The final point to note in connection with the working class in Eastern Europe is that its traditions had next to no impact on the postwar period. By one of those curious ironies of history that the area appears to specialize in, war and the Communist revolution dispersed the old working class and replaced it with another, overwhelmingly new working class.[33] The industrial explosion of the Communist era was sudden and extensive and the newly recruited workers from the land largely swamped the remnants of the prewar workers. A large proportion of them had in any case found themselves the object of rapid, even overrapid, upward social mobility because they were regarded as trustworthy pillars of the new social order. There was, therefore, no far-reaching transmission of values from the prewar to the postwar era, although there were localized exceptions to this.[34] The swamping effect was about as strong in Czechoslovakia and East Germany as it was in the other countries, where the working class was much smaller.[35] In Germany, the dislocation caused by the war, the massive demographic shifts, including migration westwards, and the submergence of the Social Democrats resulted in a state of affairs analogous to what was going on in the rest of the area, albeit it may not have been as deep-seated. Upward promotion accounted for much of the traditional working class in the Czech lands, as did the expulsion of the Sudeten Germans and the suppression of the Social Democrats. In all, then, war and the Communist revolution came to be as much of a caesura for the proletariat, in whose name the Communists launched their revolution, as it was for the rest of the population.

CONCLUSION

The Second World War constituted one of the great hinges of the East European political development. It caused massive upheavals and deep-rooted changes in attitudes, which would have resulted in corresponding changes in the political structure even without the Communist revolution.

   The question of what kind of change and what kind of political structures would have emerged without the Soviet presence is, of course, unanswerable in strict terms; nevertheless answers to the question are not wholly irrelevant, because they can point toward an understanding of the East European tradition and value systems. Thus although based on guesswork, the answers would seem to suggest a major shift of power away from the beneficiaries of the anciens régimes and toward wider popular participation. This could well have seen the construction of particularly East European types of institutions, which would doubtless have been more etatist than those evolved in the West. A certain kind of collectivism or corporatism appears to be a near-ineradicable component of the reigning political ethos that informs the behavior of some, though not all, of the population. This would not, as such, have excluded a measure of collective control over institutions, as the functioning of the *ad hoc* enterprise councils of the immediate post-1945 period in Czechoslovakia and Hungary testified.

Despite strong currents of radical populism, it is hard to see any solution of the peasant problem other than by thoroughgoing industrialization, with all its attendant dislocation. The populist solution for land reform, peasant cooperation and rest, never looked able to resolve the problem of rural overpopulation and would in any case have tended to conserve a rather anti-innovative system of values and agrarian economics. The old elites, while seriously undermined after 1945, were not destroyed (except in Poland and Yugoslavia) and could well have returned to politics to promote antimodernizing values, but also contributing political skills. These changes, therefore, would have shifted Eastern Europe away from authoritarianism toward pluralism, though it is hard to see how they would have established democracy based on parliamentary sovereignty in the short term, albeit this was by no means excluded over time. The development of Greece in the first two to three decades after the war is instructive in this respect.

The first half of the century in East Central Europe, then, saw the slow, fitful, halting construction of a modernization that was stopped and radically transformed by the Communist revolution, with its own particular modernizing objectives, myths, and utopias.

ENDNOTES

[1]This analysis owes much to Jenő Szűcs, *Vázlat Európa három történeti régiójáról* (Budapest: Magvető, 1983). A translation is in John Keane, ed., *Civil Society and the State* (London: Verso, 1988), 291–332.

[2]Canossa was only one of several such symbolic contests. Others included the humbling of Raymond, Count of Toulouse, at St. Gilles du Gard, who was whipped naked in front of the church in 1208 for his alleged involvement in the assassination of a papal legate; see John James, *Medieval France* (London: Harrap, 1986). See also Victor Turner, *Dramas, Fields and Metaphors: Symbolic Action in Human Society* (Ithaca: Cornell University Press, 1974).

[3]I have set out my views of the relationship between the European and Russian traditions in rather greater detail in my article "Central Europe: Definitions Old and New," in George Schöpflin and Nancy Wood, eds., *In Search of Central Europe* (Cambridge: Polity, 1989).

[4]William H. McNeill, *The Pursuit of Power* (Oxford: Blackwell, 1983).

[5]See John A. Armstrong, *Nations before Nationalism* (Chapel Hill, N.C.: University of North Carolina Press, 1982), and McNeill.

[6]István Bibó, "Az európai társadalomfejlödés értelme," in *Összegyüjtött Munkái*, vol. 2 (Berne: Epsze, 1982), 560–636.

[7]This is not to deny the impact of economics and the subordination of Eastern and Central Europe to Western markets, as proposed by Immanuel Wallerstein, *The Modern World System*, 2 vols. (London: Academic Press, 1974, 1980), but I would argue that the economic dependency of the area was only one factor among several in this respect.

[8]I would argue that Eastern absolutism was not as homogeneous as Perry Anderson describes it in *Lineages of the Absolutist State* (London: New Left Books, 1974).

[9]Peter Sugar, "An Underrated Event: the Hungarian Constitutional Crisis of 1905–06," *East European Quarterly* 15 (3) (1981): 281–306; and Nissan Oren, *Bulgarian Communism: The Road to Power 1934–1944* (New York: Columbia University Press, 1971).

[10]Pressure from France and Britain on the avowedly anti-Semitic Cuza-Goga government in Romania in 1937–1938 was an example. See Joseph Rothschild, *East Central Europe between the Two World Wars* (Seattle: University of Washington Press, 1974), 309–11.

[11]Andrew C. János, *The Politics of Backwardness in Hungary 1825–1945* (Princeton: Princeton University Press, 1982). See especially his introduction.

[12]Joseph Obrebski, *The Changing Peasantry of Eastern Europe* (Cambridge, Mass.: Schenkman, 1976).

[13]John Lampe and Marvin Jackson, *Balkan Economic History 1550–1950* (Bloomington: Indiana University Press, 1982).

[14]Victor S. Mamatey and Radomir Luza, *A History of the Czechoslovak Republic 1914–1948* (Princeton: Princeton University Press, 1973).

[15]Armstrong.

[16]Donald J. Olsen, *The City as a Work of Art: London, Paris, Vienna* (New Haven: Yale University Press, 1986), 58–81.

[17]Gary B. Cohen, *The Politics of Ethnic Survival: Germans in Prague 1861–1914* (Princeton: Princeton University Press, 1981).

[18]Strictly speaking, the Baltic states also fall into this category, but I shall not be dealing with them, inasmuch as they are outside my politically determined definition of Eastern Europe.

[19]Antal Garamvölgyi, "Magyarország—Nógrádból nézve," *Uj Látóhatár* 28 (1–2) (1975): 101–108; Anthony Polonsky, *Politics in Independent Poland 1921–1939* (Oxford: Oxford University Press, 1972).

94   George Schöpflin

[20]J. W. Brügel, *Czechoslovakia before Munich* (Cambridge: Cambridge University Press, 1973), 47–49.

[21]Walter Kolarz, *Myths and Realities in Eastern Europe* (London: Lindsay, Drummond, 1946).

[22]Ferenc Erdei, "A magyar társadalom a két háború között," *Valóság* 19 (4) (1974): 25–53; Jozo Tomašević, *Peasants, Politics and Economic Change in Yugoslavia* (Stanford: Stanford University Press, 1955); Anthony Smith, *The Ethnic Origins of Nations* (Oxford: Blackwell, 1986).

[23]Rothschild, 334.

[24]Nicos P. Mouzelis, "Greek and Bulgarian Peasants: Aspects of their Socio-Political Situation during the Inter War Period," in *Modern Greece, Facets of Underdevelopment* (London: Macmillan, 1978), 89–104.

[25]István Márkus, *Nagykörös* (Budapest: Szépirodalmi, 1979).

[26]Tomašević, 230.

[27]Ibid., 230–32.

[28]Zygmunt Bauman, "Intellectuals in East-Central Europe: Continuity and Change," *East European Politics and Societies* 1 (2) (Spring 1987): 162–86.

[29]Ágnes Losonczi, *Az életmód az időben, a tárgyakban és az értékekben* (Budapest: Gondolat, 1977); Miroslav Hroch, *Social Preconditions of National Revival in Europe* (Cambridge: Cambridge University Press, 1985); Obrebski.

[30]Zsolt Csalog, *Temető Összel* (Budapest: Szépirodalmi, 1977), 43.

[31]Jan B. de Weydenthal, *The Communists of Poland* (Stanford: Hoover Institution Press, 1978), 7; György Borsányi, "Ezernyolcszáz kartoték a budapesti baloldalról," *Valóság* 26 (8) (August 1983): 19–31.

[32]George Kolankiewicz, "The Working Class," in David Lane and George Kolankiewicz, eds., *Social Groups in Polish Society* (London: Macmillan, 1973), 88–89; Jan Szczepanski, "A munkásosztály összetételének változása," in *A szociológus szemével* (Budapest: Gondolat, 1977), 19.

[33]See the argument in Walter Connor, *Socialism, Politics and Equality: Hierarchy and Change in Eastern Europe and the USSR* (New York: Columbia University Press, 1979).

[34]Witold Wirpsza, *Pole, wer bist du?* (Lucerne: C. J. Bucher, 1972) argues this for Poznan, to the effect that the 1956 uprising was partly explained by the strength of the working class solidarity in the town. There is a good deal of evidence that Social Democrats played a major role during the Hungarian Revolution of the same year.

[35]On the histories of the Czechoslovak and German working classes, see William Griffith, ed., *Communism in Europe*, vol. 2 (London: Pergamon, 1966), 157–276 and 43–154, respectively.

Between Hope and Despair

Bronisław Geremek

*C*ontrasting *the crises that erupted in Hungary in 1956, in Czechoslovakia in 1968, and in Poland in 1956, 1968, 1970, 1976, and 1980, an effort is made to discover the rhythm—the political cycle—that explains the repeated outbreaks in Poland and the tragically defeated efforts of the Hungarians and the Czechs to reform their Communist systems from above. The conditions of the three countries were markedly different from the beginning; the legacies of World War II were determining in how the Soviet domination was experienced, tolerated, or resisted. The saga of Poland—particularly in the invention of Solidarity—tells how a proud and impoverished people sought to rid themselves of an alien body introduced into their midst.*

I choose to open this essay with a confession. Since I am a historian of the Middle Ages, modern history is definitely outside the field of my professional interests. The inspirations and impulses that flow to the historian from the world outside, in which he necessarily plays an active part, will influence, on a conscious or an unconscious level, many of his reflections. By the very nature of his profession, a historian is compelled to deal with things which are past; it is his task, in fact, to revive them. Hence, the importance of Marc Bloch's

Bronisław Geremek is a historian of medieval France who serves as Solidarity's floor leader in both houses of the Polish parliament.

95

opinion, following on that of his master, Henri Pirenne, that a historian is obliged to be sensitive to his own times, to the problems of his contemporaries; they constitute a lesson for him.[1]

Consequently, in the reflections I offer here on the postwar fate of Central Europe, which I have come to know either through passive experience or through active observation, I will focus on certain questions regarding the developmental tendencies in the Eastern bloc; my interest is not to narrate the dramatic events that have made Poland, Hungary, and Czechoslovakia front-page headline news in all the world press.

The political chronology of each of these countries was determined by spasmatic revolts that resulted in changes in the ruling teams and in the ways they executed power. In 1956, eleven years after the conclusion of the Second World War and three years after Stalin's death, the flame of revolt spread through Poland and Hungary; in 1968, it was Czechoslovakia's turn. Poland, in the grip of a conflict that extended over time, breaking out periodically and involving different social groups, saw the revolt of students and the intelligentsia in 1968, followed by a workers' explosion in late 1970 and by new revolt in June 1976 and again in July and August 1980. Dozens of books and hundreds of publications have treated each of the three countries and all three together; also, each of the events, again separately and together.

In this essay I have no intention of painting a general picture of each of these conflicts, so similar and so different, or of writing a political history of "the other Europe." Rather, my interest is to see if these explosions of social dissatisfaction with specific rulers and regimes had any kind of inner-time rhythm, whether, in other words, they suggest some kind of political cycle. With the perspectives provided by the great French medieval scholar Fernand Braudel, we are obliged to consider whether there is any significance in the *absence* of such explosions, any meaning in the long periods when seemingly nothing interfered with the official propaganda that trumpeted the message of moral and political unity. Looking at the situations comparatively, we must question why the social opposition in Hungary and Czechoslovakia confined itself essentially to single major conflicts while in Poland it took on a frequency that makes us ask whether we are witnessing something of a political cycle.

The political crises in post-Yalta Europe came in various complex social mazes, suggesting quite different configurations. What was the role played by the workers? What did the intellectuals do? These sociological questions lead to the problem of causes—or the alternative, if there is one—between changes decreed from above and the grass-roots nature of these transformations. In several of these crises, national aspirations came to the fore sometimes with such intensity that they turned into virtual national uprisings. The tradition of the nation-state in Central Europe is relatively new; because centuries of subjugation have built such strong national aspirations, these cannot be realized in a system of subordination. How is one to weigh the role of such sentiments? Any reflection on recent history, where the border between past and present is necessarily blurred, must be open also to the uncertainties of the future. All these spasms of the political cycle in Central Europe need to be situated within the larger crisis of the communist system.

Fundamental but seemingly elementary questions are raised by these developments. Faced with short-lived storms, a historian seeks to understand the longer-range situations, to find certain structures behind them, but also within them.[2] The implanting of Communist rule in Poland, Czechoslovakia, and Hungary had one thing in common; each was a forcible imposition of an external system, imposed against the will of the respective peoples. In no instance would democratic elections have given all power to the Communist parties, which in each case had only a small following, lacking anything resembling wide social support. In all three countries, with their strong national identities, the implanting of the communist system was a denial of their national interests[3] and their national sentiments.

The Communist campaign against all forms of nationalism, including any attachment to national traditions, involved a total rejection of all national distinctiveness. The denial of national legitimacy was the original sin committed by the Communist regimes in all these countries. The saying that communism goes with Poland as much as a saddle goes with a cow, attributed to Stalin, if used in a quite different context, applies to all the countries of Central Europe. No one of them would ever have accepted the Soviet model of power, later called real socialism, if left to itself. In every instance, the social system was wholly determined by the military advance of the Red

Army. In addressing Yugoslav Communist leaders in 1945, Stalin said, "This war is quite unlike the wars fought in the past; he who occupies a territory also imposes his own social system on it. Everybody imposes his own system as far as his army can advance. Things must be this way." To say that things could have been different is irrelevant. Stalin's philosophy of action eventually determined political reality in the whole of Central Europe. Still, there were major differences among Hungary, Czechoslovakia, and Poland, both at the start of the postwar period and in the way Stalin's moves were developed and implemented.

Hungary, for example, was one of Nazi Germany's allies in the war; its decision to join the Axis in 1941 committed the country to war for a few years. Rear Admiral Horthy, who acted as long-time regent following the suppression of Béla Kun's revolution, tried, unsuccessfully, to get out of the alliance in the final stage of the war, to no avail. Hungary paid for its involvement with the Axis in territorial losses, war reparations, and massive devastation. Given these circumstances, the country's political system was particularly vulnerable. It was here, in Hungary, that the "salami tactics"—to use the phrase of the Hungarian Communist leader Mátyás Rákosi—were first applied. It all started with an election "mistake," made in 1945, when a free election was held. The influence of the Communist party seemed to be growing; the Social Democratic party was largely subordinate to that galloping influence; there was good reason to believe that the concern over the defeat in war and the awareness of the need rapidly to resolve the country's many serious social problems would radicalize public opinion. Communist party forecasts of great success proved to be mistaken in the 1945 election: the absolute majority was won by the Small Owners' party, which gained 56 percent of the vote. A member of the Coalition Front, the Small Owners' party was hostile to the Communist party. In the next two years, however, the Stalinist political model was gradually allowed to dominate, thanks largely to successive government crises and a major expansion of the police power. Hungary became "a people's democracy."

It is impossible to ignore the role of opinion-making circles and the overall sociopsychological climate of the country in this process. One of the most acute Hungarian intellectuals, István Bibó, a historian and political scientist affiliated with the small National Peasant party, as early as 1945 pointed to the need to overcome the social and political heritage of the years of Horthy's dictatorship. Writing on the crisis of Hungarian democracy, he considered the prospects of a "revolution of human dignity," encouraging the Hungarian middle class to participate in the rebuilding of the country.[4] Following on the recent war experiences, a new political system seemed to be a historical necessity; it alone could offer new hope.

The fate of Czechoslovakia, whose fall was sealed by the Munich Pact in 1938, was largely determined by Stalin's overall European policy. Beneš, believing that he had failed to see through Stalin's game, that he had been misled, is said to have felt great remorse on his deathbed. As a matter of fact, such personal ties were largely irrelevant. After a series of dramatic developments, which included the halting of the advance of American troops and a popular uprising in Prague, the Soviet army marched into the city. Everything was then done to alter the earlier scenario to the new situation, slowly to replace the existing coalition government—for which Beneš had received firm Soviet guarantees—with a monopoly of power for the Czech Communists. In the 1946 election, the Communists finished at the top, with 36 percent of the vote, but only the carefully prepared coup d'état of February 1948 turned Czechoslovakia into a model Stalinist country.

Czechoslovakia, a nation with strong democratic traditions, constantly invoked the legitimacy of the First Republic in the first postwar years and proclaimed the need for a continuation of the old public order. It made use also of the traditional Pan-Slavic tradition, which was certainly present; Stalin alluded to it at a reception for Beneš in Moscow in 1943. There was, however, another reality—the genuine strength of the Communist party in the country. In Czechoslovakia, it was possible to withdraw Soviet troops and to hold a genuinely democratic election. The memories of Czechoslovakia's political isolation at the time of Munich, when Great Britain and France left the country as prey to the aggression of Nazi Germany, constituted an essential element in the postwar political climate. It determined the outcome of the 1946 election[5] and was very influential in generating the attitude of resignation toward the putsch of February 1948. The Czech philosopher Jan Patočka found the roots of Czech "moral disarmament" in what happened before the war, notably in the passive acceptance by the nation of the Munich decisions.

Obviously, the evolution of the postwar situation in both Czechoslovakia and Hungary was the result of an international situation marked by the West's passive approval of certain new conditions. The West's passivity was even more dramatic in the case of Poland. It is wholly reasonable that in the Poles' social consciousness the name of a Crimean summer resort should have a sinister connotation: Poland's postwar fate was sealed at Yalta, against the will of the nation. Both politically and militarily, Poland was the first country to resist Nazi aggression in World War II. Consistently, and on a truly massive scale, Poland engaged itself on the Allies' side; her legitimate authorities took for granted that the Allied promises to rebuild an independent Polish state would be kept. Because Poland was central to Soviet policy in Europe, however, the country's full subordination to the Soviet Union was necessary. Only in this way could there be a full realization of Stalin's postwar plans.[6] Stalin never fulfilled the promise made at the Yalta conference to have a "free and unfettered election" in Poland. The election of January 1947, accompanied by terror and falsehood, was rigged; there was no other way to impose Communist rule on Poland. All appearances of political pluralism, as they revealed themselves immediately after the war, were gradually destroyed—first in the climate of bloody civil war and then in the process of implementing the Stalinist model of power. The removal of Władysław Gomułka crowned this process. There was no place for a national society in the new bloc of subjugation.

The Polish cause was exacerbated by its heavy historical baggage. For many centuries, Polish-Russian relations had been marked by great hostility. Moscow's expansion to the West from the seventeenth to the nineteenth centuries took place at the expense of the Polish commonwealth; it was tsarist Russia that launched the destruction of the independent Polish state. Whole generations of Poles came to their national awareness and formed their aspirations for independence in the struggle against the Russian aggressor. When in addition the experiences of the last war are considered—the secret protocols to the Ribbentrop-Molotov pact, the invasion of Poland by the Red Army on September 17, 1939, the mass deportations of Poles, not to speak of the crimes committed on the Polish population, the best known, perhaps, the Katyń forest massacre of several thousand interned Polish officers that has become such a symbol in recent years—the Polish attitudes take on new meaning. As for the Russians, in addition to their traditional distrust of continually rioting Poles, who in the nineteenth century were seeking some sort of autonomy, events in the twentieth century gave new reason to treat Poland in a special way: it was from the hands of Poland that Soviet Russia suffered a grievous defeat in 1920; the Warsaw uprising of 1944 was at once an expression of resistance against the Nazi *Reich* but also of Polish determination to strive for real independence. Stalin's scenario for Poland was from the beginning harsher than any he prepared for other countries of the bloc then being established. The Soviet presence in Poland was never confined simply to a direct penetration of the political police, the military, and the administrative apparatus; it also took the form of stationing Soviet army units in Polish territories.

The attitudes of Polish society toward the new political order, especially among opinion-making circles and intellectual groups, reflected not only a feeling of resignation, stemming from the fact that Poland had been deserted by her Western allies, but from the conviction that it was absolutely necessary to change the country's social and political structures. The legacy of the prewar regime included memories not only of regained independence but also of disappointment and bitterness. The interwar period was a time of crisis for the European tradition. With the development of totalitarianism, the shameful product of the twentieth century, roots were given to a major deforming cancer. The "revolt of the masses," preached by philosophers of pessimism, seemed to be a historical necessity; the weakening of the heritage of elite culture was viewed as the indispensable price paid for progress. The announced social changes, with their promise of land reform and the nationalization of big industry, conformed to the programs of both liberal intellectuals and the non-Communist Left. The country, so heavily damaged by war and occupation, required a collective rebuilding effort. Given all these circumstances, the Communist authorities, forced upon Poland by entirely external factors, were able to count on the support of a certain internal consensus.

Still, the rank injustice of the post-Yalta order, the memory of the Katyń massacre, the agony of the Warsaw uprising, fought in complete isolation, could never disappear from the Poles' social consciousness. The Council for National Unity, the leading institution of the Polish resistance movement, defined its stance in an appeal to the Polish nation and the United Nations. Drafted at the moment when it had decided to disband, its message read: "The Polish Nation has retained its identity. In moments of the greatest misfortune it never broke morally or bent before anyone who would wish to govern it from outside, against its own interests and will. Fighting Poland is passing this great capital over to those who will continue to wage the nation's struggle for sovereignty with other methods."[7] This legacy has been present in Poland's entire postwar history and has turned active in every moment of crisis.

These "start-off" differences between the Communist governments in Hungary, Czechoslovakia, and Poland had consequences for their further evolution. After the first stage, in which the game of pretenses was artfully played for better or worse within the democratizing processes announced at Yalta, Stalin's strategy after 1948 was to standardize the situation. Although no one of these states was actually incorporated into the Soviet Union, they were compelled to be closely dependent on Moscow, with their economic and political systems being adapted to the Soviet model. This general trend was realized with the help of police terror, intimidation, and the development of what is best described as passive attitudes in each of these societies. Still, there were considerable differences between these countries, both in the methods used to realize the general strategy and in their effects.

The death of Stalin was not a breakthrough in the system's internal history, though it coincided with a very unfavorable economic situation in the entire Eastern bloc. The violent suppression of the riots in East Germany in June 1953 was telling testimony to the fact that nothing had changed. Indeed, in Poland, the arrest of Primate Stefan Wyszyński came six months after Stalin's death. The "thaw" that some spoke of was progressing slowly; the policy of political terror was limited gradually and unevenly in the subjugated countries. The real breakthrough came only in 1956 with mass rioting in the two countries where communism had the weakest roots, where the "monocentric" system had turned out to be both unprofitable and ineffective. The stability of the Communist authorities seemed suddenly to be in doubt.

De Tocqueville's famous aphorism that for a bad government the most dangerous moment arrives when it starts to introduce reforms seems to be fully applicable to the situation in Central Europe in 1956, and, indeed, in the last three decades. De Tocqueville also said, "Patiently endured so long as it seemed beyond redress, a grievance comes to appear intolerable once the possibility of removing it crosses men's minds."[8] With unusual perspicacity, he discerned the socio-psychological mechanism of protest which comes to operate against absolute or dictatorial rule. Major revolts in the bloc countries broke out at those times when manifestations of the decomposition of power, and the easing of the rule of force, began to be obvious. This is how the situation appeared in Hungary and Poland in 1956 and in Czechoslovakia in 1968. What was essential, however, was that the "improvement of the system" took the form of a coup engineered from above, with the seats of the central authorities of the Communist parties or governments serving as the headquarters of the general staffs of these revolutions. Hence, the first question calling for interpretation is, were the political crises in Communist Europe revolutions ordered from the top?

Each of the crises implied a change in the ruling team. In Hungary, the power crisis resulted first in the removal of the leader—Gerö replaced Rákosi—but this change was not followed by political change: the liberal-Communist regime of Imre Nagy was viewed simply as an opposition to the rulers of the Stalinist period. In Poland, following Bierut's death, the Party was headed by Ochab, from March to October 1956. It was during this period that there was rapid progress toward liberalizing the system from above. There was a weakening and even a disintegration of the secret police and the beginning of an attempt to make an accounting for the terror of the preceding period. It was during this time that a workers' riot took place in Poznań, in June 1956, whose suppression resulted in bloodshed.

The events in Hungary and Poland in the fall of 1956 merit attention, not least because they are so different. The political ferment in intellectual and artistic circles had an influence far beyond writers' clubs, universities, and newspaper offices; it was the beginning of a mass movement in which the struggle for national liberation from the empire's yoke was accompanied by calls for "genuine" or "revised" socialism. A key role was played by workers from large industrial plants, who added a dramatic dimension to the social conflict; the workers' strikes carried the sparks of either a democratic revolution or a national uprising. All these phenomena, intertwined in the events of 1956, in the order of their appearance, reveal the existence of internal tensions between those who were intent on improving socialism and those who were expressing genuine national aspirations.

As a political phenomenon, revisionism boils down to a striving for democratic socialism. The term *revisionism*, used in official Communist propaganda to describe those spokesmen proposing inner changes in the communist system, had negative connotations. It was tantamount to passing a political and ideological sentence of sorts on the communist system, and in some cases judicial as well! Still, the same term could be used correctly to define a tendency within the Communist elite that combined the affirmation of a humanistic ideology with a criticism of the policy pursued by the system of real socialism. The Twentieth Congress of the Soviet Communist party gave birth to rebellious programs drafted by the leaderships of particular parties and also by certain intellectual communities. A characteristic expression of the former was the address of Imre Nagy on July 1953, for which he was removed from power as an "opportunist." In a memo of 1955, Nagy, undeterred, outlined a policy of "communism which does not forget about man." Intellectual programs were systematically developed by Polish writers and journalists, who not only sought to separate the vision of socialism from the practice of the Stalinist system, but attempted also to map out anew the activity of the Communist party, to mobilize social imagination around the project of democratic socialism.

In the perspective of time, revisionism seems to have been a false consciousness, a grand illusion. Still, its importance for social consciousness has to be appreciated; it helped—not always intentionally—to unmask the ideology and politics of communism with the help of thinking derived from the same Marxist roots. Works of the "young Marx," of Gramsci and Lukacs, served as intellectual reference points, useful in destroying Communist ideology. The thesis about the historical role of the working class added yet another dimension to the workers' revolts against Communist rule; also, it stripped the authorities of their legitimacy, including the one that seemed so firmly rooted in their own ideological discourse. From the point of view of the future, the most important effect of revisionism was that it provoked social activism, and with it a revival of political interest; it was opposed to that passivity in public life that was both a result and a condition of the existence of Stalinist monopoly. Even the eventual defeat of revisionism served the cause of rebuilding civil society.

But it was a long way from the intellectual clubs, the Petöfi Club in Budapest and the Crooked Circle Club in Warsaw, to the workers becoming actively engaged. The workers' revolt in Poznań, for example, was hardly echoed among Polish intellectuals, while the intellectual unrest, which took place some months later, in October, met with wide workers' support only in Warsaw. In Budapest, the situation was different: the program of workers' democracy found its implementation in the establishment of workers' councils in factories. This enlivened the trade unions; later, the actual uprising united individuals from different social groups in a common armed struggle and resistance. Still, any accurate sociological analysis must make it clear that there were real divisions between the workers and the intelligentsia, stemming not only from the cultural differences be-tween the two groups, but also from the very different interests they displayed, and indeed from their very different sensitivity to certain public issues. The tactics of government, based on its party monop-oly, relied on these divergences, on the workers' distrust of the intelligentsia and its political activity.

In October 1956 Budapest witnessed a national uprising—the term is now used also by the Hungarian Communists—while in Poland the mass demonstrations led to a peaceful change in the Party leadership. In both countries, however, the democratic and liberal slogans were followed by ever more intense expressions of the validity of national aspirations. The latter expressed demands that the Russians remove themselves from direct participation in running the country—espe-cially with respect to the armed forces and the secret police. Insisting on the distinctiveness of national cultures, they emphasized the necessity of increasing the scope of national independence. In many disparate social circles, these aspirations, closely related to anti-Russian or anti-Soviet attitudes, were deeply rooted in the historical experience of Poles and Hungarians. In Poland, the reemergence of Gomułka on the political scene met certain of these demands halfway; after all, in 1949, he had been removed from power for his "rightist-nationalist leaning," for his attempt to oppose Stalin's imperial policy and defend the remnants of Polish national independence. At a mass rally in Warsaw on October 16, 1956, Gomułka's announcement that Soviet advisers would be sent home met with enthusiastic applause from the crowd.

The Hungarian uprising, a confrontation between Hungarians demanding the right to self-determination and Soviet tanks arriving to crush their striving for freedom, led inevitably to a national movement. National aspirations and slogans figured prominently in both Poland and Hungary.

The Prague Spring of 1968, while having certain distinctive features, was basically similar to the model of the Hungarian and Polish events of 1956. The program of "socialism with a human face" contained the same aspirations for democratic socialism and identical ideological illusions. The period witnessed also a revival of national consciousness among the Czechs and the Slovaks, along with an affirmation of cultural identity and a striving to expand the national autonomy. As for national slogans, they were of secondary importance until the armed intervention of the Warsaw Pact. Czechoslovakia's historical experience apparently had a role in all of this; the country's earlier and more recent history had not produced the kinds of mass anti-Russian and anti-Soviet attitudes that existed elsewhere. Such attitudes became an essential element only after the invasion; even then, however, the opposition groups rallied around democratizing and antitotalitarian programs rather than around a program emphasizing state sovereignty and national identity. Also, in Czechoslovakia, the opposition movement of the 1970s and the 1980s never extended beyond the cultural and political elite; it never assumed a mass character. The weakness of national and religious demands goes far to explain this state of affairs.

While it would be an oversimplification to treat the 1968 events in Czechoslovakia as a delayed echo of the Polish-Hungarian revolutionary wave of 1956, similarities are obvious, the more so as the slogans of the Prague Spring fit so neatly into the phenomenon of revisionism. Yet, some thought must be given to their historical context. The Czechoslovak events of 1968 voiced the last hopes of all those individuals and groups in Central Europe who had been striving to improve real socialism. The defeat of the Prague Spring was a telling lesson; it was impossible to rationalize economic policy, to liberalize the system of government or to make it more humane without rejecting the principal structures of the authoritarian construction. The situation in Czechoslovakia had repercussions in other communist countries as well, notably in Poland, but these repercussions were confined to the elite, students and intellectuals who failed to win the support of wider social circles.

The rhythm of conflict seemed to accelerate, to become more intense in Poland. The year 1968 brought a new wave of student riots and intellectual protests. The Communist party chose to counteract these with an anti-Semitic campaign calculated to win new social support. While such support never materialized, the campaign revived many ghosts from the past. In December 1970, workers' unrest broke out in the Baltic port cities, where it led eventually to the formulation of a program calling for sweeping economic and political changes. The list of demands set forth by the Szczecin workers in December 1970—a largely forgotten document today when compared with the twenty-one demands of the Gdansk workers of August 1980—has acquired a historic significance as a pioneering document. What counted, however, was not so much the formulation of a program as its success. This did not happen in December 1970. While the ruling team was replaced, the new regime aroused only limited hopes. The social climate was additionally burdened by memories of 1968 when the shameful anti-Semitic campaign was accompanied by unfortunate divisions between intellectuals and workers. The lack of unity, characteristic also of the next wave of workers' strikes in 1976, concentrated largely in central Poland, in Radom and Warsaw, was again conspicuous. Force was used to resolve all these successive workers' protests.

While in the course of the riots, rebellious participants set the Communist party headquarters on fire, the use of army units and police squads effectively put an end to all such demonstrations and strikes. Violence was used by both sides. The balance of forces, however, favored the police and the authorities; they had at their disposal all the means necessary to restore order.

In the summer of 1980, events took a quite different course. This time, the authorities resolved not to use force, though it was available to them in even more impressive strength than in preceding decades. The explanation for this behavior, in a few words, was their awareness of the critical state of the economy and a certain sense of helplessness within the ruling elite. More important, perhaps, was the changed situation of society, which had overcome its divisions, established organized structures of social resistance, and produced an independent information channel.

The most characteristic feature of the events of the summer of 1980 in Poland was society's rapid self-organization, which quite spontaneously translated its protest into a regular program and selected means of action adapted to it. The outer forms of protest seemed unchanged: price increases for basic articles, especially food staples, were met with strikes. The first occurred in Lublin in July, then spread to the Baltic port cities in August. The Lublin strike resulted in a surprisingly efficient organization of the municipal and retail trade services, with the shops being supplied with food by the local strike committees before a compromise agreement was actually signed. During the strike, local railmen blocked trains heading for the Soviet Union with Polish food exports; this, however, was more an act of passive resistance than of violence.

The August strikes in the shipyards of Gdansk, Gdynia, and Szczecin, which soon spread to most other workplaces in these cities, again produced organized strike structures and services that helped secure a normal course of life in the cities and ensure order and discipline in the striking plants. As these were all sit-in strikes, the daily life of participants had to have a certain amount of organization. This self-organizing process on the part of particular groups and the whole society fighting for their rights, became widespread; it affected certain other areas traditionally in the domain of the state. Thus, for example, because the workers' guard controlled the safety of a given factory or city, alcohol was totally banned from workplaces and from public life. The striking factories became the centers of local authority; a new kind of social representation emerged. It provided a social and political lesson of great significance. The workers' protest, characterized by great determination, was hardly an act of despair. It was a political act. In conditions of the communist system, an industrial conflict cannot be isolated; it assumes the nature of a political power struggle.

This was clearly evident in the strikers' programs, where political aspirations were explicitly articulated. The list of demands of the Gdansk workers included not only requests for specific pay and social compensation, but expressed also an awareness of the general dangers looming over the country. Hence, the demands to reform the economic system, to guarantee human rights, to free political prisoners, to curb censorship, and to broadcast Sunday Mass over the radio. The insistence on free trade unions—the most important demand from the Gdansk list—has to be placed in this context also. The new trade union saw the defense of the employees' interests as one of its tasks, but also, and perhaps more importantly, it emphasized the restoration of civil society's supremacy over the state.[9] This was a wholly political demand, undermining the structures of a system in which, in addition to the monopolistic Communist party, a workplace could accommodate only Communist-dependent organizations whose sole purpose would be to transmit Party directives down to the crew.

The national element was present in the Polish August of 1980 from the start, with great intensity. This was evident not only in the rhetoric—publications and speeches played a major liberating role in the strikes—but also in the concrete proposals put forth by the workers, and indeed, in the symbols they used. The national colors, with which the factories were decked out, were this time deprived of the company of the red banner, which had been obligatory until then. This fact alone spoke volumes about the striving for national liberation. A recurring theme in the debates on the country's economic situation was Poland's economic exploitation by the Soviet Union, real and alleged. The religious symbols placed on the gates of striking plants, together with the communal prayers and Mass, constituted yet one more expression of the wish to liberate human aspirations, to oppose the official propaganda. In this way, the August strikes gave vent to a more general questioning of the existing system—in the economy, in government, in ideology. Another novel feature of this decisive crisis was that a political solution, in the form of a compromise between the two sides, seemed to be called for.

For the first time, neither the use of brute force nor the superficial reshuffling of the ruling team was invoked to find a solution to the conflict. Instead, an agreement was reached whose main result was the establishment of a new trade union. The significance of this decision cannot be exaggerated. The birth of Solidarity and its programmatic separation from the political authorities, and above all, from the ruling Communist party, was understood to be a self-organization of civil society. A representation of the employees' interests and an antitotalitarian force from the moment of its birth,

Solidarity was recognized at once to be an all-out challenge to the totalitarian system.

The imposition of martial law by General Jaruzelski after 500 days of Solidarity's legal existence seemed to have closed, once and for all, this special chapter in Polish history. Numerous opposition circles both in Central and in Eastern Europe viewed the Solidarity experience as a lesson demonstrating that societies in the Communist bloc stood no chance of gaining their emancipation through evolutionary change and grass-roots self-organization. Seeing the geopolitical determinants as the fundamental factors defining the lot of all nations in that region of Europe, these circles believed that only political transformation on the scale of the entire Eastern bloc would enable countries like Poland and Hungary to free themselves of communism.[10]

From the perspective of the present, it is possible to say that the Solidarity chapter was not closed on December 13, 1981. The power of society's resistance to enslavement, together with the power of the political imagination of workers and intellectual elites brought about the historic changes of 1989, which not only returned Solidarity to the public scene but also returned Poland to the democratic institutions of Europe. The effectiveness of the strategy of society's self-organization and self-restraint in the struggle for the realization of its aspirations was confirmed.

However, it is impossible not to notice the significance of geopolitical factors, especially if you set aside the skepticism that has been common regarding grass-roots social activity and movements. In 1980 and 1981, comprehensive economic and political reforms proved impossible because they were not accompanied by favorable international circumstances. Such circumstances do exist in 1989: in the East, Gorbachev's policy has been promoting an overall restructuring of the system; he has approved of the changes in Hungary and Poland and has been watching impatiently the erosion of the old routine in Czechoslovakia and the German Democratic Republic; in the West, the democratic transformations in Poland and Hungary are no longer feared as being capable of destabilizing a precarious world order.

What is important, obviously, is not so much the external context of the situation in Poland or Hungary, but instead, that it is part of a general process affecting the entire communist system. From time to time opposition activists in Central Europe have launched appeals to unite the efforts of dissident groups in all countries of the Communist bloc. Many such contacts have indeed been established, but it is not this kind of conscious action that led eventually to the coinciding of major changes in this part of Europe. Rather, it is the fact that the crisis of real socialism acquired a general nature affecting the whole of the region; it affected simultaneously the economy, the government, and the ideology. Furthermore, the economic standing of the communist countries became a visible proof of the system's inefficiency.

There is a certain rhythm in the series of political crises that have taken place in the countries subjugated to the Soviet Union since the war. An analysis of these crises, especially in Poland, inevitably brings to mind certain periodic economic fluctuations. There can be no doubt that there exists a linkage between the political crises and the economic situation. It is enough to recall the Polish crises that coincided with price hikes or failures to realize successive economic plans to accept that this is so. Nevertheless, studies do not allow us to answer unequivocally what the precise nature of the relationship between political and economic cycles is. Notice must be taken of the fact that the economic situation in particular countries within the Soviet bloc show very substantial differences. In late 1989, Poland was in the grip of a far more acute economic crisis than many other countries of the bloc, but even in the GDR, whose economy has continually been supported by West Germany, thanks to which the GDR has enjoyed a period of relative prosperity, political disturbances are gradually assuming the form of sharp conflict between society and the authorities. Political crises tend to break out in Eastern bloc countries in all kinds of economic conditions. The timing of events in Poland and Hungary in 1956, and those of 1968 in Czechoslovakia and Poland, can hardly be explained in economic terms alone.

Still, there is no doubt that economic factors have had some role in these political crises, so much so that a term like *political-economic cycle* has been coined.[11] On the one hand, the phenomenon is connected with the increased role of the state in the economy and with its economic policy; on the other, there are the specific features of the planned economy, and with it the permanent conflict between the authorities—with their utopian vision of the future—and society, with its experience of the realities of daily life. The pathology of the Stalinist system, imposed on Central and Eastern Europe as a result of the Second World War, has its roots in politics; it affects first and foremost the state and public life, but it is most painfully and widely felt in the economic sphere, in daily life.

In the case of Poland, the shortening of the periods between the crises is very evident. While one may wonder about this or express surprise at the extended periods between the political crises in other countries, there is no easy explanation of either. Concrete historical factors are at play certainly, but they are extremely hard to measure or to analyze. Nor is it easy to weigh a society's patience, persistence, or even the authorities' level of incompetence or competence. The political development of East European countries displays also a dialectic between enslavement and silence, between inefficiency of the system and growing aspirations, between frustrated hopes and the rejection of conformism. In an extended time perspective, the successive crises may be viewed as the spasms of an organism seeking to reject an alien body.

Toward the end of 1989, it is obvious that the division of Europe, resulting from postwar agreements and running along ideological and political lines, has failed to pass the test of time. The structures of the last empire in the world are collapsing. The trend toward freedom in Central and Eastern Europe seems to be crystallized permanently, apparently irreversibly.

ENDNOTES

[1] M. Bloch, *The Historian's Craft* (New York: Alfred A. Knopf, 1953).

[2] F. Braudel, *Ecrits sur l'histoire* (Paris: Flammarion, 1969), 301.

[3] F. Fejtö, in *1956, Varsovie-Budapest, La deuxième révolution d'Octobre* (Paris: Seuil, 1978).

[4] I. Bibó, *Misère des petits états d'Europe de l'Est* (Paris: Harmattan, 1986), 451.

[5] T. Garton Ash, *The Polish Revolution, Solidarity 1980-1982* (London: Jonathan Cape, 1983), 1.

[6] Z. Brzeziński, *The Soviet Bloc, Unity and Conflict* (Cambridge, Mass.: Harvard University Press, 1960).

[7] A. Ciolkosz, "Zeszyty Historyczne," *Ostatnie dokumenty Polski Podziemnej* 8 (1965): 174ff.

⁸Alexis de Tocqueville, *The Old Regime and the French Revolution* (Garden City, N.Y.: Doubleday Anchor Books, 1955), 177.

⁹A. Hegedus, *Socialism and Bureaucracy* (London: Allison and Busby, 1976), 92.

¹⁰Steve W. Reiquam, ed., *Solidarity and Poland, Impacts East and West* (Washington, D.C.: The Wilson Center Press, 1988), 43.

¹¹A. Smolar, in *1956, Varsovie-Budapest, La deuxième révolution d'Octobre.*

October 1989

Bohemia of the Soul

Josef Škvorecký

T*he Communist regime which took power in Czechoslovakia in 1948 created a new type of criminal: the illegal emigrant or, to use the Party terminology, a person who left the country without permission. But these people left because their democratic and liberal state had been turned into a totalitarian dictatorship. Yet the Communists accused such emigrants of a lack of loyalty to their native country. Thus the issue of loyalties became the central issue of Czech life: Should one be loyal to the state, no matter what kind of state it is, no matter what kind of system exists within its borders, or should one be loyal to the just and democratic country as it had once existed, and as it exists now only in people's memories, yearnings, in their hearts? Should one be loyal to a geographic entity, or to a fatherland of the soul?*

My *Random House Dictionary of the English Language* defines *exile* as either "prolonged separation from one's country or home, as by force of circumstances," or "expulsion from one's native land by authoritative decree." *To emigrate,* on the other hand, means "to leave one country or region and settle in another." Although some "force of circumstances" is usually present in any decision to emigrate—except in the case of born adventurers—it is not the decisive or even predominant factor with

Josef Škvorecký is a Department of English Professor at the University of Toronto.

emigrants—as it is with exiles. In this unblessed century, *an exile* came to mean a person who leaves his homeland for political reasons, sometimes without, sometimes with, the permission of the authorities, and sometimes banished by them. An "emigrant" moves elsewhere to better himself economically.

If any group of persons fits this definition of exiles, it is the Czechs and Slovaks who left their land after the Communist coup in 1948 and after the Soviet ambush in 1968. Yet the Party press refers to them never as exiles but always only as emigrants.

The reason for this usage which seems to contradict dictionary definitions may be subconscious, but if we had access to Party archives, who knows, we might find at the beginning an authoritative decree. In any case, the roots of either the subconscious block or the *apparatchik* order are historical. In the mind of every even only mildly educated Czech, *exile* is associated with the catastrophe of 1620, when the Czech Protestant armies were decimated in the Battle on the White Hill near Prague, and the ancient, proud, and independent kingdom of Bohemia, with its Hussite tradition, became for three hundred years an oppressed province of the Austrian Empire of the Catholic Habsburgs.

After the defeat, persons of noble origin or elevated status were given a choice: either convert to Catholicism, or leave the country. Simple folks, the majority of the population, were not given a choice but an order: become Catholic, or else. The "else" soon came to mean, among other things such as the burning of witches, the burning of Protestant bibles and prayer books, the first such purification of the mind in Czech history.

*   *   *

So persons of elevated status and aristocrats went into exile, and simple folks—flocks of Moravian Brethren for instance—secretly crossed the Czech-German border and later dispersed all over the world, including large numbers to America. This is how the word *exile* is fixated in Czech minds. It evokes images of dangerous nocturnal border crossings and involuntary sojourns in foreign countries, mostly for the rest of the exiles' earthly existence.

But the word also stirs up images of great personages, of success and freedom, unattainable under the foreign rule at home. The 1620 exile wave, the first of many that were to follow, indeed could boast interesting and even great men. The most important was Jan Amos Komenský, known by his latinized name Comenius, who settled and became world famous in Holland. He was the founder of modern pedagogy, and his slogan *schola ludus,* that school should be linked not to mental torture but to play, was much later unfortunately transmogrified into educational notions that eventually led to our contemporary blackboard jungles. According to Cotton Mather's *Magnalia Christi Americana,* Governor John Winthrop invited Komenský to America to become the first president of Harvard College.[1] Though some correspondence between the two men concerning methods of education survived, the invitation is not mentioned in the letters. Nevertheless, Comenius was a scholarly star of his times, and his glory reached even the mountain huts where the diehard Protestants practiced their religion in secret, and gave them satisfaction and much needed encouragement.

There were other remarkable Czechs in this first exodus of refugees whose lives are unquestionable success stories. The Czechness of some of them may be the product of exiles' legends and of wishful thinking of those living under the boots of tyrants. What was firmly established, for instance, about Augustine Herrman, the first cartographer of Virginia and Maryland and member of the Council of New Netherlands, is that he was born in Bohemia. He may, of course, have been a Bohemian German, as the spelling he used in America indicates: Herrman. On the other hand, he signed his map of Virginia and Maryland, and many other documents, "Augustine Herrman, Bohemian." Was it to stress his allegiance to the country of the Czechs?[2] Czech or not, he certainly was a luminary. Another prominent Bohemian was Frederick Phillipse. In America he became enormously rich (in part because he owned shares in pirate ships) and he could have become George Washington's grandfather-in-law: his granddaughter Mary Phillipse Morris was proposed to by the young officer, but she refused him and married into the Loyalist family of the Morrises.[3] Such persons, whether their Czechness was real or imaginary, served as uplifting examples for the persecuted coreligionists at home. Later, American Czechs of distinction were useful to nineteenth-century liberals, who pointed to America as a land of democracy, and therefore of opportunity, and who compared life in the American republic with conditions in tyrannical, rigidly hierar-

118   *Josef Škvorecký*

chical Austria, where *freedom* was a suspicious word and social mobility an exceptional deviation.

A pattern was thus established in the seventeenth century which found its exact replicas in our own era.

*   *   *

In the party press of the more aggressive type, the word *emigrant* is accompanied by the epithet "treacherous." I don't know whether the victorious Habsburgs introduced this usage into the language after the White Hill battle had entangled them in the Thirty Years War, in which a number of Czech exiles fought in the armies of the Habsburgs' Protestant enemies. Certainly, much later, the Nazis—or at least their Czech quislings—flung it at exiles, especially after the assassination of Reinhard Heydrich, laying bare the illogicality of the usage. Can one become a traitor to one's enemies? Where should one's loyalties be? With a piece of land where we were born and which, "right or wrong," is our country? Is it, really? Right or wrong? Or should one be motivated by some other principle rather than by an accident of geography?

The Nazi quislings introduced the epithet into Czech political lingo, and the pre-*glasnost* (hopefully just the pre-glasnost) Communist media brought it up *ad absurdum*. It is best illustrated by the case of the *kulaks*. The word is Russian and means "big farmers": working farmers, not landlords, often absentees. In Bohemia a kulak could be anybody with as little as ten acres of land. By official Party decree, such laboring villagers were promoted to "class enemies" and dealt with accordingly. Some—very few—fought back, damaging farm equipment and even killing cattle before it was confiscated for the collective farms. They became "traitors." Traitorous enemies. Perhaps this is Marxist dialectics.

The most tragic victim of these dialectics was the Socialist deputy Milada Horáková. The Communists, after the takeover in 1948, reduced her Socialist party to the status of organizations such as the Cat Lovers' Club. Horáková, mother of a schoolgirl at the time, met with some Socialist friends, discussed their immediate political future, was arrested, sentenced as a "traitor," and hanged, the only Czech woman ever hanged by her own people for political "crimes." Prominent Party members received admission tickets to the execution, carried on like the audience at a box-match, and after the horror ended, departed, chatting excitedly and leaving cigarette butts and chocolate wrappers behind. An eyewitness described the scene in the writers' weekly *Listý* in 1968.

This gruesome component of the pattern of Czech exile had also emerged after 1620. Twenty-seven Protestant "traitors" of the Catholic Habsburgs, all of them persons of nobility or prominence, were executed in 1621. The spectacle was made more interesting and educational by various means. The tongue of Jan Jesenius was cut out before he was beheaded; after his body was quartered, the four pieces were put on spikes and exhibited in different parts of the city. In a similar fashion, the heads of twelve of the executed adorned spikes on the Charles Bridge tower until they rotted away. In the aftermath of 1948, atrocities fully on par with the cutting out of tongues were committed. Official reports of Party commissions cite examples of political prisoners forced to eat excrement and other such juicy improvements on seventeenth-century hangmen's imaginations. They also mention a desperate executioner who beseeched the judges to slow down on death sentences since the excessive number of his professional engagements made him a nervous wreck. One of the members of these commissions was a little known Slovak apparatchik Alexander Dubček. Perhaps this may help to explain why this gentle Communist later coined the implicitly slanderous slogan "Socialism with a Human Face."

*   *   *

The issue of the "traitorous enemy" is serious because, as I indicated, it implies the important question of loyalties. Again the White Hill battle which triggered the Thirty Years War set a precedent. Some exiles did not sever contacts with home. Secret emissaries traveled by night through the border forests between Bohemia and Germany, and further to Holland, to Sweden, precursors of modern "traitorous" agents. The Swedish Protestant armies, which almost reconquered Bohemia (they overran half of Prague), included numbers of Czechs who, under the banners of Gustavus II, fought to deliver their fatherland from Habsburg rule. When the Treaty of Westphalia was signed in 1648 and Bohemia—since the Swedes did not manage to take all of Prague—remained part of the Austrian Empire, some Swedish-Czech soldiers, their hopes of a return home frustrated, at least took with them into exile Czech women, sometimes without regard to their marital status. With them they withdrew to Sweden and to other Protestant countries, where over the centuries they melted out of recognizable Czech identity. My parental ancestor Martin Škvorecký lost his second young wife in this manner and went mad. As I wrote, I am not sure whether the Habsburgs called these soldiers traitors. They clearly were not. They just cherished freedom—which in their day meant religious freedom—more than staying at home at the price of renouncing their creed and swearing allegiance to foreign tyranny.

*   *   *

The first twentieth-century replica of the situation was World War II. Secret emissaries crossed borders again, this time in airplanes rather than on foot, parachuted into Bohemia, established links with the underground and performed acts of sabotage, some very spectacular, such as the assassination of SS-Obergruppenführer Reinhard Heydrich, the Nazi protector of Bohemia and Moravia. Czech exiles joined the French—and after the debacle of France, the British army and air force—and fought under the Union Jack in the Battle of Britain, in North Africa, and after the invasion of France in 1944, in Normandy. This first replica of the Swedish episode of Czech history was unproblematic, clear: these fighters were obviously not traitors—except in the minds of a handful of quislings—and they fought for a just cause.[4]

The pattern of martial resistance to tyranny faded after 1948 and disappeared after 1968. In 1948, when Czechoslovakia abruptly changed from a socialist democracy into a Stalinist state of horror, many still hoped that the day of glorious homecoming would arrive in their lifetime: many (not just Czechs) expected war. A few exiles enlisted with the French Foreign Legion—as their predecessors at the beginning of World War II did—but most of those willing to fight joined the Counter Intelligence Agency as "walking agents" (*agenti chodci*). Once again, determined men traveled by night through the border woods between Bohemia and Germany, establishing contacts with the anti-Communist underground, carrying messages to and fro.

But those were the early 1950s. The Communist police, incomparably better organized than whatever similar forces the Habsburgs had at their disposal, were soon able to crush underground resistance and with them, the CIA agents. About 40 percent of the populace were Party members, in those early days still frequently true believers, and therefore often ardent helpers of the security forces. In their struggle with the "class enemy" (these agents were, more often than not, Social Democrats or Socialists, workers or lower-middle-class people), the police and the border guards, naturally, used firearms. The agents, equally naturally, fired back. Many were caught and hanged. As traitors, naturally.

In the summer of 1988, as glasnost painstakingly gained minuscule ground in Prague, the old border war with the agents was used by the diehard Stalinist faction of the Party in a compaign of "warning." In a series of articles, the descendants of Oxenstierna's emissaries and Churchill's parachutists were depicted as sadistic cutthroats who volunteered for their deadly missions moved by sheer class hatred, and by money. I happen to know some survivors, and so I have an idea about the remuneration they received. Among the ones I know are sons of underground fighters executed by the Nazis. They simply saw communism for what it is and, emulating the example of their fathers, decided that to believe in democracy was not enough: one must also fight for it.

But the police writers who authored the anti-agent series in the summer of 1988 knew what they were doing. In these leftish, blindly anti-American times, there is irrational opprobrium attached to the name *CIA* in the minds of many Westerners and, after decades of Goebbelsian party propaganda, even in the minds of a number of Czechs, unfortunately, even a handful of dissidents. Thinking about the agents, they oscillate between sympathy and uneasiness. In the agents' case, the totalitarians scored a point.

From the 1968 exile wave, the martial element was totally absent. Nobody expected a war of liberation any longer. The atomic bomb became a guarantor of peace and of the survival of tyranny. There was only the Vietnam conflict. Knowing communism inside out, the Czechs had no illusion about the nature of the Ho Chi Minh regime and perceived the struggle as a just American war. A few young exiles were drafted into the U. S. Army and served in the jungles. I have never heard about any Czech draft dodgers.

*   *   *

The first true Czech emigration in the sense of the definition quoted at the beginning of this article did not emerge until the nineteenth century. Even that was not pure emigration. Most emigrants were, indeed, poor farm laborers who left for America to better themselves economically and, one day, send their children to schools, inaccessible to such trash in Bohemia. But there were among them village intellectuals, well read in the Czech liberal literature of the times, such as Josef Lidumil Lešikar, a tailor and small farmer who led one of the first bands of hopefuls to Texas in 1853. Although such people, too, intended to acquire land, work it, and become prosperous, they also yearned for life in a democracy, as Lešikar's letters testify.[5] Some were educated city intellectuals who in 1848 had fought on the barricades in Prague or participated in other uprisings, and simply had had to leave to escape prison. Like the post-1620 exiles, they boasted several excellent personages, well-known at least in Czech-American circles. Vojta Náprstek was one, a rich journalist who spent a decade publishing a German liberal paper (read by many Czechs)—the *Flugblätter* in Milwaukee, where his beautiful common-law wife was charmingly nicknamed "Náprstsquaw" (U. S. pronunciation of *Náprstková*). Another was the colorful Anthony M. Dignowitý, who had to flee to America after he had fought alongside the Poles in the 1830 uprising against Russia. A staunch abolitionist like Lešikar, he, too, was almost lynched in San Antonio but managed to escape to Washington, where he suggested to Congress a plan of an invasion of Texas which was not entirely impractical. His two sons, forcibly drafted into the Confederate Army, followed their father, defected, and joined the army of the Union. They all seem to have been "traitors" of the country of their residence.

*   *   *

That search for political and religious freedom was not absent even among the very poor is attested to by the fact that, although an absolute majority of them were listed as adherents of Catholicism—by early nineteenth century no longer an obligatory, but an establishment-preferred denomination in Austria—about half of them, as soon as they set foot in America, joined Protestant denominations or became free thinkers.

Some of these emigrants, or exiles, were defectors from the Austrian army. Being experts at nothing but soldiering, some joined the U. S. regulars. Six such exiles served and later fought under Sherman in the 13th Regiment of the United States Army. But there were also Czech volunteers who responded to Lincoln's call to arms. In Chicago in 1861 they founded the Lincoln Slavonic Rifle Company, which when the war broke out became part of the 24th Illinois Volunteer Regiment, and was under the command of the Hungarian Slovak Colonel Géza Mihalotzy, who died a hero's death at Buzzard Roost Gap near Chattanooga. Large groups of Czechs were in various regiments from the Midwest, especially in the 24th Wisconsin. They marched with Sherman to the sea, and then through the Carolinas. There Private František Stejskal encountered two liberated black slaves, who to his surprise, spoke Czech. They had belonged to a Czech sawmill proprietor near Charlestown, obviously one of the uneasy liberal slaveholders who had encouraged their slaves' efforts to acquire education. Since he had an American wife who probably refused to learn her husband's strange language, he taught it to his servants, to have, in his South Carolina linguistic loneliness, at least someone to talk to in the tongue that came naturally to him. He fell as a colonel in the Confederate Army.[6]

The Czech soldiers of the Union Army were the first Czechs since the Thirty Years War who fought for a just cause, even though in a foreign country. They established a precedent repeated in both World Wars of our century which saw large Czech units as parts of allied armies, fighting for good causes. Otherwise, for three centuries, Czechs who stayed at home, if they fought at all, did so in the interest of others, others who were never democrats.

*   *   *

After the Civil War, Czech emigration, more or less just a trickle before the war, assumed mass proportions. Many of those who decided to risk the perilous journey into the wild country of Indians made up their minds after reading enthusiastic letters written to them by friends and relatives who had preceded them. A few such letters were even printed in newspapers, but Austrian censorship soon forbade such publication. So people copied them by hand, and the epistles circulated—a kind of very early *samizdat*.

And so the Czechs went. Some ended up as failures, most considerably improved their lot, and quite a few became highly successful. But success wasn't really sweet until they traveled home to show off. Many did. The "American uncle" appeared on the Czech scene. Such showing off, however, wasn't always mere individual boastfulness. The proud new Americans who, back home, had been paupers and social zeros, demonstrated by their American journey from rags to riches the superiority of democracy over the outmoded, semifeudal system at home, with its limited freedom and huge prejudicial obstacles to upward social mobility. The American uncle phenomenon is as strong today as it was in the previous century. Miloš Forman confessed to me once that he couldn't really enjoy the triumphs of his films unless he showed them to his old friends in Prague, and even to his father's old buddies in his native town of Čáslav (his father was killed by the Gestapo). "When I screen the film in New York for the critics I'm as cool as a cucumber," he said. "But when I show it in the old Film Club in Prague—oh boy! I almost die of stagefright." Martina Navrátilová, in spite of all her victories and millions, told me she could not be really happy until she showed off in Prague, at the Na Štvanici stadium, as a proud member of the American Women's Team.

The phenomenon, of course, has to do with nostalgia. As they grew old, homesickness grabbed some of these successful American uncles and aunts; they went home to spend their declining years in the old country and, eventually, to be buried in ancestral graves. My paternal great-aunt, as a girl of seventeen, married a wealthy Czech-American. The gentleman, not unlike the Czech-Swedish soldiers two hundred years ago, yearned for a Czech wife, and so he traveled from Omaha to Bohemia and got himself a young bride. As an old widow of seventy-five, my great-aunt decided to return to her native village of Sedlčany for the above-mentioned morbid purpose. But once in Sedlčany, a different homesickness clutched at her heart—Omaha. After all, that was where she had spent most of her years, brought up her children, and buried a good husband. Once back in Omaha . . . . Altogether she made about eight Atlantic crossings, unable to decide where she really wanted to put her bones to rest. At the age of eighty-three, she expired during her ninth crossing and was fed to the fishes. Thus she crossed the border that divides reality from family legend.

As I mentioned earlier, among the simple folks eager to escape the hunger and humiliation of Habsburg Austria, there were quite a few educated or self-educated men. Thanks to them, very soon, Czech weeklies, monthlies, and later even dailies, proliferated. In Chicago, there was a large publishing house, August Geringer's, that brought out colorful farmer and family almanacs and books of all kinds—some trashy, but some of considerable importance. Since such publications breathed out the spirit of liberal democracy, their import to Austria was largely curbed. For the first time since the seventeenth century when Protestant bibles printed by the Moravian Brethren in exile were smuggled into Bohemia, Czech-American papers were imported clandestinely and read in private. Antonín Dvořák received some of his information about the distant republic where he was to become director of the National Conservatory of Music from such journals read in secret in the office of the Urbánek Music Publishing House in Prague.

All these phenomena—enthusiastic letters about the new homeland, the American uncle complex, nostalgia, and magazines and books smuggled across the border and devoured like forbidden fruit—became staples of Czech life in our enlightened century of successful fascisms.

*   *   *

The recent story of Czech samizdat and emigré publishing is, I think, sufficiently known. It has its lesser-known prehistory, reaching back to the post-1948 years, when the first refugees from communism reached the West. The conditions of exile had been much harsher then than they were after 1968, when the phenomenon of political exile became so widespread that the West developed procedures and institutions of aid designed to facilitate the transition from home to exile. In Canada, for instance, the newcomers after 1948 had to accept any sort of menial work the government asked them to do and stay with it for two years. A prominent elderly poet, Pavel Javor, for instance, worked as a kind of cowboy on the Canadian prairies. Also, the social background of these exiles was different from those of 1968. The earlier exiles had not experienced communism in power, only its beginnings. There were many more businessmen and considerably fewer intellectuals and professionals such as medical doctors or mechanical and chemical engineers in the earlier group. There was also a number of non-Communist professional politicians and World War II officers, but almost no writers. Egon Hostovský, Zdeněk Němeček, Jan Čep, Ivan Blatný—that was about all. These exiles came from a country where, until their departure, books and magazines had not been forbidden fruit; consequently, the hunger for free literature was not so biting as among the post-1968 exiles.

In spite of this difference, back in the 1950s and early 1960s there were daring publishing ventures, such as the book series *Harvest of Free Creation (Žeň svobodné tvorby)* published by Robert Vlach in Lund, Sweden. There were lively weeklies, for instance the socialist *Czech Word (České Slovo)* in Munich, and good journals of opinion like *Metamorphoses (Proměny),* a bimonthly of the Czechoslovak Society of Arts and Sciences in America, itself a creation of the post-1948 exiles. But above all, from Paris, came the excellent quarterly *Testimony (Svědectví),* edited by a liberal Catholic journalist Pavel Tigrid, easily the best post–World War II Czech intellectual journal anywhere in the world. I still remember the liberating effect of the copies Miloš Forman used to lend to me (he got them through his Western film contacts), in which one could read dispassionate logical analyses of such political events as the Slánský trial, and Tigrid's far-sighted predictions of the coming of a movement of liberalization within the Communist party, which soon actually took place.

But back home, where I was at that time, we had practically no samizdat: it was far too dangerous, and many Communists willing to rat were still around.

Quite a few of today's emigré literary stars officially published stuff they now prefer to forget—the kind of dangerous trash posing as serious poetry, for instance, which Kundera's poet Jaromil in *Life Is Elsewhere* hypnotizes himself with to become a police informer.

A few manuscripts circulated among trusted friends—Bohumil Hrabal's, mine, Egon Bondy's, Věra Linhartová's, the Surrealist yearbooks. For such manuscripts, existing only in one copy, one could be arrested, as happened to Jiří Kolář, the true father of post–World War II modern poetry and later a world-renowned collage artist. We just met in private, at Kolář's, at Jindřich Chalupecký's, in apartments belonging to members of the conspiracy against Stalinist obscurantism. Contacts with emigré journals, printing in them, was out of the question. Not until the mid-1960s, and under closely guarded pseudonyms, did some of the courageous dare to contribute.

*   *   *

The situation after 1968 was radically different. A deluge of graduates of twenty years of communism reached the West, most of them professional people who were traditional readers of fiction and poetry in Czechoslovakia—doctors, engineers, scientists, scholars, all hungry for uncensored literature. Publishing houses proliferated, and so did journals and newspapers. Parallel to this development, samizdat at home came into existence and also grew to unexpected proportions. Dissident authors, banned from publishing in establishment houses, made their manuscripts public first in the typed samizdat editions, then smuggled them to emigré publishers, who brought out the best of them in print. Dissident journals accepted contributions from exiles and vice versa. And, as for the police, nothing really drastic happened. There were harrassments, molestations, threats, repeated interrogations, even beatings by masked thugs and arrests. People were not sentenced to jail for what they wrote, but always only for various other trumped-up charges.[7]

There is no explanation except for this incomprehensible tolerance by a police that still does not hesitate to murder to say that times are changing and we are changing with them. But following, as it were, upside down, Orwell's dictum about the equality of animals, nowadays they murder only obscure people, not celebrities: a village priest suicided into the abyss of Macocha, a crackpot would-be politician who takes the Constitution at face value, people like that.

As a result of the publishing boom, both in external and internal exile, Czech literature has now three distinctive branches: official literature written and published at home; samizdat written at home and brought out only in typed editions of twenty or so carbon copies; banned literature written by dissidents both in exile and at home, published abroad, sold to exiles, and smuggled around the old country. All three branches are interesting, each for different reasons. But that would be the subject for a different article.

The ancient tripartite pattern of official literature, of the samizdat of copied letters from a better world, and of newspapers and books smuggled from Chicago, Milwaukee, and St. Paul, has grown into this saddening richness, into this schizophrenia of culture.

*   *   *

Samizdat, the distant offspring of handcopied messages, and smuggled printed matter; nostalgia and American uncles. The first two component parts of the pattern are harmful to dictatorships, and therefore to the present government of Czechoslovakia, where they are only uneasily and for mysterious reasons tolerated. The Communists succeeded in making the other two components, nostalgia and the American uncle, work for their benefit. They were unable to recruit exiles living in the United States for their campaign. The credit for this fact goes to none other but the founder of the Czechoslovak republic, Thomas Garrigue Masaryk.[8] Because of the treaty Masaryk signed with the U. S. government in the late 1920s, genuine American uncles remained the only ones untainted by the nostalgia trap set up by the Communist authorities. On the conscience of all the other pseudo-American uncles from Canada, Australia, Germany, South Africa, and Nepal, the trap leaves ugly stains. According to the treaty, persons who acquire the other country's citizenship can be, if they wish, automatically released from the bounds of their original allegiance. What motivated the two governments to enter this peculiar concordat I don't know: it may have been an effort to simplify bureaucratic procedures. In hindsight, however, the agreement appears as an almost clairvoyant feat of statesmanship, considering that at the time of signing, there was only one totalitarian state in existence, Mussolini's Italy. And that was brand new, inexperienced, and, well, Italian.[9]

The much more sophisticated post–World War II totalitarians invented the Iron Curtain. Sir Winston Churchill may have coined the term as a metaphor, but it very soon ceased to be one, although some Westerners, for many years, took it for just a locution, until the East Germans built their highly visible wall. And God knows: some of the more idiotic stay-at-home innocents may still think that talk about booby traps, electrified wire, and crossbreeds of German shepherd and wolf that roam along the futuristic palisade between Czechoslovakia and Germany, is just vile anti-Communist propaganda perpetrated by biased exiles.

The Iron Curtain is really a perversion of medieval fortified cities. Their walls used to keep out enemies of the inhabitants. The Iron Curtain keeps in the inhabitants, many of whom would run away if their precarious home were curtainless. But in one sense the Iron Curtain is, indeed, a metaphor: a figure of speech for the totalitarian laws of citizenship that make it virtually impossible to get rid of the loathsome burden. Some countries—reportedly in the USSR—tried to make such laws retroactive, which would make even ancient emigrants from tsarist Russia and all their descendants citizens in perpetuity of the Soviet Union. Allen Ginsberg would have a dual Soviet-American citizenship, and given the kind of poetry he writes—well, now under glasnost they, perhaps, would not lock him up if, as a Soviet citizen, he dared to visit the country of his forebears.

The old treaty signed by old Masaryk, which for mysterious reasons is still respected by the government of Miloš Jakeš, was indeed an act of clairvoyant statesmanship. Only American Czechs are spared the nightmare all other exiles suffer from, namely what happens if a plane with you on board makes an unscheduled landing on Czech territory. It is not an idle nightmare. If, due to weather conditions, the Vienna airport cannot accept incoming planes, they land in Bratislava, the Slovak capital, only thirty miles from Vienna. And then there is, of course, always the possibility of hijacking, which anyway is one of the Czech inventions.[10] The danger threatens passengers with passports other than American that identify their countries of birth even if they don't travel on planes flying over satellite countries—these have agreements about extradition, and their police forces closely cooperate.[11] I cannot help feeling funny whenever my plane soars above Cuba on its way to other Caribbean islands. Jan Konopásek, the one-time baritone saxophonist of Woody Herman's band, once told me how, on a flight from Stockholm to Vienna, he fell asleep, then suddenly woke up, looked out of the window, and directly under the plane saw the well-known silhouette of Hradchin Castle in Prague. What happened next was a curious linking of an open-eyed day nightmare with "the exile's dream," the recurrent nocturnal experience of all exiles, which tortures them for years. For some reason you are back home and cannot get out. Filled with terror, you drive to the airport, but the clerk of passport control examines your documents with growing suspicion. You wake up covered with sweat, and for a few seconds remain in a state of unpleasant insecurity about whether you really are back in the cage or at home in New York. Konopásek woke up, saw the Hradchin Castle, and for a few moments hoped that this was just a nightmare. But soon he woke up for a second time to realize that the castle was real (he did not know the plane's regular route was over Prague) and fainted. Mercifully, he remained unconscious until the flight attendant shook him and ordered him to fasten his seat belt because they would shortly land in Vienna.

*   *   *

If the unpleasantness were limited to the exile's nightmare, the emigré community in the West could live with it. But somebody in Prague had a devilish inspiration. The sources of the inspiration were the American uncle, nostalgia, and the special tourist rates of exchange.

The American uncle was born out of nostalgia. In the nineteenth century, when special rates of exchange were unknown and the black market did not exist, he had to be quite wealthy in order to impress stay-at-home bumpkins. But communism does everything for the poor, and the glorious rates it gives foreign visitors, combined with the thriving black money market, tolerated (except for token arrests) because the black marketeers have to spend most of their hard currency in Czechoslovakia anyway, made it possible for even rather poor uncles to assume the role of the American moneybags. It is simple: for one U.S. dollar the foreigner gets five Tuzex crowns, a special currency with which you can buy Western goods in special shops and which you can nowadays officially exchange for the regular plebeian crowns at the rate of one Tuzex crown for five poor man's crowns. Using your pocket calculator, you arrive at the tourist rate of exchange of one U.S. dollar for twenty-five crowns. On the black market, if you dare to risk it, your dollar will buy even more; there were times when for a buck you could fill your pockets with metal worth fifty crowns.[12]

But even twenty-five crowns—that's the price of a beefsteak in a fairly good restaurant. I know a rather naive man of limited resources in Toronto who, every other year, regularly boastfully makes his pilgrimage to Prague. Before the trip he stuffs his wallet with one-dollar bills. Once in Prague, he checks in at one of the good hotels, and "then I tip everybody with my one-dollar bills, and you should see them jump around as if I were a king. Later I invite my best friends to the hotel and treat them to a dinner which costs me about fifty bucks but looks like a royal feast. Sometimes I also ring up Jan, and Jan reports to me at the hotel in half an hour. He knows I'll flood him with manhattans and then send him home in a prepaid taxi." My not-very-affluent friend is a name-dropper: Jan was the late Jan Werich, the most popular Czech actor and a figure of national prominence, with whom the American uncle from Toronto went to school.

I'll return to this special uncle later.

The trouble with these journeys to paradise used to be that if you were a post-1968 exile, automatically sentenced *in absentia* to two years in jail for having committed the crime of "leaving the country without permission," you could not make the trip to this peculiar kind of fantasy land and Czechoslovakia could not get hold of your dollars, Deutschmarks, or rands. This is where the unknown bureaucrat of genius in Prague made the connection.

In the mid-1970s, the authorities issued "regulations concerning the normalization of status." What the bureaucratese meant was that the treacherous exile, sentenced *in absentia* to two years in the very cold socialist cooler, could get out of his predicament with relative ease, if: (1) he (or she, naturally: to save space I do not use the he/she pronoun) asked for presidential pardon for his crime, (2) applied for permission to be granted the status of Czechoslovak citizen licensed to live permanently abroad, (3) paid for his education, which he had received "free" in Czechoslovakia.

Step one was easy for those whose nostalgia made it acceptable for them to humiliate themselves by acknowledging they were guilty of a felony unknown in their new country of residence and made especially piquant in view of the fact that when the crime of "leaving without permission" was perpetrated, half a million foreigners in their steel chariots entered the country with no permission either.

Step two was more difficult, for it involved: (a) the filling out of long questionnaires, which could not be taken home but had to be handled at the consulate or embassy. Questions concerning the applicant were relatively few; the majority concerned the exile's friends and acquaintances: where they worked, how much they made, which emigré organizations they were members of, and so on. The reasons the questionnaires could not be taken home is, I suppose, obvious. And (b) the applicant had to sign an affidavit of allegiance to the government of Socialist Czechoslovakia, and state that, although permitted to live in a democratic, non-Socialist country, he would respect Czech laws and behave as behooves a good subject of Socialist Czechoslovakia. This may sound innocent enough, but there is a hitch: "behave as behooves a good subject" implies, for instance, that you will refrain from buying and reading uncensored Czech books and magazines published abroad, that you will not join even slightly anti-post-1968 regime organizations (which, by the way, includes even Communist emigré associations such as Czechoslovak Socialist Opposition, with headquarters in Rome, Italy) and, of course, that only at your own risk will you refuse to cooperate with organs of the state, such as its secret agents on a visit to Prague or at home if they approach you in Toronto.[13]

Step three, the paying for "free" education, was flexible. The sum depended on the kind of education the payee received and on his age. Generally, the higher the education and the lower the age, the greater the sum payable. In the early days it was reported that an M.D. of twenty-eight years had to cough up as much as ten thousand dollars. Over the years, as offer outgrew demand, the sums were much reduced. Today's average price, I am told, is less than one thousand dollars.

As for "free" education, true, there is no tuition fee at Czechoslovak universities. But access to them is far from free. They all (and there are not very many of them) practice *numerus clausus*—restricted admission policy—and the percentage of young people who study at universities is much lower than in the West. Moreover, the decisive condition for admission is not so much the student's average mark from high school as his political behavior and that of his parents and siblings. The latter condition, I am told, has been softened recently. Either everybody behaves, or the state needs good specialists.

*   *   *

The nostalgia trap was discouragingly successful, and tens of thousands of exiles were caught in it. A third term, *countrymen,* was added in Czechoslovak media to the often used *emigrants* and to *exiles,* applied only to the post-1620 refugees. Until then, *countrymen (krajané)* was reserved for the nineteenth-century emigrants to distinguish them from the "traitors" of 1948 and 1968. Now it is used also in reference to those who signed the affidavit of allegiance to the government of the Czechoslovak colony of Muscovy.

Eventually, the market for the "normalization of status" was exhausted, and so the Czechoslovak government came with a new offer. Exiles not willing to swear allegiance to Communist Czechoslovakia may now apply for "legal emigration." It requires only the plea for presidential pardon, but not the affidavit of loyalty. The successful applicants are "freed from the bonds of Czechoslovakian citizenship" *(vyvázáni z občanství)*, which I think is a telling official phrase, characteristic of "really existing socialism." They can travel to Czechoslovakia on their Western passports. Those who "regulated their status" remain Czech citizens and have two passports: the foreign one and the special Czechoslovak document. For travel home they use the latter.

But even this market seems to be exhausted now. It's being rumored that soon all exiles will be allowed to apply for visas, without either presidential pardon or a pledge of loyalty. If that happens, the whole dirty business will be shown for what it was: a cynical business venture.

I wrote that the number of exiles willing to humiliate themselves with various petitions and oaths of allegiance was sadly discouraging. But perhaps it was to be expected. Three hundred years of noncombatant life under authoritarian and totalitarian regimes and under foreign occupations seems to have done something to human souls— at least to some human souls.

And so American uncles from Canada, West Germany, France, Australia, and many other lands went and showed off, and sometimes strange things happened to them. My not-very-wealthy friend again. On one trip he visited a school friend who is now a judge. The friend offered to introduce him to an important colleague of his. The naive Torontonian agreed, was taken to a plush office, presented to a polished gentlemen, and then left with him alone—the judge, under some transparent pretext, absented himself. The polished gentleman offered the Torontonian a deal: if he collected information about other exiles and, on his next trip, reported directly to this gentleman, my friend would be given a "preferred visitor status." "I was shocked," said my friend. He said, "Excuse me, but I do not do that sort of thing!" The polished gentleman said, "As you wish," and terminated the conversation. A year later my friend phoned me. "You are an experienced person. Perhaps you will be able to explain," he said. "I have been to Czechoslovakia seven times since I normalized my status. Never any trouble with the visa. But this year, as I applied for the eighth time, I was turned down! What do you think happened?" I gently tried to explain to him what had happened.

*   *   *

All this may sound laughable but it is hardly that. It has grave moral implications, it has grave political consequences for the Czech emigré community, and it sheds a strange light on the Leninist morality of the Czech government.

Starting with the last item: the normalization regulation *de facto* confirms that crime pays. Good citizens who did not leave without permission in 1968 suffer all the limitations that go with that kind of good citizenship: they live in a police state, they cannot travel abroad freely, their money is not convertible, their children applying for admission to a university are carefully screened for political attitudes, et cetera. The "traitors," on the other hand, can have the best of two worlds: they can enjoy warm weather at Christmas in Cozumel, Mexico, and cure their rheumatism in the summer in the famous spas of Slovakia. They can live in a free society and read Solzhenitsyn, and then, during vacation time, live like feudal kings in an unfree one. For a price, of course.

It's a strange kind of government that makes treason desirable, and fidelity a disadvantage.

Since in Czechoslovakia almost everybody is approached at least once by the secret police with an offer of cooperation or an attempt at blackmail to force one into such cooperation, exiles know only too well that to describe the society of "really existing socialism"[14] as informer infested is not to spread slander. Exiles have been able to obtain copies of the notorious information-gathering questionnaires and to make them public, and the questionnaires, I am told, have since been "simplified." Several "normalized" people have confessed to having been offered cooperation. Naturally, exiles now distrust normalized persons. Friendships were broken in this way; societies split into "normalized" and "nonnormalized" groups. Amateur Czech theatrical companies, which exist in a few cities in the West, under pressure from their normalized members changed repertoires. They increasingly avoided plays by dissidents and exiles such as Václav Havel, Pavel Landovský (the brain surgeon's patient in the movie *The Unbearable Lightness of Being*, adapted from a novel by Milan Kundera), and Jan Novák and produced the standard toothless sitcoms of today's Prague stage. Participating in such light drama legitimized the continued membership in emigré organizations for the normalized who, by participating in productions of Václav Havel or Milan Uhde, would jeopardize their visas. Appearing in Prague farces, they can claim that they contribute to the spreading of "correct" contemporary culture among wavering exiles. In some towns the normalized have even founded their own clubs.

In short, the ingenious nameless bureaucrat who dreamed up "normalization of status" succeeded in splitting exiles into two mutually distrustful and embittered camps.

*   *   *

That much for some consequences the normalization edict had on emigré life; there are many more. Most painful, however, are the moral implications. The whole thing is clearly corrupt. When a free person in a free country accepts the dirty totalitarian game of playacting and humbly begs to be forgiven for a crime which he knows is a crime only in criminal societies, he demeans himself beyond words. When he then actually does behave "as behooves a good citizen" of the criminal state, he becomes an ally of criminals. All that just to be able to play the role of the rich American uncle and treat his friends to very cheap manhattans at the Jalta Hotel in downtown Prague.

The normalized know very well that what they did is far from innocent, so they have developed various strategies of defense, which range from honest confessions, to appeals to human feelings, to arrogant falsities. The honest few admit that irrepressible homesickness got the better of them, and they signed. It may have been an irrepressible urge to show off, but if it was, the lie is perhaps excusable. Those using the sentimental method claim they had to visit dying parents and therefore signed. Surprisingly, many dying parents recovered after such visits because they were still alive and kicking when their sons or daughters visited them for the umpteenth time in later years. Nevertheless, some such claims are obviously genuine. Arrogance begins with political philosophy. Some normalized countrymen claim to be economic emigrants really: they only used the opportunity the Soviet invasion unexpectedly offered, but their real motive was not so much disagreement with the domestic regime as desire for *la dolce vita* of the West. They are probably right. What is wrong with their argument is that when they came to the West as refugees, they did not disclose to immigration officers their craving for big cars and roulette tables in Las Vegas, but tried to horrify them with tales of the dangers and atrocities of communism. To what in the West is a nonexistent crime—"leaving without permission"—they added the very real crime of fraud. Strictly speaking, there are no economic emigrants from Czechoslovakia, even though some refugees may be motivated by economy rather than politics. Once they defect, in the eyes of communist law they become criminals. They become political exiles, not economic emigrants such as those who, pretending nothing, come to these shores from democratic countries, where leaving does not constitute a crime.

The most reprehensible strategy is to resort to legal philosophy: We now live in a free society, these jurists argue, and therefore, unless we transgress the law, we can do as we please. They forget, of course, that "there are certain crimes which the law cannot touch," as Sherlock Holmes so well put it. They pretend not to understand what is immoral about voluntarily signing an affidavit of loyalty to a government that incarcerates and even kills people claiming their right to the same freedoms the signers of the debasing document enjoy in their new homelands. They would also pretend not to understand William Faulkner's refusal to go on an official visit to Russia, which he justified in a letter to the State Department: "If I, who have had freedom all my life . . . visited Russia now, the fact of even the outward appearance of condoning the condition which the present Russian government has established, would be a betrayal."

And they accuse those who did not sign of a lack of love for their native country.

*   *   *

It boils down to a question of loyalties. The dilemma was best addressed by the nineteenth-century Slovak poet Jan Kollár, often quoted by those who, after the defeat of 1848, went to America and were sometimes also denounced for insufficient partriotism. In my rough and unrhymed translation it goes:

> Do not give the holy name of homeland
> To the country where we live.
> The true homeland we carry in our hearts,
> And that cannot be oppressed or stolen from us.

Another answer came from a national classic, the writer Božena Němcová, the courageous forty-eighter, a feminist and a celebrated Prague beauty. To the earlier mentioned Josef Lidumil Lešikar in Texas she wrote a letter that is never quoted in today's Czechoslovakia. She wrote:

> I want to tell you how lucky you are that you escaped from our local conditions. It was a good decision and I shall regret till the day I die that I could not make up my mind to do likewise. . . . Live happily in your new country, and never regret that you left your homeland, that you live in a foreign country—homeland is everywhere where there are people who speak our language, have our moral notions and our aims.

*   *   *

Because I am a writer, an "engineer of human souls," I was often attacked in Prague for this notorious love deficiency of the exiles. The accusations change with changing times. While in the early 1970s I used to be denounced as a cynical traitor in the pay of the CIA, now with glasnost slowly creeping even into cynical Czechoslovakia, I am just mildly reprimanded for having exchanged Czech readers who loved me for foreign readers who don't care, who can't even really understand my books, but who pay me for them richly in dollars. The idea is clearly based on the beefsteak that you can buy for one U.S. dollar in Prague.

I have often thought about loyalties and homelands, about patriotism, solidarity and honesty, and I have come to the conclusion that my homeland is Czech culture, my patriotism is for Czech culture, my loyalty is to Czech culture.

This precious commodity has been forced into exile with me by a government elected by foreign war machines.

I don't think there can be a meaningful Czech life without free Czech culture as it exists nowadays only in exile, both internal and external. Otherwise we might just as well be troglodytes. Although, judging by the wall paintings of Altamira, they enjoyed more artistic freedom than the poor Czech artists in the 1950s, who had to portray the mammoth so that it looked like a photograph. Otherwise they would have been expelled from the artists' union.

I thought about it a lot and decided that I would prefer a Czechoslovakia that would become one of the republics of the Soviet Union, if that union were a liberal democracy, to a "free" Czechoslovakia that would be what it is now. There is only one freedom: individual freedom. States, even independent states, are free only as long as their individual citizens are free. Something that, in their semantic confusion, the depressing, clench-fisted, slogan-shouting students of today don't seem to realize. If independence were identical with freedom, then Hitler's Germany would certainly be the freest state of all time. But it resembled a horror film rather than a land of humans.

Since there can be no meaningful culture without freedom, my ultimate loyalty is to freedom. Art has never been so unfree as in the modern totalitarian dictatorships. Yes, there have always been attempts to curb the freedom of the artist. Powerful tyrants threw them in jail, expelled them from their realms, even killed them. But that was all done in the disorganized amateurish manner of old times. Not until our own century was the suppression of art put on a professional basis. The author of "The Miller's Tale," who lived in the allegedly dark ages of late medieval times, would be inconceivable in Stalin's Russia. And judging by the great religious art of the early centuries of our own era, Church censors must have been incomparably better aestheticians than Stalin's. They may have made certain subject matter mandatory, but you cannot confuse a Michelangelo with a Velázquez, not to mention an El Greco, who in the days of Dzhugashvili would have ended up in Siberia. So would Josef Arcimboldi, that funny surrealist at the court of King Rudolf II in Prague. Don't talk to me about art's lack of freedom prior to the October Revolution.

*   *   *

But am I perhaps guilty of a lack of love for the sweet, hilly, lyrical landscape of Bohemia? Well, I like it. It is obviously beautiful. But a man who loves a woman only because she is beautiful, irrespective of her other qualities, may wake up to some unpleasant surprise. Beauty, as we know, is only skin deep, and the smooth, velvety skin can hide hideous horrors of the soul. Today's Bohemia is such a deceitful beauty, and I don't love her.

I love her soul, which is in her culture. And that is in exile with me. That is my loyalty.

*　　*　　*

That has always been the loyalty of exiles. Only tyrants stress geographic patriotism. Man, however, has always been a nomad in search of human life. An Asiatic primitive who crossed the Bering Strait and proliferated across the huge vertical continent, creating colorful cultures as he went from north to south. They are what remained of him. Not his homelands, not some silly, transient political formations. Culture. His soul.

*　　*　　*

And so as I think of my ancient ancestors who died in cold Sweden rather than bend their backs and enjoy the beauty that is Bohemia, or of the forty-eighters printing their pitiful magazines on foolscap in St. Paul, Minnesota, I am glad that I left without permission, that I am guilty of this good crime.

I have become a citizen of the Bohemia of the soul.

ENDNOTES

[1]Cotton Mather, *Magnalia Christi Americana*, vol. 4 (London: Thomas Parkhurst, 1702), 28.

[2]Researchers have discovered the following story in the *Memorial Book of Mšeno, Bohemia:* "A.D. 1621, the Sunday before Christ's birth, on a cold day, our beloved pastor, Abraham Herzman, went into exile with his family. . . . His noble minded and pious wife did not live to see this humiliation, having died of grief one month before his departure. . . . Before the parish house waited a vehicle, in which sat the entire family, that is son Augustine and three daughters."

"If the Augustine Herzman of Mšeno . . . is not the Augustine Herrman of Bohemia Manor," writes Thomas Čapek in *The Čechs (Bohemians) in America* (Boston: Houghton Mifflin, 1920), "it is, admittedly, a remarkable coincidence in date and name."

Besides, the spelling *Herzman* is quite ambiguous. The spelling of Czech names in the seventeenth century was by no means unified and fixed, but the combination of letters *rz* could have indicated the sound *ř*—as in *Dvořák*—which Americans find unpronounceable. If it were a German name—in which case the *rz* would be pronounced as for instance in the word *Herz* (heart)—it would have to end in two *n*'s (Herzmann). In some books the name is even spelled *Herman,* the result, perhaps, of the foreign printer's lack of the letter *ř* in his type font.

[3]Moving further in history and probably deeper into legend: according to nineteenth-century Czech emigré sources, John Brown's first wife Dianthe was also a descendant of post-1620 exiles. Her maiden name *Lusk* (a pod) was fairly common in Czech Chicago in her times—one V. Lusk, for instance, was in the presidium of a society which planned the founding of a utopian colony in the West, *Nová Čechie* (New Czechland)—and, because of Comenius's fame, Dianthe's father's first name, Amos, might have been popular among Czech Protestants. The legend, naturally, enjoyed some popularity even in Prague. Be it as it may, one thing about John Brown seems certain: among the righteous ruffians of his several armed bands during the fighting in Kansas was a Jew from Bohemia, Jacob Benjamin.

[4]The Communists did not call the Czechs who fought with the British armies traitors—but they regarded them as allies of the post-1948 traitors, and therefore as persons who were politically unreliable. Many of them who, after the war, remained in the army as officers, were fired. Those who, because of their working-class origin, escaped firing had no hope of promotion. The commander of my tank battalion, under whom I served in 1951–1953, remained a first lieutenant for years, while the new "reliable" overnight officers, all members of the Party, became captains and majors in no time. He was a capable and remarkably bitter man and became the model for one of the major characters in my novel *The Tank Battalion.*

[5]At the beginning of the Civil War, Lešikar barely escaped lynching for his pro-Northern and abolitionist views, expressed freely and in public, because the man believed in American democracy.

[6]There were other Czech-speaking blacks, war orphans adopted by families of Czech farmers in Texas. They triggered the legend of the big, fat black woman baking Czech *koláčky* (cookies) in a Texas village, which I heard from almost every compatriot who visited Texas. According to the legend, the visitor asks in English: "Can I have some?" The black cook answers in Czech: "Help yourself!" "Oh, you're Czech!" exclaims the astonished visitor (in Czech, of course). The big fat Mamma answers proudly: "Ne. Já su Moravec!" ("No, I'm a Moravian"— most Texas Czechs came from Moravia). Although I repeatedly visited Texas and roamed through many a Czech village, I never met this notorious black lady. History always ends up in legend.

[7]And, unlike in the 1950s, even some of those who publish in establishment houses did not absolutely sell their souls to the devil. From time to time one receives signals the interpretation of which is unambiguous. In the summer of 1945 I used to watch General Patton's G.I.s girl-watching on the street corners of the beer city Pilsen. When a pretty lassie passed, there would be muted cries of "Look at her!" Around the G.I.s the Pilsener zoot suitors formed an admiring circle. They understood very little English, and the subdued exclamations sounded to their ears something like "looketah," which can be transcribed into Czech as "luketa." Pretty soon that became, in Pilsen, the slang word for a pretty girl. I used it in a few stories of mine. As it usually happens, the provincial slang word soon disappeared from the language.

How else but as a signal—the kind the surrealists in Bucharest managed to broadcast to the world from the beleaguered city at the end of Nazi occupation—

am I to read the following lines from a young man's novel, published in Prague in 1983: ". . . life among the best luketas of Mlín. . . . What is it, really, a luketa? I read it somewhere. Something like a beautiful girl. . . ." How else but as a protest against the banning of books am I to understand the conclusion of a love story by a young female writer, published in 1986, which ends with the following words: "And I thought about that boy I was going to meet in Prague. Damn! Where did I read this?" The final words of my novel *The Cowards*, condemned by the Party and seized by the police, reads: "And I thought about that girl I was going to meet in Prague." Or what about the jazz critic who prefixes his story about some silly attacks on the music by a quotation from one Councillor Prudivý: "Oh these modern jazzes! It's just awful cats' music!" The unidentified and fictitious councillor uttered these words in one of my stories.

[8]His middle name was the maiden name of his wife Charlotte of the musical Manhattan family of Garrigues. Her son Jan, the post–World War II foreign minister of Czechoslovakia, apparently became the very first victim of Communist murder squads when he was suicided in 1948, only a few days after the *Machtübernahme*—a word I prefer, for the sake of bad memories, to "takeover."

[9]Risking accusations of cultural racism or pro-Fascist sentiments, I must say that, in general, Italian Fascists were less obnoxious than German Nazis. The difference is graphically illustrated in Fellini's *Amarcord*, that nostalgic evocation of beauty and bliss that is youth, even youth under murderous regimes. These regimes simply cannot murder everybody or murder all the time, and the innocently egocentric youth lives for the moment. Do you remember? The Fascists of Fellini's native town hold a rally on the town square, and suddenly, from the church steeple, come the provocative sounds of the "Internationale," played on a gramophone by the local diehard Socialist. The Fascists drag the elderly man to their party secretariat, and there they . . . force him to drink a sizable bottle of castor oil and let him run. He does not run fast enough with embarrassing consequences. It's easy to imagine what the Nazis would have done to such a political daredevil. The scenario might have been identical up to the point when the door of the party secretariat closes behind the unfortunate man. Inside he would have been beaten to death or, if the storm troopers were in a good mood, shot.

I have also a personal recollection of the difference. As a boy, I spent two months in a Czech children's colony in the celebrated Adriatic seaside resort of Grado. Our pension stood between the villa of the Hitler Jugend on the left, and, on the right, the house of the Balilla, Mussolini's version of the Hitler Youths. The Hitler Youths would have nothing in common with us: they ignored our Czech existence as if we were the air, and started each day with a noisy *appel*. Afterwards they departed on a forced march, which brought them back a few hours later, exhausted but elated in the trademark *(echt)* Prussian military way. The Balilla rascals defeated us at soccer, bartered food specialties, and even tried to steal kisses from our girls. (Our colony was coeducational, and so was the Balilla group. The Hitler enclave was strictly male.) In the evening, the three herds of youngsters sang. Sonorous, threatening sounds from the left, perhaps also due to the absence of girls' voices. Sprightly, cheerful Italian melodies, beautifully sung from the right. As far as I could tell, they had only one political song in their repertoire: it had a line in it I thought I understood, "Vivat Duce" or something like that. And even that song had a lively, nice melody.

We contributed to these evening concerts renditions of contemporary Czech hit songs, such as the tango "Oh, Play To Me, Gipsy!"

[10]It was first practiced by a group of desperate "class enemies" in the early 1950s who forced the pilot of a Prague-Karlsbad commuter plane to cross the border and land in Munich.

[11]The nightmare turned into reality in several well-known cases, the most notorious being the abduction of the son of the Czech Wimbledon star Jaroslav Javorský. The young man defected, leaving his fiancée behind. As soon as he got West German citizenship, he traveled to Bulgaria, where he was to meet his girl, smuggle her across the Bulgarian-Yugoslav border, and take her to Germany. His plan leaked out; both he and the girl were arrested and deported to Prague, where Javorský served a jail term of several years.

Other dangers await young men born of exiled parents in the old country but taken abroad as infants. Relying on their foreign citizenship, they travel to Czechoslovakia to visit grandparents. Usually nothing happens, but there were several cases—the government wanted to hurt or blackmail parents active in emigré organizations—when boys were seized and drafted into the Czech army. They were permitted to leave only after they had completed their two-year term of service. For a young man born in and used to a permissive society, such military service is no picnic indeed.

For these reasons, exile organizations in Canada successfully petitioned for a change in Canadian passports. They no longer list the bearers' countries of origin. Since many Czechs have German names and vice versa, this practice might save them in case of an unscheduled landing in Prague or in Havana.

[12]These rates were valid in the 1970s; they have changed slightly since then. I don't know the current conversions because, stripped of my citizenship for writing books, I have never been allowed to travel back to Czechoslovakia. To tell the truth, I have never even tried. The thought of having to deal with Communist bureaucracy gives me goose pimples, or maybe condor pimples, if the huge birds have any.

[13]I found out about this effect of the affidavit in a peculiar way. One good customer of our publishing firm, the Sixty-Eight Publishers Corp., suddenly began to order two copies of every title instead of one. Since I know him personally, I phoned him to find out the reason for this generosity. "Well, you know Franta," he said, referring to a mutual acquaintance. "He normalized his status, and now he is afraid that they could steal your customer's file, might refuse him a visa. So he asked me to buy the books for him."

In a similar fear of consequences, some stopped hearing the Sunday Mass in the St. Wenceslaus Church in Toronto, and switched to non-Czech parishes. "They" might have their informers even in the House of the Lord. I wonder how many Westerners have an idea about how long the fingers of Czechoslovak security are.

[14]This is the official party and government description of the system in today's Czechoslovakia. Taken semantically and in the context of Czech history, it is a concession of defeat, slightly offensive, just as Dubček's description of his intended system—"socialism with a human face"—slanders the twenty years of "socialism" that preceded it in Czechoslovakia. In the 1970s, the Stalinist president Novotný changed the name of the state from the Czechoslovak Republic (CSR) to the Czechoslovak Socialist Republic (CSSR). On that occasion he also officially

proclaimed that socialism in Czechoslovakia had been achieved, and described the system as "achieved socialism" *(dovršený socialismus)*. He was using the term in its utopian meaning as a semiparadise from which the road to the full-blown paradise of "achieved" communism is short and relatively straight. Then, of course, came the reform movement (after the Soviet invasion, described as "creeping counter-revolution") with its economic, political, and legal revelations about shortcomings, blunders, and crimes that were going on long after Novotný's grandiloquent announcement about the successful accomplishment of the final step toward communism. Afterwards came the invasion, and to pretend that the society had really arrived at semi-utopia was impossible even for the brazen neo-Stalinists. So the pragmatic term *really existing socialism* was coined, I believe, by Communist party ideologues in France, and accepted, indicating that this is what we have: reality, not utopia. Lectures and articles about the nebulous society, which in the late 1950s was declared to be within reach and which was described as a heaven where "everybody works according to his abilities, and everybody will be rewarded according to his need"—these "philosophical" orations about the pie in the sky, so popular with party ideologues, disappeared from the repertoire of meetings and manifestations and were replaced by simple eulogies to the wisdom of the *realsozialistisch* government.

October 1989

POSTSCRIPT

Momentous changes have occurred in Czechoslovakia since I wrote this essay. However, the events of November 1989 merely have made the article more thoroughly historical rather than rendering it inaccurate or outdated. Much of what I wrote was already history; now even those passages that described what was then a painful and tragic time have fortunately become history as well.

August 1990

Political Change and National Diversity

Ivo Banac

Always *territorial and historical, the nationality question in Eastern Europe is still an overriding political concern in most of the region. Multinational Yugoslavia typifies the region's history of postwar nationality policies, which have alternated between the political and institutional recognition of national diversity and various ideological attempts at national homogenization. With an eye to the past, can the growth of pluralistic democracy linked to national statehood overcome both nationalist and Communist urges for centralism and unitarism?*

History has shown that federalism in America and Switzerland was only a transitional independence of states or cantons to their complete union. Federalism proved quite expedient as a transitional step from independence to imperialist unitarism, but it became out of date and was discarded as soon as the conditions matured for the union of the states or cantons into a single integral state. . . . As in America and Switzerland, Comrade Stalin *concluded, federalism in Russia is destined to serve as a means of transition—transition to the* socialist *unitarism of the future.*
                                      —*Pravda*, April 4, 1918

For modern homogenizers, whether in the service of capital or social revolution, Eastern Europe has always been a challenging mixture of

---

Ivo Banac is Professor of History and Master of Pierson College at Yale University.

145

lands and peoples rudely huddled together, but resistant to amalgamation and assimilation. The demise of the Leninist project has
demonstrated to what extent Eastern Europe remains a region of
cultural and national diversity. Everything about the area continues
to be disputed, even the name. Is it East Central Europe, as the precise
scholars will have it? Could it instead be a part of some larger
Mitteleuropa, which is said to include the two Germanies and
Austria, but not the predominantly Eastern Orthodox countries? Is it
simply Eastern Europe, an area that is occasionally drawn out to
include the western rim of the Soviet Union, and perhaps the whole
of European Russia? Or is *Eastern Europe* just a synonym for Soviet
satellites, a category into which Yugoslavia and Albania do not fit,
despite their systemic similarities with Soviet socialism?

Matters are not improved when we take up each one of the
region's ancient lands. Is Poland more complete with Silesia than with
its lost Eastern territories? Does Czechism define Bohemia-Moravia?
How Hungarian is Trianon Hungary? What is Serbia in a territorial
sense—the Rascian-Macedonian lands of Stefan Uroš II Milutin
(reign, 1282–1321), or the Danubian domains of Stefan Lazarević
(reign, 1402–1427)? What are the implications of Bessarabia's
Moldavian heritage? Where are the bounds of the Italian area? Does
Yugoslav history begin in 1918, or is 1918 its culmination?—The
questions are always historical and territorial, but their importance is
in the troubled relations among national groups, between Slavs and
non-Slavs, Magyars and Romanians, and, no less, among the various
Slavic nationalities, between Poles and Russians, Czechs and Slovaks,
Serbs and Croats, Serbs and Bulgars.

Put together, these questions concern the issues of nationality.
They appear oddly out of place in the context of Marxism-Leninism,
the ideology that in 1945 became the principal East European
political fact, but they befit the circumstances of Eastern Europe.
They fit an ill-defined and contested area, where several great empires
held sway until 1912–1918, thereby retarding the process of national
independence and nation building. They fit the ideologies of nationalism and debates over the issues of national identity that have
dominated the political and cultural concerns of the East European
peoples much after Western Europe put such questions aside. They fit
the enduring contest between national homogenization and national

diversity, between assimilationism and pluralism. They are the summa of the nationality question.

Since medieval times the East European lands, or more precisely the lands of the Hungaro-Croat and Polish crowns, have lagged behind the economic and cultural development of Western Europe. The rustic and nonurban vastness of the East, which, according to the Renaissance Latinist Janus Pannonius, "had many villages, but not a single city" *(Pagos complures, oppida nulla gerit),* lent itself to concentrated grain production for export. This lucrative business brought on the belated phenomenon of "second serfdom," which reached its culmination in the seventeenth century, at the time when Western peasantry was loosening the bonds of agrarian serfdom. The economy of grain export, which increasingly was translated into social and political contingency, retarded the process of urbanization and the growth of manufacture and the middling strata. Instead, it further enhanced the corporate spirit of the gentry, especially its magnate upper crust, precisely at the moment when absolutism became the measure of royal (usually foreign) governance.

The seesaw between the absolutist state and its gentry opponents was recast in the nineteenth-century national movements. Not only were these movements inspired and frequently led by the gentry, but they perpetuated a democratized edition of upper-class corporatism in several other ways. First, they represented a coalition of interests in which social harmony was seen as the measure of national survival. Second, they preserved the political culture of the gentry within a new elite—the specifically East European intelligentsia, which was increasingly seen as the modern embodiment of gentry legitimacy in political leadership. Third, the programs of these national movements frequently did not transgress the bounds of struggle for state independence. Social reforms were thereby diminished, including those that could benefit the area's overwhelmingly peasant majorities. Fourth, class corporatism was transformed into national collectivism, which, in turn, frequently and unwittingly undermined the democratic goals of national movements. In the most dramatic historical crises of the nineteenth and twentieth centuries this meant the choice between an alliance with equal neighbors and the dominance (usually in partnership with some outside power) over subordinate tenants. Most East European leaders, certainly from Ferenc Deák and Gyula Andrássy in 1866 to the shapers of "independent"

Eastern Europe in 1918, opted for the latter. This choice became preponderant along the whole political diapason, no less among Béla Kun's Communards in 1918 than on the nationalist Right.

In the Orthodox Balkans, where the Ottomans destroyed the Christian landed elites, native leadership was vested exclusively in the Orthodox churches. Orthodox prelates substituted not only for the gentry, but for its tasks in national culture and historical memory. As a result, the nineteenth-century anti-Turkish uprisings (in Serbia, Greece, and Bulgaria) were by definition both confessional and national, which translated into a lasting suspicion of religious and national diversity. They were also social, and brought about an economy of peasant smallholders, intolerant of class differences. Small wonder that the golden age of national statehood in the Balkans (from the Congress of Berlin to the First World War) was also a period of extreme national tensions and attempts to correct history not just by pen, but by state policy. Expulsions and exoduses of whole populations, culminating in the Balkan wars of 1912–1913, were the sad epitaph to the lifting of the Turkish yoke.

Just as the demise of Ottoman power spelled no relief in Balkan nationality tensions, the national question of the interwar period meant the reversal of the earlier roles in the whole of Eastern Europe. The dominant Magyars were parceled out among several "successor states," where they frequently fared no better than the Slovaks and Romanians in Kálmán Tisza's dualist Great Hungary. The hegemonicons of revived Poland and contrived Czechoslovakia were, respectively, the formerly subordinate Poles and Czechs. In Yugoslavia, whose vast nationality problems became the metaphor for the whole region, hegemony was exercised by the Serbs. Hitler's New Order reversed some of the reversals, thereby "benefiting" the Slovaks, Hungarians, Croats, Bulgars, and Albanians. Like the Russian *matryoshka* dolls, there was always a successively smaller toy-baby in the litter. For the Communists, the point was not to interpret the meaning of competing national ideologies, but to break the cycle of national oppression and revanchism.

That is what the Communists thought they were doing in 1945. They came to power in the wake of wartime horrors, in which chauvinism showed its particularly ugly fascist face. In fact, the genocidal toll of German rule, most notably in the Nazi plan to destroy the Jews, as well as population losses attributed directly to the war, postwar forcible population transfers, and incidence of political emigration changed the face of Eastern Europe. Poland, which was literally transferred westward, lost some 4.5 million to 6 million people in the course of the war, some half of them Jews. In addition, some 2 million persons were involved in mutual repatriations between Poland and the USSR, and some 2.3 million Germans were expelled from Poland after the war. The population of the present territory of Poland declined by 7 million, or 12 percent, between 1939 and 1950.[1] Not counting the loss of Subcarpathian Ukraine (annexed by the USSR in 1945) with a population of 800,000, Czechoslovakia lost some 250,000 people, of whom 138,000 were Jews. In addition some 3 million Germans and Hungarians were expelled from Czechoslovakia after the war.[2] Despite changes in Hungary's territory from 1939 to 1945, the direct Hungarian war loss is estimated at 420,000, almost half of it Jewish.[3] Moreover, some 250,000 Germans left Hungary after the war, while some 228,000 Hungarians were repatriated from Czechoslovakia, Romania, and Yugoslavia.

The demographic impact of the war is most difficult to estimate in the Balkan countries. The population of Romania (present territory) was 14,281,000 in December 1930 and 15,873,000 in January 1948. There are estimates that Romania lost more than 300,000 people by the middle of 1943.[4] Some 400,000 Romanian Jews perished in the course of the war and some 175,000 Germans died on or quit Romania's territory.[5] Bulgaria seems to have incurred the most modest wartime losses, probably not significantly more than some 30,000 military casualties. A large number of Bulgaria's Turks was expelled to Turkey after the war.[6] Estimates of Albania's losses are most unreliable and range from 9,000 to 30,000 casualties.[7] But it is Yugoslavia that has the most controversial history of statistical accounting of its wartime losses. The official figure of 1,700,000 is increasingly challenged. According to recent statistical analyses Yugoslavia lost 1,014,000 people (or 5.9 percent of its population). Serbs lost 487,000 (6.9 percent), Croats 207,000 (5.4 percent), Bosnian Muslims 86,000 (6.8 percent), and Jews 60,000 (77.9 percent) of their conationals.[8] Most of these losses were sustained in the course of internecine conflicts among the South Slavs that included widespread massacres and selective, nationally based terror. Under the circumstances, in Yugoslavia and elsewhere, the Communists found it easy enough to point to "bourgeois nationalism" as one of the principal villains in East European history. But their habit of helping the homogenization of the client East European states through expulsions and national engineering could also be seen as part of the old nationalist arsenal.

The Communists also came to power in the wake of Soviet victory and (except in Yugoslavia and Albania) military occupation. The internationalist policy of the Soviet Union had to be measured against a record of Soviet imperialism. From 1939 to 1945 the USSR acquired not only the Baltic republics and sizable portions of eastern Poland, but also Romania's Northern Bukovina and Bessarabia, Czechoslovakia's Subcarpathian Ukraine, sizable pivots along the Finnish frontier, and the northern part of Germany's former East Prussia, that is, some 180,000 square miles, or a bit more than the two Germanies and Austria combined. In addition, the Soviets practiced economic and cultural imperialism in the East European countries. Progressive social reformers, who looked on the Soviet Union as a country that has solved the economic and social problems which assailed interwar Eastern Europe, soon discovered that their countries were as drained of their resources under the Soviets as they were under the Nazis and the earlier Western capitalists. They also discovered that the sort of honor that Stalin reserved for the Russian nation in the Soviet Union, where the Russians were called the *naibolee vydajuščajasja nacija* (the most prominent nation) and the *rukovodjaščij narod* (the leading people), applied also in the fledgling Soviet bloc. Moreover, the Soviets encouraged not only the worship of everything Russian, but the reproduction of their own hierarchies of nationhood in each of the bloc states. According to Milovan Djilas, immediately after the war Stalin's ambassador to Yugoslavia goaded the "Serb functionaries, as if in jest, with their neglect of the Serb nation's 'leading role.' "[9]

One of the basic contradictions of the Soviet system in Eastern Europe was that its ideological brunt could not be borne by Moscow. The struggle against "bourgeois nationalism" could be directed only against the opponents of Russification, not the Russifiers. Small wonder that the resistance in Eastern Europe—both elite and grass-roots—for a long time was essentially national. The difference was that the components of "national communism" (national, but not systemic, opposition) more often were present in elite resistance. Yugoslavia led the way in 1948, followed by Poland and Hungary in 1956, Albania and Romania in the 1960s, and Czechoslovakia in 1968. Throughout Eastern Europe, not just in the countries that confronted or broke with the Soviet Union, the elites were alert to the legitimizing potential of carefully crafted national programs. These programs were not always meant as a challenge to Moscow; a more "national" regime could be a more effective ally. Frequently, however, they were meant to substitute for or forestall democratization. They were examples of what might be called bureaucratic nationalism.

The crisis of East European socialism, which was evident since the mid-1950s, thus helped the national revivals in two ways. Ever since the time of entry into the Soviet bloc, grass-roots opposition, mainly outside but also inside the ruling parties, had the restoration of national sovereignty as part of its inherent—though not always articulated—platform. This sort of defensive national program was always directed against Soviet supremacy, but also had various local targets. In Czechoslovakia it was directed against Czech supremacy, in Yugoslavia against the dominant position of the Serbs, and by the minorities of all countries against the privileges of majority nations. The grass-roots national movements and stirrings usually accompanied the periods of democratization, but had the potential of restoring the features of presocialist national ideologies with all of their attendant features, including exclusivist integral nationalism. To the contrary, the national program of the elites, generally tended in the direction of "bureaucratic nationalism." Increasingly, as the crisis of official ideology deepened, bureaucratic nationalism, too, incorporated many features of old national ideologies. The prewar national question was being reproduced under the conditions of crisis socialism, but with a twist. The ability of the party-state to homogenize its territory surpassed the possibilities of prewar bourgeois nationalists.

The development of bureaucratic nationalism in Eastern Europe coincided with the stagnant Brezhnev era and had many bizarre aspects, including the fostering of cults of great native tyrants, such as that of the Wallachian prince Vlad the Impaler (reign, 1456–1462) and the Albanian dynast Ali Pashë Tepelena (1741–1822), the Ali Pashaw of Jannina in Byron's "Childe Harold."[10] Of course, there were also more positive heroes. Emperor Trajan, who conquered the Dacians for Rome, thereby laying the foundation of Romanian Latinity, was described as a symbol of Hispano-Romanian friendship during Ceauşescu's visit to Spain in 1979: "The deep-seated and durable affinities of Latin origin, language and culture, [were] so brilliantly, symbolically embodied by Emperor Trajan, born on Iberian soil...."[11] Traditional Albanian hero Skanderbeg (1405–1468), "although a feudal lord ... understood better than others of his class in Albania and abroad that for as long as the Ottoman enemy stood at the gates of the Homeland, not his narrow personal feudal and class interests, but the interests of the entire Albanian society must be placed, first." He was presumably the prototype of the modern Albanian leadership in defending the homeland "not only against the savage enemies from the East, but also against the cunning robbers of the West" and in being "the founder of the United Albanian State."[12] And in the German Democratic Republic they increasingly celebrated Luther (no longer a mere "ideologist of German burghers" and the opponent of the peasants in the Peasant War of 1525), Frederick the Great (no longer a mere Frederick II), and even Otto von Bismarck. The ruling East European ideology was becoming a hybrid of socialist and nationalist collectivism.

Bureaucratic nationalism represented a reach not just for legitimacy, but also for superiority, especially over the Russians. The Dacian state, whose two-thousand-fiftieth anniversary was celebrated in 1980, was the direct ancestor of Romania. Moreover, after the Romans left Dacia between 271 and 275 A.D., the "slave statal organization imposed by the imperial authority completely disappeared from the Dacian land, life was ruralized and the sole form of organization of the entire Daco-Roman people north of the Danube remained the commune, the age-old Dacian tradition.... On arriving in the Romanian territory, the Slavs got for the first time into contact with the forms of communal organization, which they adopted later on, and of statal organization."[13] On the thirteen-hundredth anniversary of the Bulgarian state (1981) the Bulgarian party and state leadership proclaimed, "We are legitimately proud of the fact that Bulgaria was the homeland of the Slav [Cyrillic] alphabet and culture, that we are descendants and successors of the brothers Cyril and Methodius and their disciples."[14] In the course of the celebrations Politburo member Liudmila Zhivkova noted that Ivailo's uprising, the late thirteenth-century peasant insurrection led by a swineherd called Ivailo, whom the peasants proclaimed tsar, was

"Europe's first anti-feudal uprising, one of the few peasant uprisings in the world ending victoriously and raising the leader to supreme state power."[15] In another claim to primacy made during the anniversary year, it was stressed that Dimiter Blagoev, the founder of the Bulgarian Communist party, "studied in Petersburg, where he founded in 1883 the first social-democratic organization in Russia."[16] And speaking at the official anniversary rally, the party and state leader Todor Zhivkov noted that "a former printer, Georgi Dimitrov, together with Vasil Kolarov stood at the head of the first world antifascist uprising—the September uprising [of 1923]; at the Leipzig trial he delivered the first shattering ideological-political and moral blow at fascism." Zhivkov concluded his speech with a slogan unusual for a Communist leader: "May our mother Bulgaria be blessed!"[17]

In fact, examples of bureaucratic nationalism were most noticeable in the least democratic states with a history of national homogenization. The long-standing policies directed against the minorities in Albania, Romania, and Bulgaria, and most recently the repression of the Hungarians in Romania and the expulsion of Turks from Bulgaria, were not just examples of drastic surgery in which Communists frequently delighted (and which were possible in the context of Stalin's legacy in nation removing). These policies represented the practical application of a new ideology—that of disillusioned "real socialism," ready to cohere with nationalism in direct resistance to democratization. This was no longer vintage Stalinism, with its revolutionary voluntarism, extremist zeal, and boundless optimism. This was an attempted synthesis of national legitimacy and post-utopian state socialism in which collectivism lost its class component and became nationalized.

The growth of nationality rights, the development of federalist and autonomist forms of governance, and the creative periods in national culture always accompanied periods of democratization. Yugoslavia's federal reform began in earnest in the mid-1960s, Czechoslovakia was federalized in 1968, and Hungary started paying serious attention to its Slavic minorities in the 1980s. In a similar vein, repression of mass national movements, as well as attacks against institutionalized diversity, such as Romania's abolition of the Mureş-Magyar Autonomous Region in 1968 and the denigration of the autonomous status of Vojvodina and Kosovo within Serbia in 1989, represented moves away from the policies of democratization. Yugoslavia, culturally and nationally the most varied country in Eastern Europe and now in the midst of its most far-reaching structural and nationality crisis, continues to serve as the most forcible laboratory of national diversity in the region. The nationality relations in Yugoslavia, the subject for the remainder of this essay, demonstrate the links between national homogenization and political monism. They also demonstrate to what extent the old national ideologies have been revived.

The political legitimation of Yugoslav Communists cannot be separated from their efforts at solving Yugoslavia's long-standing national question. As early as December 1942, Tito linked the prospects of his National Liberation Movement (NOP) with the resolution of the nation question:

> Our national-liberation struggle would not be so determined and so successful if the peoples of Yugoslavia did not see in this struggle, today, not only the victory over fascism, but, too, the victory over everything that was typical of the old regimes, the victory over those who oppressed and aim to continue oppressing the peoples of Yugoslavia. The term "national-liberation struggle" would be only a phrase, moreover deception, if it did not have—in addition to its general Yugoslav sense—a national sense for each separate people, that is, if—in addition to the liberation of Yugoslavia—it did not also mean the liberation of Croats, Slovenes, Serbs, Macedonians, Albanians, Muslims, etc., if the national-liberation struggle did not have the content of liberty, equality, and fraternity for all the peoples of Yugoslavia.[18]

Soviet-style federalism was the essence of Tito's nationality policy. As a result, the Yugoslav national question was transformed from the prewar conflict of opposing national ideologies into the postwar conflict over the structure and composition of the Yugoslav federation. Ever since the concluding phases of the war, when Tito shifted attention from the needs of each of Yugoslavia's constituent nationalities to those of the larger federal whole, the national question has been played out mainly within the constitutional-structural frame. Before 1944 Tito and the leadership of the Communist party of Yugoslavia (KPJ) took care to appeal to each nationality in terms of its own individual aspirations. In the course of 1944 and in the immediate postwar period the focus shifted to the new state and its aspirations. This shift was translated into a pragmatic state of federalism.

Before the end of the war, Tito's emerging federation counted eight "lands," as the future republics were called in this still formally monarchist period. Besides the regular members of the postwar federation (Serbia, Croatia, Slovenia, Macedonia, Montenegro, and Bosnia-Hercegovina, in the hierarchical and nonalphabetical order that had been in use since November 1943) there were two additional federal units—the Sandžak and Vojvodina—which lost their equal status in 1945. In the first half of that year Tito's leadership partitioned the Sandžak between Serbia and Montenegro and decided that Vojvodina must enter into the framework of composite Serbia as an autonomous *pokrajina* (province). As for Kosovo, the Communist party of Yugoslavia never intended to treat it as a federal unit. It was handed to Serbia as an autonomous *oblast* (district), a status inferior to that of Vojvodina. There remained the question of borders of the six federal units that were frequently contested, as in the dispute between Serbia and Croatia over the disposition of Srem (Srijem).

The conflicts of 1945 revealed all the contradictions of Tito's nationality policy. In principle, Tito's federalism was the negation of prewar Serbian hegemonism and wartime chauvinisms. Yet Tito operated in accordance with the Soviet federal model, which not only was more apparent than real but actually put a premium on the power of the center. Small wonder that Tito failed to see the sense in many of his comrades' attempts to solve Yugoslavia's nationality question by means of formal axiomatic constructions such as national parties, regional committees, land assemblies, federal units, and borders. The building of national institutions might carry weight with the non-Communists, but the running of Yugoslavia would in no way differ from the running of the ruling party.

Still, if national sensitivities had to be stroked, they initially had to be Serbian sensitivities. Partisan support was thinnest in Serbia, which was quite won over to the idea propagated by the Chetniks, Serbian anti-Communist guerrillas, that the Partisan movement was not just an aggressive Communist organization, but a Croat nationalist one at that. Indeed, Serbian public opinion shunned the Communists less for their illiberality than out of fear that Serbian identity would perish in a federal Yugoslavia. From 1944, therefore, Tito increasingly restrained the federalist expectations of the non-Serb segments in the Partisan movement. In time he learned the Yugoslav variant of Hegelian *Aufhebung*. Federalism could be ordered in such a way as to preserve the substance of centralism.

Tito's growing support for centralism and espousal of Yugoslav unitarism, that is, the policy of amalgamating the South Slavic nationalities into a single Yugoslav supranation, became one of the obstacles in the path of reform after the break with Stalin in 1948. In late December 1952, at the height of Yugoslav anti-Stalinism, Tito still held that the power of religion prevented the goal of a "firm, monolithic state and the amalgamation of nationalities." Speaking to a group of foreign correspondents, he noted that it would be an error for each of Yugoslavia's six republics to look after their individual interests:

> I would like to live to see the day when Yugoslavia would become amalgamated into a firm community, when she would no longer be a formal community, but a community of a single Yugoslav nation, in which our five peoples would become a single nation. . . . This is my greatest aspiration. You had a similar process of establishing a single nation in America, where a single nation was created from English and other nations.[19]

Socialist unitarism of the future, which Tito preserved from the Soviet nationality program, did not go unchallenged, even in his closest company, within the Party leadership. In 1957, Edvard Kardelj, the second man of the Yugoslav politburo, wrote a new introduction to the first postwar edition of his overriding study *Razvoj slovenskega narodnega vprašanja* (Development of the Slovene National Question), published in 1939. Almost two decades after the publication of his work, Kardelj warned that "bureaucratic centralism," connected with its "ideational-political manifestation of great state hegemonism," was still vibrant in Yugoslavia. Moreover, based on the bureaucratic-centralistic tendencies, there appeared new attempts at the revival of "old chauvinistic 'integral Yugoslavism,'" as a tendency of negating the existing South Slavic peoples and aimed at affirming some sort of a new 'Yugoslav nation.'" Kardelj denounced the "absurdities of such tendencies," which "necessarily undermine the genuine fraternal relations among the independent peoples of Yugoslavia" and warned that the "remnants of old Great Serbian nationalism" were seeking contact with unitarism under the cloak of Yugoslavism.[20]

The nationality aspect of the struggle for Yugoslav reform was joined by Kardelj at the low tide of Titoism. From 1945 to the break with Stalin in 1948 Yugoslavia practiced a form of Soviet administrative centralism, which was slowly abandoned on the theoretical level after 1950. The Sixth Party Congress (1952), when the party was renamed the League of Communists of Yugoslavia (SKJ), marked the high point of struggle against Stalinism. This struggle, in turn, was slowly abandoned after Stalin's death, the Djilas affair (1954), and partial reconciliation with Moscow (1955–1956). From 1954 to 1961 Kardelj led a lonely struggle against revived antireform centralism and unitarism. By the end of the period, and helped by Tito's growing anxiety about the strength of Stalinism in the Communist world (the Sino-Soviet split), Kardelj prevailed in the inauguration of a new round of economic and political reform. The experiment ended in a temporary reversal. The so-called minireform of March 1961 provoked economic chaos and a virtual split in the leadership in March 1962. Tito appeared to take up the cudgels on behalf of the centralists, who were led by Aleksandar Ranković, the party's organizational secretary, who was also responsible for the security apparatus. More by political instinct than by any elaborate theory, Tito sensed that his erratic behavior in 1962 destabilized the system. In July 1962 he definitely joined Kardelj's reform faction. The reasons for Tito's shift are complex, but essentially had to do with the realization that his federal system was in danger of being devoured by creeping Serbian hegemonism after the passing of the Partisan generation.

The removal of Aleksander Ranković in 1966 signaled Tito's victory over "domestic conservative-centralist forces" that were entrenched in Serbia. There followed a series of moves that restricted the prerogatives of Ranković's machine and legitimized greater national liberties for the Croats, the Bosnian Muslims, and the Albanian minority. In fact, Tito's unstudied way of handling the national question led him in the 1960s and 1970s to espouse the same formal axiomatic constructions (rotating party and state presidency, exact proportionality in party and state organs by republic and province of origin, limited tenure of office) that he eschewed in the 1940s. Despite the reversals of 1971–1972, when Tito removed the liberal leaders throughout Yugoslavia and initiated a campaign against Croat nationalism, the trend toward decentralization prevailed and was enshrined in the constitution of 1974. More important for the subsequent course of Yugoslav development, the period that ended in 1974 completed the party's assimilation of the old South Slavic national ideologies. It is significant that the three topmost Yugoslav politicians of that period—Tito, a Croat; Kardelj, a Slovene; and Ranković, a Serb—increasingly espoused positions typical of the national ideologies of their respective nationalities.[21]

In keeping with the fundamental contradiction of Croat national ideologies, which aimed at making an integral whole of separate South Slavic nationalities while simultaneously maintaining the tradition of Croatian state and historical right, Tito's integrationism was in tension with his support of Croatia's historical continuity. His espousal of Yugoslav unitarism in the immediate postwar period repeated the history of that originally Croat tendency, which culminated in the Nationalist Youth of 1912. His abandonment of unitarism in the 1960s opened the way for the affirmation of republic-based national movements (1969), but did not lessen the pressure for integrationism (note the purge of Croat national Communists in 1971).

Kardelj's antiunitarism was more consistent because it was dependent on his Slovene preoccupation with national individuality, expressed through the distinct Slovenian language. Unlike the Croats, the Slovenes never had a national state. Their statehood was precisely the result of the Slovene Partisan movement, which developed in isolation from Tito's supreme headquarters. The protection of the Slovene republic, based on the affirmation of separate Slovene culture and language, was present in Kardelj's thinking only a shade less ardently than among the more radical Slovene national democrats of the 1980s. Ranković's Serbian-based unitarism, practiced with various degrees of success in most of Yugoslavia, but most forcefully in Kosovo, Vojvodina, Bosnia-Hercegovina, and Montenegro, maintained many links with the assimilationist and scientist trends of Serb national ideologies. Small wonder that the fall of Ranković signaled not just the collapse of unitarism, but the affirmation of all non-Serb national individualities, especially among the new so-called South Slavic nationalities (Bosnian Muslims,

Macedonians, Montenegrins) and the national minorities (Albanians, Hungarians).

The constitution of 1974, following in the wake of the Croat "mass movement" of 1971, meant to reaffirm the party's support of federalism, but also to impose party control over the growing national movements. Its provisions lifted Serbia's autonomous provinces of Vojvodina and Kosovo to a level almost identical to that of the republics, prompting Serbia's opposition, which has been particularly strong since Tito's death in 1980. The Kosovo street protests of 1981 and the alleged mistreatment of Kosovo's Serbs by the province's Albanian majority were merely pretexts for the revision of Tito's constitutional handiwork, which was caricatured as following in essence the slogan "Weak Serbia = Strong Yugoslavia."

For all that, the 1980s were notable for the final assault on unitarism. This time the challenge came not so much from Croatia, whose purified party leaders continued to maintain the policy of "Yugoslav synthesis," or even from the forceful antiunitarist initiatives of Slovenia.[22] For the first time since 1918 Serbia was challenging the ideology that permitted its varying predominance within Yugoslavia, albeit not at the cost of abandoning the procentralist attachments. The chief ideological statement of Serbian antiunitarism was the "Memorandum of the Serbian Academy of Sciences" (1986), which alleged that Serbia had been discriminated against within Yugoslavia, both politically and economically. The concerted activity of Slovene- and Croat-led "anti-Serb coalition," the document claimed, continued the traditional "Serbophobia" of the Communist movement. Under the circumstances Serbia (and the Serbs as a nation) had a right to determine their own national interest.[23] In a similar vein, Dobrica Ćosić, Serbia's leading writer and chief national ideologist, has stated that he has "not been convinced for a long time that an a priori Yugoslavism is in Serb interest":

> Let us stop once and for all to liberate, save, and safeguard others, to keep convincing them that they would perish without us. If they do not wish to live with us in a democratic federation, let us respect their wish to be alone and happy.

After all the trials that the Serbs encountered in the twentieth century, Ćosić concluded, "it is difficult to understand why the Serbs today reasonably and persistently fail to aspire to a state without national questions, national hatreds, and Serbophobia."[24] The course of Serb homogenization was expanded still farther in a proposal by a group of Orthodox churchmen who drafted a Serbian ecclesiastical-national program. Their proposal stressed that:

> history once again asks the Serbian State and the Serbian Church to gather their people everywhere, both those within the country and those scattered throughout the world. History asks that the cause of this people's future be served by a final overcoming of all of our accursed divisions and migrations, by having us forgive one another and by seeking reconciliation among ourselves over the overplowed ambushes, fratricidal graves, and killing fields. All Serbs must know today: the higher interests of the Fatherland at this moment override all of our political, ideological, regional, and other divisions.[25]

Serbia's successful policy of diminishing the autonomy of Vojvodina and Kosovo in 1989 represented the first step toward the republic's full homogenization. The nationalists in Serbia's leadership accomplished this after a purge of their moderate opponents in September 1987. The distinguishing feature of the new leadership was not just the pursuit of bureaucratic nationalism, but the takeover of the Serbian party apparatus on behalf of an openly nationalist program.[26] Serbian leader Slobodan Milošević has in the meanwhile subverted the leadership of Vojvodina, Montenegro, and Kosovo, pushed through a centralist constitution for Serbia against the vociferous opposition of Kosovo Albanians, pursued a policy of permanent military occupation and police repression in Kosovo, stirred up the most primitive and self-pitying nationalist passions through total control of the information media, and started a campaign of psychological warfare against the federal center and the western republics. In his speech at the Field of Kosovo on the six-hundredth anniversary of the Ottoman victory over the Serbs, Milošević accused all the postwar Serbian leaders of "humiliating Serbia":

> The concessions which many Serb leaders made at the expense of their people could be accepted by no people on earth, neither historically, nor ethically. Especially since the Serbs throughout their history never conquered or exploited anybody else. Their whole national and historical being throughout their history, through the two world wars, as well as today is—liberating.[27]

The opposition to diversity and the pursuit of homogenization belie Milošević's support of democracy. He clearly believes that the goal of any society is the establishment of absolute unity:

> I . . . ask the critics of homogenization, why are they disturbed by the homogenization of peoples and human beings in general if it is carried out on the basis of just, humane, and progressive ideas, in one's own interests, and is of no harm to others? Is this not the meaning, the aim, to which humanity has always aspired? Surely the sense of the human community is not to be unhomogeneous, divided, even when its aspirations are progressive and humane?[28]

The postwar Soviet model in Eastern Europe prompted a form of socialist national homogenization that has of late been overtaken by bureaucratic nationalists. Whereas the old homogenizers believed they served the goals of socialist revolution against bourgeois nationalism, their successors are increasingly applying nationalism in the struggle against national liberty and democratization. The prescriptions of the homogenizers—old and new—could never be maintained by democratic consensus and only contributed to the further destabilization and fragmentation of multinational countries like Yugoslavia. Perhaps the time has come to think of alternatives to both nationalist and socialist unitarism in the perennial search for the solution to the nationality questions of Eastern Europe. The most attractive road out of the current impasse is by means of democratic (con)federalism, which would acquire the legitimacy of a consensual contract. This is actually an old idea, favored (just to mention the case of the South Slavs) by the Illyrianist reformers and other seminal thinkers who upheld the historical identity of each East European nationality. Historical identity predicated independent political organization, that is, national statehood, though not on any authoritarian model. Democratic statehood presupposes both democracy and historical frontiers. Without democracy, national statehood can become an underpinning of nationalist despotism; without historical frontiers, statehood becomes the prey of outside nationalist irredentism. But in addition to its political-historical aspect, democratic (con)federalism also must have its cultural side, with the stress on the mutual East European links. Anything less is impossible to maintain and will certainly perpetuate the endless seesaw between socialist unitarism and nationalist turmoil.

162   *Ivo Banac*

ENDNOTES

[1]Leszek A. Kosiński, "Demographic Characteristics and Trends in Northeastern Europe: German Democratic Republic, Poland, Czechoslovakia, and Hungary," in Huey L. Kostanick, *Population and Migration Trends in Eastern Europe* (Boulder, Colo.: Westview Press, 1977), 26–27.

[2]Ibid. Also see Gregory Frumkin, *Population Changes in Europe since 1939* (London: Allen & Unwin, 1951), 50–51.

[3]Egon Szabady, *The Population of Hungary* (Budapest: Demographic Research Institute, 1974), 36–37.

[4]Frumkin, 129–30.

[5]Elemér Illyés, *National Minorities in Romania: Change in Transylvania* (New York: Columbia University Press, 1982), 25–27.

[6]Nissan Oren, *Revolution Administered: Agrarianism and Communism in Bulgaria* (Baltimore: Johns Hopkins University Press, 1973), 87, 105.

[7]See Stavro Skendi, ed., *Albania* (New York: Praeger, 1956), 51; Janez Stanič, ed., *Albanci* (Ljubljana: Cankarjeva založba, 1984), 144; and Anton Logoreci, *The Albanians: Europe's Forgotten Survivors* (London: Gollanz, 1967), 82–83.

[8]Bogoljub Kočović, *Žrtve Drugog svetskog rata u Jugoslaviji* (London: Naše delo, 1985), 124–26. An alternative statistical analysis estimates the loss of 1,027,000 people, including 530,000 Serbs, 192,000 Croats, 103,000 Bosnian Muslims (which would indicate the percentage loss of 8.1 percent of their total, the greatest among the South Slavic nationalities), and 57,000 Jews. See Vladimir Žerjavić, *Gubici stanovništva Jugoslavije u drugom svjetskom ratu* (Zagreb: Jug. viktimolo ško društvo, 1989), 70–75.

[9]Milovan Djilas, *Vlast* (London: Naša reč, 1983), 116.

[10]The standard synthetic history of the Ceauşescu era describes Vlad as a ruler who "had won European fame. His feats of arms, his energy, and the sternness with which he put down all opposition, placed him among the outstanding political figures of his age, although he became the prototype of the bloodthirsty tyrant under the name of 'Dracula.' " See Andrei Oţetea, ed., *The History of the Romanian People* (New York: Twayne, 1972), 200.

[11]"A New Stage, Brilliant Page in the Annals of Romanian-Spanish Relations," *Lumea* (Bucharest), 1 June 1979, 3.

[12]"Legendary Hero of the Albanian People," *New Albania* (Tirana) (1) (1985): 16–17.

[13]Lucian Chiţescu, "The Romanian People's Origin: The Unitary Character of its Development on the Same Ancestral Territory," *Romanian News* (Bucharest), 11 April 1979, 9.

[14]"Address to the Bulgarian People on the Occasion of the 1300th Anniversary of the Founding of the Bulgarian State," *13th Centennial Jubilee of the Bulgarian State* (Sofia: Sofia Press, 1981), 10.

[15]Liudmila Zhivkova, "Opening Speech," *13th Centennial Jubilee of the Bulgarian State,* 39.

[16]Vassil A. Vassilev, *Bulgaria—13 Centuries of Existence* (Sofia: Sofia Press, 1979), 134.

[17]Todor Zhivkov, "Slovo za Bulgariia," *Slaviani* (Sofia) (1) (1982): 5, 8.

[18]Josip Broz Tito, "Nacionalno pitanje u Jugoslaviji u svjetlosti narodnooslobodilačke borbe," *Sabrana djela* (Belgrade: Komunist) 13 (1982): 99.

[19]"Religija razdvaja Srbe i Hrvate," *Novosti 8* (Belgrade), (3 August 1989): 16.

[20]Edvard Kardelj (Sperans), trans. Zvonko Tkalec, *Razvoj slovenačkog nacionalnog pitanja,* 3d ed. (Belgrade: Komunist, 1973), xxxvii.

[21]On the principal characteristics of South Slavic national ideologies, see Ivo Banac, *The National Question in Yugoslavia: Origins, History, Politics* (Ithaca, N.Y.: Cornell University Press, 1984), 105–15.

[22]For the main Slovene attitudes toward the national question in Slovenia and Yugoslavia, see the thematic issue titled "Prispevki za slovenski nacionalni program," *Nova revija* (Ljubljana) 6 (57) (1987): 1–246.

[23]"Memorandum SANU," *Duga* (Belgrade) (June 1989): 34–47.

[24]"Ima li smisla pristajanje na svaku Jugoslaviju?" *Borba* (Belgrade) (13 June 1989): 6.

[25]Editors, "Predlog srpskog crkvenonacionalnog programa," *Glas Crkve* (Valjevo) 5 (3) (1989): 11. The proposal called for the overcoming of dry European democracy and old theocracy in favor of a "genuine theodemocracy."

[26]For the best analysis of what happened in Serbia, see Branka Magaš, "Yugoslavia: The Spectre of Balkanization," *New Left Review* (London) (174) (1989): 3–31.

[27]"Ravnopravni i složni odnosi uslov za opstanak Jugoslavije," *Politika* (Belgrade) (29 June 1989): 3.

[28]Slobodan Milošević, *Godine raspleta* (Belgrade: BIGZ, 1989), 334.

September 1989

POSTSCRIPT

"Political Change and National Diversity" was written before the collapse of the Communist order in all of the East European countries except Albania and, arguably, the Balkan countries of predominantly Eastern Orthodox religious tradition (Romania, Bulgaria, Serbia, Montenegro). The Balkan exceptionalism notwithstanding, bureaucratic nationalism has been dealt a mortal blow. Hybrid national leaders of the Milošević stripe have become endangered species. For all that, the dangers of homogenization have not lessened—nor has the attractiveness of democratic (con)federalism. Western policymakers would do well to discourage the increasingly vociferous campaign on the menace of nationalism of Eastern Europe—a campaign that is often mounted by commentators who do not appreciate the subtleties of East European regional history—in favor of seeking positive alternatives. The task of the 1990s is to combine the spirit of democratic discourse with the rich sense of nationhood that is characteristic of Eastern Europe.

September 1990

In Search of a Paradigm
Elemér Hankiss

As the search goes on for a new social and economic model to launch Eastern Europe on to a new course of development, it is increasingly unclear which "organizational principles" can be adopted. In Hungary, where competing principles have vied with each other for decades, none has held the field for very long. Attempts to introduce market mechanisms have only contributed new confusion to the system, and have not been markedly efficient. To reduce substantially state ownership of property, thought to be a prerequisite to economic recovery, has proved to be extraordinarily difficult. While the collapse of Communist ideology has favored the return of a certain kind of nineteenth-century conservative liberalism, doing this after forty years of despotism has not proved easy.

State socialism is bankrupt in Eastern Europe. Governments, ruling parties, parties of the opposition, experts, and expert committees are desperately searching, at least in Poland, Hungary, and Yugoslavia, for a new paradigm, a new social and economic model with which to launch these countries onto a new course of dynamic development. These three countries—and to less extent the Soviet Union as well—are now teeming with controversy about what course to take, which

Elemér Hankiss is Director of the Center for the Sociology of Values at the Institute of Sociology of the Hungarian Academy of Sciences in Budapest.

socioeconomic model to adopt or develop. Dozens of plans and programs have been proposed and are being discussed.[1] In Hungary, the proliferation of these alternatives has created chaos in economic and political thinking and in political maneuvering.

This proliferation and mingling of heterogeneous social and economic models, or organizational principles, is not something new in Hungary. In a different form, and in a different configuration, it has plagued this country for thirty or forty years. A multitude of basic sociopolitical organizational principles emerged in the 1950s and 1960s and have been at work—with changing intensity—ever since: the one-party system, neocorporatism, oligarchy, clientelism, paternalistic enlightened absolutism, and elements of democracy. Now this hybrid state of the country is further complicated by the emergence of new models and organizational principles before the old ones have disappeared.

In the first half of this article, I shall specify what I mean by the term *organizational principles* and analyze the role various organizational principles play in Western societies. In the second half, I shall focus on the role these principles play in one East European society, in Hungary. It is a hybrid society where the interaction of heterogeneous organizational principles obstructed economic and social development throughout the 1960s, 1970s, and early 1980s and where, nowadays, this hybridization renders the transition to a democratic polity and a market economy extremely difficult.

ORGANIZATIONAL PRINCIPLES

Having several organizational principles, or logics, at work in a society is not peculiar to Hungary or to East European socialist societies in general. Western-type societies, too, have serious problems in functioning according to heterogeneous, and in some cases incompatible and conflicting, organizational principles. In this respect, there are interesting comparisons and contrasts to draw between these two types of societies.

The idea that different societies, cultures, and socioeconomic formations have underlying configurations of organizational principles is not at all new. In the philosophy of history, in cultural history, in German *Geistesgeschichte*, in the American functionalist systems analysis of the 1940s and 1950s, and in the French neo-Marxism of the 1960s, there were already serious attempts at discerning and describing these patterns and principles. In the 1970s the West German sociologists and political scientists Claus Offe and Jürgen Habermas were the first to develop the concept of the organizational principle into an important research tool for the study of contemporary societies. Offe analyzed capitalist and noncapitalist systems in terms of "steering mechanisms," "steering principles," "form elements," and "form principles" present in highly developed industrial societies and spoke of the "kinetic laws" and "logic" of capitalist development.[2]

Habermas stated that the formation of a society is always determined by a basic "organizational principle" that delimits the space within which the society may change without losing its identity—the space within which the system of the productive forces, the system of steering mechanisms, and the system of values securing social identity may change and develop. In the same context, he defined organizational principles as "highly abstract regulations which come into being in unlikely evolutionary thrusts, as emerging features that characterize a new stage of development."[3]

In the 1980s the concept of organizational principles emerged also in East European studies. Andrew Arato, in a paper on the problem of civil society in contemporary Poland, used the concept as common currency: "Eastern European societies, whose new organizational principle is authoritarian state socialism," he said, and "Societal corporatism . . . involves a reconstitution of a version of civil society and is not compatible with the system's organizational principle."[4] Ferenc Fehér and Ágnes Heller analyzed the "logic" of various social and economic systems and distinguished, for instance, the "logic of capitalism" from the "logic of industrialism."[5] Włodzimierz Brus discussed the change in the "regulatory principles" of socialist economies.[6] In the mid-1980s, the concept emerged also in the writings of East European political scientists. Mihály Bihari, for instance, a leading Hungarian political scientist, speaking of social and political changes that had taken place in his country, stated that:

> The typical principles of political mechanisms in [Hungarian] socialism are historically abiding political and social organizational principles, which have changed in the course of various economic, political, and cultural reforms but the substance of which has remained unchanged.[7]

A large variety of terms clusters around the concept of organizational principles: "structures," "patterns," the "laws" or "logic" of development, "form elements," "form principles," "steering mechanisms," "highly abstract regulations," the "features of a new stage of development." In this paper, I shall use the term *organizational principles* in the following ways:

- In the early stages of the emergence of a new social formation, organizational principles may be nothing more than transitional patterns of the changing power relations. But once the power relations have more or less settled, these patterns tend to be codified into laws, norms, regulations, rules of the game.

- The organizational principles of a new social formation are shaped by socioeconomic forces. But once they have developed, they begin to help coordinate these various forces and regulate the new socioeconomic system. (S. N. Eisenstadt and René Lemarchand speak of a process of "crystallization."[8])

- I propose to use the term *organizational principle* instead of *organizing principle* because the latter might be understood to indicate that these principles are primary facts and that social formations are their results. In my understanding, organizational principles of an emerging socioeconomic formation come into being in the very process of this development. They are in no way pre-existing. There had been no blueprints of West European feudalism before feudalism developed in Western Europe; there was no blueprint for capitalism before the emergence of capitalism; and, since the failure of the bolshevik model, there has been no blueprint for the type of society that will evolve in Eastern Europe.

- In the various historical and socioeconomic contexts, organizational principles tend to cluster into more or less stable configurations. We may speak, for instance, of a liberal capitalist configuration and an East European state socialist configuration.

WESTERN SOCIETIES

There are historical and socioeconomic contexts in which various organizational principles operating in a given configuration harmonize with one another or are at least more or less congruent with one another. And there are other contexts in which incompatible organizational principles conflict with one another.

Interaction of Organizational Principles in One Subsystem

Two or more organizational principles may operate within the very same subsystem—for instance, within the economic or the political system. According to Karl Polanyi, several organizational principles, or "modes of exchange," operate in all modern economies; market exchange may be the dominant mode, but the principle of reciprocity and that of redistribution also play a fairly important part.[9] Larissa Lomnitz and other experts of the Latin American scene have shown how the principle of reciprocity is working side by side with market exchange mechanisms in the lives of urban marginal populations as well as in those of Chilean and Mexican middle-class communities.[10] Jeremi Boissevain, Ernest Gellner, J. Waterbury, S. N. Eisenstadt, René Lemarchand, and others describe the simultaneous working of client-patron networks and other sociopolitical mechanisms in a wide range of societies.[11] Alan Cawson has recently analyzed the English political system as a kind of "dualism" in which "parliamentary structures and corporatist processes 'co-exist' " and a third organizational principle, the redistributive one, is working too.[12] Csaba Gombár, a Hungarian political scientist, has devoted a paper to the study of the three main "ordering principles" in late twentieth-century politics, that is, to "pluralism," "corporatism," and "direct democracy."[13] Many more examples of the simultaneous working of two or more organizational principles in the same economic or social context could be added. Most of the authors stress the relative incongruence and, at the same time, the complementarity of the interacting organizational principles.

The Economic versus the Administrative Subsystem

Organizational principles interact and interfere with one another not only within particular subsystems but also between separate subsystems. Offe gives us a classic example in his analysis of the growing "structural non-correspondence" between the two main organizational principles operating within late capitalist societies.[14] He argues that in late capitalism market mechanisms are no longer able to secure system integration; this inefficiency gradually increases the importance of the centralized administrative subsystem. The process leads, however, to serious tensions because the organizational principle of the emerging administrative subsystem is incompatible with that of the market system. The new principle is based on state regulations and not on exchange mechanisms; it "decommodifies" commodities produced by the market economy; it applies "bureaucratic labor" and not "wage labor"; it produces use value and not exchange value; it withdraws a growing proportion of the social product from the sphere of private investment decisions and redistributes it according to nonmarket principles. Offe speaks in this connection of a "structural breach" between the economic and the administrative subsystems. These discrepancies and incompatibilities of the two subsystems, this necessary and inevitable "interdependence of two self-excluding form principles," is, according to Offe, at the root of the permanent and deepening crisis of late capitalist societies.[15]

The Economic versus the Political Subsystem

The best-known case of conflict between economic and political subsystems is the controversy about the relationship between capitalist economies and democratic or nondemocratic polities. Marx presupposed a close relationship between capitalism and the emergence of bourgeois democracy. Recently, this thesis has been questioned by many critics. According to Jean L. Cohen, for instance, "Marx collapsed two quite distinct dynamics of modernity—capitalist rationalization and the countervailing process of democratization initiated through social movements."[16] Offe speaks of "the Marxist (neo-Marxist) thesis that bourgeois democracy and the capitalist mode of production stand in a precarious and immanently indissoluble relation of tension."[17] Bob Jessop quotes a passage from Rosa Luxemburg in which she argues that in various historical contexts capitalism was coupled with various political formations.[18] Similar ideas were expressed later by many social and political scientists.[19] According to Goran Therborn, both pluralistic and nonpluralistic systems of leadership selection, or "formats of representation," may combine with a capitalist economy, and Giovanni Sartori, studying contemporary political arrangements, enumerates a whole range of party polities that may link up with capitalist and socialist economies.[20]

The Economic versus the Sociocultural Subsystem

The coordination of economic and sociocultural subsystems is as problematic and almost as varied as that of economic and political subsystems. The disorders and breakdowns of this coordination have become one of the major issues in studies concerned with developments in late capitalism.

Some of the major texts in this respect are to be found in Daniel Bell's writings on the cultural contradictions of capitalism, where he describes the erosion of the moral and behavioral principles of traditional bourgeois societies ("the Protestant sanctification of work" and the norms of "efficiency," "optimization," and "functional rationality") and the spreading of "hedonism," "permissiveness," "anticognitive" attitudes, and "instinctual values." These new norms and values are, according to Bell, incompatible with the needs of a highly developed industrial economy. "This cultural contradiction, in the long run, is the deepest challenge to society," he says.[21] Writing about the same phenomenon, but heading toward a different conclusion, Herbert Marcuse, too, speaks of a deep cleavage between the capitalist economy and the emerging new behavioral patterns of the age.[22]

In Habermas's formulation, the sociocultural system in late capitalism is no more able to provide the economic system with the motivations and values (e.g., "achievement motivation," "proprietary individualism," "exchange values orientation") that are indispensable to its normal functioning.[23] On the other hand, the sociocultural system generates new needs that the economic system cannot satisfy.[24]

The Political versus the Sociocultural Subsystem

The fact that the political and the sociocultural systems within a society do not necessarily harmonize with one another has been well known since Emile Durkheim and Max Weber. It is only since the mid-1960s, however, that social scientists have understood the extent of their incongruence and its implications.

According to Raymond Aron, for instance, the discrepancy between ideals and institutions is more or less inevitable since "every industrial society is obliged in some fashion to invoke egalitarian ideas. . . . They spread egalitarian ideas and create hierarchical structures."[25] He, and many others in his wake, attributed this phenomenon to the survival and persisting social importance of the ideals of the bourgeois revolution and, on the opposite side, to the needs of an industrial state. The revolution declared the right and duty of every citizen to participate in social decision making and in the democratic process in general; this has remained ever since the declared ideology, and an important integrative force, in Western democracies. The actual functioning of the capitalist economy and bourgeois polity, however, has always required a rather authoritarian form of the exercise of power. This discrepancy between ideals and institutions has led to the generation of mixed political culture. Gabriel Almond and Sidney Verba describe bourgeois political culture in terms of a "double bind":

> If elites are to be powerful and make authoritative decisions, then the involvement, activity, and influence of the ordinary man must be limited. . . . The need for elite power requires that the ordinary citizen be relatively passive, uninvolved, and deferential to the elites. Thus the democratic citizen is called on to pursue contradictory goals; he must be active, yet passive; involved, yet not too involved; influential, yet deferential.[26]

Huntington describes the same phenomenon in France: "Perhaps the outstanding aspect of French political culture is its dual character. On the one hand, there is a tradition of elitism, hierarchy, and sharp class divisions. On the other, there is the French Revolution's legacy of liberty, equality, and fraternity." And then he goes on to quote William Schonfeld's "two-France theory" about the fact that Frenchmen's attitudes and behaviors are governed by two different sets of organizational principles. Or in his own words, "each Frenchman has two distinct sets of dispositions toward political authority: he both fears, dislikes, distrusts, and seeks to avoid submission to authority and concurrently needs, seeks, and depends upon political authority."[27] As far as American society is concerned, Huntington devotes a whole book to the study of the "gap" between "the American creed" and "political authority" or, in other words, between American ideals and American institutions, between ideals like liberalism, democracy, individualism, openness, and equality, on the one hand, and authoritarian, secretive, and inegalitarian institutions on the other. In the same line, Murray Edelman, and later M. Parenti, Claus Offe, Niclas Luhmann, and others analyzed and demonstrated the incongruence of the symbolic versus the institutional systems of advanced industrial societies.[28]

✳   ✳   ✳

I have attempted so far to substantiate the hypothesis that there are several organizational principles or logics working, and conflicting with one another, in Western societies. I now turn to Eastern Europe and particularly to Hungary.

A HYBRID SOCIETY: HUNGARY IN THE KÁDÁR ERA

Kádár's Hungary had two features that distinguished it from its counterparts in the West: a great number of organizational principles simultaneously at work and a strange hybridization which may have had something to do with the nature and interaction of its organizational principles.

East European societies are generally supposed to be streamlined and controlled by a unique and strong central system, by the logic of the one-party state. They have been described accordingly as "Leninist monisms" by P. C. Schmitter, as "mono-archies" by W. Brus, and as "mono-organizational societies" by T. H. Rigby. But this homogeneity lasted, at least in Hungary, only a couple of years. The emergence of new organizational principles began in the early 1950s. By the 1960s and 1970s, a proliferation of heterogeneous organizational principles was pervading all the domains of Hungary's economic and social life.

In its economy, two new systems began to operate beside the system of command planning and redistribution, with their own logics, their own organizational principles: the system of market mechanisms introduced by the 1968 reforms and the system of the "administrative market." This latter term refers to behind-the-doors negotiations between party and state bureaucracies, on the one hand, and various economic and social actors, on the other. This was the most important marketplace in the country. Terms concerning production capacities, plan-fulfillment promises, conflict potentials, various amounts of conformism, and social consensus were negotiated with investment funds, bonuses, exemptions, favorable prices, wage limits and regulations, political power, career, influence, and prestige in mind.[29] According to another approach, the different logics of the first versus the second economy were the two main organizational principles in the national economy: "The 'duality' of the country means that there are two economies here, operating according to different principles and regulated by different means."[30]

In the sociopolitical field, too, there was a plurality of organizational principles at work. There was the principle of etatist-

bureaucratic governance: the "bureaucratic authoritarianism" of
Andrew C. Janos, the "participatory bureaucracy" of R. V. Daniels,
the bureaucratic "state capitalism" of A. G. Meyer and M. Djilas.
There was the principle of corporatism or neocorporatism of S. P.
Huntington, V. Zaslavsky, and others. There was the logic of
"oligarchic dominance" of K. Jowitt and T. H. Rigby, the logic of
"clientelism" of S. N. Eisenstadt and R. Lemarchand, and others, and
the logic of "enlightened absolutism" of W. Brus, F. Fehér, A. Heller,
and G. Markus. And there was the logic of "incipient," "mirage,"
"institutional," "bureaucratic," "centralized," or "one-party" pluralism of authorities like G. H. Skilling, E. Morawska, J. F. Hough, and
A. Nove.[31] And so on. How did this proliferation of various, and
often incompatible, organizational principles come about in such a
strictly controlled socialist society? Let me adduce here some of the
possible causes and/or explanations.

The Dysfunction Hypothesis

The highly centralized, dirigist one-party system struggled with
serious dysfunctions from the very beginning. Its rigid and hierarchic
institutional system was unable to cope with the problems of
governing a complex modern society. Through the cracks and gaps of
the system, alternative organizational principles could penetrate it.
They began to regulate social and economic domains (e.g., the second
economy) which were outside the reach of the official institutional
system and in areas where this system had proved inadequate.

The Adaptation Hypothesis

Since the mid-1950s, the country had increasingly difficult problems
of adjustment. Adaptational constraints forced the party and the
government to give more and more autonomy to various economic
and social actors and to implement reforms. These processes, too,
may have activated alternative organizational principles.

The Immune Reactions Hypothesis

According to this hypothesis, there was a struggle going on between
the elite and various social groups from the very beginning.[32] The
elite, with its utopian plans, attacked society, and society in turn tried
to elude these attacks or to neutralize their negative effects as much as

possible. These "immune reactions" activated various kinds of alternative organizational principles.

The Double Deal Hypothesis

Those in the ruling elite did not much mind that their original model and logic did not work well enough because the emerging new organizational principles (the oligarchic, the clientelistic, etc.) channeled power and profit back to them. The activation of the oligarchic and the clientelistic organizational principles, for instance, seems to have been inevitable in the post-totalitarian period of East European societies. Despotic central control had to be relaxed and centralized bureaucratic power had to be decentralized without giving any power or any rights to the population, without creating institutions of democratic participation and interest intermediation, without setting into motion efficient mechanisms of social auto-regulation. Between a weakened central power and a paralyzed society, oligarchic and client-patron networks began to proliferate and became more and more important as the channels of power, influence, and interest intermediation.

None of these causes can easily be dismissed. Each of them may have played a role in the generation of this welter of organizational principles. Something, however, remains unexplained: the phenomenon that may be called the hybridization of organizational principles in Eastern Europe.

We have seen that heterogeneous organizational principles interact and interfere with one another in each complex contemporary society and lead to tension, ungovernability, and, according to some critics, even to a "crisis of crisis management."[33] But in Eastern Europe, the simultaneous action, interference, and conflict of various organizational principles have led to a chaotic and confused situation in which the various organizational principles have stuck in embryonic, undeveloped forms that have produced inefficient mixtures. Several authors have investigated this hybrid character of East European societies.[34]

F. G. Casals described state socialist societies as "syncretic societies." According to him, they are syncretic because the Leninist revolution "implanted a postcapitalist class structure in an economy that was precapitalist as regards the level of its productive forces. . . .

Owing to the property vacuum, the general syncretism of that society does more than just survive: it penetrates into the foundations of the economy, engendering syncretic production relations. . . . Stalinist production relations combine elements proper to socialism, to capitalism, and especially to precapitalism."[35] In similar fashion, Kenneth Jowitt described the Soviet society as a "striking amalgam of charismatic, traditional, and modern features. . . . The novelty of Soviet (and more generally of Leninist) institutions is that they do regularly generate modern elements and as regularly enmesh them with and subordinate them to charismatic-traditional frameworks."[36] And we could adequately describe East European societies also with the features of Fred W. Riggs's "prismatic society," though he used this concept to describe the mixed and confused structures of post-traditional societies.[37]

In Hungary, hybridization was particularly strong. This may be attributed to various causes.

Transitory Situation

Hungary underwent cataclysmic changes after World War Two and in a swiftly changing world has not yet regained her equilibrium. In this state of constant change and uncertainty, none of the organizational principles operating in this country has become clearly formulated or dominant, not even those that were parts of the so-called official paradigm, which received a major blow in the mid-1950s and has been disintegrating since the late 1960s.

Peripheral Position

Hungary lies on the periphery of the advanced industrial world and as a result, has been exposed, throughout these four decades, to the socioeconomic logics of both highly advanced and less advanced countries. It has been unable to fully adopt or develop any of them.

In-between Position

Since the late 1960s, Hungary has been in a kind of social and economic research laboratory that has experimented with combining socialist organizational principles and the logic of market mechanism and sociocultural (though not yet political) pluralism. This has led to half-measures, abortions, freakish solutions, to hardly functioning or dysfunctioning organizational principles.

Forced Immaturity

Due to the lack of an open political and public sphere where various social interests can compete with one another, the organizational principles underlying these interests could not mature and formulate themselves; they were kept in a diffuse informality and their interaction remained confused, muddled, hard to disentangle.

The Politics of Kádár's Liberalization

Kádár and his team were able, and willing, only to "liberalize" the country, not to liberate it. In this context, liberalization is a process in which the ruling elite gradually widens the sphere of things permitted, the space where people can feel themselves more or less free, but it does so without granting the rights, or without tolerating the assertion of rights, that would guarantee these new opportunities and liberties. The ruling elite made great efforts to achieve opposite goals simultaneously: to grant more freedom to society but at the same time to increase its own power; to try to gain people's cooperation without giving them any guaranteed rights; to try to make the society and the economy more innovative but, at the same time, to claim, and preserve, the right to make all the important decisions. The ruling elite hesitated between the necessity for reform and the fear of all kinds of change that might jeopardize its own interests. These unhappy double binds of contrary objectives led to amalgams, to various economic, social, and political "hybrids," characterized usually by low efficiency as far as both the objectives of liberalization and the conservation of power were concerned. In Table 1, I give some examples, indicating in each case the two goals under which these mixed formations took shape. Not forgetting the fact that the goals in the right-hand column were never publicly acknowledged policy objectives but exercising, no doubt, a strong attraction for a substantial proportion of the population, let me briefly describe some of these hybrids.

"Quasi pluralism," for instance, was a mixture in which the one-party and the etatist-bureaucratic organizational principles were dampened by the logic of paternalistic and enlightened absolutism, which, in its turn, permitted, within certain well-confined areas, the

TABLE I. **Contradictory Goals and Their Hybrid Outcomes**

Goal 1		Goal 2
To safeguard and conserve the statist, centrist, one-party monopolistic paradigm and related objectives.	The hybrids	To cautiously advance in the direction of the pluralistic, democratic paradigm and related objectives.
Monism: the party has the monopoly of power.	Quasi pluralism Bureaucratic pluralism Centralized pluralism Oligarchic pluralism	Pluralism: democratic interaction of social actors.
Total dependence of society on central power.	Relative autonomy of social actors	Autonomy of social actors.
Central planning.	The administrative market The bargaining society The second economy	Market mechanisms.
Centralized interest representation: there is only one common and indivisible social interest and this is safeguarded by the party.	Quasi corporatism Clientelism Paternalism Crypto-politics	Heterogeneous group interests; their free interaction produces an optimal approximation of the integrated social interest.
Centralized decision making; no participation.	Covert participation (i.e. influencing policy implementation) Participation only as "consultants" or as "clients" behind acting patrons	Participation in decision making.

working of a strongly mitigated form of pluralism. "Bureaucratic pluralism" was the simultaneous working of the etatist-bureaucratic, the oligarchic, and the corporatist organizational principles. The "administrative market" was an arena where the heterogeneous logics of the market economy and the redistributive economy and those of the bureaucratic, one-party, oligarchic, clientelistic, and neocorporatist forms of governance competed with one another in an informal and chaotic way.

"Relative autonomy" was the outcome of a process of power delegation without effective guarantees. It was a state of delicate equilibrium, where both parties had to act very carefully. On the one hand, the elite had to restrain its power; it had to "arrest . . . the process of control," but it had to keep standing by for action.[38] On the other hand, the social or economic actor had to exercise its autonomy only as far as it did not offend the interests of the elite, or, at least, it had to maneuver carefully lest it trigger the elite's alarm reactions.

The interference of incompatible organizational principles in the Hungary of the 1960s, 1970s, and early 1980s created confusion and tension in all spheres of life. It confused and hybridized various social roles. The manager of a company, for instance, had to compete on the market, and in this role he had to work according to the logic of the market. But, at the same time, he was dependent on the state bureaucracy and had to observe the rules of the game of the etatist-bureaucratic system. As a Party member, he had to conform to the logic of the one-party system, which was not the same as that of etatism. As a member of the oligarchy, he had to act according to the oligarchic organizational principle. As the client of various patrons, and the patron of various clients, he had to play the game of clientelism. When the opportunities of a free-market economy are opening up, it is necessary, but at the same time very difficult, to get rid of this multiplicity of roles and attitudes.

The same was true of ordinary citizens. In the morning, they worked as the employees of a state-owned company and had to conform to the logic of the planned and redistributive economy; in the afternoon, they toiled in the second economy, as independent small producers or entrepreneurs and observed the rules of the market; if they needed permits, they went to the city hall and played the role of subservient subjects of the etatist-bureaucratic system; if they wanted to find places for their children at good universities, they had to go to their patrons and skillfully play the game of clientelism.

All these were radically different and even incompatible logics or rules of the game. The confusion of roles and logics of behavior was so great that people had difficulty comporting themselves and interacting with other people. That they hardly knew how to greet and address one another is just one small example.

I conducted a survey in this field in 1980. I found, for instance, that the managing director of a state-owned company addressed his female employees by their first names, usually by their nicknames; the female employees addressed him as "Comrade Director." (In other words, the director acted according to a traditional, quasi-feudal code, while the employees observed the rules of the one-party paradigm.) The same duality of norms could be observed in the director's comportment with his driver, whom he addressed by his first name (just as the lord of the good old days addressed his liveried coachman), while the driver addressed the director as "Comrade Director." The director addressed his official visitors coming from other companies or from state and party agencies as "Comrades So and So" (that is, he acted within the framework of the one-party logic); but if the visitor belonged to the same "clan" as he, then he used the "thee and thou" form, instead of the official "you" and in this way added oligarchic connivance to the communication. He addressed the unknown and unprotected petitioner as "the comrade," in sentences like "What does the comrade want?" And with this impersonal "comrade," and with the third person singular, he relegated him or her to the ranks of the grey and anonymous pariahs of the existing system of despotism, but he did not exclude this comrade from the existing system of socialism. In the good old postwar revolutionary years, his predecessor would have morally and politically annihilated a petitioner by labeling him "Mr. or Mrs. So and So," "Sir" or "Madam," excluding him or her as a class enemy from the then young and self-conscious socialism. Coming back to our director: he addressed his poorer and helpless clients as "Uncle" or "Mother So and So," "old man" or "aunty," fitting them into the age-old terminology of traditional clientelism. He addressed the minister and the university professor as "Comrade Minister" or "Comrade Professor," but he addressed his physician with a different, middle-class or bourgeois reverence, as "Sir."[39] Similar symptoms of the thoroughgoing hybridization of Hungarian society in the Kádár era could be multiplied almost *ad infinitum*.

TRANSITION TO MARKET ECONOMY AND DEMOCRACY

It was relatively easy to destroy the institutions and structures of a market economy and a democratic polity in the late 1940s, and it has turned out to be an extremely difficult task, and a long process, to rebuild a market economy (since 1968) and a democratic polity (since late 1987).

The Economy

I have shown Claus Offe speaking of the emergence of the state redistributive system as an alien principle in West European market economies. Let me now point out that in East European societies the relationship is reversed: the market principle is the alien body within the centralized, redistributive economy; it is the market principle that may bring about "subversive structural changes"; it "commodifies" goods and services, which were redistributed as nonmarket goods and services before; it produces exchange value and not use value (at least not in a direct way); it "withdraws a growing proportion of the social product" from the sphere of redistribution and distributes it according to the market principle; and so on.

In Hungary (and in Eastern Europe in general) this process has proved to be even more difficult and more conflict ridden than in the West. Already, in the mid-1960s, economic necessities pushed Hungary toward the reintroduction of market mechanisms; the political system, however, and the vested interests of the ruling elite behind it, thwarted or at least slowed down this process and—instead of laying down the solid foundations for a market economy—contributed to the development of a confused economic system.

When they came to power in the late 1940s, East European elites substituted state ownership for private ownership as the basic institution of their societies. The idea was that state ownership would be more efficient in mobilizing social and economic resources than private property had been. But, as a matter of fact, after a relatively short period of time in which the concentration of resources led to dynamic economic growth (and to the dynamic growth of human sacrifice and suffering), the system began to function badly. State ownership did not fulfill the hopes it had raised. Its motive force proved to be very low or counterproductive; it mobilized only the bureaucracy and thereby impeded normal economic and social growth.[40]

The inefficiency and failure of the new motivational principle were apparent already in the early 1950s when the ruling elite was forced to implement first minor and then major changes. It had to reintroduce old, or introduce new, elements into the system so as to fill up the gap left by the absence of an effective dominant motive force. These elements were, however, alien to the state socialist economy. Consequently, the ruling elite did its best to neutralize their subversive effect and to slow down the whole process—so much so that, with all these delays and half-measures, it ultimately led the country, in the mid-1980s, to the verge of bankruptcy. Let me briefly survey a few stages of this process.

Campaigns—First, the elite used campaigns to boost workers' sagging or missing motivation and to step up production. These campaigns failed. Each was focused on only one objective, to the detriment of all others. This strategy played havoc with the complexities of a modern society and created an atmosphere of confusion and irresponsibility.

Rhetoric—After 1948, with slogans like "Yours is the country; you work for yourself," the ruling elite strived to create the missing motivation by convincing people that bureaucratic state ownership was in reality social ownership and so they had a stake in the system. But slogans like this lost their impact—if they ever had any—after the first, feverish months of postwar reconstruction.

Incentives—Personal and group incentives, even if they led to social differentiation and inequality, were accepted and legitimized already in the 1930s in the Soviet Union (under Zaslavsky in 1982) and were adopted in the 1950s by the Hungarian elite as well. In this way they reintroduced, if not private property, at least private interest as a factor to motivate people to work in a more efficient and responsible way.

Personal Property and Consumption—The creation and gradual extension of a market of personal and family consumption was a clever and more successful strategy than those mentioned above.

People were allowed, however, only to consume what they had earned and were not permitted to invest their money in the productive process. Such investment would have meant the direct reintroduction of the principle of private property, the alien body *par excellence*. But with the consumer market cut off from the productive process, consumer motivation could not become a truly propelling force in the economy.

The Second Economy—The emergence of the second economy, first obstructed, later cleverly tolerated by the elite, reintroduced private property as a motive force to the productive process. Its efficiency appeared very soon, and the elite could not dismiss or ban it. But the elite kept considering private property as a principle alien to the system and held it within close boundaries by fragmenting it into small pieces (only small family-sized enterprises were allowed) and by cutting it off from all sources of credit and investment funds.

Economic Reforms: The "Simulation" of Market and Private Property—After several years of expert work, discussion, and political tug-of-war, the so-called New Economic Mechanism was introduced in 1968. This was a program which, without ever openly stating it, aimed at establishing an economic system that would simulate the operation of a market based on the principle of private property and competition.[41] Within the given bureaucratic system and power relationships, however, the New Economic Mechanism inevitably failed to achieve its goals. Directors did not become really cost- and price-sensitive, market- and profit-oriented, and they did not become responsible managers of their companies. They have been prompted ever since by their own and their employees' interests, not so much to maximize the medium- and long-term profits of their companies on the market as to improve their positions on the administrative market, that is, within a complex network of bargaining with state and party bureaucracies. In other words, the potential of private property and the market principle could not unfold within the framework of the still-surviving state socialist paradigm.

Recent Reforms—The fatal crisis of the mid- and late 1980s forced the ruling elite to stop delaying real, and radical, reforms. A feverish activity began to develop the basic institution of a market economy. The new *Company Law*, passed at the November 1988 session of the Parliament, gave the green light to private and group entrepreneurship and inaugurated the free competition of a wide range of ownership forms; state ownership, cooperative and corporate ownership, self-managing companies, public and community ownership, and private ownership are now allowed to compete for funds, investments, and consumers. The membership of private and group enterprises rose from 67,576 in 1982 to 530,270 in 1987 (the new system of taxation, introduced on 1 January 1988, broke this positive trend only temporarily). The reorganization of the stock exchange, which had been closed on 21 March 1948, began on 19 January 1988; its formal opening is scheduled for January 1990.

This spectacularly fast emergence of the basic institutions of a market economy does not mean in itself that an efficient market economy is already functioning in Hungary. Not at all. On the one hand, the entangled networks of the hybrid economy of late Kádárism are obstructing the operation of market forces. The system of state redistribution still plays a major role in the economy; the administrative market still controls a substantial portion of economic and social interactions; oligarchic and clientelistic networks still survive and interfere with market transactions. On the other hand, new economic models and organizational principles have recently emerged and are conflicting with one another in a rather chaotic way. In 1987 and early 1988 "manager socialism," "self-managing socialism," "entrepreneurial socialism," and "shareholder socialism" were the star models; recently they have been squeezed out by Western models such as Thatcherite or Friedmanite liberalism, the social democratic welfare state, Japanese- or South Korean-type capitalism, the Finnish and the Austrian models, and so on.

One of the most difficult tasks is to decide what to do with state property. In the late 1940s and early 1950s practically everything was nationalized in Hungary—industrial and commercial companies, mines and banks, farms and real estate. For forty years, all these assets and organizations were controlled, and quasi-owned, by the Party oligarchy.[42] This quasi-ownership, or—using Felipe Casals's term—"ownership-in-abeyance," created an economic system in which everything had to be regulated in its tiniest details, from outside, from the political sphere, by omniscient bureaucrats and ultimately by an infallible leader. All this led to chaos, total inefficiency, and the perpetual regeneration of despotism.[43]

It is generally accepted in Hungary that the radical reduction of the share of state ownership is an imperative and a precondition of economic recovery. The question is how to achieve this task. Parties and people are divided over this issue. Or, rather, they are confused about it. Should state companies be "reprivatized," that is, given back to their original owners? But where are these owners or their inheritors? Should they be *privatized* (sold to new owners)? But where to find those who, after forty years of state socialism, have the capital to buy several thousand companies? Should they be "socialized," that is, given to the workers and employees, who would manage them?[44] Should they be transformed into joint-stock companies? But what to do then with the shares? Sell them on the stock exchanges at home and abroad? Give them to local communities, foundations, pension funds, hospitals, or universities? Or should a small portfolio be given, by birthright, to every Hungarian citizen?[45] What would be the economic and social consequences of one or the other solution?

The same hesitation and confusion can be observed about the future of land as well. Should state farms and state cooperatives be preserved as they are, or should they be transformed into real cooperatives or joint-stock companies? Should they be dissolved and their land be given back to the original owners? Should the land be sold to the highest bidders? Or should it remain in the possession of the cooperatives, which would lease it to the highest bidders? Should it be given in the ownership of local communities? The division of society over these issues is well illustrated by the outcomes of a national survey done in June 1989, displayed in Table 2.

Let me stress that these are not incompatible solutions; various ownership forms could coexist and compete with one another. But there is a long way to go, and extremely difficult social, political, and economic problems to be resolved, before they, together, may become the sound basis of a well-functioning market economy. At present, hectic attempts at realizing this or that program, opting for this or that ownership form to the detriment of others, have further augmented the chaos of the late years of Kádárism, even if this is a fertile and promising chaos as compared with the sterility of the hybrid society of the 1960s and 1970s.

Politics

In the mid-1980s, Hungary was still a hybrid society entangled in, and stifled by, a web of etatist, one-party, oligarchic, clientelistic, corporat-

TABLE 2. **Basic Policy Issues**
Based on a sample of 1,000

Question: Nowadays there are many discussions on the future of state enterprises in Hungary. In your opinion, what would be the correct solution?

—Giving back the enterprises to the original owners.	9%
—Selling the enterprises to the people promising most, even to foreign contractors.	29%
—Giving the enterprises to the workers of the enterprises; self-direction.	26%
—Keeping the enterprises in state property.	33%
—Don't know or no answer.	4%

Question: In your opinion what should be done with agricultural land in Hungary?

—The land should be given back to the original owners.	18%
—The land should be sold to people promising the most for it.	7%
—The land must remain the property of the agricultural cooperatives; no change is needed in the present system.	28%
—The land must remain the property of the agricultural cooperatives, with the possibility of free selling and leasing.	33%
—The land must become the property of local communities.	10%
—Don't know or no answer.	4%

Source: Gallup, Parliamentary Reports Ltd., Institute of Market Research, June 1989.

ist, and other networks. The chances for "dehybridization" were, at that time, not good at all. I shall deal with one of the reasons now.

The members of the ruling elite were deeply interested in keeping the country in this diffuse and hybrid state since they had thoroughly colonized and intertwined this system with their parasitic networks. The administrative market, one-party and etatist institutions, oligarchic and clientelistic networks were all channeling power and wealth back to them. They could feel themselves safer within this hybridized society, and profit more from this confusion, than they could either in the restoration of a pure, strongly centralized, rigid, bolshevik one-party system or in the development of a pluralist system with the clearly defined interaction of various interests and various sociopolitical logics.

The dramatic, if not tragic, deterioration of the country's economic situation in the mid- and late 1980s, however, undermined the monolithic power of the ruling elite and triggered the transition to a parliamentary democracy. Since the autumn of 1987, committees of experts, the government, Parliament, the new parties, the Round Table of the Opposition,[46] and the Trilateral Talks between the Communist party, the Opposition, and various other social organizations[47] have all been working—with various intensities and for various interests—on the creation of the basic rules, laws, and institutions of a new, democratic polity. Transition, however, still has serious difficulties. The hybrid institutions, structures, and networks of late Kádárism are still around. The nomenclature was formally abolished in early 1989, but its members still occupy almost all important positions in the country. Oligarchic and clientelistic networks have been a bit rumpled, but they are still working. Behind-the-doors politicking is still going on.

There is a certain confusion also in the field of the new political forces. Since late 1987, a number of new parties have emerged and begun to fight against Communist rule. The strongest among them—the Hungarian Democratic Forum (MDF)—won the four by-elections (the first by-elections since the general elections in 1985) against the Communist candidates in June, July, and August 1989, and according to forecasts, the parties of the opposition will, in all likelihood, defeat the Communist party at the coming general elections (in March or April 1990). The new parties have hardly had time to make themselves known in the country, but nevertheless recent public opinion polls indicate them as clear winners. (See Table 3.) But in spite of these positive signs and achievements, these parties still struggle with difficulties; they are rent by inner divisions; they have not yet built up their national networks and constituencies; they lack funds, expertise, and well-known spokespersons. What is more important, they have not yet found their identities and their places in the political spectrum. They have not yet drawn up their detailed programs and have not clearly outlined the sociopolitical model they want to establish in this country. They are simultaneously attracted by heterogeneous or even contradictory models. The Federation of Free Democrats (SZDSZ) openly admits that its program is based both on liberal and social democratic ideas; the Hungarian Democratic Forum is making serious efforts to integrate liberal capitalist and anticapitalist populist elements; the Communist party has drawn up a radically liberal, Thatcherite economic program, but at the same

TABLE 3. **Voting Intentions at the Coming General Elections**
       Based on a sample of 1,000

Question: If a national election were held this Sunday, which party would you vote for?

Hungarian People's party [MNP]	2%	
Christian Democratic party [KDNP]	3%	
Hungarian Independence party [MFP]	4%	
Association of Free Democrats [SZDSZ]	4%	} 41%
Association of Young Democrats [FIDESZ]	5%	
Independent Smallholders' party [FKgP]	7%	
Social Democratic party [SZDMP]	7%	
Hungarian Democratic Forum [MDF]	9%	
The Hungarian Socialist Workers' party [MSZMP]	26%	
Other	4%	
Don't know or no answer	28%	

Source: Gallup, Parliamentary Reports Ltd., Institute of Market Research, June 1989.

time, it is flirting with the idea of becoming a European-type socialist party or a we-promise-everything-to-everybody-type people's party.

This may be a normal state of affairs after forty years in a political wasteland. During the electoral campaign, the necessary political articulation will presumably take place. But at present, the residuals of Kádárite hybrid society and this recent diffuseness of political ideas and models obstruct, or at least slow down, the establishment of a democratic political system in Hungary. And since time may be running out, this hesitation may jeopardize the very success of the process of transition.

Values

Jürgen Habermas, in analyzing the cultural crisis in Western societies, has demonstrated that, on the one hand, the sociocultural system in late capitalism was unable to provide the economic system with the motivations and values that were indispensable to its normal functioning ("achievement motivation," "proprietory individualism," "exchange value orientation") and that, on the other hand, the sociocultural system generated new needs that the economic system could not satisfy.[48]

East European societies struggle with similar, but much more serious, problems of discrepancy between values and the needs of their economies. Let me focus again on Hungary.

When the Communists came to power in 1948, they launched a frontal attack against the traditional value system. They dismantled the traditional value-generating institutions (churches, communities, associations, social movements); they disintegrated the families; they stigmatized, persecuted, drove underground the values of the previous economic and sociopolitical system, including values relating to private property, market activities, and capital accumulation and to personal autonomy, freedom, and responsibility.

The Communists intended to replace these values with those of collective discipline, altruism, and revolutionary consciousness, but they failed almost completely. They failed because they stuck to their anachronistic revolutionary ideology and values in an age of socialist conservatism and cautious reformism; because the almost total inefficiency of their economic system ruined the working morale and generated nationwide negligence and irresponsibility; because their authoritarian social and political system excluded people from public life and created an alienated, individualistic, consumption-oriented, privatizing society.

To show the extent of this extreme individuation of Hungarian society, let me quote here some figures from the European Value Systems Study, which was conducted in more than twenty countries in 1982.[49] Table 4 gives the average values of responses to questions concerning attitudes of individualism versus altruism and sociability. As can be seen, Hungarians turned out to be surprisingly more individualistic than their European counterparts. To the question "Is there anything you would sacrifice yourself for, outside your family?" for instance, 38 to 64 percent of the English, French, Germans, Spanish, and Italians answered, "No, I would not sacrifice myself for anything outside my family." In Hungary, the corresponding figure was 85 percent. To the question "Would you raise your children to have respect for other people?" the European average of positive answers was between 43 and 62 percent, while the corresponding Hungarian figure was 31 percent. Similar differences between the average of the European figures and the Hungarian data can be observed in the other items as well.

TABLE 4. **Individualism and Privatism in Ten European Countries**
European Value Systems Study, 1982

	England	Ireland	France	Belgium	Germany	Holland	Spain	Denmark	Italy	Hungary
You may trust people.	43%	40%	22%	25%	26%	38%	32%	46%	25%	32%
Is there anything you would sacrifice yourself for, outside your family? No!	60	55	64	61	53	54	38	49	45	85
Parents have their own lives; they should not sacrifice themselves for their children.	18	15	17	21	28	15	13	39	27	44
Child-rearing principles:										
—Respect for other people.	62	56	59	45	52	53	44	58	43	31
—Loyalty, faithfulness.	36	19	36	23	22	24	29	24	43	10
How do you prefer to spend your leisure time?										
—Alone.	11	12	10	9	8	12	7	8	20	10
—With the family.	48	39	47	51	52	49	53	53	36	72
—With friends.	27	27	22	18	27	15	23	12	29	10
—Going out, seeing people.	11	12	8	7	5	12	4	4	8	3

Source: Stephen Harding, David Philips, and Michael Fogarty, *Contrasting Values in Western Europe* (London: Macmillan, 1986).

The deepening economic crisis has recently forced the ruling elite to liberalize the economy, to introduce more and more elements of the market system, but the attitudes and values necessary to the smooth functioning of this system are not around. As we have seen, the traditional value system was destroyed; efforts to create a new, socialist and collectivist value system have failed. The values of consumerism and privatism, which have gained ground since the early 1970s, are not capable in themselves of motivating and regulating a dynamic economic revival. The values and the ideology necessary for such a revival, those of a new "Protestant ethic" based on discipline, responsibility, rationality, efficiency, frugality, and accumulation (and not consumption) orientation have not yet emerged.

The confusion is increased by the collapse of the Communist ideology and by the fact that the Communist leadership is making desperate efforts to surreptitiously replace its bankrupt bolshevik ideology with a sort of nineteenth-century conservative liberalism. The egalitarianism of orthodox Marxism is being replaced with an inegalitarian ideology that is ascriptive and meritocratic at the same time; the substantive egalitarianism of orthodox Marxism is being replaced by the bourgeois concept of the equality of chances. The sacred dogma of full employment is being relinquished and the necessity of unemployment is acknowledged and justified in almost talmudic terms; dethroning state ownership as the highest form of ownership, private property is being rehabilitated; replacing blue-collar, physical work as the sacrosanct type of work, entrepreneurship has suddenly become the most valuable social achievement. If we consider the fact that these new bourgeois values are professed by the representatives of the Communist oligarchy, who still rule the country by force—more and more leniently, though—and who try to convert their bolshevik bureaucratic power into a new type of power that would efficiently work in the coming market economy and democratic polity, then we shall understand that this new strategy contributes to the confusion reigning nowadays in the field of values.

*   *   *

Anachronistic and hybrid institutions in the economy and politics, a value system in disintegration and confusion, uncertainty and hesitation about what economic and political model to choose and realize: people and parties in Hungary have to overcome these problems if they want to escape from the present economic and social crisis. It may have been easy for the Communists to destroy the market economy and democracy in the late 1940s; the Hungarian and the Polish cases show us how extremely difficult it is to rebuild them now, after forty years of open or latent despotism.

ENDNOTES

[1] I have described this search for a workable model in a recent book: *Kelet-európai alternatívak* (Budapest: Magvető, 1989). The English version of the book is *East European Alternatives: Are There Any?* (Oxford: Oxford University Press, forthcoming).

[2] Claus Offe, *Strukturprobleme des kapitalistischen Staates* (Frankfurt am Main: Suhrkamp, 1972), 50, 51, 32, 8, 18, 9.

[3] Jürgen Habermas, *Legitimationsprobleme im Spätkapitalismus* (Frankfurt am Main: Suhrkamp, 1973).

[4] Andrew Arato, "Civil Society Against the State: Poland 1980–81," *Telos* 47 (Spring): 46, 37, 43.

[5] Ferenc Fehér and Agnes Heller, "Class, Democracy, Modernity," *Theory and Society* 12 (1983): 211–44.

[6] Włodzimierz Brus, "Political System and Economic Efficiency: The East European Context," in Stanislaw Gomulka, *Growth, Innovation and Reform in Eastern Europe* (Madison, Wis.: University of Wisconsin Press, 1986), 24–41.

[7] Mihály Bihari, *Politikai rendszer és szocialista demokrácia (Political System and Socialist Democracy)*, (Budapest: University of Budapest, Faculty of Law, 1985).

[8] S. N. Eisenstadt and René Lemarchand, eds., *Political Clientelism, Patronage and Development* (Beverly Hills: Sage Press, 1981).

[9] Karl Polanyi, *The Great Transformation* (Boston: Beacon Press, 1957, 1968), 43–68.

[10] Larissa Lomnitz, "Reciprocity of Favors in the Urban Middle Class of Chile," in George Dalton, ed., *Studies in Economic Anthropology* (Washington: American Anthropological Association, 1971): 93–106. See also Larissa Lomnitz, *Networks and Marginality: Life in a Mexican Shantytown* (New York: Academic Press, 1977).

[11] Jeremi Boissevain, *Friends of Friends: Networks, Manipulators, and Coalitions* (Oxford: Basil Blackwell, 1974); Ernest Gellner and J. Waterbury, eds., *Patrons and Clients in Mediterranean Societies* (London: Duckworth, 1977); Eisenstadt and Lemarchand.

[12] Alan Cawson, *Corporatism and Political Theory* (London: Basil Blackwell, 1986), 126–49, 155.

[13]Csaba Gombár, *Állampolitikai rendezöelvek és a helyi társadalom* (State Political Ordering Principles and Local Society), unpublished manuscript, Budapest, 1985.

[14]Claus Offe, *Strukturprobleme des kapitalistischen Staates*, 37, 40–44.

[15]Ibid.

[16]Jean L. Cohen, *Class and Civil Society: The Limits of Marxian Critical Theory* (Oxford: Martin Robertson, 1983), 226. (Originally published in Amherst, Mass.: University of Massachusetts, 1982).

[17]Claus Offe, *Contradictions of the Welfare State* (London: Hutchinson, 1984), 66.

[18]"When capitalism began, as the first production of commodities, it resorted to a democratic constitution in the municipal communes of the Middle Ages. Later, when it developed into manufacturing, capitalism found its corresponding political form in the absolute monarchy. Finally, as a developed industrial economy, it brought into being in France the democratic republic of 1793, the absolute monarchy of Napoleon I, the nobles' monarchy of the Restoration Period (1818–1830), the bourgeois constitutional monarchy of Louis Philippe, then again the democratic republic, and again the monarchy of Napoleon III, and finally, for the third time, the republic . . . . No absolute and general relation can be constructed between capitalist development and democracy. The political form of a given country is always the result of the composite of all the existing political factors, domestic as well as foreign. It admits within its limits all variations of the scale from absolute monarchy to the democratic republic." Rosa Luxemburg, *Rosa Luxemburg Speaks* (New York: Pathfinder Press, 1970). Quoted in Bob Jessop, "Capitalism and Democracy: The Best Possible Political Shell?" in *Power and State* (New York: St. Martin's Press, 1978), 10–51.

[19]E. Mandel, *Late Capitalism* (London: New Left Books, 1975); Barrington Moore, Jr., *The Social Origins of Dictatorship and Democracy* (London: Allen Lane, 1968); Nikos Poulantzas, *Political Power and Social Classes* (London: New Left Books, 1972); Nikos Poulantzas, *L'Etat, le pouvoir, le socialisme* (Paris: PUF, 1978).

[20]Goran Therborn, *What Does the Ruling Class Do When it Rules?* (London: New Left Books, 1978), 185–211; and Giovanni Sartori, "The Typology of Party-Systems—Proposals for Improvement," in Erik Allardt and Stein Rokkan, eds., *Mass Politics: Studies in Political Sociology* (New York: Free Press, 1970), 324–28.

[21]Daniel Bell, "The Cultural Contradiction of Capitalism," *The Public Interest* 21 (1971): 15ff.; and Daniel Bell, *The Cultural Contradiction of Capitalism* (New York: Basic Books, 1975), 33–84.

[22]Herbert Marcuse, *One-Dimensional Man* (Boston: Beacon Press, 1964).

[23]Habermas.

[24]Ibid., 113–20.

[25]Raymond Aron, *Eighteen Lectures on Industrial Society* (London: Weidenfeld and Nicholson, 1967), 234.

[26]Gabriel A. Almond and Sidney Verba, *The Civic Culture* (Princeton: Princeton University Press, 1965). See also Habermas, 107–08.

[27]William R. Schonfeld, *Obedience and Revolt: French Behavior Toward Authority* (Beverly Hills: Sage Press, 1976), 137–42. Quoted in Samuel P. Huntington, *American Politics: The Promise of Disharmony* (Cambridge: Harvard University Press, 1981), 50.

[28]Murray Edelman, *The Symbolic Use of Politics* (Urbana: University of Illinois Press, 1964); M. Parenti, "The Possibilities for Political Change," *Politics and Society* (1) (1970): 79–90; Offe, *Contradictions of the Welfare State*; Niclas Luhmann, *Legitimation durch Verfahren* (Berlin: Neuwied, 1969); Stanley Hoffmann, "Paradoxes of the French Political Community," in Stanley Hoffman et al., *In Search of France* (Cambridge: Harvard University Press, 1963). Parenti, for instance, described the discrepancy between ideals and institutions in the following way: "One might think of ours as a dual political system: first, there is the *symbolic* input-output system centering around electoral and representative activities including party conflicts, voter turnout, role playing and certain ambiguous presentations of some of the public issues which bestir presidents, governors, mayors and their respective legislatures. Then there is the *substantive* input-output system, involving multibillion-dollar contracts, tax write-offs, protection, rebates, grants, loss compensation, subsidies, graces, giveaways, and the whole vast process of budgeting, legislating, allocating, 'regulating,' protecting, and servicing major producer interests, now bending or ignoring the law on behalf of the powerful, now applying it with full punitive rigor against heretics and 'troublemakers.' The symbolic system is highly visible . . . . The substantive system is seldom heard of or accounted for."

[29]László Antal, *Gazdaságirányítási es pénzügyi rendszerünk a reform útján (Our Economic Policy and Financial System on the Way of Reforms)*, 2nd ed. (Budapest: Közgazdasági, 1985); László Lengyel, "Végkifejlet" ("Endgame"), *Valóság* 29 (12) (1987): 27–42; and Erzsébet Szalai, *Gazdasági mechanizmus, reformtörekvések és nagy-vállalati érdek (Economic Mechanism, Reform Endeavors, the Interest of Big Companies)*, (Budapest: Közgazdasági, 1989).

[30]R. István Gábor, "Második gazdaság: a magyar tapasztalatok általanosíthatónak tűnő tapasztalatai" ("The Second Economy: Lessons that Can Be Drawn from the Hungarian Experience"), *Valóság* 28 (2) (1985): 20–37.

[31]See Huntington; and Victor Zaslavsky, *The Neo-Stalinist State: Class, Ethnicity, and Consensus in Soviet Society* (Armonk, N.Y.: Sharpe, 1982); S. N. Eisenstadt and René Lemarchand, eds., *Political Clientelism, Patronage, and Development* (Beverly Hills: Sage, 1981); and Ferenc Fehér, Ágnes Heller, and György Markus, *Dictatorship Over Needs* (New York: St. Martin's Press, 1983).

[32]László Bogár, *A fejlődés ára, Gazdasági nehézségeink főbb okainak történti aspektusa (The Price of Development, Historical Aspects of the Major Causes of Our Economic Difficulties)*, (Budapest: Közgazdasági, 1983).

[33]Offe, *Contradictions of the Welfare State*.

[34]Laśzló Lengyel; Csaba Gombár, *Velleitásaink* (Budapest: Institute of Social Research, Research Reports, 1987); Csaba Gombár and Laśzló Lengyel, "A társadalmi reform kérdéseihez," *Társadalomkutatás* 1 (1986): 112–24.

[35]Gombár and Lengyel.

[36]Kenneth Jowitt, "Soviet Neo-traditionalism: The Political Corruption of a Leninist Regime," *Soviet Studies* 35 (3) (1983): 275–97.

[37]Fred W. Riggs, *Administration in Developing Countries: The Theory of Prismatic Society* (Boston: Houghton Mifflin, 1964).

[38]Juan J. Linz, "An Authoritarian Regime: Spain," in Eric Allardt and Stein Rokkan, eds., *Mass Politics: Studies in Political Sociology* (New York: Free Press, 1970), 257–83.

[39]Elemér Hankiss, *Diagnózisok* (*Diagnoses*), (Budapest: Magvető, 1982).

[40]Among the best works dealing with this problem are Felipe Garcia Casals, *The Syncretic Society* (White Plains, N.Y.: Sharpe, 1980); Fehér, Heller, and Markus; János Kornai, *Economics of Shortage* (Amsterdam: North Holland Press, 1980); and János Kornai, "The Hungarian Reform Process: Visions, Hopes, and Reality," *Journal of Economic Literature* 24 (1986): 1687–1737.

[41]László Antal, *Gazdaságirányítási és pénzügyi rendszerünk a reform útján*; and Kornai, "The Hungarian Reform Process."

[42]Fehér, Heller, and Markus speak of state property in Eastern Europe as of a specific form of "corporate property" of the ruling elite. "No individual belonging to this elite would have, on his own, any effective power or right to dispose over the means so owned—and most definitely none would be able to transfer or alienate any part of them to others." They have only the "power of disposition," which does not include the right of "alienation in respect of the bulk of this property . . . . " But the *raison d'être* of state property is not so much economic exploitation (though "the bureaucracy does appropriate an increasing share of the total national income"), but the maximization of the elite's power and its control over society. Costs and profits are measured by the decrease and increase in their power, and not in economic losses or gains. This is why state ownership and the economic system built on it are doomed to inefficiency, waste, and ultimate failure. See Fehér, Heller, and Markus, 56–79.

[43]Casals.

[44]The idea of workers' self-management, which was at the core of radical reform thinking in the 1950s and 1960s, and which lost its appeal in the 1970s and 1980s, has recently popped up in Hungary in the programs of conservative left-wing groups and—in the wake of the first serious strikes in the country—in the thinking of militant workers' groups.

[45]According to a new consulting firm, Financial Research Ltd., the best solution would be to translate all state companies into joint-stock companies and to distribute the shares, according to a carefully prepared blueprint, among local communities (villages, towns, cities) and various institutions (foundations, universities, hospitals, pension funds, holdings, etc.). These new owners would, in all likelihood, keenly watch the managements of the companies in which they had shares and would force them to make profit (see Antal). Pál Juhász, and other economists as well, have warned that the institutional and human preconditions of the new system are not given yet. A rich network of financial experts and of institutions, banks, holdings, brokers, counseling, investing, and accounting firms would be necessary to handle the transactions of several thousand share-holding

communities and institutions. The organization of such firms and the training of experts began in 1988, but there is still a long way to go.

[46]This is a temporary alliance of eight parties of the oppositions and the League of Independent Trade Unions.

[47]These talks began in June 1989 and have the function of preparing the first free elections in Hungary since 1946.

[48]Habermas, 113–20.

[49]The survey was conducted, in more than twenty countries, by the European Value Systems Study Group. For details, see Stephen Harding, David Philips, and Michael Fogarty, *Contrasting Values in Western Europe* (London: Macmillan, 1986).

September 1989

POSTSCRIPT

Elemér Hankiss, like Bronisław Geremek and so many others, lives a life today very different from the one he knew at the time he wrote the essay. In August 1990, he left his scholarly retreat at the Hungarian Academy of Sciences to assume responsibilities as president of Hungarian television. Since then, as he wrote a month later, "I have ceased to be a normal man and a decent scholar and have been working, day and night, on the transformation of an anachronistic, 'state socialized,' [and] rigid . . . organization into an institution which could help the process of democratization and Europeanization and, at the same time, provide people with valuable entertainment." Professor Hankiss's new responsibilities have left him little time to do much else.

However, it is significant that despite the dramatic events of the past year, Professor Hankiss's article needs little revision or addition. It has become obvious that though the Hungarian nation wants desperately to transform its socialist bureaucratic system into an effective and competitive market economy, it must still, in Hankiss's words, "struggle with the heavy and destructive heritage of the paradigm" described in this chapter.

Stephen R. Graubard
October 1990

Reform Economics: The Classification Gap
János Mátyás Kovács

Reform economics seems perpetually slipping: between political power and academic life, government and opposition, East and West. While theories from the latest reform cycle always claim to break through the usual "plan" and "market" strategies, questioning reveals the slippage. For the historian struggling to classify, socialist reform economics appears—despite its apparent radicalization—less a revolutionary breed than a mutation of the old doctrines.

But in that crystal scales let there be weigh'd
Your lady's love against some other maid
That I will show you shining at this feast,
And she shall scant show well that now seems best.
—William Shakespeare, Romeo and Juliet

According to a joke circulating in Eastern Europe, socialism is the longest path from capitalism to—capitalism. Few in the West know that this witticism reflects also a certain bitter nostalgia on the part of unreconstructed Stalinists for the good old days prior to the first reforms, when socialism was still "true" as opposed to a later stage when it became only "real." Until recently, socialist reform economists would

János Mátyás Kovács is a Research Fellow of the Institute of Economics at the Hungarian Academy of Sciences in Budapest and Visiting Scholar at the Institute for Human Sciences in Vienna.

have rejected this sarcasm, proudly maintaining that they wanted nothing to do with capitalism; their way led not to capitalism nor even to one of its social-democratic versions but to a better socialism.[1]

They also had to cover a great distance on a dangerously winding road to realize in what direction they were going and to gather enough strength by the end of the 1980s to present the iconoclastic program of marching back or ahead to capitalism (euphemistically referred to as moving toward a mixed economy.)[2] Socialism, the reformer-*routinier* in Hungary, Poland, or Yugoslavia says nowadays, has been a tiresome detour, which under the pretext of destroying the feudal relics of East European societies, has done its best to reinforce them. Economic and political reforms ought therefore to display antifeudal features: they should create (not merely reconstruct) a workable market economy, through reprivatization and the dismantling of state controls, and a pluralist (democratic) political system, by transforming the authoritarian and/or oligarchic nature of the Party-state. The reforms are to give rise to (and not merely revitalize) a "civil society" and a *Rechsstaat* while—and this is the Achilles' heel of the program—probably leaving the ultimate power of the "enlightened monarch" intact.

Interestingly enough, the pragmatism and sometimes the cynicism that are called for on the practical side of reform making are not rarely mixed with that standard revolutionary trait, lack of self-irony, when it comes to theorizing about the reformation process. The vacuum has been filled by the antireformers; the critique of the scholarly performance of the reform economists, unfortunately, became a privilege of the neo-Stalinists.

In light of the controversial achievements of reform making in the East, reform economists do not dispute the fact that—to use the language of the early reformers—the meshing gears of "plan" and "market" tend to squeak. Nevertheless, reform economists look for the causes of maladjustment outside the mechanism, and not in the logical structure of their discourse. The "external enemy" appears on the political side of the plan, as an agent who pours sand between the gears. Thus, as far as the basic principles of reform theory* are

---

*In what follows, I use the expressions *reform theory, reform concept, reform program, reform blueprint,* and *reform project* interchangeably. In this context *theory* does not necessarily mean "scientific theory"; it simply denotes the opposite of reform practice.

concerned, there seem to be no major obstacles to making a winning combination of plan and market, if one succeeds in disciplining the reluctant planners, in getting them to acknowledge the logic of liberalizing (deregulating) so that the share of the market in the mix increases.

Many reform economists as well as their Western observers would say that this problem is to be solved by a pragmatic (political) theory of transformation rather than by an abstract (economic) theory of the market. In their opinion, from the point of view of pure economics, reforms have been a fairly clear issue from the very outset. What the reformers have always needed, so goes the argument, is a kind of "applied economics," that is to say, the invention of intelligent economic policies for the transition to a market economy, clever mechanisms of deregulation and artful political techniques (democratic as well as elitist) to implement them. The planners have to be convinced that—as paradoxical as it may sound—reducing emphasis on the plan is in their interest as well.

The militant reformer would continue: leaving behind the familiar stages of radicalization (or secularization, if you wish), we can ignore the word magic of introducing the "socialist law of value," "perfecting the economic mechanism," or "regulating the market," and develop the idea of the coexistence of the "minimal (or medium) state" and the "maximal market."[3] To accept this new concept, one also needs less logical reflection than economic expertise, political radicalism, and ideological clear-sightedness.

With the passing of time, East European reformers have lost most of their illusions concerning changes coming from above, the enlightened self-constraint of the Party-state, and the self-generating power of reform. In this learning process, reform economists have touched on the principal taboos of Stalinist political economy. Secularization has in turn helped refine the applied economics of the reform in scientific terms: based on the original combination thesis of plan and market, the reform concepts have become more and more complex and systematic. Now we are witnessing the consolidation of a new social-liberal paradigm of economic science.[4]

Such is the optimistic vision of the evolution of reform thinking as portrayed by its representatives when they are not ground down by the day-to-day struggles of reform making. However, students of the history of socialist economic thought tend to grow suspicious of any theories claimed to be near to perfection.*

Suspicion No. 1: After almost four decades of semiperfect theories, we may doubt whether "reform economics" (RE)—as we call this branch of socialist political economy in Hungary—is able to solve the scientific problem of harmonizing the principles of liberalism and collectivism in a genuine and coherent economic theory, if the reform concepts remain within the framework of the traditional discourse of combining plan and market.

Suspicion No. 2: Even if we accept a priori that the reform programs have been refined in terms of their scholarly messages because of the relaxation of political and ideological constraints, the knowledge we have of these nonscientific specifics of reform thinking may be neither relevant nor up-to-date.

I am afraid that these reservations lead us to discover a twofold gap in the conventional classification of reform theories. On the one hand, in exploring the ambiguous nature of RE as economic science, perplexity grows when we try to classify reform concepts in the history of economic thought. On the other hand, the internal typologies of reform economics have often been confined to the comparison of the political and ideological variables such as naiveté, moderation, and radicalism, and the differences in the conceptualization of the plan-market mix have been ignored.

*   *   *

In what follows, a Hungarian economist working on the history of socialist economic thought tries to give an overview of the *Dogmengeschichte* of contemporary economic reforms in Eastern Europe. The subject, however, extends beyond the expected limits both in time and space; in our case, contemporary history begins in 1921

---

*Compare the relationship between classical and Marxian economics, utopian and "scientific" socialism, Marxism and Leninism, Marxism-Leninism and Stalinism, Maoism and Titoism, et cetera.

with the introduction of the New Economic Policy (NEP) in Moscow, and the frontiers of Eastern Europe stretch as far as Beijing.

BETWEEN TWO DISCOURSES

As long as RE restricts itself to the traditional plan and market (PM) discourse (and it is well-known that until recently the authors of reformist concepts such as "market socialism," "the self-managed market economy," and "the regulated market," have been cautious about touching on the main taboos of the discourse, namely those of reprivatization and political pluralization), the scholarly performance of its disciples will very likely continue to exhibit serious flaws.

In a recent essay I tried to confirm Suspicion No. 1 by raising a couple of "compassionate doubts" about the consolidation of a Grand Theory of socialist economic reform.[5] Based primarily on the more than thirty-year history of the Hungarian school of reform economics, my critical remarks centered on the following topics:

Mixed Doctrines—The PM discourse opens an extremely large umbrella under which a multitude of often diametrically opposed schools and ideas can find a place for themselves, ranging from neo-Marxism, some sugar-coated Stalinism and optimal planning, through a kind of old Manchester liberalism and moderate deregulation theory, all the way to a neo-Keynesian-type social-democratic concept of *Soziale Marktwirtschaft*, or the idea of the corporate state. What the historian sees under this umbrella is a strange mixture rather than a fruitful combination of alternative doctrines.

Speculative Institutionalism—The confusion of mutually exclusive approaches is not the sole reason the delimitation of RE is almost impossible. A close look at the evolution of socialist reform thinking reveals, surprisingly, no magnum opus of the reformist school. The writings that are usually considered the basic works of RE are in most cases obsolete, or they transgress the limits of the PM discourse. The literature of reform economics looks fragmented, unbalanced, and eclectic from the standpoint of the different fields of economic theory as well as from that of countries and periods of time.

The eminent authors come as often from academic circles as from the sphere of politics or business administration, not to mention the mass media and belles lettres, so the messages of RE appear on very different levels of scholarly abstraction and quality. But even in pointedly scientific works, reform ideas are pigeonholed in thematic subcategories, the description of the economic system to be reformed is frequently confused with normative statements about the future, and there are large gaps in empirical analysis on the microeconomic level as well as in the understanding of the behavior of the higher echelons of the Party-state.

Paradoxically, RE is not empirical enough to provide a synthetic description of the Soviet-type economies being reformed, yet it is too empirical to impede abstract analytical research on them. Reform economists tend to apply the institutionalist instruments offered primarily by Marxian economics, without testing their validity in comparison with the "new institutionalism" of the West (property rights and transaction cost economics, public choice theory, concepts of nonprofit organizations, political business cycles, principals and agents, theory of deregulation). The result is a kind of speculative institutionalism, based as often as not on soft, pseudoabstract categories such as "plan," "market," "enterprise autonomy," "self-management," and "material incentives." These govern reformist thought about interpreting and predicting economic behavior through mechanisms, interests, organizations, and power relations without either appropriate empirical or analytical backing. In Eastern Europe even the fragmented liberal traditions of economic thought have not been fully reconstructed, and the civilizing effects of neoclassical economics are still extremely weak.

The "Bad" Market—The liberal critique of the state economy and collectivist planning, dominant in the debate on socialist economic calculation in the 1920s and 1930s, has been only partially refuted by the reformers. Oscar Lange's doctrine of "the market simulated by the plan," which was the origin of the PM discourse, has proved, at most, mathematically defensible.

The reformers originally conceived of the plan as a sterile institution: they held not the plan but the conservative politicians, the hard-liners, who were not considered to be involved with the plan-market combination, responsible for blocking marketization. The assumption, however, that even the most reform-minded, market-oriented planner disturbs—*ex officio*—the spontaneous order of the market process sounds heretical even nowadays when in reform economics the desired scope of planning is relatively narrow. For a reform economist to say "plan *or* market" instead of "plan *and* market" is still a neo-Stalinist attack on, and not a liberal critique of, the PM discourse.

The market was also regarded by the early reformers as a neutral institution, something indifferent to property rights. It was a widespread assertion that the market can be recreated in the state sector as a whole and that if the market does not work there adequately, it is not the lack of private ownership but the intrinsic failure of the market that is to be blamed.

In the reformers' view, the grand concepts of "plan" and "market" were able to embrace everything: on the one hand, from the rationalization of certain techniques of state dirigism to indicative planning, and on the other, from the abolition of forced procurement in agriculture to the use of the stock market. Nevertheless, on the level of economic theory they were portrayed, at best, symmetrically. In the beginning, the supremacy of planning was not disputed in reformist circles. However, even later, when the "bad" market succeeded, by and large, in emancipating itself in reform thinking, the basic philosophy remained intact; the principle of giving the market a (revocable) chance to help where the plan fails has so far not been definitively replaced by that of giving the plan a slight (revocable) chance where the market fails.

Instead, the reformers tend to entertain the possibility of establishing a kind of symmetry between the "good plan" and the "good market." In the PM discourse there is still no room for the idea that plan and market cannot be balanced in a speculative equation, because the plan in Soviet-type economies is more "contagious" than the market: a drop of planning is able to spoil a barrel of market. Then, plan and market would be within a hair's breadth of turning into plan without market.

Using the analogy of modern capitalism to support the combination thesis, reform economists have from time to time entertained the hope of creating a mixed economy "with an Eastern appeal," i.e., with the *differentia specifica* of the plan having the larger share in the mixture. The question of how large it should be has usually been answered in allusive terms, suggesting that all kinds of the combination are viable from the standpoint of economic rationality. The authenticity of RE has been based on this assumption rather than on the perhaps more realistic one that under certain conditions plan and market are as capable of impairing each other's positive effects as they are of improving them.

Since the invention of the convergence theorem, decades have passed, and the fact that it is much easier to liquidate or distort the market in the West than to establish it in the East has become a common experience of the reform economists. Now there are signs in the literature of a switch from the pattern of modern capitalism to that of early capitalism, when it managed to get rid of the feudalistic restrictions on the market. According to the new slogan, the market (not socialism) has to be built up, and perhaps the old dogma of the "bad" market that has to be corrected by the "good" plan is starting to be abandoned. However, it has not been generally admitted until recently that even a markedly smaller proportion of the state than ever envisaged by the reformers is capable of destabilizing the model of the mixed economy (consider the end of the Keynesian revolution).

New Paradigm—Although we may assume—with some foundation—that these imperfections stem from the essentially hostile political environment in which reform thinking must make its way, it would be wrong to disregard the logical contradictions inherent in RE's attempt to harmonize the economic principles of liberalism and collectivism under real socialism.

If the supporters of RE want it to become a general economic theory of real socialism, first they will have to deal with this inevitable question: how can Marxism, even if promoted with increasing reservations, be coupled with liberalism? This question will be raised on every level of economic theory, beginning with the philosophical-methodological preconditions (how can the holistic and deterministic approach of Marxism be associated with the essential individualism and subjectivism sustaining liberal thought?) and proceeding to concrete proposals for mixing economic institutions in a Soviet-type society (how can the Party-state be harmonized with medium- or large-scale private property and/or with autonomous forms of collective ownership?). That is to say, in addition to facing the problem of how to reconcile different interpretations of liberty, equality, tolerance, virtue, rationality, common good, and private initiative in the two systems of discourse, reform economics has to clarify analytically the underlying issue of whether the market can work at all in a modern economy without large-scale private ownership and political pluralism.

Surrogate capitalist amidst fundamentally collectivist property rights and limited reprivatization, a simulated market with a quasi-deregulationist state, informal (latent) pluralism within a formally monolithic political system: are these unstable combinations appropriate for providing a solid base for a new paradigm of economic science?

We will search in vain for a new paradigm if we suspect that, to use Kuhnian language, the consensus within the scientific community of reform economists is rooted in political solidarity rather than in the similarity of the scholarly principles under the umbrella of RE, and that the values represented by the reformers are ambiguous, the concepts applied are shaky, and the methodological apparatus of economic research is eclectic.

Deregulation Theory, in the Middle of the Road—Let us see if reform economics can be described in a less ambitious way. Instead of forcing the definition onto the level of pure economics, why not consider this branch of economic thought a genuine normative theory of economic deregulation? No doubt, RE is authentic as a peculiar mixture of liberal and collectivist doctrines, but only as such, for most of its liberal components are imported. As a consequence, its authenticity by and large amounts to the fact that the liberal ingredients of the mix have to do with the "pacification" of a unique kind of war economy—that is, to the liberalization of Soviet-type state economies where the fabric of regulation is incomparably more comprehensive, intricate, and durable than in most contemporary Western war economies and where state controls have become an organic (self-reproducing) part of the system.

Unfortunately, however, within the framework of the PM discourse, RE does not come near to being a sophisticated normative theory of deregulation either. In the absence of a comprehensive critique of the point of departure (Stalinism or War Communism) and of a clear picture of where to arrive, it is only the process of dismantling controls that is discernible in this transformation program.[6]

In other words, RE is able to describe the transformation only up to a certain point: it allows us to step off the pavement and zigzag more or less safely among the cars in the middle of the road, but it cannot show us what is on the other side of the street. As a strange theory of transformation-without-end, reform economics can be considered a pretheory, a pilot program that clears the way for a postreform economics.

Sophistication—As years go by, RE has refined its scientific premises and conclusions in the course of a lengthy trial-and-error procedure (although its followers have been more active in learning-by-doing than in learning-by-reading). By analyzing *in vivo* the government failures and market distortions in Soviet-type economies (disequilibrium, overcentralization, hierarchical bargaining, the shadow economy) the reformers can even make a contribution to the understanding of similar phenomena of overregulation in the West, which can often only be examined in smaller scale, almost *in vitro*. From the point of view of Western mainstream economics, one might characterize reformist economic science as borderline-case economics, a sort of economic knowledge that issues warnings against any recurrence of borderline cases.

However, the fact that reform economists have made great advances in comprehending and predicting the economic reality of Soviet-type societies, and in systematizing the ends and means to change it, does not necessarily lead to the solution of the basic theoretical dilemma of the PM discourse: why would the reformers prefer the "bad" market to the "good" old plan?

In answering this question, a reform theorist may choose one of two possibilities. If he remains within the framework of the PM discourse, the prohibition of large-scale private property and political pluralism, the idea of the bad market will eventually hinder the scholarly evolution of RE (the scientific explanations will be incomplete, the reform proposals inoperational, etc.); but if he violates these prohibition rules, he enters a new discourse. He leaves the concept of the socialist market economy, for, let us say, that of the social-democratic version of the social market economy. In other words, this move undermines the main political and ideological principle of RE, i.e., reformism within real socialism. If RE truly evolved, it would cease to exist. To put it pathetically, its initials would stand not for *reform economics* but for *revolution economics*.

It is, however, by no means proved beyond a doubt that by crossing the frontiers of real socialism one reaches the realm of a new scientific paradigm of economics. In any event, if reform economists stop flirting with half-solutions like explaining the behavior of the state economy with a fragmented understanding of the Party-state, searching for the surrogate capitalist, or creating concealed pluralist structures, there might be an opportunity to follow a great many lines of thought started three or four decades ago to their logical ends.*

We may also hope that entering a new discourse will narrow our classification gap, for we will be able to rely on the vast knowledge gathered on welfare economics when we situate postreform economics in the history of economic thought. So far, RE has resisted classification because it has oscillated between Marxism (Stalinism) and liberalism. This situation has excluded the possibility of qualifying reform economics as a coherent species of social-liberal economic thinking. For the time being, RE cannot be portrayed as other than a mutant subspecies of the doctrine of *Soziale Marktwirtschaft* (social market economy).

TOWARD COMPARATIVE REFORM CONCEPTS

Overdue Reservations

Now let us examine Suspicion No. 2 and see what is meant by *classification gap* when we turn to the typology of the individual reform concepts.

To characterize the dominant types of reform economics, most analysts have so far taken the easy way of regarding nearly every species of reformist thought as a distinct type. Now we have "Langeism" and "Libermanism," "Illyria" and "Pannonia" (the Yugoslav and Hungarian versions of reformist thought), "computopia," "planometrics," even "Galbraithian socialism." We can play with abbreviations such as "NEP," "NEM," and "NÖS." We tend to be well acquainted with the "naive" and "routinier" types of reform theorists, the "moderates" and the "radicals," the "perfectionists" and the advocates of "crucial" reforms, the "market-type" and the "technocratic" reformers, those representing "entrepreneurial,"

---

*It is, of course, quite another matter whether this intellectual border crossing between the two discourses can also be accompanied by political action, or whether the PM discourse—despite all of its scholarly imperfections—will remain the intellectual basis for the only pragmatic program for the liberalization of Soviet-type economies and societies.

"etatist," or "self-managing" market socialism, while we remain unfamiliar with the internal logic and the interrelations of these different forms of classification.[7]

Important as it is to construct these types with the hope of further generalization, these attempts do not yet seem very promising. Composing the types of reform theory based on the practical reform moves, that is, disregarding the apparent asynchronism of reform and reform economics (see the fashionable model of the "three waves" of reform); comparing cases from periods far apart in time (note the use and abuse of the NEP model); applying an excessively broad concept of reformism into which even the markedly statist ideas of "computopia" and "Galbraithianism" can be fit; taking, as in a democratic census of racial minorities, almost everyone who declares himself to be a reformer at his word, etc. These dubious techniques of classification may discourage those who would gladly believe in some "rational" criteria for delimiting the field of reform economics.

I have reservations about the way reform programs are usually compared. First, the traditional models of socialist economics are too loosely defined (thus, the process of separation from them is indeterminate);[8] the goals are also veiled in mist (therefore the degrees of approximation to the ideal cannot be compared either).[9] Second, the dimensions of comparison are often arbitrarily chosen and highly judgmental; the intratheory variables indicating the scholarly performance of reform economics are usually neglected or confused with the technical details of economic and political liberalization; the variables are too comprehensive (they are formulated in terms of the PM discourse), inoperational, and mostly of binary nature; and the interrelations among the variables are frequently ignored.[10] Third, attempts at measuring the variables are scarce, and the comparisons are often made along different dimensions; whole countries and time periods are characterized by a single type.[11] Fourth, the main types are defined in advance, deductively; the inductive test of assumptions is often lacking. Fifth, the comparisons are mostly static; if, however, they are dynamic, the principles of commensurability and the concept of evolution are not clarified.

Why shouldn't we start classification with the understanding that reform economics is amorphous and has intrinsic ambiguities? Why shouldn't we proceed gradually, following the standard methodological rules for historical taxonomy?[12]

1. Defining the basis for comparison.

2. Selecting the relevant dimensions and subdimensions of comparison (defining the variables and their potential values).

3. Measuring the movements within the individual dimensions and distinguishing the directions of the movements.

4. Constructing subtypes within the dimensions.

5. Combining the subtypes in order to construct main types.

6. Defining ways to compare the main types if the *ceteris paribus* principle cannot be applied.

7. Solving the problem of static versus dynamic comparison.

Understandably, expecting taxonomic rigor in retrospect would be cruel on the part of succeeding generations.

As long as the reform theory initiatives were scattered over countries and decades and there was hardly any communication between the reform economists, as long as the number of cases lending themselves to prolonged observation was not large enough to make fair generalizations on their basis and the adventure of separating from the Stalinist model was fresh, and as long as paradoxes of reform thinking, the confusion of theoretical patterns, and the controversial political roles of the reform economists were still obscure, it was only natural that the comparers would be inclined to improvise. They optimistically assumed in advance that it is possible to create a coherent reform concept, so they were simply not interested in the intratheory characteristics of RE.

Now at the end of the 1980s, however, we have learned a lot about the long and the short waves of reformation, for we have seen reform experiments even in the most exotic countries of real socialism, abortive reforms, half-reforms, distorted and reversed reforms, fierce discussions among alternative schools of reform economics, and supranational communication among reform economists. We have also experienced the most varied ideological commitments on the part of the reformers (the cynical as well as the romantic ones). In other words, we have witnessed the evolution of economic reform thinking as a new culture in Soviet-type societies. The observer can hardly avoid becoming a self-made comparative "anthropologist" to investigate this folklore.

Naive, Moderate, and Radical Liberals

Provided the assumption is true that to raise the scholarly level of reform theories, reform economics has to exit from the PM discourse, we face a new question: do reform economists really want (and are they at all able) to burn their bridges behind them?

A great many of them say that in the world of reformist ideas they already started their trips back from real socialism a long time ago by taking one of the "third ways." In testing this assertion, the historian of economic thought has to admit how little is known about this expedition.[13] Throughout our writings we operate with a series of journalistic truisms about the political and ideological constraints on reform economics, which we tend to consider proven.

Naive, moderate, and radical reformers—the analysts used to select these subspecies of reform economists and arrange them one after the other along a line allegedly leading out from the PM discourse.[14] In the implicit assumptions of this arrangement, there is an imaginary scale of liberalism on which one can measure how far a given reform economist has moved away from the concept of the Stalinist centrally planned economy (the conventional basis for comparison), and the reform economist is a sociologically neutral creature who is governed primarily by the values of his scientific convictions—convictions that have an ideological component but are essentially uncompromised by vested interests.

If, however, this is not the case, and the comparison of the distances from the Stalinist model is indeterminate, and the reform economist turns out to be a "political animal" as well, we soon find ourselves wrestling with classification problems.

Why? First because it is uncertain whether we can adequately define the yardstick for measuring the degrees of radicalism. What is to be considered the basis for comparison? Taking the ideal Stalinist economy as a point of departure, one ignores its historical predecessors, War Communism and NEP. In this way one can easily forget the fact that, if compared with the ideal type of War Communism, i.e., to a model of completely centralized and demonetized state economy, even the Stalinist political economy can show features of "naive" reformism (in property rights, financial regulation, second economy, consumer markets)—true, much more naive than NEP.

If we place Stalinism at the origin of the system of coordinates of reform thinking, there remains no room for the post-Stalinist relapses back to the War Communism model (as in Albania, Cambodia, Cuba, and China). What is more, relying on their allegedly decentralist (democratic) blueprints, some observers may be tempted to classify these instances of backsliding as reform experiments. The same mistake can be made in appraising the computopia approach of the Soviet school of mathematical economics, where the strong claim for rationalizing the planning procedures often makes the analysts forget about the model of an overcentralized phalanstery that is also promoted by the disciples of this school.[15]

Paradoxically, a much graver problem arises if one does not disregard the Soviet 1920s, because—War Communism and Stalinism being more or less identified with each other—NEP is so often misinterpreted as a prototype of the "naive" reformism of the 1950s and 1960s. In this case NEP becomes a model to imitate despite the fact that its general philosophy was more "naive" than the average PM discourse of the last few decades in excluding the market from the state economy, but at the same time, more "radical" in tolerating it during the transition period in the form of an enormous private sector which dominated the Soviet economy in the 1920s.[16]

As a matter of fact, this historical question mark leads us to a bigger—methodological—one concerning the measurement of radicalism: whatever the departure point in the comparison, the changes in the political and ideological considerations of the reformers take place in various dimensions at different speeds and sometimes in opposite directions.

To put it plainly, who was the more "radical" reform economist in, for example, 1966: was it the theorist of the Cultural Revolution in China, being a dedicated supporter of the decentralized commune system with mass mobilization but a relentless critic of the market? Or was it the follower of the aborted Kosygin reform in the Soviet Union proposing the abolition of the *uravnilovka*, the promotion of consumerism, and the loosening up of mandatory planning, but retaining the centralist and etatist nature of the reform? Who was less "naive," the Hungarian economist of the forthcoming New Economic Mechanism (NEM), trusting in the quasi-automatic deregula-

212   *János Mátyás Kovács*

tion effects of marketization without a simultaneous political reform, or the Yugoslav representative of the 1965 reform, who believed in the fruitful combination of liberalization and self-management? Or were they, perhaps, equally "naive" in not being able to foresee that the formally centralized structures of the state economy are just as well suited to distorting the liberal reform initiatives and promoting a counter-reformation as the formally decentralized ones if one-party rule is left intact?

Should we consider the Hungarian scholar János Kornai, who—while he was practically unaffected by the renaissance of Marxism—warned the NEM reformers against some laissez-faire illusions about marketization less "moderate" than the Czech economist Ota Sik? Although at that time Sik was more modest in his recommendations for economic liberalization than most of his Hungarian and Yugoslav colleagues and strongly committed to Marxian political economy, during the Prague Spring he came close to adopting the idea of multiparty democracy.[17]

Who won the contest for reformist radicalism in the early 1980s: the Polish emigré Włodzimierz Brus, the Yugoslav Branko Horvat, or the Hungarian Márton Tardos? The first, while still seeking ways to retain the principles of central allocation of capital in his reform concept, looked rather permissive in his assessment of reprivatization and militant in his support of political pluralization; the second seemed to insist on the concept of self-managing socialism, i.e., on decentralization without a multiparty democracy and reprivatization; and the third was promoting a decentralized holding system of capital allocation but did not favor self-management and had reconciled himself to one-party rule.[18]

A legion of misleading questions—without answers, of course. To prevent misunderstandings, I would not doubt the logical possibility of comparing reformist thought along the naiveté-moderation-radicalism line if the principle of *ceteris paribus* applied. There are, however, several reasons in general that it cannot:

Limited Liberalization—There is no guarantee that reform thinking moves in each dimension in the same direction (or that in all dimensions but one there is no movement at all) even if we remain on the abstract level of the PM discourse and study only the overall economic, political, and ideological dimensions. This is largely due to the fact that the majority of reform concepts are, by definition, fragmented and compromised in advance. So it is almost natural that a forward movement in one dimension is coupled with a backward step in another. As often as not, reform ideas are born in the course of political struggle, in countries with gloomy economic prospects, and under the threat of the destabilizing effects of the necessary liberalization measures. In addition, the implementation of these measures requires making a deal with the current regime (or with the reform economist's own conscience as he may feel guilty about violating Communist ideals) in order to reconcile it.*

As a result, the historian may find built-in "reform brakes" (as we put it in Hungary) in every dimension of change. Although the call for political pluralization and ideological secularization in most reform concepts indicates the presence of proposals for economic liberalization as well, we cannot take for granted that the reverse is also true. Reform economists frequently have to buy an amount of deregulation with an amount of political orthodoxy and ideological conservatism, or—*horribile dictu*—with a portion of reregulation.

How else could we understand, for instance, the ambiguity of the Polish reform blueprints in the early 1980s, which were to combine the bitter truth of political monoliths (even militarization) with far-reaching market liberalization? The same applies to a series of reform concepts in Yugoslavia, where for a long time permanent tribute to the ideology of self-management had to be paid for an entrance ticket to the "dirty" world of marketization. Or let us go back again to the 1920s in the Soviet Union, a period in which the NEPist initiatives for deregulating war structures (primarily in agriculture and commerce) were taken simultaneously with measures to retain (in heavy industry) the system of strict central management, to build up the main institutions of the coming reign of Stalinist planning, and to gradually do away with the remnants of limited political and ideological pluralism of the first few years after the revolution.[19]

We can also take, as an example of exchanging deregulation for reregulation, Hungary in the late 1970s and early 1980s. It was symptomatic of how uncertain the ex-reformers of NEM had become when, in 1978 and 1979, they had trouble evaluating the official

---

*I come back to this point in the subsection about bargaining.

reform package, "the new path of growth." This was an attempt to legitimate strict central management ("manual control") of the economy, which informally restored a part of mandatory planning by shattering a few old idols (lifting the ban on small entrepreneurship, amalgamating the branch ministries in industry, joining the International Monetary Fund and the World Bank).[20]

Relevant Subdimensions—Another reason the *ceteris paribus* principle is so often not operational is that far more dimensions require comparison than have in the past been studied. The historical analysis of reform economics is lagging to a considerable degree behind the discipline of comparative economic systems. Dimensions that by now are routinely examined in the course of comparative research into reform processes[21] are usually overlooked in appraising the various types of reform thinking with which these economic processes are intertwined.

Yet we did have the opportunity to learn that, for example, it is by no means the same if in a reform concept economic liberalization stands for the computerization of planning, for counterplanning, for the reduction of the number of planning targets, or for the final liquidation of mandatory planning. Moreover, there is no small difference between two blueprints for reform when one of them envisages the formal abolition of mandatory planning, but—leaving the institutional system of economic management intact—provides for an informal restoration of central planning targets, and when the other includes an elaborate system of indicative planning backed up by a series of institutional guarantees against recentralization.[22]

Moreover, it is worth distinguishing those reform projects which stop at deregulation of commodity markets from those which go further and want to liberalize the capital and labor markets as well; those which concentrate their liberalization efforts primarily on the rural economy from those which embrace the whole economic system; those which are based on the idea of the advantages of large economic organizations from those which favor smaller ones; those which allow the second economy to prosper from those which try to limit the "black" or "grey" economic activities of the population.

Please note that these subdimensions are not the whims of hair-splitting taxonomists. The fate of entire reform packages has been dependent on how the deregulation components of a given reform concept were placed in subdimensions like these, not to mention the positive or negative interference between the components. It is well known that liberalization measures have to reach a critical mass for them to become a reform process. This amount includes greater or lesser doses of economic deregulation, without the cumulative effects of which reformation can come to a standstill and be reversed. Precisely which subdimensions (and within them, which movements) prove vitally important to keep the reform going is subject to debate. However, the twists and turns of the Hungarian and Yugoslav reforms (the most lasting ones in socialist economic history), the liquidation of NEP, and the recent slowdown of reform in China all serve to warn us of the dangers of focusing only on a few subdimensions and ignoring the multifarious nature of deregulation programs.

Sometimes it even matters that a small link is missing in the chain of liberalization because of the logical interconnections of the economic system. When reforms fail, they do not necessarily fail in the main dimensions of economic deregulation, ideological heresy, and political pluralization. The fiasco can be invisibly prepared in various subdimensions. How high is the proportion of free prices? How big are the income differentials between enterprises? What is the share of investments financed by the center? To what extent are imports liberalized? How much income goes through the channels of state redistribution? We know from experience that dozens of similar questions can (and must) be raised if we want to decide whether a reform concept is workable.[23]

All in all, if we venture to assess alternative blueprints of economic deregulation, we find so many important subdimensions that it is very unlikely that the changes in these will indicate the same direction, providing an unambiguous comparison. What is more, within the subdimensions simple alternatives are scarce or meaningless: one cannot make do with a yes-or-no answer when, in examining a reform project, one tries to decide how far, for example, wage policies are going to be deregulated. For that, one needs a scale of ordinal measurement and/or the construction of intermediary types of liberalization (regulation of the average wage level, control of the gross amount of wages, wage bargaining).

So far, I have mentioned only the particulars of economic deregulation. What if we also start taking into account the nuances of political liberalization, from the intricacies of property rights through the interrelations of the political parties, the government, and the trade unions, the composition of the state bureaucracy, or the fine techniques of bargaining, all the way to the degree of the external dependence of the country experimenting with reforms? What if ideological secularization comes under scrutiny as well, including the movement away from Marxism or Stalinism with regard to economic and political liberalization: the proportions of etatist, autonomist, and liberal values in the world outlook of the reformers; modernization versus national identity; and socialist, religious, and "profane" liberalism?

*   *   *

Economic liberalization with political counterreforms, regulation through deregulation, ideological conservatism mixed with political innovation, economic counter-reform through political decentralization—these unexpectedly contradictory movements shown by the above-mentioned examples used to disconcert the ambitious comparer. Moreover, things grow ever more complicated as we leave the national types of reform thinking in a given reform cycle and approach the problem of surveying the country-by-country and cross-period differences in terms of degree of naiveté, moderation, or radicalism. However, the real complications are caused by the reform economist himself who tends to combine naive, moderate, and radical traits in his own thinking.

Serving Many Masters

The previous subheading included the word *liberals*, a term that the historians of reform thinking regularly avoid qualifying. It is not my intention to parody socialist liberalism, the ambiguities of which originate, in the last analysis, in the intermediary position of the reform economist between political power and academic life, government and opposition, East and West. My aim is to demonstrate here how unstable the political liberalism of the reform economist is and to what extent this instability hinders the construction of a sophisticated typology of reform economics.

If we study the reformer's social background, his interests, peer groups, and alliances (and the degrees of their institutionalization), his bargaining techniques, compromises, and willingness to take risks, we see a diversity of features stemming from day-to-day cooperation and conflict with the political authorities.

Diffuse Roles—The reform economist has many masters to serve. He is a historian and a fortune-teller (he would say cynically both a jester and an alchemist at the royal court), a critic of orthodox politics, a man of letters, and a public relations manager helping the neologist wing of those in power. Sometimes he is a human relations expert when his socialist commitments oppress his commercial spirit. He is a representative of the academic community, a spokesman for social groups interested in economic and political liberalization, an ersatz oppositionist who channels nonofficial views to the government, and a lobbyist for his own interests in the maintenance of his personal status in reform.[24]

Many or all of these functions can be performed on one and the same day. In Poland, Yugoslavia, and Hungary, where the activities of the reformers have become more or less institutionalized under ideologically rather indulgent conditions, it would not have been pure coincidence even some months ago if we had found the following entries in the diary of a prominent reform economist:

8:00—Proofreading of the manuscript of a new reform blueprint (coauthor is, perhaps, a leading member of the Communist party Central Committee).

10:00—Discussion of the government's recent reform package in one of the economic commissions of the Party or the government.

12:00—Lunch with delegates of the World Bank (informing them about the plans of the government).

14:00—Meeting with "liberal" Communists criticizing the Party leadership (preparing a manifesto for publication).

16:00—Panel discussion organized by sociologists at the Academy of Sciences (title: "Harmonization of the Measures of Economic and Social Reforms to be Proposed to the Government").

18:00—Dinner with East German economists (defending the new reform endeavors of the government against their ideological misgivings).

20:00—Meeting with leading oppositionists (to finalize the text of a petition rejecting the government's new reform package and organize the publication of the critical remarks in *samizdat*).

Of course, this does not imply that a heterogeneity of political commitments makes the reformer a turncoat hypocrite. Without becoming substantially more schizophrenic than the average socialist citizen, ideally, he can be simultaneously a mild oppositionist in the eyes of the ruling apparatus and a mild *apparatchik* in the eyes of dissidents.[25] Without fundamentally compromising the intellectual content of the blueprint, he can adjust the severity of self-censorship according to whichever role he is playing (being almost "naive" when selling the reform project of the government to the East, "moderate" when negotiating an agreement with his coauthor from the Central Committee, but ultra-"radical" when talking with Westerners or colleagues from the opposition).

Bargaining—This content can also change from one day to another. As reform is often subjected to an iterative bargaining process at the upper echelons of the Party-state, the reform economist—following the conventional rules of political rationality in Eastern Europe—takes off in a balloon of maximum requirements (a "radical" strategy) in order to be able to jettison what is not of vital importance from the reform basket later on. In this way he arrives at a moderate strategy. He is able to extend and contract the reform concepts depending on the degree of resistance expected from the partners in the bargaining game, and if necessary, to resort to a kind of guerrilla warfare. He may withdraw today from the battle to legalize unemployment in order to rally his forces for tomorrow's offensive over introducing a stock market.

The bargaining power of the reform economist largely depends on the degree of institutionalization of his expertise (advisory activities), on the pattern of recruitment in the Party-state apparatus (the upward mobility of the scholars), and on the extent to which the ruling elite is willing (and able) to open channels of communication between itself and the intellectuals and autonomous social groups. Where the rulers, having once or twice already been disastrously misled by their own apparatus, want to rely on quasi-independent experts as well; where members of the Politbureau and the government can become directors of research institutes and vice versa overnight; where a certain amount of tolerance, common sense, and pluralism is required to earn the benevolence of the West; and where (and this is a crucial element) the reforms recommended by the economic experts have proved advantageous (and the counter-reforms disadvantageous) for those in power—in such countries reform economists can carry a lot of weight.[26]

Where there is a fierce ideological countercurrent, reformers can turn "naive" in several respects. In the interests of reaching consensus in reform, the reform economist can in good faith formulate a great number of his ideas in Marxian language (calling for instance, the entrepreneur an ambitious innovator who is getting rid of the bureaucratic patronage of the state) and lower his sights (contenting himself with simulated prices, smaller income differentials, weaker antitrust regulations).

To exaggerate slightly, the reformer plays politics in a formally monolithic regime and represents various imaginary organizations: political parties, employer associations, sometimes even trade unions. As long as the diverging interests in the Soviet-type societies are not protected by real political institutions, the reform economist will be a substitute not only for dissidents but also for politicians of a peasant party, for conservative liberals, or for social democrats. He can be the mediator between the workers and employers as well. He can be very "naive" in trusting in crucial political reforms coming from above, fairly "moderate" in negotiating with the trade unions about inflation, and at the same time very "radical" in demanding legal representation for the enterprise managers or greater participation by the public in major investment decisions.

So we have arrived at our difficult questions again.

Can we, for instance, simply give the Hungarian reform concept of the New Economic Mechanism the label "naive" knowing that its introduction in 1968 was preceded by four years of preparations, in the course of which many of the less "naive" ideas (small entrepreneurship, import liberalization, withdrawal of the Party from business life, etc.) were filtered out, while "radical" proposals such as the abolition of mandatory planning and central supply of materials or the generating of big-income differentials were retained at least for some months following the inauguration of the New Economic Mechanism?

Or let us take the recent reform drive in China. Is an economic reform concept really "radical" if, through the "family responsibility system," it thoroughly marketizes agriculture and is very tolerant toward small- and medium-scale private ownership, but in the lengthy bargaining process over "urban reform" restricts itself to a dual (half-administrative) setup in managing industry, and reform making is under the strict control of a charismatic party leader?

Can the notions of "naiveté" and "radicalism" be applied to describe what is going on now in the Soviet Union? There reform economists have already outlined the most comprehensive economic reform in the country's seventy-year history, but in the wavering bargaining game of the last three years they have only reached agreement on experiments with self-financing, quality control, the rearrangement of ministerial powers, the supporting of small industries, the loosening up of the *kolkhoz* system—in other words, on fragmented issues. At the same time, they are witnessing bold attempts at ideological liberalization that may promote economic deregulation in the future, while the Party has not abandoned the traditional techniques of mobilization from above.

Reform paradoxes—As bargaining shows, the liberalism of the reform economist can become rather elitist at a certain stage of the negotiations. Later it may exhibit more democratic features. He might favor economic decentralization and privatization to gain support from the lower and the middle classes but avoid antagonizing the upper classes by not questioning their main political prerogatives. He can even mix the elements of authoritarianism and populism depending on whether he wants to implement reforms with the help of the "monarch" against the "people" or the other way round.

Nevertheless, the reform economist is unable to behave like a clever businessman who knows exactly what he expects from a deal. The reformer—serving many masters at the same time—is locked into the logical paradoxes of reformation, which often make the costs and benefits of bargaining indeterminate. If the reform economist opts for the minimum strategy (appearing to be naive) and accepts partial changes initiated by the rulers, he may lose popular backing as he throws his reform concept to the mercy of those in power. If, however, he chooses the maximum ("radical") strategy representing a genuine reform movement from below, he risks severe opposition on the part of the ruling elite.

So the reform economist has to maneuver between naiveté and radicalism. However, any intermediary solution may lead to a restoration of the prereform situation either because it is not sufficiently backed from below (as in the case of price liberalization and growth of income differentials), or because it is markedly distorted from above (in Yugoslavia and Hungary the regional party organizations and state agencies took over the enterprises again after the liquidation of mandatory planning), or both. Or there is a consensus but the chosen compromise (e.g., simulated world market prices) is not logically viable.

One also cannot disregard the fact that the reform economist has to disentangle these paradoxes while he solves the parallel dilemma of whether to start a reform project in a slump or during an upswing— that is, at a time when those in power can be more easily persuaded to accept even radical changes but the destabilizing effects of these reform moves may be stronger, or when one can only expect very moderate reforms from above while the risks of throwing the economy off balance are smaller.*

Needless to say, slumps can also bring about political crises in which the traditional meanings of *naiveté* and *radicalism* when applied to reform thinking are further twisted.

How should we characterize, for instance, the consolidation (austerity) packages that Polish, Yugoslav, and Hungarian reform economists have proposed over the last few years in the introductory chapters of their reform programs? These packages—following concerted action from the center that was not submitted to democratic control—resulted in a sharp drop in living standards. Were these reformers naive to rely on state intervention, somehow believing that the state would be successful at crisis management and then voluntarily yield its place to market forces? Were they perhaps radical as they tried to convince the respective governments that these austerity measures would be effective only in the long run if they were gradually combined with far-reaching liberalization (ranging from the complete monetization of the economy and the legalization of the second economy to large imports of private working capital), and if the state made up for what would be taken out of the people's

---

*According to a joke in Hungary, there are two cases where the government does not venture to make reforms: when the economic prospects are bright and when they are gloomy.

pockets with "injections" of human-rights legislation (relaxed travel restrictions, multiple-candidate elections, toned-down censorship)? Or were they simply moderate and reasonable as they did not demand all-out deregulation during a deep economic crisis? Why apply the different degrees of radicalism to assess reform concepts if the instigators of these concepts frequently have no say as to how radical they want to be?

Reform Cycles—In countries like the Soviet Union and China (and perhaps East Germany and Czechoslovakia), where the political roles of the reform economists have been considerably less (or not at all) institutionalized, the reformers tend to modify their concepts with greater interruptions. They try to exploit the rare but recurrent opportunities provided by the rather irregular reform cycles; more exactly, by the weakening of the ideological control over the economics profession in the course of economic slowdowns and recessions.

During these transitional periods of "permitted freedom," reform thinking starts to flourish. Does this recurrent prosperity of ideas necessarily lead to a kind of cyclical radicalization of the reform concepts?

Has, for example, Liberman's proposal for self-financing, formulated in the early 1960s, become essentially more radical by being more extensively adopted by the advisers to Gorbachev than by Kosygin's aides? Was Hungarian reform thinking more naive in the 1960s, when Tibor Liska was still an outcast because of his blueprint for "entrepreneurial socialism," in comparison with the present-day official reform rhetoric, which includes his singular language even in the communiqués of the Politbureau? How should we compare the naiveté of the proposals Ota Sik made in 1967 and 1968 with that of the subdued suggestions of his followers during the Czechoslovak *perestroika*?

Self-Censorship—Every concept of liberalization formulated by a reform economist is wrapped in an ideological and a political membrane of censorship. If a reform program manages to pierce one of them, there is still no guarantee that it can infiltrate the other one. Which breakthrough should we regard as more radical: the ideological or the political one? Should we consider the concept of the regulated market, which, after long years of polemics, has finally won the approval of the official ideologues in many East European countries but has always been played down by the politicians (sometimes the same people), more naive than that of privatization (household plots, second economy, intra-enterprise associations, etc.)? Privatization often sounds heretical even now, but it has nevertheless enjoyed tacit political support on the part of the *nomenklatura*. That is another question without a comforting answer.

A number of Hungarian reform economists said in 1983–1984: if we may not abolish the administrative privileges of state agencies in decision making on capital allocation by creating holding enterprises which would be responsible only to a democratically elected parliament, why should we not use a detour and introduce a self-management scheme into a large number of enterprises? Why not promote the deregulation of the capital market first by breaking the monopoly of the national bank? Is this a forced substitution of one reform proposal for another? Yes, undoubtedly. Does it lead to the continued shelving of the idea of autonomous capital ownership within the state economy? Yes, it does. Is this substitute proposal a less radical, more second-best solution than the original holding concept? Maybe yes, maybe no. In principle, self-management techniques can have less efficiency in allotting capital but more in dissolving the organizational pillars of the traditional administrative management than marketization within the state economy. (At least this is how two influential groups of reform economists in Hungary discussed this substitution issue.)[27]

Finally, an example of the synergism of economic and political reforms. Can we be certain, as so many analysts have been recently, that any concept of market-oriented reform is more radical if it also includes proposals for the transformation of totalitarian rule to an oligarchic or a democratic system of governance? The history of East European reforms (as well as current developments in China) often display just the opposite logic. In the absence of the first push given by the enlightened and powerful "monarch," the reform process cannot even gather the necessary momentum to get going. Moreover, once reformation begins, the "landlords" and the "governors" show a strong propensity to reverse its direction if they are not prevented from doing so from above. Or from below. It is probably not by chance that reform economists, fearing the short-term lack of interest (or hostility) of the population, do not flirt with the idea of holding a referendum on reform matters (particularly, after the Polish experience). Would they have been radical if in the initial phase of the reforms they had tried to shatter the idols of Tito, Kádár, or Deng? Were they naive or moderate when they censored themselves before being censored by others?

No doubt, after exhausting those possibilities of marketization, which involve only modest political liberalization (mostly at lower levels), reform economists need changes in such matters as general property rights and the structure of political representation in order to keep the reform process going. Many of them are currently taking the risk of stepping over the boundaries of the PM discourse in Eastern Europe. But they also know that economic reforms can blossom on the ruins of crushed political revolutions.*

COLORING IN THE MAP

Arguments that are meant to describe a classification gap are supposed to offer at least one or two salient dimensions of comparison designed to narrow that gap. Obviously, salience is in the eye of the beholder. It is to be hoped that this article has highlighted a number of areas worth exploring and instruments worth applying if we are going to construe a timely typology of reform thinking under real socialism. I think that in both the scholarly features of reform economics, and the sociology of the reform economist, comparative research ought to be initiated or revitalized. I believe that the dimension of economic liberalization should be freed of the dominance of general surveys of political and ideological radicalization of reform thinking.[28]

At this point we still know more about how not to compare reform programs than about how to compare them. Nevertheless, we do not have to worry about the large blank spots on the map of reformist

---

*To prevent misunderstanding, it must be stressed that doubts concerning comparisons of the various degrees of radicalism of reformist thought should not discourage us from analyzing the long waves of radicalization in large aggregates. Few would dispute the fact that over the last three decades, socialist reformers have mixed their original role of privy councillor of the Party with, to an increasing extent, that of the popular tribune. Similarly, if we wanted to know whether, for instance, the "average" Polish reform economist was more naive in 1956 than he is nowadays, it would be very difficult to answer no. But this *no* is composed of many affirmatives and still more *maybe's* uttered in the course of short-term comparisons of reform concepts.

folklore: in most of the Eastern bloc countries the path between capitalism and capitalism is so tortuous that, unfortunately, we will have plenty of time to color those areas in.

This pessimism may surprise the reader who is now charmed by the current "revolution" in Eastern Europe. No doubt about it, the reform economists of yesterday are becoming the "transform" economists of today, experiencing the fact that the Soviet-type systems are not only reformable (as they have until recently expected) but possibly also transformable. The unbelievably rapid liberalization process and the disintegration of the Party-state encourage the reformers to leave the political boundaries of the PM discourse. This development considerably reduces the ambiguity in their sociological position, discussed above. However, the border crossing in political terms does not necessarily lead to similarly speedy changes in the scholarly message of the former reform economists. The fact that many of them have joined the Solidarity government in Poland, or that most of them have grouped themselves around the opposition parties in Hungary, has accelerated their move toward liberalism. Nevertheless, this liberalism is still burdened by strong social commitment, corporatism, and populism, which can only be partly attributed to the present crisis in Eastern Europe. The conspicuous theoretical uncertainty, the great number of ersatz solutions prevailing in the current debates on privatization, and the reemergence of the idea of self-management in countries undergoing political liberalization show how great this burden is. Look at the reformer if you want to understand the transformer.

ACKNOWLEDGMENTS

I wish to express my gratitude to Włodzimierz Brus, Elemér Hankiss, Michael Kaser, Aladár Madarász, and Márton Tardos for their comments on an earlier draft of this paper. I owe special thanks to Cara Michelle Morris for reading the text and to the George Soros Foundation in New York for its financial support.

ENDNOTES

[1]See, e.g., W. Brus, "Socialism—Feasible and Viable?" *New Left Review* (1985): 153; Branko Horvat, *The Political Economy of Socialism* (Armonk, N.Y.: M. E. Sharpe, 1982); O. Sik, *Der dritte Weg* (Hamburg: Hoffmann und Campe, 1972).

226   *János Mátyás Kovács*

²Hungarian economists have probably been the most successful in making official reform policy reflect this approach. See I. Szelenyi, "Eastern Europe in an Epoch of Transition—Towards a Socialist Mixed Economy?" in V. Nee and D. Stark, eds., *Remaking the Economic Institutions of Socialism* (Palo Alto: Stanford University Press, 1989).

³See, for example, T. Bauer, "Reforming or Perfectioning the Economic Mechanism?" *European Economic Review* (1987): 31; J. Kornai, "Individual Freedom and Reform of the Socialist Economy," *European Economic Review* (1988): 32; T. Kowalik, "On Crucial Reform of Real Socialism," *WIIW Forschungsberichte* (October 1986).

⁴See, for example, Nove's concept of "feasible socialism" or Sik's "third way" program. See also the answers of A. Bajt, K. Dyba, B. Horvat, and G. Lisichkin to the questions of *Acta Oeconomica,* in "On Socialist Market Economy," *Acta Oeconomica* (1989): 3–4. These expectations are rather strong in Hungarian economic thinking. See J. M. Kovács, "Compassionate Doubts about Reform Economics," in J. M. Kovács, M. Tardos, eds., *Reform and Transformation: Eastern European Economics on the Threshold of Change* (London: Routledge, forthcoming). (Cf. the works of I. T. Berend, J. Bognár, A. Bródy, I. Gábor, R. Hoch, L. Lengyel, and L. Szamuely quoted there.) See also the answers of B. Csikós-Nagy, F. Kozma, and T. Nagy in "On Socialist Market Economy," *Acta Oeconomica.* J. Kornai's oeuvre is a remarkable exception: it contains a series of warnings about the logical obstacles to the harmonization of the planning and market principles. See, e.g., "The Dilemmas of a Socialist Economy," *Cambridge Journal of Economics* (1980): 4; "Bureaucratic and Market Coordination," *Osteuropa Wirtschaft* (1984): 4.

⁵What follows is a catalogue of deliberately provocative statements. For references and a more nuanced interpretation, see Kovács, "Compassionate Doubts about Reform Economics."

⁶As regards the comparison with Stalinist economics, I hasten to add three remarks: (1) the imperfections of RE do not help the case of its rival, Stalinist economic thought, for because of the latter's "subscientific" nature, the question of scholarly coherence cannot even be raised; (2) scientific incoherence does not necessarily impede practical reform moves; rather, it can even promote them; and inversely, (3) if reforms fail, the internal imperfections of the original reform concept are, in general, a minor cause of the fiasco. Compare the debate between E. Mandel and A. Nove in E. Mandel, "In Defence of Socialist Planning," *New Left Review* (1986): 159; A. Nove, "Markets and Socialism," *New Left Review* (1987): 161; E. Mandel, "The Myth of Market Socialism," *New Left Review* (1988): 169.

⁷Cf. Bauer, "Reforming or Perfectioning the Economic Mechanism?"; A. Bergson, "Market Socialism Revisited," *Journal of Political Economy* (October 1967); M. Bornstein, "Introduction; Economic Reform in Eastern Europe," in M. Bornstein, ed., *Comparative Economic Systems, Models and Cases* (Homewood, Ill.: Irwin, 1979); G. Grossman, *Economic Systems* (Englewood Cliffs, N.J.: Prentice-Hall, 1966); "Continuities and Change in Centrally Planned Economies," in A. Brown, E. Neuberger, M. Palmatier, eds., *Perspectives in Economics* (New York: McGraw-Hill, 1971); J. Kornai, "The Hungarian Reform Process: Visions, Hope and Reality," *Journal of Economic Literature* (December 1986); H. Leipold, *Wirtschafts und Gesellschaftssysteme in Vergleich* (Stuttgart: Fischer, 1980); E.

Neuberger and W. Duffy, *Comparative Economic Systems* (Boston: Allyn and Bacon, 1976); A. Nove, *The Economics of Feasible Socialism* (Boston and London: Allen & Unwin, 1983); R. Selucky, *Economic Reforms in Eastern Europe* (New York: Praeger, 1972); B. Ward, *The Socialist Economy: A Study of Organizational Alternatives* (New York: Random House, 1967); J. Wilczynski, *The Economics of Socialism* (London: Allen & Unwin, 1977); P. Wiles, *Economic Institutions Compared* (New York: Wiley, 1977); J. Zielinski, *On the Theory of Socialist Planning* (Oxford: Oxford University Press, 1968); A. Zimbalist and H. Sherman, *Comparing Economic Systems* (Orlando: Academic Press, 1984).

[8]Cf. the lack of historical specification of prereform economics in most of the typologies (Leipold, Neuberger and Duffy, Selucky, Wilczynski, etc.) and in Brus's concept of the "centralized system," Kornai's "bureaucratic coordination," and Bauer's "direct planned economy." See W. Brus, *The Market in a Socialist Economy* (London and Boston: Routledge and Kegan Paul, 1972); J. Kornai, "Bureaucratic and Market Coordination"; T. Bauer, *Planned Economy, Investments, Cycles* (Budapest: KJK, 1981) (in Hungarian). For a critique of the latter, see A. Soós, *Plan, Campaign, Money* (Budapest: KJK, 1986) (in Hungarian).

[9]Cf. Kovács, "Compassionate Doubts about Reform Economics," about the invention of the concept of the "permanent reform" in recent reform thinking in Hungary.

[10]Cf. the dominance of inquiries into the centralization-decentralization dimension, and the confusion of decentralization with marketization in early comparative studies (e.g., Grossman, *Economic Systems*; Wilczynski, *The Economics of Socialism*). Sophistication and radicalization are used as interchangeable terms even by Kornai, in "The Hungarian Reform Process: Visions, Hope and Reality." For broad dimensions, see, e.g., Zielinski's concepts of "state-parametric" and "market-parametric" reforms or Selucky's distinction between market and technocratic reforms. The works of Mesa-Lago, Montias, and Wiles show the inevitable proliferation of subdimensions. Mesa-Lago's "continuum model" is a notable exception to the rule of binary comparisons. See C. Mesa-Lago and C. Beck, eds., *Comparative Socialist Systems* (Pittsburgh: University of Pittsburgh Center for International Studies, 1975).

[11]For comparisons made along seemingly one and the same dimension, see, e.g., Wilczynski, in *The Economics of Socialism*, who includes "planometric centralization," "selective decentralization," and "supplemented marketization" in a chain of evolution of socialist economics. For country types, one can point to the ever lively interest in the Yugoslav and the Hungarian models. The concept of reform waves and the identification of the NEP with the Soviet 1920s demonstrate some negligence in the periodization of reform theories.

[12]Cf. K. Boulding, *Beyond Economics* (Ann Arbor: University of Michigan Press, 1968); A. Eckstein, ed., *Comparison of Economic Systems; Theoretical and Methodological Approaches* (Berkeley: University of California Press, 1971) (see the contributions of M. Bornstein, A. Erlich, L. Hurwicz, T. Koopmans, and J. Montias, H. Levine, and B. Ward); C. Mesa-Lago and C. Beck, *Comparative Socialist Systems* (see the contributions of W. Dunn, A. Korbonski, C. Mesa-Lago, J. Montias, and W. Welsh); J. Montias, "Types of Communist Economic Systems," in C. Johnson, ed., *Change in Communist Systems* (Stanford: Stanford

University Press, 1970); N. Spulber, "On Some Issues in the Theory of the Socialist Economy," *Kyklos* (1972): 25; A. Przeworski and H. Teune, *The Logic of Comparative Social Inquiry* (New York: Wiley-Interscience, 1970); F. Fleron, ed., *Communist Studies and the Social Sciences, Essays on Methodology and Empirical Theory* (Chicago: Rand McNally, 1969); O. Zinam, "The Economics of Command Economies," in J. Prybyla, ed., *Comparative Economic Systems* (New York: Appleton-Century-Crofts, 1969); R. Kanet, ed., *The Behavioral Revolution and Communist Studies* (New York: Free Press, 1971); H.-J. Wagener, *Zur Analyse von Wirtschaftssystemen* (Berlin: Springer, 1979).

[13]Lacking a comparative history of reformist ideas under real socialism, we can only refer to works (mostly journal articles) that deal with a single reform concept from a certain period in the life of a given country. Not infrequently these articles are collected in what I would call quasi-comparative volumes. See, e.g., M. Bornstein, ed., *Plan and Market, Economic Reform in Eastern Europe* (New Haven: Yale University Press, 1973); H. Leipold, ed., *Sozialistische Marktwirtschaften* (Munich: Beck, 1975).

However stimulating these studies may be, the valuable empirical material gathered by their authors prove too weak to bring the abstract-deductive approach, which dominates the few comparative projects being made, back down to earth. See, e.g., W. Brus, "The Political Economy of Polish Reforms," *Praxis International* (July 1985); D. Duff-Milenkovitch, *Plan and Market in Yugoslav Economic Thought* (New Haven: Yale University Press, 1971); G. Golan, *The Czech Reform Movement* (Cambridge: Cambridge University Press, 1971); C. Jozefiak, "The Polish Reform, An Attempted Evaluation," *WIIW Forschungsberichte* (April 1986); J. Kornai, "The Hungarian Reform Process: Visions, Hope and Reality"; T. Kowalik, "On Crucial Reform of Real Socialism"; P. Sutela, *Socialism, Planning and Optimality* (Helsinki: Finnish Society of Sciences and Letters, 1984); L. Szamuely, "The First Wave of the Mechanism Debate in Hungary 1954-1957," *Acta Oeconomica* (1982): 1–2; "The Second Wave of the Economic Mechanism Debate and the 1968 Reform in Hungary," *Acta Oeconomica* (1984): 1–2; A. Zauberman, *Aspects of Planometrics* (New Haven: Yale University Press, 1967); A. Zauberman, *Mathematical Theory in Soviet Planning* (London: Oxford University Press, 1976).

[14]See, e.g., Bauer, "Reforming or Perfecting the Economic Mechanism?"; Bornstein, *Comparative Economic Systems, Models and Cases*; Kowalik, "On Crucial Reform of Real Socialism"; Nove, *The Economics of Feasible Socialism*; Wiles, *Economic Institutions Compared*. The singling out of this dimension is as old as the first uprisings in the GDR, Hungary, and Poland during the 1950s, when the early steps of moderate de-Stalinization (the "first wave" of reform) led to political radicalization in these countries. From that time on, reform economists have among themselves distinguished between the "moderate," the "naive," and the "radical" members of their community. This distinction, which has spread throughout the popular literature of Sovietology, is actually very useful for a reformer in the East who is trying not to get lost in the daily political maneuvers of reform making. Moreover, if we look at even the least political typologies of reform concepts, we will find in most of them the adjective *radical* as a synonym for the more comprehensive and consistent deregulation programs (market reforms), and *moderate* as a synonym for limited and sporadic adjustments (administrative perfecting).

It was Kornai who in "The Hungarian Reform Process: Visions, Hope and Reality" first experimented with borrowing these categories from the language of political journalism for a scholarly work on the general typology of reformist thought in Hungary. Kornai with fairness warns his readers of "some arbitrariness" in his classification scheme. It will not, I believe, be his fault if in the future the concepts of "naiveté," "moderation," and "radicalism" dominate the classification of reform thinking, without the restrictions applied by Kornai.

[15]Cf. the not completely unambiguous evaluation of the "Rätedemokratisches Modell" in Leipold, *Soziale Marktwirtschaften,* and of the Cultural Revolution in China in Neuberger and Duffy, *Comparative Economic Systems,* and in Zimbalist and Sherman, *Comparing Economic Systems.* Similar uncertainties can be revealed in the interpretation of "planometrics" by Wilczynski, *The Economics of Socialism,* and "Cybernetics, Automation and the Transition to Communism"; by Beck and Mesa-Lago, *Comparative Socialist Systems;* by Neuberger and Duffy, *Comparative Economic Systems;* and by Zauberman, *Aspects of Planometrics* and *Mathematical Theory in Soviet Planning.* See Sutela, *Socialism, Planning and Optimality.* M. Keren's paper, "Concentration Amid Devolution in East Germany's Reforms," in Bornstein, "Plan and Market: Economic Reform in Eastern Europe," is a good example of how one can avoid overestimating decentralization and underestimating centralization in a hybrid reform move.

[16]Cf. V. Bandera, "The New Economic Policy (NEP) as an Economic System," *Journal of Political Economy* (1963): 3; M. Lewin, *Political Undercurrents in Soviet Economic Debates* (Princeton: Princeton University Press, 1974); L. Szamuely, *First Models of the Socialist Economic Systems* (Budapest: Akademia Kiadó, 1974). For a critique of the NEP analogy, see J. M. Kovács, *Ahistorical Parallels: the NEP and the NEM* (Budapest: Institute of Economics, 1982) (in Hungarian).

[17]Cf. J. Kornai, *Anti-Equilibrium* (Amsterdam: North-Holland Publishing Company, 1971); O. Sik, *Plan and Market under Socialism* (White Plains, N.Y.: International Arts and Sciences Press, 1967) and *Der dritte Weg,* 1972.

[18]See W. Brus, "Is Market Socialism Possible or Necessary?" *Critique* (1981): 14; "Political Pluralism and Markets in Communist Systems," in S. G. Solomon, ed., *Pluralism in the Soviet Union* (London: Macmillan, 1983); "Socialism—Feasible and Viable?"; B. Horvat, *The Political Economy of Socialism;* M. Tardos, "Development Program for Economic Control and Organization in Hungary," *Acta Oeconomica* (1982): 3–4; "The Conditions of Developing a Regulated Market," *Acta Oeconomica* (1986): 1–2.

[19]See J. M. Kovács, *Ahistorical Parallels: the NEP and the NEM.*

[20]See J. M. Kovács, "In the Thick of Reform Bargaining. A Public Debate on the 'Reform of the Reform,' " *Valóság* (1984): 3 (in Hungarian); "Reform Bargaining in Hungary," *Comparative Economic Studies* (1986): 3.

[21]See, e.g., the contributions of A. Korbonski, C. Mesa-Lago, J. Montias, F. Pryor, J. Triska and P. Johnson, and W. Welsh to the volume edited by Beck and Mesa-Lago, *Comparative Socialist Systems.*

[22]See, e.g., T. Bauer, "Reforming or Perfecting the Economic Mechanism?"; Morris Bornstein, ed., *Economic Planning East and West* (Cambridge, Mass.: Ballinger, 1975); W. Brus, *Praxis International* (1985).

230   *János Mátyás Kovács*

[23]See L. Antal, *The Hungarian System of Economic Management and Finances in the Course of the Reform* (Budapest: Közgazdasági, 1985) (in Hungarian); W. Holesovsky, "Planning and the Market in the Czechoslovak Reform," in Bornstein, *Plan and Market, Economic Reform in Eastern Europe*; C. Jozefiak, "The Polish Reform, An Attempted Evaluation."

[24]Obviously, a closer look at the sociological character of the reform economists reveals a great many intragroup differences. We find among them former Communists and present-day dissidents, Party members and outcasts, Marxists and liberals, "enfants terribles" and well-established political speechwriters, scholars, and politicians, etc.—and naturally quite a few people who swing back and forth between these roles. Similarly, the ideologies accompanying the roles are also highly complex: interestingly enough, legitimation and critique, cooperation and conflict, technocratic values and humanist attitudes, elitism and democratic approach, pragmatism and romanticism, etc. are simultaneous components of the reformist world outlook.

[25]See L. Lengyel, "On the History of the 'Turnaround and Reform,' " *Medvetánc* (1987): 2; M. Tardos, "Reform—Hic et Nunc?" *Mozgó Világ* (1983): 2; T. Sárközi, *In the Wake of a Reform of the Economic Organizations* (Budapest: KJK, 1986) (in Hungarian). A symptomatic case is that of the leading Hungarian reform economist (quoted also in this paper) who about a year ago wrote the new austerity program of the government during the day and then criticized it that evening.

[26]Cf. J. M. Kovács, "Reform Bargaining in Hungary."

[27]Cf. Sárközi, *In the Wake of a Reform of the Economic Organizations*. To distinguish between self-management-oriented and so-called managerial types of reform concepts has always been a troublesome task because both of them exhibit anti-etatist, anticentralist features. By now, however, separation seems almost impossible as the managerial reform proposals in China, Hungary, and Poland are regularly permeated with various ideas of workers' participation, industrial and parliamentary democracy, and civil initiatives.

[28]It is to be hoped that this kind of comparative scheme will be one of the results of the research project "Plan and/or Market (A Comparative Study of Reform Economics in Soviet-Type Societies)," that Márton Tardos and I have launched in Vienna and Budapest. Cf. J. M. Kovács, M. Tardos, *Reform and Transformation.*

May 1989

POSTSCRIPT

What is left to be said about socialist economic reforms after the victory of antisocialist political revolutions? The simple fact that revolutionary change proved possible in Eastern Europe has devalued, in retrospect, every effort made by the reform economists in the past to liberalize the Soviet-type economy within the framework of the Soviet-type polity. Their theoretical concepts have begun to appear in historical studies of socialist economics under the heading of "the most successful failure," as one of my Hungarian colleagues recently said.

Should one now defend the economic reformers, emphasizing their pioneering role in criticizing the utopia of communism or in the dismantling of the party-state economy? I think this will be the task of future historians when real socialism will unfortunately be again portrayed—as in the 1950s—as one of the two great totalitarian experiments in the twentieth century. Then a few good words will have to be put in for the virtues of reform economics in order to prevent it from becoming identified with its all-time enemy, the Stalinist political economy.

At this moment, however, it seems more important to focus on the surviving ambiguities of reformist thought during the first phases of transition from socialism.[1] I have written that under socialism, economic reforms can blossom on the ruins of crushed political revolutions. Now we are realizing that victorious revolutions do not necessarily lead to extremely liberal economic reforms (and a breakthrough of neoliberal thought) under postsocialism. At this point, economists in Eastern Europe have just started to experiment with the "unmaking of the omelet." They are not sure that this experiment will succeed— if what has been impaired can be repaired at all.

At the same time, however, these economists—from Leszek Balcerowicz to Václav Klaus or János Kornia—are convinced that (1) the state has a significant role to play in controlling privatization and marketization (cf. the concept of "regulated deregulation") and (2) a *social* market economy, and not a market economy as such, must be the final goal of the transition. They list a series of legitimate reasons, ranging from the controversial tasks of the transformation all the way to the need to prevent the capitalization of the *nomenklatura* privileges to explain why they do not advocate a "plunge into liberalism."

Evidently, the simultaneous tasks of crisis management, liberalization, and democratization force the former reformers to continue searching for compromises, now between "public" and "private" and not as earlier between "planned" and "market." Although their liberal imagination is no longer constrained by the taboos of the Soviet-type economy in the course of the

232 *János Mátyás Kovács*

day-to-day engineering of the transformation process, the economists may be confronted with parties and governments that show a propensity to pursue rather authoritarian-corporatist policies. Will the transformers reconcile themselves with the emerging "new interventionism" in Eastern Europe? Or, on the contrary, will they find the new political limits almost as uncomfortable as the old ones and opt for more liberal and less social concepts than any of those of *Soziale Marktwirtschaft*? Who would venture to make forecasts after 1989?

ENDNOTE TO POSTSCRIPT

¹See J. M. Kovács, "From Reformation to Transformation: Limits to Liberalism in Hungarian Economic Thought," *Eastern European Politics and Societies* (1990); "Das Grosse Experiment des Übergangs, Über die Grenzen unseres ökonomischen wissens," *Transit* (1990).

September 1990

Central Europe or Mitteleuropa?

Jacques Rupnik

With the collapse of the Berlin wall, discussion of Central Europe takes on new meaning. Since 1945 Soviet domination in East Central Europe has been legitimated by an alleged German threat. Now that Soviet domination is crumbling, old and new questions are raised about the German role in East Central Europe. Are we in fact witnessing the early end of a divided Germany, and indeed of a divided Europe? What, then, will be the culture of this region? Will a new version of Mitteleuropa emerge, and with it a new kind of German influence?

As the Berlin Wall comes down, the echo of falling dominoes can be heard all over East Central Europe. The disintegration of "the Yalta system" (the retreat of Soviet Russia) brings with it old and new questions about the German factor in the Central European equation. The democratic tide which since September of 1989 has shaken the very foundations of the German Democratic Republic has made more obvious than ever the direct connection between political change in East Central Europe and "the German question." For historical reasons, it is impossible to reclaim Central European identity without its essential German component; and as one nation with two states, Germany remains the symbol par excellence of a partitioned continent.

Jacques Rupnik is Senior Fellow at Fondation Nationale des Sciences Politiques (C.E.R.I.) in Paris.

"Whether we like it or not," wrote Sebastian Haffner,[1] "today's world is the work of Hitler. Without Hitler no divided Germany and Europe, without Hitler no Americans and Russians in Berlin." And without Hitler, one is tempted to add, no Sovietization of Central Europe. The fate of the Central European nations has been shaped by the two dominant powers, Russia and Germany. Stalin would never have conquered Central Europe if Hitler had not been let in first. Thus the flip side of "the Russian question" (Soviet domination over half of Europe) is the German question (a divided nation which in the long run cannot accept that Europe remains divided).

The ghost of Central Europe is back to haunt the lands of what used to be known as "real socialism." From Prague to Budapest, from Cracow to Zagreb, and evoking powerful echoes in Vienna and Berlin, the rediscovery of Central Europe will remain one of the major intellectual and political developments of the 1980s and will no doubt be a vital ingredient in the reshaping of the political map of Europe in the post-Yalta era.

Central Europe represents, on the one hand, an assertion of a historical and cultural identity distinct from that imposed for forty-five years on the nations of the other half of Europe by the Soviet empire. On the other hand, it is also part of the continuing political search for an alternative to the partition of Europe.

The protagonists of the debate range from writers such as Milan Kundera, Czesław Miłosz, and György Konrád to Pope Karol Wojtyla,[2] and from dissidents on the Eastern side of the divide to ecolo-pacifists (Greens) on its Western flank. Though it originated in the post-Solidarity depression, it took on a new, more political dimension with the formidable acceleration of change in the Gorbachev era. The return of Central Europe as an idea is an attempt by the nations of the area to think of themselves as subjects, not merely as objects, of history.

The current search for a Central European identity as an alternative to the Sovietized present tends to put emphasis on ascertaining the area's otherness from Russia. "The tragedy of Central Europe" is seen as having come from without. The German question does not allow such a convenient cop-out; it forces the protagonists also to confront the tragedy that has come from within.

The rediscovery of Central Europe is more than nostalgia for a lost innocence, more than "the invention of a tradition."[3] It is above all an attempt to rethink the predicament of the area beyond official Marxist clichés as well as old nationalist stereotypes. Its starting point is often an attempt to reclaim a world that is lost, a culture that was and is fundamentally pluralist, the result of centuries of interaction between different cultural traditions.

CULTURE VS. NATIONALISM: FROM KOKOSCHKA TO MODIGLIANI

Odon von Horvath, author of the famous *Tales from the Vienna Woods* (1930), gave himself as a typical example of the Central European mix: "If you ask me what is my native country, I answer: I was born in Fiume, I grew up in Belgrade, Budapest, Pressburg, Vienna and Munich, and I have a Hungarian passport; but I have no fatherland. I am a very typical mix of old Austria-Hungary: at once Magyar, Croatian, German and Czech; my country is Hungary, my mother tongue is German."[4]

Czesław Miłosz writes in a similar vein about the ethnic and linguistic mix of his hometown before the war: "The Poles say Wilno; the Lithuanians, Vilnius; the Germans and the Byelorussians, Wilna. The inhabitants of the town spoke either Polish or Yiddish; the other languages—Lithuanian, Byelorussian, Russian—were spoken only by small minorities."[5] Though the city was predominantly Catholic, there were also Jews, Calvinists, and Russian Orthodox.

Another Polish writer, Adam Zagajewski, was born in Lwów-Lemberg-Lvov in 1945 just as the Red Army moved in, and of the three possibilities to spell the name of the city, only one officially remained. Though too young to remember the cultural diversity that characterized the town of his ancestors, he writes about their forced departure from Lwów with the same sense of loss for the vanishing pluralist world of prewar Central Europe as do writers from the previous generation.[6]

The Central European city as a bridge and a divide now survives only in literature. Today Gdansk-Danzig is a Polish city identified with the birth of Solidarity, and few of its present-day inhabitants are even aware that it used to be a place of contact between Germans, Poles, and Katchubs (one of the oddest and most ancient of Central European minorities surviving on the margins of two worlds), described in *The Tin Drum* and other novels by Gunther Grass.

Prague, the birthplace of Franz Kafka and Jaroslav Hasek, the author of *The Good Soldier Schweik*, was a meeting ground of Czech, German, and Jewish cultures, with the latter often acting as a bridge across the Czech-German divide. Kafka's father's mother tongue was Czech but Kafka wrote in German. (To make things even more complicated, Czechs often had German names and vice versa.) "I am 'hinternational,' " wrote Johannes Urzidil, reminiscing in his *Prager Triptychon* on his Prague childhood. "One could live 'behind' nations [hinter is German for 'behind'] and not just below or above them."[7]

Prague as a cultural frontier, writes Central Europe's leading literary historian, Claudio Magris, was "felt by its inhabitants in their bodies as a wound."[8] And Kafka as a German-speaking Jew in the Czech capital epitomizes the "in-betweenness" of the Jewish community caught between its traditional allegiance to Germanic culture (and language) and the new assertiveness of the Slavic nation of Central Europe.*

Perhaps no one has summed up more movingly the grandeur and the tragedy of that German-Jewish symbiosis than Elias Canetti, who in one of his wartime aphorisms says, "The language of my intellect will remain German—because I am a Jew. Whatever remains of the land that has been laid waste in every way—I want to preserve it in me as a Jew. *Their* destiny too is mine; but I bring along a universal human legacy as well. I want to give back to their language what I owe it. I want to contribute to their having something that others can be grateful for."[9] (1944!)

It has been argued that the artistic and intellectual creativity of Central Europe was related not just to its mere ethnic diversity, but to the interaction and even the rivalries among the various national cultures. Here Canetti's words about his universalistic allegiance to the German language should be read in parallel with an essay by Béla Bartók written at the same time and entitled "Race and Purity in

---

*Since the late eighteenth century German was the lingua franca of enlightenment in Central Europe. Prague's Charles University, founded in 1348, and the University of Czernowitz, founded in 1875 in the far-off Austrian province of Bukovina, illustrate the changing status of that language in Central European universities. At Czernowitz (as in Konigsberg, now Kaliningrad, the town of Kant and Hannah Arendt), German was the academic language, but the students included Jews, Romanians, Ukrainians, and Magyars. In Prague the University became divided along national lines with a Czech-speaking branch established in 1882 to which a certain professor Masaryk was called from Vienna.

Music." The essay, written in 1942, transcended the problems of musicology per se. In sharp contrast to those for whom folklore was a means to exalt the supreme virtues of national distinctiveness, Bartók stressed "the continuous give and take of melodies" among the Hungarians, Slovaks, and Romanians over the centuries. "When a folk melody passes the language frontier of a people, sooner or later it will be subjected to certain changes determined by the environment and especially by the differences of language. The greater the dissimilarity between two languages in terms of accents, metrical conditions, syllabic structure and so on, the greater the changes that, fortunately, may occur in the 'emigrated' melody. I say fortunately because this phenomenon itself engenders a further increase in the number of types and sub-types . . . ."[10]

Thus in the process of spreading, musical elements (as well as other spheres of cultural life) become richer, more complex, offering new possibilities for artistic creativity. Bartók argued that the richness of Central European folk music was "the result of uninterrupted reciprocal influences" and concluded that "racial impurity" was therefore "definitely beneficial."

The implications of Bartók's insights might help explain the explosion of intellectual and artistic creativity in Central Europe since the turn of the century. In addition to the interaction of emerging and competing national cultures, there also existed a genuinely supranational or cosmopolitan outlook, often identified with the Jewish community. Many of the great names associated with Viennese *fin-de-siècle* cultural life were Jewish and not originally from Vienna: Freud, Mahler, Musil, and Husserl came from lands that are today part of Czechoslovakia.[11] Joseph Roth, the author of one of the finest novels about that period, *The Radetzky March*, came from Polish Galicia. Budapest, Prague, and Cracow were not just suburbs of Vienna, but rather part of a cultural network strongly connected with Vienna.

Hermann Broch suggested that, at the turn of the century, an "enlightened" Jewish bourgeoisie had replaced the Catholic aristocracy as the main force behind the development of a universalistic, cosmopolitan Central European culture. (The baroque tradition had been implanted in the far corners of the Habsburg Empire, leaving us architectural boundaries of Central Europe stretching from Prague to Vilnius and from Cracow to Ljubljana.) At the turn of the century, the bearers of a common culture that was often German in form but universalistic in content were liberal, middle-class Jews caught between the Empire and the emerging nations.

The Austrian Empire was par excellence the embodiment of that supranational concept of Central Europe. Roth quipped: "All nations of the Empire could call themselves Austrian, except the Germans"; it was the last state based on a supranational idea which, as Franz Werfel put it, expected its citizens "to be not just Germans, Czechs or Poles, but to acquire a superior, universal identity."[12] The disintegration of this culture (and of the above-mentioned German-Jewish symbiosis) coincided with the destruction of the Austrian Empire as a supranational state in the face of competing nationalisms.

The current rediscovery of that Central European culture thus also entails an implicit rejection of ethnic nationalism (and its by-product, anti-Semitism). It has little to do with the superficial nostalgia for an embellished imperial past illustrated by the popularity of the Viennese exhibition "Traum und Wirklichkeit" (later presented in Paris under the title "Vienne: l'Apocalypse Joyeuse"). Indeed, Viennese longing for the ersatz of a distant past tends to be all the more fervent when it coincides with a rather selective memory concerning more recent history (as the Waldheim case has shown). For Milan Kundera, as before for Stefan Zweig, the disintegration not only of a supranational state but also of a pluralist culture foreshadows the coming of a European crisis.[13] It is a metaphor for a vanishing Europe whose spirit now survives only in the memory of those "unhappy few" Central European "Dichter und Denker" recovering from a double hangover: that of nationalism followed by that of communism.

The cultural and political rediscovery of the idea of Central Europe, which started in Budapest and Prague, has now also reached Vienna and Berlin. Karl Schlögel's essay, appropriately called "The Middle Lies in the East" (*Die Mitte liegt ostwarts*), gave this rediscovery the most perceptive reading from Berlin.[14] The overcoming of borders—real and imaginary—is understandably a highly attractive theme in a divided country in search of its identity.

The reinterpretation of German history became in the late 1980s the focus of a major political and intellectual debate. In East Germany it brought a rereading of Prussian history. In West Germany it focused on the "exceptionalism" of Nazism. But to reassess modern German history in a wider European context requires, according to Schlögel, seeing it first of all as part of the history of Central and Eastern Europe—German history as the history of an eastward expansion: "One can deal with the history of Prussia only in connection with the history of Poland, and vice versa; with the history of the University of Leipzig, founded in 1409, only in connection with the earlier developments at the University of Prague; the founding of Berlin as part of the German settlement policy in the East; civilizing and Germanizing trends, both fruitful and catastrophic."[15]

For these historical reasons, as well as contemporary political ones, German intellectuals tend to be more familiar and more involved in the Central European debate that originated in the East than their counterparts in London, Paris, or Madrid. Moreover, revising German history and reclaiming a Central European heritage raises questions about the motives involved, even (or especially) when they are not clearly stated. Many Eastern neighbors must have wondered what Peter Glotz, a leading spokesman for the Social Democratic party, meant when he advocated (in *Neue Geselschaft*) that West Germany should act as "guarantor [*Machtgarant*] of Central European culture."[16]

Schlögel's and Glotz's observations (like the recent East German rehabilitation of Prussian history), reflect the two traditional faces of German influence in Central Europe: a long history of interaction and the tendency to seek hegemony; a duality still present in Central European perceptions.[17]

Two Czech historians, Jan Kren and Vaclav Kural, authors of a major (*samizdat*) study of the subject, speak of a "community of destiny" in their survey of the often conflictual relationship between the Germans and the Slavic nations of East Central Europe.[18] If one of the features of Central Europe is national fragmentation, the inadequacy of ethnic and state boundaries, then Germany too is an integral part of it. In this perspective the German minorities (*Volksdeutschtum*) are both an important component of the Central European space and an integral part of the German nation (*Gesamtvolk*).

In their Eastern neighbors the Germans evoked a mixture of fear and attraction, a model of Westernization and a threat of domination.[19] On the one hand, the threat of Germanization was very real. In the Habsburg Empire under Joseph II, it was assimilation through "enlightenment": the German language gained supremacy in schooling and administration. In Poland, Germanization was carried out by the much more ruthlessly implemented Prussian *Kulturkampf* of Bismarck and later of Hitler.[20]

Yet at the same time the German presence was also identified with modernization, the development of towns and the spread of Western civilization. In the words of Kren and Kural, "The same way France has long been identified with the idea of revolution, Germany represented in Central Europe a development model of industrial capitalism as well as its socialist alternative."

With the other nations of Central Europe the Germans share a similar pattern of nation building: they are a *Kulturnation* in search of a political identity. Hence some of the common features of Central European nationalism were a feeling of insecurity, revealed in recurrent debates about the national character, and the tendency for nationalism to invade social and cultural life. But whereas in the German case the nation-building process in the nineteenth century led to the unification of Germany, for the Slavic nations from the Baltic to the Balkans it was centrifugal, leading to political fragmentation.

Although the nationalism of the Slavs developed in reaction to the rise of German (and Hungarian) nationalism, the Slavic pattern mirrored the German one: it was Herderian, romantic, and ethnolinguistic. A nation was defined by "ethnos," by language, and an often mythicized version of its history.*

The conflict between these adverse—yet in some respects also similar—nationalisms (as well as the parallel conflict between Prussia and Austria over the solution of the German question) eventually brought about the destruction of Central Europe as a pluralist and multicultural society. The two phases of that disintegration coincided with the two world wars, which originated in Central Europe.

In the first stage, the very idea of Mitteleuropa as defined in Friedrich Naumann's influential book published in 1915 became

---

*Guiding the initial phase in the early nineteenth century were ethnographers (such as Vuk Karadzic, expert on the folklore of the South Slavs and author of a famous ethnographic dictionary published in 1818), linguists (such as Josef Jungman, who compiled the first Czech dictionary), and romantic poets (Poland's Mickiewicz was perhaps the most widely admired).

merely a code word for a German sphere of influence from the Rhine to the Danube or "from Berlin to Bagdad," as Masaryk saw it.[21] Especially for Poles the word *Mitteleuropa* remains associated with the German *Drang nach Osten*. This indeed was Masaryk's reading of German intentions; "the New Europe" of independent democratic nations which he and R. W. Seton-Watson conceived of in London during World War I was precisely meant as an alternative to a German-dominated authoritarian Mitteleuropa.[22]

The new Central Europe of 1918–1938 was conceived of not only without Germany but against it. A pro-Western buffer zone between Soviet Russia and Germany, it was the product of exceptional circumstances: the power vacuum created by the simultaneous World War I collapse of Germany and Russia. And it lasted only as long as these exceptional circumstances did.

In the 1930s Hitler used the German minorities to challenge the Versailles settlement and seek a new *Lebensraum* in the East. Conversely, when German domination was replaced by Soviet power, Stalin used the idea of protecting the Slavic nations against the common German enemy to legitimize his conquest. A policy of de-Nazification—identified with de-Germanization—became an instrument of Sovietization in Central Europe.

Munich in 1938 and Potsdam in 1945 provide two landmarks, two faces, of the break of Central European nations' relations with Germany. It was a trauma not just for the Poles and the Czechs, who were the first victims of Nazi Germany's expansionism, but also for the nations whose nationalism compromised itself with Germany. Hungary's irredentism and opposition to the Versailles treaty boundaries helped to turn it into the last, if reluctant, ally of Hitler. The claims of the Romanians on Soviet-annexed Bessarabia led them to fight with Nazi Germany on the Eastern front. The anti-Czech nationalism of the Slovaks and the anti-Serbian separatism of the Croats led them to seek independence under the sponsorship of Nazi Germany.

The interwar concept was a Central Europe without Germany. The post–World War II concept was a Central Europe without Germans. The expulsion (or transfer, as it was called at the Potsdam conference in 1945) of over 10 million Germans was the main result of this policy: 6 million when Poland's borders were shifted to the West (Pomerania, Silesia, and East Prussia); nearly 3 million from the

Czechoslovak Sudetenland; and several hundred thousand from Hungary, Romania, and Yugoslavia.[23] In Hungary, the German transfer was considered secondary to "the Transylvanian question" (the Hungarian minority in Romania) and the proposed "population exchange" with Slovakia. The Hungarian primate, Cardinal Mindszenty, expressed doubts about the wisdom of the expulsions. But in Poland and in Czechoslovakia, following the unspeakable suffering inflicted by the Germans during the war, the expulsions had the support of the overwhelming majority of the population. It was seen as a painful yet necessary outcome of a centuries-old conflict of which Hitler's barbarism was the culminating point.

Thus, 1945 and the ensuing Soviet domination brought with it both a Stalinist "final solution" of the German problem and an end to the "private civil war" waged among Central European states since 1918. The method, as the common wisdom of the day had it, might not have been a very elegant one, but it seemed the necessary price for future peace in Europe.

For more than forty-five years, the main problem in Central Europe was less a German than a Russian one. This fact, as well as the current reexamination of nationalist ideologies of the past, has encouraged a reassessment of the trauma of 1945. Jan Josef Lipski, in a lucid and courageous analysis of Polish nationalism written at the height of the Solidarity period, invited the Poles to rethink their relationship with their neighbors. The expulsion of the Germans is for him "an injustice," at best "a lesser evil" sanctioned only by "the necessity to organise the life of millions of Poles forced to leave their country" (the Eastern territories, now part of the Soviet Union). Lipski summed up on the Polish-German relationship as follows:

> For centuries we've held many grudges against the Germans: German emperors used to invade our country to keep it in submission; the Teutonic knights were the nightmare of the Prussians, the Lithuanians, the Pomeranians and the Poles; Prussia, Russia and Austria divided the First Republic. National and religious persecutions in the lands occupied by Prussia already foreshadowed what was to come during World War Two. We shall not dwell on the enormity of Hitlerian crimes in Poland. Despite all this, since we identify with Christian ethics and European civilisation, somebody had to come and say concerning the Germans, "We forgive and ask for forgiveness." In the dependent situation of our country, it was the highest independent moral author-

ity which said it: the Polish Church. Despite all our resentments, we must make this sentence ours.[24]

Czech soul searching over the expulsion of the Germans is both more tormented and farther reaching in its conclusion. The issue was cautiously raised during the Prague Spring of 1968, but the real debate was only launched a decade later, with a samizdat essay by a Prague-based Slovak historian, and Charter 77 signatory Jan Mlynarik. Entitled "Thesis on the Expulsion of the Czechoslovak Germans," it sparked heated debate which focused on three issues challenging the hitherto accepted orthodoxy. First was the moral question: by endorsing the theory of "collective guilt," President Beneš, and more generally the whole Czech postwar political elite, broke with Masaryk's humanist principles on which democratic Czechoslovakia had been founded in 1918.[25]

Next came a political problem. The expulsion of the Germans was the dubious centerpiece of Beneš's alliance with the Communists under Stalin's sponsorship. In the twentieth century, population transfers have been the specialty of two totalitarian great powers, Nazi Germany and Stalinist Russia. Mlynarik posed the question of whether by depriving its non-Slavic minorities of civic rights (including the right to vote) on ethnic grounds, the newly restored democratic Czechoslovakia was not in fact succumbing to the logic of exclusion characteristic of its two totalitarian neighbors. In other words, was not the expulsion of the Germans the first step in the slide toward the establishment of a totalitarian system in 1948?

Finally, there is the question of national identity. In his monumental *History of the Czech Nation*, Frantisek Palacky had argued that the "meaning" of Czech history was to be found in the interaction and rivalry of Czechs and Germans of Bohemia and Moravia. The expulsion of the Sudeten Germans put an end to that conflictual coexistence that went back to the thirteenth century and thus represented a radical caesura in the nation's history. What was supposed to be the meaning of Czech history, asked Czech historian Milan Hauner, now that its partner (adversary or interlocutor) had disappeared from the horizon?[26] Was not therefore, in this perspective, the expulsion of the Germans a Pyrrhic victory for the Czechs?

The question could apply not just to the Czechs; it holds for the whole of Central Europe. One of the essential features of Central

Europe was the historic presence there of Jewish and German minorities. Using Poland as the base for the Holocaust, Hitler destroyed the Jews. Stalin expelled the Germans. What was then supposed to be the meaning of *Central Europe* without two of its vital common denominators?

The complex Central European ethnic puzzle was simplified through murder, migration, and forced assimilation. What was left in 1945 was a series of ethnically "pure" states incorporated into the Soviet empire. The great dream of right-wing nationalists finally came through under the Communists.

Central Europe used to be about multinational states that claimed to be multinational. It was then turned into multinational states that claimed to be merely national. Finally, it became a series of nation-states which actually (almost) were ethnically homogeneous nation-states. Summing up this evolution, Ernest Gellner observed fittingly that Central Europe before the war resembled a painting by Kokoschka made of subtle touches of different shades; after the war it was turned into a painting by Modigliani, made of solid single-color patches.

It is in Central Europe that since the nineteenth century the conflict between two ideas of the nation and of culture has been the most acute. The first, inspired by the ideas of the French revolution, was a democratic, political definition of the nation as a community of citizens. The other was the German, romantic, "blood and soil" concept of the nation. Conversely, two ideas of European culture were at stake: the universalistic, humanist concept of European culture defined by Julien Benda as the "autonomy of the spirit" versus the concept of culture as identity, or *Volksgeist*, unique to each nation.[27]

The transition from the "traditionalist," ethnolinguistic or cultural, concept of the nation to the democratic idea of the political nation between 1848 and 1918, associated for Czechs, Hungarians, and Poles respectively with the names of Tomás Masaryk, Oscar Jaszi, and Jósef Pilsudski, was merely an apparent success. The noncorrespondence of ethnic and political borders, the permanent state of insecurity, the almost pathological fear for the "fate" of the national community, account for the persistence of a combination of defensive (vis-à-vis the Germans) and aggressive (vis-à-vis minorities, especially those that were Jewish) features of Central European nationalism. Thus "the German hysteria," as István Bibó described the rise of German nationalism from the trauma of the defeat at Iena to the 1930s, had also produced its East Central European counterparts. In this sense, Hitler, the Austrian, was also a product of Mitteleuropa.

Bibó, the Hungarian political thinker who became in the 1980s a key inspiration for independent-minded intellectuals in Hungary, wrote three seminal essays between 1943 and 1946: "The Reasons and the History of German Hysteria," "The Jewish Question in Hungary," and "The Misery of the Small East European States." These are indeed the three closely intertwined components of "the tragedy of Central Europe."

This tragedy did not start with the arrival of the Red Army in 1945 and the Sovietization that came with it. The Holocaust, the destruction on national grounds, had preceded destruction on a class basis. Totalitarianism from the Right prepared the ground for totalitarianism of the Left. It did not come just from without, from the East; it also came from within. In 1945 in Central Europe, all, even apparent victors, were in some way vanquished.

ALTERNATIVES TO PARTITION

Reflecting, in the late 1940s, on the meaning of the postwar partition of Europe, the Polish historian Oscar Halecki introduced a subtle distinction to the conventional wisdom about Eastern and Western Europe. In his study *The Limits and Divisions of European History*,[28] Halecki observed that the Soviet expansion into Europe had pushed Western Europe into a close association with the United States and created a new Atlantic community. He daringly compared that trend with the period at the end of the first millennium when the Islamic conquest of Spain was offset by the extension of Christendom to Poland and Scandinavia. The development of the Atlantic dimension, which admittedly has for Western Europe gained after the war, could be seen as a compensation for the loss of "the other Europe."

But Halecki's most interesting insight, forty years ago, concerned the lasting cultural and historical division within each camp, the Western and the Soviet. Challenging the then dominant "bloc" approach, he distinguished between what he identified as West Central Europe, consisting of the defeated German-speaking countries, and East Central Europe, comprising the lands between Germany and Russia.

Twenty years later it would probably have been dismissed on the grounds that the experience of socialism in the form of an identical social, economic, and political system was allegedly reducing the difference between the Soviet Union and its allies. And to distinguish sharply between Western and West Central Europe seemed even more obsolete, given that old rifts had been healed by de Gaulle's partnership with Adenauer and that the West Germans were behaving like model pupils of the postindustrial society and the American way of life.

Today, however, the validity of Halecki's insight seems easier to confirm. The differences between what he called East Central Europe and Soviet Russia are as great as ever. In terms of history, and cultural and political traditions, the real Iron Curtain runs further East than commonly assumed—along the Russian border with the Baltic countries.*

The 1980s have also revealed a growing latent dissatisfaction in West Germany with its postwar Atlantic identity. The debates there on the Central European theme often combine anti-Americanism (and Gorbymania) with a dose of *Heimat* provincialism.[29] The renewed discussion of the German question and the priority given to relations with East Germany; the loosening of old-fashioned ideological stereotypes about the East bloc, used too often as a negative legitimation for an insecure democracy; and the "Euro-missiles" controversy, with the two Germanies stockpiling weapons over which they had no control, have all contributed to the ongoing reassessment of Germany's role in Europe. In this context, Germany's rediscovery of Central Europe, of cultural and economic affinities with its Eastern neighbors, became compensation for its eroding Western (Atlantic) self-definition.

In 1987 the Friedrich Ebert Foundation (associated with the Social Democratic party) organized a conference entitled "*Mitteleuropa*: Dream, Nightmare, Reality." On the invitation was a map of the two

---

*What is the difference between Poland and the Baltic countries in their relations to Moscow? Five years. Now that on the fiftieth anniversary of the Nazi-Soviet pact the illegitimacy of Soviet rule in the Baltic has been exposed, the Baltic states' demands for greater autonomy combine with their return to Central Europe and the gradual restoration of relations with their main historical partners, the Poles and the Germans.

Germanies, Poland, the Baltic countries, and the former lands of the Austro-Hungarian monarchy. Karl Schlögel, one of the speakers at the conference, said that the word *Mitteleuropa* should be a "provocation" in front of "the wall in our heads." The term certainly represents an unspoken farewell to the postwar settlements.

Here cultural trends clearly blend with political aspirations. The interaction between East and West Central Europe has developed in at least two areas where the spillover into politics is obvious: one is the growing concern about the environment; the other is the parallel search for alternatives to the partition of Europe.

The Greening of Central Europe

Acid rain; the slow death of the Central European forests; the hotly contested plan to build two dams on the Danube in Hungary, Austria, and Slovakia; and the fallout from Chernobyl brought into the open the scale of the ecological disaster facing the area as well as the realization that environmental issues are oblivious to borders. The cooperation of the Greens in the two Germanies has spread to the whole of Central Europe, especially Czechoslovakia, Hungary, Austria, and Slovenia.

Perhaps nowhere today is popular concern over the environment so acute, so desperately felt as a matter of survival, as in Central Europe. It is undoubtedly the most polluted area in the industrial world, with East Germany, Czechoslovakia, and some areas of Poland on the verge of ecological disaster. In 1982, East Central Europe (excluding the Soviet Union) emitted over 40 million tons of sulphur dioxide, well over double the amount of the European Community countries.[30] Pollution is sometimes associated with level of industrial development, but the German case disproves the theory: though its industrial development is much lower, East Germany's per capita sulphur dioxide pollution (the highest in Europe) is four times higher than that of West Germany.

According to a 1983 study by the Czechoslovak Academy of Sciences, a third of the forests in the Western half of the country are dead or dying and another third are at risk. If urgent measures are not taken, 30 percent of all animal life and 50 percent of all plant life will be threatened. A third of all rivers are biologically dead. The water is contaminated with a high level of nitrates. Nearly half of the country's population lives in ecologically devastated areas. Prague is one of them.

According to an official report, the average amount of fly-ash fallout in greater Prague is between 220 and 240 metric tons per square kilometer. The top values sometimes exceed 1,000 metric tons per square kilometer. Moreover, fly ash contains high concentrations of heavy metals and other poisonous elements. Recently a two-stage warning system, which goes into effect when pollution reaches dangerous levels, was introduced in the Czechoslovak capital.

These official documents have been made public by the Charter 77 movement, which in 1987 released a lengthy document entitled "Let the People Breathe."[31] According to the charter, whose documents are not known for excessive dramatization, the situation has reached a point where "national survival" is at stake.

One of the issues that has most inflamed public passion and also provoked the best-organized opposition is the Gabčíkovo-Nagymaros hydroelectric power station currently under construction. The whole landscape between the Slovak capital of Bratislava and the Hungarian city of Budapest is to be "reshaped"—destroyed say the Hungarian Greens. Their fears range from water pollution in Budapest to a flood threat posed to the city in the event of an accidental break in the dam. They also point to the likely disappearance of the Hungarian rural communities on the Slovak side of the Danube and question the financial wisdom of a venture whose main purpose seems to be to secure cheap electricity for Vienna.

Between 1984 and 1986 the unofficial Hungarian environmental movement, called the Danube Circle, gathered thousands of signatures of people protesting the construction of the dam. In the spring of 1986, the Hungarian police broke up a joint demonstration of Austrian and Hungarian environmental activists on the site of the planned power station. But the situation changed in the post-Kádár era: the Greens not only acquired the right of city, but their campaign, fueled by the democratization process in the country, eventually made an impact. First Parliament, and then the government, was brought to reexamine the issue. Whereas under Kádár it seemed impossible for Hungary to back down from an agreement with neighboring countries not to antagonize Czechoslovakia, such a decision became a possibility, even a necessary concession, for a retreating Communist government facing transition to a multiparty system. To be sure, the Hungarian decision to cancel the project contributed to the growing tension between the two countries because of their conflicting domestic policies, to Dubček's interview on Hungarian television, which could be seen in Slovakia, or to the Hungarian party's self-criticism of its involvement in the suppression of the Czechoslovak Spring of 1968; but it will remain as the first major victory of an independent Green movement in East Central Europe.

The Greens' conception of grass-roots "antipolitics," based on concrete issues, and the distrust of party machines and the circumvention of the state bureaucracy appeal especially to young people who feel alienated from the regime but do not belong to the political opposition and the milieu of "dissident" intellectuals. The development of single-issue politics and the "greening" of Central Europe became one of the major developments of the 1980s. Yet it will be interesting how it will fare in the context of the current return of "real" politics: will it lose its specific identity and become absorbed by the transition to a pluralist, democratic political system, or will it seek institutionalization on its own on the West German model?

The Uses and Abuses of the German Question

The second area in which the concerns of Europeans on both sides of the divide converged or partially overlapped was the relationship between disarmament and the issue of the partition of Europe. In the context of missile deployments in both East and West Central Europe in the first half of the 1980s, cooperation involved Western (particularly German, but also British and Scandinavian) peace movements and dissidents from "the other Europe." It started as a debate about the meaning of détente, peace, and human rights; it turned into a reassessment of Yalta, the Central European status quo, and the German question.

Reflecting on the connection between Soviet domination of his country and the division of Germany, former Charter 77 spokesman Jiri Dienstbier wrote:

> Long after the war, the division of Germany served the internal consolidation of the Stalinist regimes. After the terrible experiences of the war, many anti-communists accepted an anti-German and pro-Soviet political orientation as a lesser evil. . . . The events of 1968 dealt

a heavy blow to this way of thinking, especially since, unbelievably and perhaps thoughtlessly, the East Germany army took part in the invasion, so that for the first time since the Second World War a German Army entered a foreign territory.... The unification of Germany is still a spectre which haunts Europe.[32]

Since 1945, the Soviet bloc leaders have justified the division of Europe by conjuring the bogey of German "revanchism." There were the "good" de-Nazified Germans building socialism in East Germany, and there were the "bad" Germans, in the Federal Republic presented as nostalgics of the Third Reich.

However strong the anti-German feeling initially was, especially in Poland and Czechoslovakia, it gradually gave way to anti-Russian sentiment. The realities of Soviet domination and the emergence of West German *Ostpolitik* help account for this evolution. There was also growing popular aversion to government manipulation of the German issue to justify the unjustifiable. The Warsaw Pact invasion of Czechoslovakia was presented as a prevention of a "revanchist plot" (even the Russian soldiers expected to fight the Germans). In Poland the repression against students in March 1968 was accompanied by denunciations of an alleged "Germano-Zionist" conspiracy. There was a strange innovation on the part of official propaganda: could waning anti-German feeling be propped up by anti-Semitism? Tadeusz Walichnowski, head of the police academy in Warsaw, obviously thought so when he published a book entitled *Israel and the FRG*, in which most dubious parallels were made. In short, until 1967, Israel was accused by the official propaganda of behaving like the German revanchists. After the Six-Day War the Germans were accused of behaving like Israelis!

The anti-German rhetoric gradually died down, however, in the post-1969 atmosphere of détente and Chancellor Brandt's Ostpolitik. Following the signing of treaties recognizing the Oder-Neisse border with Poland in 1970, Western recognition of the GDR in 1972, a treaty with Czechoslovakia describing as null and void the Munich Agreement in 1973, and simply in view of the fact that the Federal Republic was led by an anti-Nazi Nobel Peace Prize winner, the "German threat" argument became out of date. And it seems likely to remain so unless Chancellor Kohl's preelectoral appearances at gatherings of Silesian refugees under the banner "*Schlesien bleibt unser"* (Silesia is ours) give occasionally unexpected ammunition to tired propagandists. Or unless the prospect of a reunified Germany revives old fears.

The thinking behind German Ostpolitik was that, in the aftermath of 1968, one had to accept the status quo in order to be able to transform it in the long run, and the existing borders in order to make them more permeable. The inter-German approach was extended to the whole of Central Europe. Détente between states, it was assumed, would also help to bring about internal improvements in the Soviet bloc countries.

Note that there was gradual improvement, not fundamental change. The basic tenet of the German, particularly the Social Democratic party's concept of détente, was that inter-German relations constituted a model for the coexistence of the two Europes.[33] Now the Central European idea became a useful extension of the model: it helps, as Pierre Hassner put it, to "Europeanize" the German problem or, if you prefer, to "Germanize" the European question. Hence the idea of a web of mutual dependence and joint responsibility for peace in Central Europe. This, of course, has an economic dimension (trade, credits), of which the East Germans, but also the Poles in the 1970s and the Hungarians in the 1980s, have been the prime beneficiaries.[34]

The "security partnership" was considered the centerpiece of this policy: the draft treaty on the ban of chemical weapons that was signed between the SPD and the East German Communist party was presented as an example to be followed in the whole of Central Europe. The SPD's signing, in 1987, of a joint ideological platform with the very orthodox and anti-*perestroika* East German ruling party was presented as an even higher stage in this development: the bridging of the historical divide between Communists and Social Democrats as a step toward overcoming the ideological partition of Germany and of Europe. Totally underestimating the illegitimacy of the East German regime, the SPD, in dealing with the ruling Communist parties, has gone further than most Western Communist parties. And in view of the massive rejection of SPD ideology and policies by the East German people and even attempts to recreate a Social Democratic party in East Berlin, the SPD line appears to be not only an irrelevant but a pathetic illustration of the shortsightedness of *realpolitik*.

It also reflects a major misjudgment of the linkage between the German and the Russian question in Central Europe. The rapprochement between the two Germanies, between West Central and East Central Europe, depends on West Germany's understanding with the Soviet Union. This general point requires two qualifications. First, although launched in the late 1960s by a Brandt-led SPD, the basic features of Ostpolitik were followed when the Christian Democrats came to power in the 1980s. The staying power of Genscher symbolizes that continuity. Second, East Germany has often been considered merely a Soviet pawn in Soviet West German policy. Now, in the Gorbachev era, with East Berlin's stability unsettled from the West, from the East the effects of *glasnost* and perestroika, but also from below, the value of the pawn may decline to a point where a "for sale" sign will have to be put up. Meanwhile, the East German regime appears as an actor in the Moscow–Bonn–East Berlin triangle, whose relative autonomy has faded proportionally to the exposure of its fragility.

Stability in the neighboring lands of so-called real socialism used to be considered a vital precondition for inter-German rapprochement. Change was meant to be so gradual as to be acceptable to Moscow. In the 1970s relations with the Gierek regime in Poland was often presented as the perfect illustration of the low-key approach to détente at work. The emergence of Solidarity was its paradoxical and most unexpected by-product, and Jaruzelski's military coup certainly marked its demise. Poland's "self-limiting" revolution of 1980-1981 was anathema to the German concept of détente, and the Poles remember that on December 13, 1981, the primary concern of Helmut Schmidt and Eric Honecker was that General Jaruzelski's military coup not spoil their progress in inter-German relations. The restoration of "order" and "stability" in Warsaw was perceived in both Germanies as a prerequisite for the pursuit of *Deutschlandpolitik* and for East-West détente. Now with a Solidarity-led government in Poland, the promoters of this approach have been overtaken by events and left in the cold. A similar point could be made about the recent changes in the GDR: they might have been indirectly helped by the legacy of the above-mentioned "realistic" approach to Ostpolitik. The result completely disproves the SPD theories about East Germany and invalidates a concept of inter-German relations between states at the expense of society. All the more so in the case of an artificial state such as East Germany. After fifteen years of Ostpolitik from above comes reunification from below.

There were two types of responses in East Central Europe to this German-centered concept of détente. One was very suspicious toward the concept of stability of neighboring countries. The other was the conviction that since in the West only the Germans actually mind the East-West divide, there should be a parallel search for alternatives to the partition of Germany and of Europe.

Overcoming Yalta without a Return to Rapallo?

Is Eastern Europe under the shadow of a new Rapallo? This was the most provocative question Hungarian philosophers Ágnes Heller and Ferenc Fehér raised in an essay assessing the meaning of what the authors saw as the "neutralist" drift of the German Left for the countries of the other Europe.[35] According to their reading, the "ecolo-pacifism" and neutralism of the Left is merely German nationalism in disguise; the real goal is German unity at the price of "self-Finlandization." A drawing together of the two Germanies in a neutralized Central Europe implies American withdrawal from Europe. It can only be achieved on terms acceptable to the Soviets, since for geographical reasons there can be no real equivalence between American and Soviet withdrawal. Moreover, it would provide for the Soviets a "necessary *cordon sanitaire*" around an unruly East Central Europe. In other words, such an approach has many drawbacks and few very hypothetical advantages: it could mean a Finlandization or a "Hong-Kongization" in the West and improved stability in the East.

"A new Rapallo—why not?" asked Rudolf Bahro, the East German dissident, now active in the West German Green movement. For the German Left the price of such an arrangement might well be acceptable, especially in the Gorbachev era. But, as Fehér and Heller have argued, such an inter-German and Soviet-German attempt to heal the wounds of Yalta would most likely take place over the heads of the Poles, Czechs, and Hungarians.

East and West German attitudes toward Solidarity and even more toward martial law have confirmed in Warsaw the suspicion that, as often in history, a German-Russian rapprochement could only be anti-Polish. The Polish opposition journal *Nowa Koalicja* (New Coalition) favors cooperation of dissidents from all over Central Europe, but leaves the GDR out of the "new coalition" considering that "the natural representative of the interests of East German citizens is the German Federal Republic," in other words, a Central Europe preferably without the Germans. This view is strengthened by the widespread impression the Poles have had since 1981 that inter-German rapprochement tends to ignore Polish aspirations for freedom. Now that Solidarity has (and that perhaps the SPD may) come to power, this legacy may have repercussions for the relations between the two countries: German realpolitik giving overriding priority to state-to-state relations (as opposed to contacts with society) has proved in the long run not to be the most realistic policy. This Polish mistrust of Germany has by no means vanished with the recent changes in Moscow, Warsaw, and East Berlin. In the words of Adam Michnik, "The end of the Stalino-Brezhnevite order in Central Europe has paradoxically reinforced in Poland the obsessive fear of a new Sovieto-German variant against the interests of Poland."[36]

One of the most significant documents in the launching of the Central European debate on the link between the German question and the overcoming of the division in the heart of Europe was the *Prague Appeal*, published by Charter 77 signatories in 1985 on the eve of the fortieth anniversary of the end of World War II:

> We cannot ignore the existence of certain taboos. One of them is the division of Germany. If we cannot, in the perspective of the unification of Europe, deny anybody the right to unification, this applies to the Germans too. This right should not be used at the expense of others nor should its use disregard their fears. Let us declare unequivocally that the solution cannot lie in any kind of revision of the present European borders. In the context of a European rapprochement, borders should become less important, and not provide the occasion for nationalist relapses. Let us nevertheless recognize the Germans' right to decide freely if—and under what form—they desire the union of their two states within their present borders. As an extension of Bonn's agreement with its Eastern neighbors and of the Helsinki agreement, the signing of a peace treaty with Germany could become a signficant instrument in a positive transformation of Europe.[37]

The main idea of the *Prague Appeal* was that Germany is no longer dangerous, while the partition of the continent into two antagonistic military blocs is. This became the basis for a dialogue between Western pacifists and Eastern dissidents that centered on the connection between peace and human rights. The result was a joint document submitted to the delegations at the Third Helsinki Review Conference in Vienna in November 1986.[38]

This document is remarkably revealing about East-West intellectual and political communication in the 1980s. The result of a trade-off between the concerns of Western peace activists and those of dissidents, the *Appeal* can be considered as the manifesto of the "greening" of Central Europe. Its common starting point is the rejection of the Western habit of identifying Europe with the European Community and, conversely, of calling Eastern Europe the countries that "by geography as well as political and cultural traditions belong to Central Europe."

The link between peace and human rights came clearly from the dissidents: the idea of a détente "from below" involving societies rather than governments. Indeed, the document suggests that the measure of East-West détente between states is the degree to which détente exists between state and society.

The Western pacifists' input was the symmetrical treatment of the two superpowers, one involved in Afghanistan, the other in Central America. Their military industrial complexes are the main source of conflict. The document suggests that both withdraw their troops and missiles so that Europe can break free of its bipolar straitjacket and become a place where all peoples and nations "have the possibility to organise their mutual relations as well as their internal political, economic and cultural affairs in a democratic and self-determined way. It should be clear that the German question is a European question and therefore efforts to solve it should be part of a democratic programme to overcome the bloc structure in Europe."[39] It was the first joint document conceived across East-West as well as East-East borders and concerned not just a protest or a commemoration of a particular event but an alternative vision of Europe.

A Central Europe under the double ecological and military threats of two parallel systems of domination—that seems to be the German Greens' contribution to the Central European *Zeitgeist* of the 1980s. The United States and the Soviet Union are often perceived as external, non- or at most semi-European powers. "What were once role models have become mere guardians," said Peter Bender, whose writings on Germany and the "Europeanization of Europe" should be read along with György Konrád's critique of "the Yalta legacy."

Central Europe is a laboratory for the competitive decadence of the two rival alliances.

Fundamental differences appeared, of course, between Western peaceniks and Eastern dissidents. In his famous 1985 essay "The Anatomy of a Reticence," Václav Havel discussed why the political naiveté and utopianism of the former are not easily swallowed in a Central Europe long since grown allergic to any promises of a "radiant tomorrow." The very word *peace*, because of its place in the official ideology and propaganda, arouses "distrust, skepticism, ridicule, and revulsion" in the population, says Havel—distaste not for the goal of peace but for its official association with the "struggle against Western imperialism."

Other voices among the dissidents' proclaimed that the alleged symmetry between the two superpowers and the two political systems is based on false premises. Not only is there no geographical symmetry between the United States and the Soviet Union vis-à-vis Europe, but as Janos Kis noted, the nature of the two systems cannot be compared either.

Why have so many dissident intellectuals been prepared to put aside their "reticence" toward the Western Left and get involved in what might seem to be a dubious dialogue? One pragmatic reason is that, for most of the 1980s, "peace and human rights" seemed the only game in town. In the 1970s, calls for human rights were voiced within the Helsinki framework of East-West détente; in the mid-1980s they had to be presented in the context of the dominant East-West issue of the moment, the superpower arms race. After "no détente without human rights," the slogan of the 1980s became "peace and freedom are indivisible."

As prospects for internal change, after the crushing of Solidarity, seemed distant, the focus of peoples' hopes for the better part of the 1980s tended to switch to external factors. The loosening of the Soviet grip, it was hoped, could be fostered by a mutual disengagement from the center of Europe by the two superpowers. The way to overcome "the Yalta legacy" is through the denuclearization of a "neutralized" Central Europe. Seen from Paris, this looks like a nightmare raising the specter of German reunification. But seen from Prague, Budapest, and above all East Berlin, *neutralism* is by no means a dirty word.

All this is now being overtaken by the pace of change in East Central Europe. In the Gorbachev era the Green discourse, or "antipolitics," has been overtaken by the upsurge of democratic politics, which after Poland and Hungary has now reached East Germany and Czechoslovakia. After the Central Europe of nostalgia associated with a search for a historical-cultural identity and the Central Europe of utopia in the guise of denuclearized neutrality, now comes a time for a political concept of Central Europe as an answer to the current process of dismantling communism and de-Sovietizing the Western periphery of the Soviet empire. The combination of the massive exodus and of mass protest in East Germany has now made explicit the connection between political change in East Central Europe and the German question. The idea of Central Europe as part of a wider process of Europeanizing Europe is not devoid of ambiguities and misunderstandings. All the main protagonists—the democratic opposition, the Germans and, of course, Mikhail Gorbachev—have their hidden agendas. For the democratic opposition in East Central Europe, the agenda is primarily a quest for autonomy, for emancipation from the Soviet empire. In West Germany, the new interest in Mitteleuropa is related to the search for a solution to the German question, which entails greater distance from the United States and the West. At the same time it implies a degree of understanding with the Soviet Union. The fact that these different concepts of Central Europe, east and west of the political divide, have been rediscovered almost simultaneously does not imply that they are compatible (let alone desirable).

A middle Europe emerges which does not match up with either of the two competing visions of Europe: that of a unified West European market after 1992 (with its de facto barriers between East and West) and that of Gorbachev's "common European house" stretching from the Atlantic to the Urals. Rather, it is a third Europe, straddling the two Cold War alliances as their internal cohesion and perhaps their *raison d'être* deteriorate. What would be the role of the Warsaw Pact with a democratic Poland and a neutral Hungary? As for NATO, it used to be said that this alliance was meant to "keep the Soviets out, the Americans in, and the Germans down." The prospect of German reunification would for all practical purposes mean the end of the Atlantic alliance.

The future shape of this reemerging of Central Europe will depend on the linking of the democratization process in East Central Europe with the German question. With the Berlin Wall coming down and *Unter den Linden* no longer enjoying the status of the most spacious deadend street in Europe, it must have dawned on even the most Stalinoid *apparatchiks* in the Prague bunker that their days are numbered. There seems to be a domino effect in the disintegration of Communist rule in East Central Europe. And when Prague goes, the de-Sovietization of the area will become irreversible. The Germans are the European nation with the deepest long-term interest in altering the postwar status quo. It is also the nation best equipped to fill the Central European power vacuum and thus to recover its traditional sphere of economic and cultural influence in the area. This change would, of course, ultimately depend on Soviet consent, which means keeping German political ambitions toned down.

But how would Germany's Eastern neighbors see the return of Germany? Though all compete for German economic involvement, they are watching with some concern that the reunification debate bring with it also the question of the borders, especially when they hear statements—admittedly not the most widespread—such as those of Theo Weigel, the finance minister in Chancellor Kohl's government: "The German Reich in its 1937 borders still exists in law. . . . The territories East of the Oder-Neisse border are an integral part of the German question. . . . It will remain open legally, politically and historically so long as there will be no peace treaty."[40] Such statements are bound to refuel old anxieties of the Eastern neighbors about a greater Germany which once stretched "from the Meuse unto Memel, the Tyrol to the Baltic sea." West Germany's self-limitations, its capacity to articulate the opening to the East with its role in the European Community will be decisive in the shaping of East Central European attitudes to German reunification.

Adam Michnik, the editor of *Gazeta*, put the Polish view (but one could extend it to others as well) this way: "The Polish minimum for German-Polish relations must today be formulated as follows: the reunification is a matter for the Germans themselves, but also for all the nations which have payed [sic] with their blood the crushing of the Third Reich. It thus depends on the guarantee that the Germans can never be a threat for anybody." It is with this in mind that Michnik made perhaps the most explicit statement by a Pole in favor of German reunification: "It is our duty to state that the Germans have the right to have a state corresponding to their own wishes."[41] Michnik admits that his is a minority view in Poland, but his view is an act of faith in the capacity of democracy in Central Europe to overcome the old demons of nationalism.

An East Central Europe stabilized with West Central European (German and Austrian) assistance would be a double-edged weapon. On the one hand it would challenge West European cohesion and America's commitment to Western Europe. Gorbachev is a master at using the internal weaknesses of his empire as foreign policy assets in Western Europe: the process of de-Sovietization would be "compensated" for by German neutralism and American isolationism. Gorbachev's "common European house" would be a more fragmented one and one more open to change. It would also be a Europe that would have room for Russia but not for America.

On the other hand, a neutralized Central Europe, by reducing what Moscow perceived as an external threat to the Soviet Union, could facilitate democratic change in East Central Europe. The end of the Yalta system implies the symmetrical decay of the two alliances and the overcoming of the partition of Europe and of Germany. But it leaves open the question of what is to come in its stead: a new Central Europe as a community of nations between Germany and Russia or a new version of Mitteleuropa as a German sphere of influence.

ENDNOTES

[1]Sebastian Haffner, *Anmerkungen zur Hitler* (München: Kindler, 1978).

[2]Milan Kundera, "Un occident kidnappé—ou la tragédie de l'Europe centrale," *Le D'ébat* (November 1983): 3–22, also published as "The Tragedy of Central Europe," *New York Review of Books*, 26 April 1984.

[3]Eric Hobsbawm and Terence Ranger, *The Invention of Tradition* (Cambridge: Cambridge University Press, 1973).

[4]Quoted in Jean Claude François, *Histoire et fiction dans le théâtre d'Odon von Horvath* (Grenoble: Presse Universitaire, 1978), 31.

[5]Among the numerous writings by Miłosz on the multicultural uniqueness of the Baltic countries, see chap. 9 of his *Captive Mind* (London: Secker and Kasburg, 1953) and his novel *The Issa Valley* (New York: Farrar, Straus & Giroux, 1981).

[6]Adam Zagajewski, "Nekde i nikde" (Somewhere and Nowhere), *150 00 SLOV* (17) (1987): 32–34.

[7]Johannes Urzidil, *Le Triptique de Prague* (Paris, 1988).

[8]Claudio Magris, "La Mitteleuropa et ses rèves," in *La Lettre Internationale* (20) (1989).

[9]Elias Canetti, *The Human Province* (London: Pecador), 53, or (New York: Farrar, Straus, and Giroux, 1986).

[10]Béla Bartók, *Essays* (London: Faber and Faber, 1976), 29–32.

[11]Michael Ignatieff, "The Rise and Fall of Vienna's Jews," *New York Review of Books*, 29 June 1989.

[12]In F. Werfel's words, "The idea of the Austrian Empire required from the men who composed it their own transformation . . . . It implied that they were not just Germans, Czechs, Poles but men with a higher, universal, identity . . . . The renunciation of the unlimited affirmation of the self . . . ." In F. Werfel, *Aus der Dammerung einer Welt*, quoted by V. Belohradsky in his essay "La precession de la légalité ou l'Empire d'Autriche comme métaphore," *Le Messager Européen* (1): (1987): 252.

[13]Stefan Zweig, *Le Monde d'hier* (Paris: Pierre Belfond, 1948) (first ed. in German, 1944).

[14]Karl Schlögel, *Die Mitte liegt ostwarts* (Berlin: W. J. Seidler, 1986).

[15]Schlögel in *Frankfurter Allgemeine Zeitung*, 21 February 1987.

[16]See also Peter Glotz, "Deutsch-bohmische Kleinigkeiten oder: Abgerissene Gedanken uber Mitteleuropa," *Neue Geseischaft* (7) (1986): 584–85.

[17]Claus Hammel's play *Die Preussen Kommen* was first performed in Berlin in January 1986.

[18]A substantial part of Kren and Kural's study was published under the title *Integration oder Ausgrenzung, Deutsche und Tschechen, 1890–1945* (Bremen: Donat & Temmen, 1986).

[19]In 1945 A. J. P. Taylor wrote: "No one can understand the Germans who do not appreciate their anxiety to learn from, and to imitate, the West; but equally no one can understand the Germans who does not appreciate their determination to exterminate the East." In *The Course of German History* (London: Methuen, 1982), 3.

[20]See Sylvia P. Forgus, "German Nationality Policies in Poland: from Bismarck to Hitler," *East European Quarterly* (March 1986).

[21]T. G. Masaryk, *Nova Evropa* (Prague: G. Dubsky, 1924) (written in 1917).

[22]H. Seton-Watson, *The Making of a New Europe* (London: Methuen, 1983).

[23]Alfred M. de Zayas in *Nemesis at Potsdam, The Anglo-Americans and the Expulsion of the Germans* (London: Routledge & Kegan Paul, 1977) gives somewhat inflated figures for the transfer. The disappearance of German minorities is now being contemplated with the dramatic surge in the number of ethnic Germans emigrating from the Soviet Union and Eastern Europe. As many as 600,000 of an estimated 3 million ethnic Germans remaining there are expected to settle in West Germany by 1990. Gorbachev's easing of restrictions as well as

economic collapse in Poland and the repressive policies of the Romanian government have turned the flow of migrants into a flood. While assimilation of East German refugees in West Germany is relatively easy, that of Germans from East Central Europe is proving difficult, providing a focus for the campaign for the extreme nationalism of the Republican party.

[24]Jan Josef Lipski, "Examen de conscience," *Esprit* (1987) (first published by the NOWA samizdat press in Warsaw in 1986).

[25]Jan Mlynarik (Danubius), "Tézy o vysídlení Československých Něvmcov," *Svědectví (57) (1978): 105–34.*

[26]See Milan Hauner, "The Meaning of Czech History: Masaryk vs. Pekar," paper presented at the T. G. Masaryk conference at London University 13–16 December 1986 (publication forthcoming).

[27]See the first part of Alain Finkielkraut's essay *La défaite de la pensée* (Paris: Gallimard, 1987). On Herder's view of the Slavs, see chap. 16 in his *Idées pour la philosophie de l'histoire de l'humanité* (Paris: Aubier, 1962).

[28]Oscar Halecki, *The Limits and Divisions of European History* (London and New York: Sheed & Ward, 1950).

[29]Anti-Americanism and Gorbymania are abundantly documented by opinion polls of the past five years. Although a clear "majority" does not want American troops to leave, 79 percent want all nuclear weapons eliminated from Western Europe. See Josef Joffe, "Les Allemands et leur sécurité," *Libération*, 11 April 1989.

[30]See Jan Winiecki, *Economic Prospects—East and West* (London: Centre for Research into Communist Economics, 1987).

[31]"Let the People Breathe: Czechoslovakia's Ecological Crisis," *East European Reporter* (3) (1987): 15–20.

[32]"Pax Europeana (On the Thinkable and the Unthinkable)," *Labour Focus on Eastern Europe* (1) (1985), quoted by Peter Brandt and Gunter Minnerup, in "Eastern Europe and the German Question," *Labour Focus on Eastern Europe* (July-October 1987): 8. For a more elaborate Czech view of the German problem, see Alexander Ort, *Evropsky dum 1989* (Prague: Samizdat, 1989), 57–66.

[33]See Pierre Hassner's essay on the two Germanies in the context of East-West relations in the *Revue française de sciences politiques* (June 1987).

[34]See an unpublished paper by Centre d'études prospectives et d'informations internationales, "L'Effet Habsbourg" (December 1986 and June 1987). The study examined the resurfacing of traditional patterns of trade in the economic relations of Austria and Germany, with the countries of East Central Europe.

[35]Ferenc Fehér and Ágnes Heller, *Eastern Europe under the Shadow of a New Rapallo* study no. 6 (Wien: Research Project Crises in Soviet-type Systems, 1984).

[36]A. Michnik in *Der Spiegel*, 16 October 1989.

[37]The *Prague Appeal* was published in *La Nouvelle Alternative* (1) 1986: 32–33.

[38]The manifesto was signed by leading dissidents in Czechoslovakia (Havel, Benda, Simecka, Uhl), in Hungary (Kis, Konrád, Haraszti, and Demszky), in East Germany (Templin, Eppelmann, Poppe), and in Poland (Onyszkiewicz, Romas-

zewski, Lipski, Czaputowicz—but not Kuron and Michnik), noted in *East European Reporter* (1987).

[39]Published in the *East European Reporter*.

[40]Quoted in K. Christitch and D. Audibert,"Faut-il une seule Allemagne?" *Le Point*, 23 September 1989.

[41]A. Michnik in *Der Spiegel*, 16 October 1989.

In an interview with the author (in Rome on 28 October 1989) Michnik gave three reasons for coming out in favor of German unity: (1) as a nation that has been partitioned for over a century, Poland cannot wish partitioning on anybody else; (2) one cannot call for a reunified Europe without Germany being reunified in one form or another; (3) it is necessary to take away from the Communists their last nationalist argument for an alliance with Moscow. Democratic change in the GDR will mean that West German funds, that Poles or Hungarians, are likely to be "diverted" to East Germany. This is not likely to strengthen popular support for German reunification in neighboring countries of East Central Europe.

The visit of Chancellor Kohl to Poland in November 1989 highlighted the impact of the question of German reunification on Polish-German relations. First, the visit was preceded by a controversy about a planned visit to the German community. The actual visit was heralded in Bonn as "historic": the meeting of two Christian Democrats, Kohl and Mazowiecki, was meant to be the equivalent for German-Polish reconciliation of de Gaulle's meeting with Adenauer for Franco-German relations. Yet meanwhile history was made in the streets of East Berlin. The West German chancellor interrupted his visit to Poland to be in Berlin for the opening of the Wall. German reunification clearly had precedence over Polish reunfication.

The Polish government merely stated that the question of German reunification should not imply changes in existing borders; it should be placed in a "European context" so that it would not "threaten European security" (reported in *Le Monde*, 12–13 November 1989).

August 1989

POSTSCRIPT

Many Eastern Europeans wonder if Soviet domination will be replaced by German domination. In spring 1990, the Czechoslovakian ambassador to the United States in Washington made a deliberately provocative statement: "The German-speaking world (the two Germanies and Austria) will now achieve what the Habsburgs, Bismarck, and Hitler failed to achieve: the Germanization of Central Europe . . . through peaceful and laudable means, of course. And by logic of commerce rather than conquest."[1]

Postscript translated by Victoria Foster.

It is not territorial conquest but economic *Lebensraum.* Eastern Europeans hope to be aided by Germany and to be lifted from an economic marasmus; but at the same time they fear being vanquished by this uncertain savior. For Central Europe this is a classic dilemma; Germany has always been perceived as either a source of modernization, a doorway to the West, or as a menace to sovereignty and national identity.

News of Germany's reunification was received with mixed feelings in Warsaw, Prague, and Budapest. After the joy of seeing the wall disappear—the symbol of a divided Europe—there was an element of envy, based on the impression that those who contributed least to the fall of communism would leave it quickly and undergo a smooth transition to a market economy. East Germans did not participate in the "international" of dissidents including Solidarnosc, Charter 77, and the Hungarian Democratic opposition. However, the East Germans would be able to enjoy a parliamentary democracy and even European integration without having fought for it, thanks to the existence of West Germany. In Warsaw, it was immediately clear that West German funds would go to their East German cousins rather than to the restructuring of the Polish economy.

However, the rapidity of the absorption of the East German economy and its integration into the European Community also serve as tangible proof that if there were Western political desire, transition would be possible within a time framework acceptable to the East. Apparently no one in Brussels realized that after East Germany, once the most orthodox and least dissident of Central European societies, was integrated there would no longer be a justifiable argument against its membership in the European Community.

However, it is on the political level that reunification revealed the attitudes and stakes that will be involved in the building of relations between Germany and its neighbors in the years to come. Two approaches to the German problem are apparent, although there is obviously an entire range of intermediary positions; the Czech approach gives the benefit of the doubt to the Germans and the Polish approach fears the repeat of history.

The day after his election, Czechoslovakian President Václav

Havel visited Berlin and Munich, symbolic places in the collective memory of the Czech people. Havel, contrary to public opinion, made strong statements in the name of collective guilt against the expulsion of the three million Sudeten Germans living in Czechoslovakia. At a privileged historic moment, these actions took on the promise of reconciliation. The meeting of Havel and von Weizsäcker in Prague on March 15, 1990 (the date of Hitler's invasion of Czechoslovakia in 1939), was a meeting not only of two heads of state but also of two political moralists who were trying together to turn a new page in the history inherited from World War II. Their discussion will remain in the annals of politics as a meeting between ethics and history. In this historical framework, Havel, in effect, bet on the democratic future of Europe.

The Polish approach does not differ greatly from that of well-known dissidents such as Adam Michnik. Michnik spoke in favor of the reunification of Germany in October 1989 (before the fall of the Berlin Wall), giving three principal reasons. First, as a nation that had itself been divided for more than a century, Poland could only hope for such an end. Secondly, there could not be a reunified Europe without a reunified Germany. Lastly, anti-Germanism is the final trump card of the Communists under Jaruzelski in their attempt to preserve an anchor to the east of Poland. Barely two months later, however, Michnik wrote in the *Gazeta:* "German-Polish relations must be formulated in the following manner: Reunification is not only a German question but also a question for all those nations who paid for the defeat of the Third Reich with their blood. Reunification would, therefore, necessarily depend upon a guarantee that Germany would not constitute a threat to anyone."[2]

How is it possible to explain this change in tone, this passage from hope to fear? The growing anti-Polish nationalism in Eastern Germany is partially responsible; but, above all, the hesitations of Helmut Kohl concerning the Oder-Neisse border succeeded in reviving old Polish fears and favored the return to a classic Polish stance: balance the German threat through political relationships with France and Russia. One has the surprising picture of Prime Minister Mazowiecki and his jailer of yesteryear General Jaruzelski, side by side in Paris asking President Mitterrand to help them obtain Polish participation in the Four-Plus-Two negotiations on Germany. By the same token, there is the notable lack of Polish eagerness to require the withdrawal of the Red Army from Poland. In a matter of days, for strategic electoral reasons, Chancellor Kohl has succeeded in doing what Communist propagandists have failed to do for over forty years: reviving a fear of Germany.

The Polish and Czech approaches reflect not only two different readings of the Germany question but also two different visions of the international system. For Havel, reunified Germany signifies the end of an antagonistic alliance system and the emergence of a new security system in Europe. The Polish attitude is a return to classic geopolitics: balance Germany by forming alliances with those who also fear a confident and dominant Germany. These approaches also bring to mind crucial questions about future relations between Germany and East-Central Europe. Will Germany be a bridge between the two Europes, a vehicle of integration for the "other Europe" with the expanded European Community? Or will Germany dominate a "Balkanized" Mitteleuropa economically and culturally, transforming it into a German sphere of influence? Will it "Germanize" the East or "Europeanize" it?

ENDNOTES TO POSTSCRIPT

[1]Charles Krauthammer, "The German Revival," *The New Republic* 202 (13) (26 March 1990), pp. 18–21.
[2]Adam Michnik, *Gazeta* (7 December 1989).

September 1990

Ethnicity and Faith in Eastern Europe
Ernest Gellner

raveling through the Soviet Union today, visiting regions as distinctive as Byelorussia, Georgia, and Estonia, is to be aware of the potency of tradition, long-standing social habits, deep-seated religious beliefs, often linked to passionate sentiments of nationality. Where an area has been part of the Soviet Union since the beginning, conditions and memories differ from those common in regions incorporated more recently, in the 1940s. Whether, under the pressures of perestroika, *ethnic associations will help revive civil society, but restrain aggressive nationalisms, is an open question.*

BYELORUSSIA

Western Byelorussia had been under Polish rule and domination between the two world wars. Staying with Byelorussian peasants, on a visit from Moscow, one had no feeling that the time was remembered with resentment. On the contrary, the Poles had left behind precisely the kind of romantic image with which they are associated and with which they like to be associated. "The *pan*," I heard, "was a real gentleman. When he went out to dinner he went with his groom, and whilst the pan ate with his host, the groom was to be entertained in the kitchen. Before the pan sat down to the table, he would go into the kitchen to see that his groom was treated right. If he were not—well then the pan would leave at once, no matter what they said, no matter how much they begged him."

Ernest Gellner is Professor of Social Anthropology at Cambridge University.

267

The pan on occasion interfered in the marriage arrangements of the peasants. One of my informants had a grandmother who had been married off to a local craftsman, who had been lukewarm about the whole business but had allowed himself to be urged into it by the lord. The bride was extremely young and had been a maid in the household of the pan. She gave birth to a child soon after the wedding. In his old age, it is said, the pan was given to melancholy, and used to wander around the countryside murmuring the name of the erstwhile maid. So, some two centuries after Beaumarchais and *Figaro*, the relationship of the quasi-feudal lord and the peasantry was still expressed in the old symbolism of *droit du seigneur*. But what is interesting is that the story was told me by the offspring of the peasantry, not with resentment, but with a kind of sentimental admiration. He was a real pan.

A curious recollection, which I cannot properly explain and which fits no stereotype known to me, is that in Polish days, the insurance companies seemed to be either gullible or generous. One way to improve one's housing in those days was to burn down one's cottage. The compensation paid by the insurance company was good enough to enable one to build oneself a new and better house. Perhaps insurance compensation was based on what it cost to have a house built by professionals, and peasants, used to building houses themselves with kin and local assistance, knew how to do it more cheaply.

Society in those days was markedly plural. For one thing, the pan provided small holdings, or *khutors,* for veterans of the Polish Legion who had fought, initially under Austrian patronage, for Polish independence during the First World War. But in any case, there had locally been both Orthodox and Catholic communities. The Catholics considered themselves a kind of gentry even when, economically, they were no better off than the Orthodox. In local speech, a different term is used for "church" according to whether it is Orthodox or Catholic: *tserkov* or *kostel.* An Orthodox priest is remembered who tried to campaign for the conversion of the Catholic peasantry. In the village, there had been a number of inns run by Jews where one could rest horses and drink. Now there are none: here as in Russia, there is that curious lack of public or communal space, driving people to accentuate the privacy and home-based nature of social relations. There is of course the *kolkhoz* club, but these places tend to be used in a formal and stilted way and to contribute little to informal socializing. (In a village where I used to walk regularly and which survives, as if by miracle, in the lovely woods left between two new suburban developments in outer Moscow, the only time it was even possible to penetrate into the village club was in the spring of 1989, when it was all tarted up to house, rather ceremonially, the booths in national elections.)

In the local town, the quarter around the market had been inhabited mainly by Jews. The synagogue building still stands. Relations between Byelorussians and Jews seem to have been markedly less bad than those between Ukrainians and Jews. In Minsk, at the place where the Germans carried out mass executions, the memorial carries an inscription in Hebrew letters, in marked contrast to the much more portentous memorial in Kiev at Babi Yar, which gives offense by its failure to indicate in any way that the victims were Jewish.

The Jews and the Poles have gone. The Poles fled or were deported. The Jews perished during the German occupation. Byelorussian nationalism, as nationalisms within the Soviet Union go, is relatively muted. Byelorussian parents are not averse to sending their children to Russian schools, which gives their children better access to advancement and what is, after all, a world language and the idiom of an enormous political unit. (Such an attitude is unthinkable in, say, Estonia or Georgia.) In the village, the older inhabitants remembered having to have their schooling, such as it was, in Polish; but they remembered it without any bitterness. On the contrary, they were eager to try out their Polish on me. The village retained an attractive insularity: if a man did not speak Byelorussian, why then naturally he must speak Polish. (They did not actually go as far as a little chief in the Moroccan Atlas who once told me that there were only three languages in the world—Arabic, Berber, and French—but they were not too far from a similar state of mind.) In the nearby town, the historic local Polish church, an early specimen of Polish baroque, is well preserved despite the absence of a congregation, and the inscriptions in Polish and Latin commemorating erstwhile local dignitaries and their achievements, and thus testifying to an order which is no longer, are piously preserved. The seat of the greatest local nobles, the Radziwils, a great polonized Lithuanian lineage lately intermarried with the Kennedys, is now preserved as a monument and a convalescence home.

The peasants of Byelorussia are somewhat better off than suburban Muscovites, if we can judge by the range of goods available in the village stores. These Byelorussians have a mild contempt for the Great Russians, whom they consider somewhat addicted to sloth, feckless and inefficient. "It is *we* and the Baltics who feed Russia," they exaggerate. One should add that they still *are* peasants, albeit peasants with electric shavers and television sets and electric lights, and on occasion, a rickety car. But the horse-drawn plough is still much in use on their rather extensive private plots. The interior arrangement of the house still has a peasant quality: basically it is treated as one space, with but curtain partitions to give visual but not acoustic privacy. The master has a better bed, on his own, somewhat apart. And there is no sign of peasant land hunger: no great enthusiasm for the new institution of long-term land leasing, which is meant to turn kolkhozniks into farmers. On the contrary, the kolkhoz provides a certain basic security, and the large private plot a source of extra food for the family and, through sales, of income. There seems little eagerness here to exchange this measure of security for the risks of real private enterprise—risks not merely of economic failure or bad harvest, but also political. If people leaving the shelter of the kolkhoz were offered in return ten acres freehold, a small tractor, and a signed copy of Gorbachev's works, I suspect that there would be few takers. Who knows when the present astonishing political climate may be reversed? Why rush into this risk? One distinguished Soviet expert on rural life was told by the Ukrainian villagers whom he had known well for many years, "They drove us into collectivization. Let them drive us into *perestroika!*"

GEORGIA

As far as this attitude goes, the situation is very similar in Georgia. I spent some time in a mountain community in the recesses of the Caucasus, barely a day's walk from the 5,000-meter-high watershed. Here pastoralism is important, and the renting out of both livestock and pasture was proposed from on high, without eliciting a great deal of enthusiasm. The leasing of the various elements and facilities which go into pastoral production did not come all at once or convincingly, and the countrymen remain skeptical.

The Byelorussian peasants were indeed hospitable: no visit for ethnographic inquiry failed to provoke a groaning table, and often some astonishingly smooth home brew (*samogon*, "own-fire," a word constructed on the same principle as *samizdat*, "own-publish," though of course preceding it). But Georgians are not just hospitable; with them hospitality is a way of life and a religion. One Georgian toast runs: "May a time never come when a Georgian is not willing to put himself in debt for the sake of entertaining a stranger!" The Georgians must be the most Durkheimian people in the world: they virtually never eat or drink, unless it be to establish, enhance, affirm, and sacralize a human relationship. They do not drink without toasting someone or something first, and they drink a good deal. Nor are their toasts brief: they are elaborate and when performed by a skilled *tamadan*, or toastmaster, they can be great works of art. Their artistry is, however, more perceptible, and more perceived, at the beginning of a meal, when some measure of sobriety still allows the perceptions of listeners and speaker to retain a degree of sharpness. By the end of the meal, toasts tend to be long and repetitive, and as the New York psychoanalyst has observed, who listens?

In the Soviet Union, generally speaking there is a difference between the so-called seventy-year-old and the forty-year-old areas of Soviet power: there is a perceptible difference between the areas that have been parts of the union ever since the Revolution, and those that were incorporated in it only at the end of the Second World War. The difference between seventy and forty years seems to affect the nature of social memory profoundly: the forty-year-ers have a sharp sense of what the other world is like, and the seventy-year-ers have largely lost it. They know no other. But Georgia, though in fact the Red Army reconquered the Menshevik Georgian Republic a few years after the October Revolution, has the atmosphere of one of the forty-year-old zones of Soviet power. Social memory is somehow more vigorous and tenacious in the Caucasus. All that toast-sustained network of relationships largely survived both Stalinism and stagnation. It should be added that statues of Stalin survive in Georgia and that during the first thaw, long ago there were disturbances directed against the denigration of Stalin. Georgia is a kind of joyous Mezzogiorno. The country is plausibly believed to be Mafia-ridden, but it is a Mafia with a smile, which prefers to persuade by means of cordial conviviality.

The drink-confirmed links of kinship, affinity, and patronage embrace both the living and the dead. Though the Georgians, like their Armenian neighbors, embraced Christianity very early and are proud of it, their religion retains a strong Mediterranean, community-celebrating, quasi-pagan quality. Georgian Christianity, unlike the Islam which almost surrounds it, appears to feel no strain between its unitarian-theocentric and its communal-pagan elements. It is not merely that in the mountains, operational shrines abound which are much in use for sacrifices but quite untouched by any Christian symbolism, or that prestations at shrines which do have some Christian symbolism include such instruments of mundane joy as playing cards; the churches, and above all the cemeteries adjoining them, express and articulate communal organization and solidarity, rather than the relationship of solitary souls to a unique deity. The cemeteries are divided into family plots, each protected by its metal railing, and within each plot there tends to be a table, for the benefit of the living eager to drink with and to the dead. In the Georgian heaven, the dead are provided with self-filling wine goblets, and their perpetual topping-off is conditional on the living continuing to drink toasts to their deceased predecessors. Once they fail to do so, the topping-up mechanism no longer operates. This of course imposes an obligation on the living to continue drinking toasts to the dead, and the obligation is taken seriously. Celebration with wine in no way devalues or renders slightly humorous what is being honored, as it might in the West: the victims of the massacre of April 9, 1989, an event felt deeply and bitterly by the Georgians, are also commemorated by the habitual toasts. Tamara Dragadze's recent book on Georgian villages in the Caucasus[1] has splendid illustration of this spirit. A commune was once organized in a certain village, and it was explained to the villagers that this meant a unit of communal production and consumption. The villagers rapidly caught on to the idea of communal consumption; the Georgians are quite unbeatable at communal consumption. They practiced the principle with enthusiasm, and the commune had to be disbanded after a month, its resources having been dissipated.

A Georgian intellectual provided me with a potted socioeconomic history of Georgia. The country fell into the lap of the Russians at the beginning of the nineteenth century. Shortly before, the capital had been devastated by a Persian invasion, and the Georgians, for a long time caught between Shiite Persia and Sunnite Turkey, preferred their fellow Orthodox Russians. Within a small number of years, a Georgian prince commanded an army corps at Borodino against Napoleon. The memory of the princely family of the Bagrations continues to be honored, and there is no suggestion that this was some kind of reprehensible collaboration. But the Russian viceroy of Transcaucasia in Tbilisi set up a brilliant court, and the Georgian nobility and gentry, rather numerous, rapidly sank into debt in their eagerness to take part in this scintillating social life. As a result of this indebtedness, the finer houses in the old town of Tbilisi gradually passed into the hands of the Armenians. However, just as this process of the impoverishment of Georgian gentry and the enrichment of Armenians was about to be completed, a revolution was arranged, and now all those fine old houses are inhabited neither by Georgian aristocrats nor by Armenian merchants. Instead, they are occupied by the offices of the proliferating bureaucracy of the Soviet regime. So it has all come out even in the end.

In the small township in the recesses of the Caucasus, a Jewish community continues to flourish, even though depleted in its numbers by emigration to Israel. Once there were 800 families; now there are 350. Traveling between the two countries is not unduly difficult, and I have met a number of visiting Israeli Georgians, including Israeli-born children who nevertheless speak fluent Georgian; the community remains compact in Israel. The relationship between Jewish and Christian Georgians appears to be wholly relaxed and without tension, and the Georgians take pride in insisting on their own record of tolerance of minorities. As one Georgian told me, "We treated the Jews as equals, like everyone else. So much so that, in the nineteenth century, the Jews were serfs, just like the others—no discrimination at all. Now where else in Europe did you have Jewish serfs? Just tell me that." I met an Anglophone Georgian Jew who emigrated fifteen years ago, met his English wife in Israel, and now lives in Hertfordshire. This was his first return visit to his ancestral homeland, and his strongest impression was of the astonishing extent to which housing had improved during the intervening decade and a half. Georgian Jews, somewhat contradictorily, claim local residence since the *first* exile, but at the same time classify themselves as Sephardim. Georgians are eager to have an Israeli consulate in Tbilisi and to establish a regular flight to Lod. A delegation from the

274 *Ernest Gellner*

Georgian Academy of Sciences has been to Israel, and altogether, there is a tendency to think of the two countries as being natural allies, sharing the same predicament of very nearly being islands in a Muslim sea.

The Georgian self-image is that of tolerant hosts who welcome minorities, as long as these don't go as far as to claim the land as their own and do not aspire to detach it from Georgia. As a Georgian observed, "Now take the Ossetians. They are only here, on the southern, Georgian slopes of the Caucasus, because in the nineteenth century our nobles were short of manpower and invited Ossetians from the North, from beyond the Caucasus watershed, to work here as shepherds. But you know how it is—they bring their cousins, they settle down, and start thinking South Ossetia is their own, and want to detach it from Georgia, and join up with North Ossetia, though they have more cultural freedom with us than with the Russians." (North Ossetia is an autonomous region within the Russian Federal Republic.) Our bus had to cross stunningly beautiful South Ossetia on its way to the mountain township, and there was some nervousness because on occasion, vehicles with Tbilisi number plates had been stoned in Ossetia. The only thing the Ossetians did to us, however, was to sell us some corn on the cob. In Georgia proper, I received my corn on the cob for free from the stall, as soon as my foreign status was noticed.

But, tolerant and generous hosts or not, minorities continue to be the major problem facing Georgian nationalism. Georgia constitutes a geographic and a historic unity between the Caucasus and Anatolia. But within this unity, a very large proportion of the territory, something of the order of a third, is inhabited by a wide variety of minorities. The most tense, indeed murderous, relationship at present is with the Abkazians, only barely kept within bounds by the Red Army; but the number of potential conflicts is far larger.

Among the theoreticians in Moscow hoping to work out some kind of solution for the Soviet Union's acute ethnic problem, there is a kind of spectrum ranging from the centralists to the autonomists, so to speak. The centralists are not necessarily Russian chauvinists: they may simply be people giving priority to the rights of individuals over the right of cultures. Nationality should be a private matter, like religion; as one of them put it to me, "My nationality is my business." Take it out of the public sphere. Such men favor the exclusion of the often resented specification of nationality on personal documents. This entry actually operates as a kind of freezing of ancestral ethnicity, insofar as people have the option of only one of the two categories of their parents (if their parents are not of the same group), with the curious consequence that some people are classified as belonging to a group whose language they do not speak and with which they may not otherwise identify. (The fact that in Western documents, *nationality* generally means citizenship has led some Soviets to conclude that in Western terminology, *nationality* means only citizenship, which of course is not the case.) But such a practice would weaken the independence of the ethnic republics, especially in as far as upholders of this position also insist on the right of individuals to use the one dominant language when dealing with the bureaucracy. One consequence of the recent ethnic revival is that some bureaucratic documents, penned in languages unintelligible to their recipients, have begun to circulate.

In contrast with these centralists, whether or not motivated by a kind of human universalism, there are those who, though also motivated by generous liberal sentiments, would bestow autonomy on all local cultures, including rather small ones, and would permit or encourage them to develop local institutions, including separate schools. The interesting thing about the Georgians is that they feel a cordial dislike for *both* ends of this Moscow spectrum, and view their representatives with utmost distrust. One lot would weaken Georgia vis-à-vis the Russians, the other vis-à-vis the local minorities. Let the Russians go practice either universal brotherhood or cultural pluralism within the border of their own republic (they can do with both), but let them not meddle with our own special conditions here south of the Caucasus, they say.

ESTONIA

In Estonia, the atmosphere is altogether different—not that national sentiment is any less vigorous than it is in the Caucasus. In Tallinn, I bought a tourist memento—a mousetrap, not normally the kind of thing on sale in a shop dedicated to amber beads, ethnic jewelry, and so on. The mousetrap is painted in the Estonian national colors (those of the "bourgeois" interwar republic, naturally). In its iron grip, the mousetrap holds a wooden rat, painted red and further embellished with the crossed hammer and sickle. This provocative object was bought, not in some underground hotbed of nationalist irredentism, but in an official, government tourist gift shop set up by the legal authorities. The national "bourgeois" flag also flies proudly over the highest tower in both Tallinn and Tartu.

The sense of national identity and devotion to the national culture is as strong by the shores of the Baltic as it is in the Caucasus, but the mechanism by which it is sustained is different. In Georgia, a highly ritualized conviviality sustains a network of relationships which have survived both Stalinism and stagnation. A highly distinctive national culture is its idiom. The Estonians are not, like the Georgians, a "historic" nation with a national state and a dynasty to look back to. (On the Baltic, only the Lithuanians can claim such status.) Originally the Estonians did not even possess an ethnic name, but referred to themselves as those who live on the land, as distinct from the Teutonic or Swedish nobility and burghers. The lovely old town of Tallinn is built as if intended to illustrate the Marxist model of society: on the hill, there are not one, but two walled cities adjoining each other. The one on top housed the nobles, and lower on the slope, walled in against the upper town as well as the surrounding countryside, stood the burghers. Those who lived on the land, the Estonians, were outside. The plain outside the old walls is now covered, not by peasant holdings, but by a busy industrial city and port with a very strong Russian element in the population, and the nobles' dwellings, as in Tbilisi, house the bureaucracy.

The strong sense of national culture is carried not by formalized sustained drinking and eating, but in the standard approved manner in which the "new," "nonhistoric" nations of Eastern Europe attained consciousness. The National Theater in Tallinn is a shrine to the culture, and the ethnographic museum in Tartu (the Cambridge of Estonia) ensures, quite literally, that no part of the national culture will be forgotten. The museum proudly boasts no fewer than 100,000 objects—in other words, no fewer than one for every ten Estonians. The museum is sustained by a large network of conscientious ethnographic informants: this much-loved culture will remain well documented. Folklore and song festivals sustain both theater and museum.

If Georgians have panache, Estonians have virtue. They too are united in their nationalism: the national spirit has captured the Party.

There is a good Freudian drama to be written about the Estonian reassertion: the most fiery leader of the national movement is the daughter of the man who was crucial to establishing Soviet power in the first place. A man who claimed to me that he had always been an open nationalist, and hence was isolated in the old days of Party conformism, said that he now still feels isolated. The same people who more or less ostracized him previously were now still in command of the scene, but had inverted the meaning of the old slogan "The Party and nation are one." This had always been the official position, but it is now repeated with an ironic tinge: the national spirit has captured the Party.

The Estonians have a cool and rational strategy and, in so many words, hope to achieve their ends without loss of life. If that means some delay, it is worth it. In the new year, Estonia begins its economic autonomy, accompanied by marked internal liberalization. They, if anyone, can bring off the liberal *Wirtschaftswunder*. If they do, a kind of de facto independence should be within their grasp at least. (Even as things are, you need your documents to make purchases in the better-stocked Estonian shops: raids by shoppers from less fortunate parts of the Soviet Union are not allowed.)

The Baltics are both the allies of perestroika and one of its great dangers. They are in the vanguard of economic reorganization, and its greatest hope, for they may demonstrate its viability and provide a model. But their secessionism at the same time risks destabilizing the Soviet Union politically. When Peter the Great conquered the Baltic provinces, he conferred privileges on the barons to ensure their loyalty, and they served the tsars well. Gorbachev may need to confer analogous privileges on the reviving Baltic bourgeoisie. But he is also pushed into opposing secession. He may yet have cause to echo Lincoln, and justify thwarting the Baltic confederates by saying it is necessary to ensure that perestroika of the people, by the people, and for the people shall not perish from the earth.

There is a difference between the Baltic and the Caucasian attitude toward the Russians. Though Georgians may deny it in their present mood of bitterness over the events of April 9, 1989, the massacre in the main street of Tbilisi, there is an affinity between the Russian and the Georgian culture. Georgians are like Russians but more so. Many Georgian customs, and above all Georgian cuisine, have entered the Russian life-style. Georgians are proud of the fact that one of

Pushkin's hostesses was a Georgian lady established in St. Petersburg, that the Rostov family in Tolstoy is based on a Georgian family, and of the Caucasian involvements of Tolstoy and Lermontov. The two cultures are intertwined. In Estonia, on the other hand, Russian culture is an object of indifference rather than hostility. If the Georgians had the Bagrations at Borodino, the Estonians had at least two Baltic nobles there in command of army corps, but no one cares. (They weren't ethnic Estonians anyway.) It is hard to get students to take an interest in Russian literature, though the Russian literature department at Tartu, with Professor Lottman, must be the most distinguished in the world.

The Estonian ethnic and minorities problem is not, like that of the Georgians, a result of the persistence of an ancient ethnic patchwork. (The German minority, which in any case left at the time of the Ribbentrop-Molotov agreements, was too small, however dominant, to count in a modern society. Many of the few remaining Swedes left by an agreement made under Hitler, and very few of them are still there now.) The real problem arises from a massive industrial immigration during the Soviet period, and is almost entirely concentrated in Narva (where the Russians constitute a massive majority), in Tallinn (where they constitute something in the neighborhood of half the population), and in the industrial and mining northeast of the country (which in any case includes Narva). All these areas are located on the northeast coast of Estonia. Many of the recent ethnic squabbles arise from Estonian attempts to introduce laws limiting electoral participation by length of residence, laws whose effect, and aim, is to disfranchise as many Russians as possible. In opposing these devices, it is not difficult for the Russians to claim that they have a kind of justice on their side.

SUMMARY

In the course of the post-Napoleonic settlement at the beginning of the nineteenth century, Eastern and Southeastern Europe was divided among three great empires. Though each of them was in varying measure associated with a given language and ethnic group, not one of them could really be called a national state. Each of them was based on a faith: one on Sunni Islam, another on Counter-Reformation Catholicism, and the third on Orthodoxy. Not one of them was legitimated by ethnic homogeneity. All of them included complex patchworks of populations of diverse languages and religions, often distributed by social role rather than territory. The emergence of nationalism gradually produced a number of new states, autonomous and eventually independent, in the buffer zone between these empires. There were five or six of these by the time the post-Napoleonic settlement ended with World War I.

Each of these three empires was defeated by the end of that war and left on the scrap heap of history, notwithstanding the fact that they had been on different sides in that war. Two of them effectively abandoned the faith which had once helped establish them and sustain them as a viable and binding political principle. The moral vacuum so created was largely filled by the new political principle of nationality, which required each nation to have its state, and the boundaries of each state to coincide as much as possible with the limits of an ethnic culture, and to act as the protector of that culture. Given the complex patchwork of ethnic boundaries, compounded by the fact that ethnic groups often occupied niches in the social structure rather than compact territories, this principle, though passionately embraced, simply could not be fully implemented. The failure to apply it engendered much bitterness, as did attempts to apply it. From the end of the first world war to the period immediately following the end of the second, a series of very brutal methods helped ensure that the map of this part of the world came to correspond more closely to the requirements of the nationalist principle: in addition to the relatively benign method of assimilation (voluntary or otherwise), both forcible massive transplantations of population and genocide took place. Under cover of World War II, and during the period of retaliation following it, measures normally unthinkable and internationally unacceptable could be adopted, which dramatically adjusted the ethnic map so as to make it correspond better to the nationalist requirement of homogeneity. So the map now does correspond to it far more closely than before, though even now, less than completely. Where it fails to do so, ethnic conflict continues to fester.

This, in substance, is the political history of the territories of two of those three empires in the period between 1815 and 1948. But something quite different happened in the third empire. It recovered from its military defeat of 1917 and reemerged by 1920, under entirely new political and ideological management. It emerged with a new faith, which its leaders held with a passionate conviction, and which enabled that political unit to become, once again, an effective ideocracy rather than a nation-state. In consequence, this third part of the area did not follow the same line of development as the other two-thirds, which went from a faith-based to a nation-based polity. In large measure the region shared the social and economic development that normally leads to nationalism: a professional, mobile, atomized society. The spread of universal literacy, and a type of economy in which men live both their working and their private lives through their school-transmitted culture, depend on it and therefore identify with it passionately. But the new secular religion, and above all the Caesaro-papist regime it engendered, were strong enough to inhibit and suppress overt nationalism. In fact, the new political structure was more than Caesaro-papist: it not only combined the political and ideological hierarchies; it also fused them with the economic *apparat*. A single bureaucracy ran state, faith, *and* production: there simply was no sphere of social life left from which a countervailing civil society could emerge. Genuine ethnic associations were suppressed along with all the others.

After the period of its initial establishment, the system went through two stages: the terror of Stalinism and the period of stagnation. First terror, then squalor. The first period was a time of faith as well as fear: it was not merely that fear sustained the faith, but that faith also sustained the instruments of fear. During the second stage, however, during stagnation, the system was gradually discovered to be economically ineffective, not perhaps in comparison with the past, but certainly by the international standards of our time. This relative deprivation and weakness obliged it, by the mid-1980s, to seek to reform itself. The path of reform taken was that of internal liberalization—incomplete, vacillating, and unsure, but nonetheless substantial and significant. It involved the abandonment of the monopoly and centralization of political, ideological, and economic life. If we have had too little production and too much coercion, then if we diminish coercion, perhaps we shall have more production. This is the underlying intuition of perestroika. It doesn't strictly follow, but it seems well worth trying, especially since no one has been able to think of any alternative method.

In the course of this inner loosening, it was also discovered that all faith had quietly evaporated in the course of the stagnation. During the Khrushchevian transition from Stalinism to stagnation, faith was still there: but by the time stagnation was being repudiated by Gorbachev, it had gone.

What idea was left to guide the new direction? There was nothing but a mixture of pragmatism and a formal, halfhearted perpetuation of the old pieties. And what was to be the social base of the new pluralism? Only one really effective and quickly operative catalyst of new loyalties and associations was available: that very nationalism which had been suppressed during the period of secular messianic faith. The nationalism whose emergence has been made possible by perestroika also constitutes its greatest menace.

In the enormously varied and complex pattern of cohabitation of Soviet ethnic groups, the three I have sketched out impressionistically represent three very characteristic types (though they are not exhaustive). Byelorussia resembles certain areas outside the Soviet Union: Poland or the Western (Czech) part of Czechoslovakia. Genocide and expulsion or transplantion have ensured that the ethnic problem is now minimal. Here a fairly homogeneous unit does, closely enough, satisfy the imperatives of nationalism. The vogue of ethnic revival could of course go on forever, like a recurring decimal. If Byelorussians are distinct from Russians, then Byelorussians in turn have a distinct dialectal minority in the south of their country, the Polishchuks. Presumably there also exists a variant dialect within Polishchuk.

Georgia resembles the Soviet Union as a whole, as well as certain parts of Eastern Europe (Yugoslavia, Transylvania): it has not benefited sufficiently from Hitler's and Stalin's crimes. The Germans hardly crossed the Caucasus range, and as for Stalin, though he did indeed commit crimes in Transcaucasia, he did not commit them on a scale sufficient, or methodically enough, to achieve an ethnic *Gleichschaltung* in the region. Given the number of ethnic groups in the area, and the complex nature of their interrelationships, this would have taken some doing.

Estonia exemplifies another pattern still. The complexity it has inherited from the agrarian past is not such as to trouble its present tranquility. The once dominant German minority has in any case left. Had it stayed, it would not have been numerous enough to make an impact on contemporary conditions. The problem Estonia faces does not spring from the tendency of preindustrial society to multiply cultural boundaries so as to mark role and status and thus to produce differences which become national ones during industrialization; Estonian problems spring rather from labor migration under industrialism. The fairly recent in-migration of Russians to new industrial zones has left an intractable problem.

The overall consequence? The Russian third of Eastern Europe now has to face the same ethnic tensions and problems that the other two-thirds faced many decades earlier. It faces them in quite different and novel conditions, at a moment when the central power is trying to achieve a *Wirtschaftswunder* by means of an attempt, far from total, to revive and breathe life into the civil society which it previously destroyed. In the course of doing so, it has released the genie of nationalism. It is not clear whether it is possible to revive civil society *and* to keep nationalism within bounds, or whether the revival will really have the desired economic effects. A civil society recreated almost by decree within the interstices of industrial socialism may not resemble the old one which had emerged spontaneously within the cracks of a feudal order, and it may not have the appropriate economic ethos. The situation is complex, explosive, and, on this scale, quite unprecedented. One may try to specify the factors which contribute to it, but one can hardly predict its outcome.

ENDNOTE

[1]Tamara Dragadze, *Rural Families in Soviet Georgia* (London and New York: Routledge, 1988), 189.

October 1989

To the Stalin Mausoleum

Z

While the world is much preoccupied with Gorbachev, his successes and his prospects, fundamental questions about the capabilities of the Soviet political and economic system to achieve the structural reforms promised by* perestroika* are ignored. Z reports on what the expectations of* glasnost *and perestroika have been, why the accomplishments fall so far short of the much-heralded intentions. With respect to democratization, economic restructuring, and growth, and the complex and diverse nationality issues, the historical record of seventy years of Sovietism permits only great skepticism about the possible outcomes of perestroika; the internal contradictions of the system are simply too overwhelming.*

The most dangerous time for a bad government is when it starts to reform itself.
—Alexis de Tocqueville, anent
Turgot and Louis XVI

I

The Soviet socialist "experiment" has been the great utopian adventure of our century. For more than seventy years, to millions it has

---

Z is a sometime observer of the Soviet scene. The writing of this article was completed on December 12, 1989.

meant hope, and to other millions, horror; but for all it has spelled fascination. Nor does age seem to wither its infinite allure.

Never has this fascination been greater than since Mikhail Gorbachev launched *perestroika* in the spring of 1985: a derivative painting in the Paris manner of 1905, a Beatles' vintage rock concert, or a *Moscow News* article revealing some dark episode from the Soviet past known to the planet for decades could send tremors of expectations through the West if it were datelined Moscow. So conservative-to-centrist Ronald Reagan, Margaret Thatcher and Hans-Dietrich Genscher have vied with the liberal-to-radical mainstream of Anglo-American Sovietology in eulogizing Gorbachev's "modernity." Even though after seventy years, the road to the putative "radiant future" of mankind no longer leads through Moscow, the road to world peace still does. And who is against world peace?

But this is not the whole explanation: Moscow is still the focus of a now septuagenarian ideological fixation. On the Right there is the hope that communism may yet repent of its evil totalitarian ways and evolve into a market democracy of sorts (into the bargain putting down the Western Left). On the Left there is the wish that the "experiment" not turn out to be a total loss (if only so as not to comfort the Western Right) and yet acquire something approximating a human face. So on all sides alleged connoisseurs of the *res sovietica* are anxiously asked: Are you optimistic or pessimistic about the chances for perestroika? Can Gorbachev succeed? Will he survive? Should we help him?

These questions, however, presuppose answers with diverse ideological intonations. To what is no doubt a majority in Western opinion, Gorbachev's reforms mean that Stalinism and the Cold War are over and that democracy is at hand in the East, bringing with it the end of global conflict for all. For a smaller but vocal group, the Cold War is indeed over and the West has won, a victory that presages the global triumph of capitalism, the end of communism, indeed even the "end of history."[1] A third group, once large but now a dwindling phalanx, holds that communism remains communism for all Gorbachev's glitter, and that *glasnost* is simply a ploy to dupe the West into financing perestroika until Moscow recovers the strength to resume its inveterate expansionism.[2]

Yet the two dominant Western perspectives on Gorbachev have one element in common: the implication that our troubles with the

East are over, that we are home free, at the "end of the division of Europe" and on the eve of the Soviet Union's "reintegration into the international order," a prospect first advanced by Gorbachev but eventually taken up by a hesitant President Bush. So in an odd way the perestroika pietism of the Gorbophiles and the free-market triumphalism of the Gorbophobes converge in anticipation of a happy dénouement of a half-century of postwar polarization of the world.

And, indeed, in this avalanche year of 1989 we are surely coming to the end of a historical epoch. It is hardly so clear, however, that we are entering a simpler, serener age: decaying superpowers do not go quietly into the night. It is not even clear that we are asking the right questions at all about Gorbachev. Certainly Western Sovietology, so assiduously fostered over the past four decades, has done nothing to prepare us for the surprises of the past four years.

Nor is the predominant Western question about Gorbachev's chances for success the most pertinent one, or at least the first we should ask. The real question is: Why is it that seventy years after 1917—which was to have been the ultimate revolution, the revolution to end all further need of revolutions—Gorbachev proclaims *urbi et orbi* that Soviet socialism urgently requires a "new revolution," a "rebuilding" of its fundamental fabric? What is so drastically wrong as to require such drastic action? And what, after four and a half years of increasingly frenetic activity, has in fact been accomplished?

The most natural way to approach this question is to focus on personalities and policies: on Gorbachev and his "conservative" opponents; on "perestroika," "glasnost," and "democratization." And it is this preoccupation which explains the cult of his personality in the West. But if fundamental revolution is now really on the Soviet agenda, then our focus of inquiry ought to be the *longue durée* of deep structures and abiding institutions. And these, as Gorbachev constantly reminds us, were created "sixty years ago," a euphemism for Stalin's "Year of the Great Break," 1929. For this was the beginning of the forced collectivization of agriculture through "de-kulakization," together with "full steam ahead" in industry for a "First Five-Year Plan in four years," policies that created the Soviet system as it exists in its main outlines to the present day. In short, Gorbachev is calling into question the very basis of the Soviet order and the historical matrix of what until now was called "developed" or "real" socialism. Perestroika is thus not just a reform of a basically sound structure, but the manifestation of a systemic crisis of Sovietism per se.

II

It is precisely because during the past twenty-odd years mainline Western Sovietology has concentrated on the sources of Soviet "stability" as a "mature industrial society" with a potential for "pluralist development" that it has prepared us so poorly for the present crisis, not only in the Soviet Union but in communist systems everywhere.[3] Instead of taking the Soviet leadership at its ideological word—that their task was to "build socialism"—Western Sovietology has by and large foisted on Soviet reality social science categories derived from Western realities, with the result that the extraordinary, indeed surreal, Soviet experience has been rendered banal to the point of triviality.

Much of this was done in the name of refuting the alleged simplifications of the post–World War II "totalitarian model," itself deemed to be the product of the ideological passions of the Cold War. Thus, beginning in the mid-1960s successive waves of revisionists have sought to replace the totalitarian model's emphasis on ideology and politics with an emphasis on society and economics, to move from "regime studies" to "social studies," and to displace "history from above" with "history from below."[4] This reversal of the totalitarian model's priorities of explanation has yielded a Soviet Union where the political "superstructure" of the regime derives logically from its "social base" in the proletariat and a peasantry being transformed into urban workers, with a new intelligentsia emerging from both classes. This inversion of the actual roles of state and society obviously gives the Soviet world a normal, almost prosaically Western, character and a democratic cast as well.

At the cost of some simplification, it is possible to say that this social science approach (with a fair admixture of Marxism) has produced a consensus that the Soviet historical trajectory leads "from utopia to development."[5] In this perspective the key to Soviet history is presented as "modernization" through "urbanization" and "universal education"—a process carried out in brutal and costly form, to be sure, especially under Stalin, but the end result of which was the same as in the West. Often this social science reductionism holds that the Stalinist excesses perpetrated during an essentially creative Soviet industrial transformation represented only a passing phase, an "aberration," which under Brezhnev gave way to "normalcy" and "institutional pluralism" expressed through such "interest groups" as the army, industrial managers, or the Academy of Sciences.[6] Indeed, Stalinism itself has been viewed by the more thoroughgoing revisionists not as an aberration at all, but as an essentially democratic phenomenon, stemming from a "cultural revolution" from below, within the Party and the working class, and resulting in a massive "upward mobility" that produced "the Brezhnev generation." In this view the whole revolutionary process may be summed up as "terror, progress, and social mobility," with the modest overall cost in purge victims falling in the "low hundreds of thousands."[7]

A corollary to this revisionist picture is that Gorbachev's "restructuring" will be the crowning of the edifice of Soviet modernity. Thus, all that is required to humanize the Soviet Union is a measure of "reform" in the ordinary sense of reorganization: that is, a "calibrated" decentralization and a gradual debureaucratization of administrative structures, or more specifically, a reduction of the role of the central plan and the *nomenklatura*, or those administrative and managerial posts reserved for appointment by Party committees.

Such, indeed, was the expectation behind Gorbachev's early policies, as in the new Party program (now forgotten) voted at the Seventeenth Party Congress in February 1986 and expressed in his book *Perestroika and New Thinking* in the fall of the next year. This was still the expectation two years later of the main line of American Sovietology; indeed, this Sovietology to a degree reflected Soviet thinking in the Moscow social science institutes of the Academy of Sciences.[8] But the border nationalities crisis of 1988 and the union-wide economic crisis of 1989 have made these anticipations, though hardly four years old, already superannuated. As for the blatant fantasies—to use a charitable term—about democratic Stalinism, they are clearly destined for that same trashcan of history to which Trotsky once consigned the Provisional Government of 1917.

As the crisis year 1989 draws to a close, it is—or ought to be—patent that both the Soviet regime and its Western analysts are in for an agonizing reappraisal of long-standing assumptions about

Soviet "stability." More precisely, the time has come to take a fresh look at the starting point of Western Sovietological analysis: namely, the two bases of the totalitarian model, ideology and politics, and at the ways in which these factors have modeled the institutions and the mentalities created by seventy years of "utopia in power."[9] For if the fact of glasnost demonstrates the Soviet capacity to return to human "normalcy," the revelations of glasnost prove incontrovertibly that for the past seven decades Russia has been anything but just another modernizing country. As we now know, both from Gorbachev's economists and from televised shots of empty shelves in Moscow stores, the Soviet Union, though clearly a failed utopia, is neither a developed nor a modern nation. It is rather something *sui generis*, a phenomenon qualitatively different from all other forms of despotism in this or previous centuries.

It is for this reason that the term *totalitarian*, coined by Mussolini with a positive connotation to designate his new order and first applied in a negative sense to Stalin's Russia by Trotsky, was taken up by Hannah Arendt to produce a general theory of perverse modernity. And she did so because the blander term *authoritarian*, serviceable, say, for a Salazar or a Chiang Kai-shek, simply would not do for the gruesome grandeur of Stalin, Hitler, or Mao. Contrary to current opinion, Jeane Kirkpatrick did not invent but simply continued this distinction, though she added the corollary that totalitarian regimes are far more permanent than authoritarian regimes, a proposition with which the struggling intellectuals of Eastern Europe thoroughly agree, since as yet no country, not even Poland or Hungary, has successfully completed its exit from communism.

The Sovietological revisionists of the West, however, find Kirkpatrick's distinction scandalous, in part because of the conflation it effects between communism and fascism (though the Soviet novelist Vasili Grossman does exactly this in his enormously popular *Fate and Life*) and in part because Stalin must be presented as an aberration from the Leninist main line of Sovietism, for if he is integral to the system, then the prospects for its democratic transformation are dim indeed. But this sanitization of the Soviet regime into mere authoritarianism, at least for the period after Stalin, is achieved only at the cost of a fundamental conceptual confusion, if not an outright caricature of the totalitarian concept. Totalitarianism does not mean that such regimes in fact exercise total control over the population; it means rather that such control is their aspiration. It does not mean they are omnipotent in performance, but instead that they are institutionally omnicompetent. It is not Soviet society that is totalitarian, but the Soviet state.

This conceptual confusion results from taking as the defining criterion of a regime the degree or quantity of repression, not its nature or quality. Thus, since Khrushchev shrank the dimensions of the Gulag and Brezhnev killed or imprisoned far fewer people than did Stalin, the Soviet regime is deemed to have evolved from totalitarianism to authoritarianism (or as some would put it, "post-totalitarianism"), say on the model of Greece under the colonels or of Pinochet's Chile. But this view neglects the central fact that the structures of the Party-state, with its central plan, its police, and its nomenklatura, have remained the same—as Gorbachev's more liberal supporters, such as Sakharov, have constantly complained. Consequently, the milder face of Sovietism after Stalin—and the quantitative change is quite real for those who live under it—simply offers us, in Adam Michnik's phrase, "totalitarianism with its teeth knocked out."[10]

Paradoxically, just as the "T word" was being expunged from Western Sovietology around 1970, it became current in Eastern Europe: Hannah Arendt was translated in *samizdat*, and Soviet intellectuals now routinely refer to the whole system, including its Leninist phase, as totalitarian, and to the Brezhnev period as classical or stable Stalinism.[11] Even more paradoxically, it is when communist totalitarianism began to unravel under Gorbachev that the inner logic of the system became most transparently clear to those who have to live under it.[12] To resort, à la Marx, to a quotation from Hegel: in matters of historical understanding "the owl of Minerva takes flight only as the shades of night are falling." It is this twilight, Eastern view of the evolution of the Soviet experiment from 1917 to Gorbachev that will be adopted here, in an effort to present a historicized update of the original, and in truth too static, totalitarian interpretation.

III

It is impossible to understand anything about Gorbachev and perestroika without taking seriously the origins of the Soviet system in a utopia. The utopia, of course, was never realized, but this is not the point. For applied utopias do not simply fail and fade away; the effort to realize them leads rather, through a perverse cunning of reason, to the creation of a monstrous antireality, or an inverted world. So the great Soviet adventure turned out to be, in the words of an early Polish observer, a grim "mistake of Columbus." This unforeseen landfall led to the creation of a new politics, a new economics, and a new Soviet man, which are at the root of the present crisis of perestroika.

The utopia in which the Soviet system originated is integral revolutionary socialism. This is not to be confused with simple egalitarianism, although this is obviously involved under so protean a label as "socialism." Nor is it to be confused with mere social democracy (a term for which both Marx and Lenin had a distinct aversion), for this is clearly compatible with a mixed economy and constitutional government. Rather, integral revolutionary socialism in the Marxist tradition means full noncapitalism. As the *Manifesto* puts it, "The theory of the Communists may be summed up in the single phrase: Abolition of private property." From this it follows that the product of private property—profit—and the means for realizing this profit—the market—must also be abolished. For property, profit, and the market dehumanize man and fetishize the fruits of his labor by transforming both into reified commodities. It was to end this scandal that the most deprived and dehumanized class, the proletariat, received the world-historical mission of bringing about the socialist revolution, whereby mankind would at last be led out of "prehistory" into genuine human existence in the oneness and unity of a classless society. And all of this is supposed to come about through the inexorable logic of history, operating through the self-enriching alienation of the class struggle. This set of beliefs—the core tenets of Marxism—has been characterized by Leszek Kołakowski as "the greatest fantasy of our century."[13]

But the logic of history does not work this way (if indeed it exists at all); and although private property and the market can be abolished, their demise will not come about automatically. Therefore, the hand of history must be forced by the creation of a special instrument, "a party of a new type," with which Lenin declared he "would overturn all Russia." Thus, utopia can be achieved only by an act of political will exercised through revolutionary coercion, in short by quasi-military means. Utopians of this ruthless temper, however, can get a chance at power only in extreme crisis, amid the collapse of all structures capable of resisting them. Such an exceptional state of affairs came about in Russia in 1917, when under the impact of modern war, the old order unraveled with stunning rapidity to the point where Lenin's Bolsheviks simply "found power lying in the streets and picked it up." True, they enjoyed a significant measure of worker support at the time and their ranks were largely filled with former workers. But this does not mean that what they themselves called, until well into the 1920s, the October overturn (*perevorot*) was any the less a minority coup d'état staged against a background of generalized, particularly peasant, anarchy, and not a "proletarian revolution" in any meaningful sense of that term.[14]

The Bolsheviks then had to confront their utopia with reality in the form of economic collapse and civil war. Under the combined pressure of the military emergency and the logic of their ideology, between 1918 and 1920 they produced the world's first version of noncapitalism, "War Communism." Nor at the time was this viewed as an emergency expedient. For Lenin, socialism would emerge out of the fullness of capitalism; the "imperialist war" was the highest phase of capitalism; General Ludendorff's militarization of the German economy during the struggle was therefore the supreme form of capitalism and by the same token, the matrix of the new socialist order. So nationalizing the entire urban economy under the Supreme Economic Council (the ancestor of the present Soviet industrial ministries and of "Gosplan"), the Bolsheviks amplified Ludendorff's practices in Russia and abolished profit and the market. To this was added the "advanced" American method of Taylorism for the rational organization of work and an ambitious program for building power stations under the conviction that "socialism equals Soviet power plus electrification." At the same time, the Bolsheviks experimented with rural collectives, or *Sovkhozes*, and thereby adumbrated the extension of their statist model to the countryside and the entire population; and in the meantime they simply pillaged alleged "petty bourgeois kulaks" for grain under the policy of "class warfare" in the villages. In fact, during War Communism the Bolsheviks created the first rough draft of what later would be called a planned, or more accurately a command, economy.[15]

Simultaneously, Trotsky hit upon another essential component of the new system, the political commissar. The vocation of the Party is political and ideological, not technical and professional in any of the activities necessary for the functioning of society. Since the Party was at war, the most important professional expertise at the time was military, expertise the Bolsheviks lacked, while most trained officers in the country were former members of the Imperial Army and hence unreliable. So the new people's commissar for war simply conscripted the officers he needed and flanked them with trustworthy Party monitors, such as Stalin, Kirov, Voroshilov, and Orjonikidze, all future leaders of the 1930s. In this way a dual system of administration was created in the army, but one that could easily be adapted to economic and other civilian tasks, where Party figures would supervise industrial managers, collective farm chairmen, educators, scientists, writers—indeed, everybody and everything. This is the earliest origin of the *apparat* and its nomenklatura right of appointment to all functional posts of importance in society. Dual administration thus adumbrates the end of "civil society," by which Central Europeans and Soviets mean social groups capable of self-organization independent of the state. This mode of control is the essence of the Party-state, a system wherein the functional, governmental, or "soviet," bureaucracy is monitored from behind the scenes by a parallel and unaccountable Party administration that has the real power of decision.

The period of War Communism produced a second monitoring apparatus as well, this time for "enemies" of the whole system—the Cheka, or political police. Conceived by Lenin as early as November 1917 to wage class war against those who were certain to resist the Bolsheviks' unilateral seizure of power, the Cheka was originally directed against "feudal" or "bourgeois" parties, but was soon turned against erring, "petty bourgeois" socialist parties as well as recalcitrant workers and peasants who supported them. But there was no structural reason in the system to prevent the Cheka's eventual use against enemies within Bolshevik ranks themselves. For as the Civil War raged on, it became increasingly apparent that the Party and its leadership represented (to use Kołakowski's language again) not the "empirical proletariat," but a "metaphysical proletariat" that had the world-historical mission of leading mankind to socialism. Thus, whenever workers or peasants rejected the Party's power, as in the Kronstadt revolt of 1921, they were automatically revealed as "petty bourgeois" and disposed of *manu militari*.

And so by 1921 all the essential institutions of Sovietism had either been created or sketched in: the Party-state with its monopoly of power, or "leading role," as it is now called; the dual administration of soviet and apparat, both backed by the Cheka; the central plan and the agricultural collective; and a propaganda monopoly in the service of the dictatorship of the proletariat, with its single "correct" ideology and the cult of technological Prometheanism. It is difficult to believe that a system of such internal coherence and logic should be the passing product of military emergency, although this is now the dominant view in Western Sovietology. In any event, it is this model that, in fact, was to become the main line of Soviet development, from Stalin to the eve of perestroika. And this, as the Soviets used to say in their earlier, more ideological days, is surely "no accident."

But War Communism would become the Soviet norm only after what turned out to be the temporary retreat to the mixed economy of the New Economic Policy (NEP) in the 1920s. For War Communism, though it permitted the Bolshevik victory over the Whites, also produced one of the worst social and economic collapses of the twentieth century. In the course of the Civil War, some 15 million to 19 million people perished from war, terror, famine, and epidemic— or more than in all of World War I. By 1921 industrial production had virtually halted, money had disappeared, and organized exchange had given way to barter. To be sure, a part of this primitivization was due to six years of war; but it was due in even greater part to the ideological extravagance and incompetence of Bolshevik policy, which continued with fanatical grimness for months after the war had been won.[16]

IV

The limited return to the market under the NEP was a success in reviving the country, but not in leading it to socialism. This contradictory circumstance has given rise to endless speculation and controversy about the true nature of the system in the past, and thus about the proper tasks of perestroika in the present. The central questions are these: Is the "hard" communism of War Communism and Stalin the norm or a deviation in Soviet history? Or is the "soft" communism of the NEP this norm and therefore the model for perestroika—a perspective in which Stalinism, together with its

Brezhnevite prolongation, becomes the deviation from which perestroika is the hoped-for recovery? Finally, which of these two
communisms, the hard or the soft, is the legitimate heir of Lenin and
October? Or to put the whole debate in one classic question, Was
Stalin necessary?[17]

In strictly temporal terms there is no doubt about the answer to
these questions: three years of War Communism, twenty-five of
Stalin, and eighteen of Brezhnev clearly add up to the empirical norm
of Soviet history, and it is the eight years of the NEP (together with
bits and pieces of the Khrushchev period) that are the "aberration,"
or, if one prefers, the metaphysical norm of "real" Leninism; and this
overwhelming preponderance of hard communism must have something to do with the logic, if not of history, then at least of the Soviet
system. Yet these questions are not really about chronology; they are
about essences, and through these about present attitudes and
policies toward Soviet reformability.

The case for the NEP as essential Sovietism rests on the fact that
Lenin inaugurated it and did so with the admission that War
Communism had been an error, or at least a premature attempt at
attaining socialism. In his dying months, moreover, he gave his
blessings to "cooperatives" (a concept he did not flesh out) as the
means for arriving at socialism. Nikolai Bukharin then developed
these hints into something of a system in the mid-1920s and thereby
became the true heir of Lenin. Stalin (attacked by name, moreover, in
the founder's "Testament") thus rose to power only as an intriguer
and a usurper.

In this view the true Leninist-Bukharinist course, which enjoyed
majority support in the Party by mid-decade, drew from the horrors
and errors of War Communism the lesson that the regime's first
priority should be to preserve the "revolutionary alliance of workers
and peasants" allegedly forged in October. To this end, the Party was
to conciliate the 80 percent of the population that was peasant by
orienting the "commanding heights" of state industry to meet rural
consumer needs and thereby to accumulate through the market the
capital for the industrial development necessary to achieve mature
socialism. In this way the socialist sector, since by definition it would
be the more efficient, would outcompete the private, peasant sector;
the rural cooperatives would be gradually transformed into genuine

collective farms; and the whole nation would thus "grow into socialism," in the sense of the full transcendence of capitalism.[18]

There are numerous objections to this view over and above the puerile fetishization of Lenin involved and the bizarre notion that the supreme achievement of October Revolution was the discovery, in 1921, of the virtues of cooperatives and the market. The first major objection is that never during the NEP and Bukharin's brief ascendancy did the Party play the economic game according to market rules: it constantly resorted to "administrative" means to manipulate both supply and demand since it feared the peasants' power over the economy, and hence the state, through their purchasing power, or more simply their freedom to grant or withhold the supply of grain. The second major objection is that the empirical evidence about the resistance of the peasants to the forced requisition of grain during War Communism, and their refusal even to market it under the NEP, especially after 1927, whenever the price ratio was unfavorable, indicates their inveterate distrust of Bolshevik arbitrariness. Never under a Bolshevik monopoly of power would they have entered collective farms voluntarily. Given these circumstances, a collision between the Party and the peasants was at some point inevitable, and the NEP was inherently unstable. Ultimately, either the Party would have to give up on integral socialism and share economic, and eventually political, power with the peasants through the market—in short, opt for mere social democracy—or it would have to crush peasant independence, and along with it the market, and march toward full socialism by coercive, "administrative" methods.

By the end of the 1920s it became imperative for the country to embark on a program of intensive industrialization and heavy capital investment, if only to replace an obsolete plant that had not been renewed since 1913. This imperative was translated into a plan and given an ideological aura as the "building of socialism." Bukharin advocated that this transition be financed in cooperation with the peasantry and through the mechanisms of the market. Still, it was necessary to raise industrial prices after 1927 in order to get the plan started at all. The response of the distrustful peasantry was immediate: a "production strike," as the regime called it, and thus also a "procurement crisis," which forced rationing on the cities at the moment the plan was launched.

The choice before the Party was clear: either follow Bukharin's policy and capitulate to the peasants, a course leading eventually to the abandonment of the Party's monopoly of power, or revert to the military methods of War Communism, but in institutional, permanent form as collective farms, or *kolkhozes.* Stalin, as General Secretary, chose the latter course as the only one compatible with maintaining the Party's monopoly of power. And in this he was thoroughly Leninist.[19]

The monopoly of power, and not any one economic program, whether hard or soft, had been the cardinal Leninist principle since 1917, indeed since *What Is To Be Done?* was written in 1902. This was the reason Lenin carried out the October coup rather than wait for elections to the Constituent Assembly, which he knew he could not win. The decision to coerce the peasantry had good Leninist precedent also: when their "production strike" of 1918 threatened the new regime with starvation, Lenin resorted to "class warfare in the villages" and then to *prodrzvyorstka,* or grain requisition. True, he later came to reconsider this decision; but he never reconsidered the Party's irrefragable right, conferred by the logic of history, to a monopoly of power.

And Stalin's decision was good Trotskyism, too. "Full speed ahead" for industrialization has always been the Left's program, as was making the peasant pay for it through a "primitive socialist accumulation of capital" carried out on their backs. To be sure, the Trotskyite Left had always paid lip service to the notion that collectivization would have to be voluntary. But this position did not derive from consulting with the peasants while theorizing on the matter; and when Stalin encountered peasant resistance, the Trotskyites supported him in the use of coercion, as indeed their whole previous record indicated they would do, for the sake of the Party and of socialism. Stalin's decision even turned out to be compatible with basic Bukharinism, for when the chips were down in 1929 Bukharin went along with the new "General Line" and served the leader devotedly for seven more years. He even penned what was considered to be the crowning achievement of "built socialism," the Stalin Constitution of 1936, proudly exhibiting the historic pen to an emigré friend in Paris the same year during his last days of freedom; for to him, as to all the others, *partinost,* or Party spirit, meant more than any economic program or policy toward the peasants.

So to answer the famous question "Was Stalin necessary?" it must be reframed in terms of a second question: Necessary for what? If one means necessary for Russia's industrialization, then the answer must be no. In strictly economic terms Bukharin's program would no doubt have done as well, if not better, at modernizing Russia, and at far less cost, both human and material—a proposition that may be advanced with a high degree of certainty by analogy with the state-guided development of Finance Minister Witte in Russia during the 1890s, or of Meiji Japan, or of post–World War II South Korea. But if one means necessary to achieve industrialization in a form compatible with preserving the Party's monopoly of power, then the answer must be yes. Only the coercive Stalinist method of institutionalized War Communism could break the ever-present peasant threat to this monopoly by extending Party control from the cities, where Lenin had left it, to the countryside and the entire population. The real choice in 1929 was to do approximately what Stalin did or to give up on utopia and the Party monopoly of power.

So the Great Break of 1929 resulted from a political, not an economic, decision, and one which for the first time established the iron primacy of politics over economics in all aspects of Soviet life. Thereby the Party became genuinely totalitarian in its policies, if not always in its performance. Private property, profit, and the market had been suppressed, or driven underground and branded as "speculation" and "corruption." "The leading role of the Party" was established in all types of social activity, a status written into law in the Constitution of 1936; this leading role was the Party's very *raison d'être*, the concrete realization of utopia in actual history.

That the man Stalin presided over this realization no doubt made it more brutal, costly, and ultimately paranoid than it otherwise might have been. But too much can be made of his warped personality and lust for power in accounting for the extraordinary events of the 1930s. Stalin's power stemmed not from the drives of his psyche, but from a set of institutions: the monopolistic, monolithic Party operating on the principle of "democratic centralization," or command from the top down, and on the myth of the historical inevitability of socialism. The Party, as an institution, cried out for personification in a Leader. Trotsky or some other ruthless Civil War commissar could well have filled Stalin's role and done the job of building socialism in his place. And this attempt had to be made at some point because the myth that socialism could be built was the *raison d'être* of the Party's leading role, the justification of its monopoly of power. But since the myth is only that, any leader acting on it would be compelled to a massive use of force and violence. Thus, in the Leninist world we have not only the Stalin-sized Mao, but a whole series of pocket Stalins, such as Ceauşescu, Kim Il Sung, and Castro. It is difficult to blame all of this on Joseph Djugashvili's psyche.

V

The building of socialism was conducted like a military operation and was carried out on two main "fronts," to use the language of the time. The first was the agricultural front. Between 1929 and 1935 some 85 percent of Russian peasant households were herded into collective farms, or kolkhozes, and transformed into state serfs, obliged to turn over to the regime a fixed quantity of produce without regard for what the annual harvest left to the producers. Peasant resistance was such that millions of so-called kulaks and their families were deported to Siberia; and in 1932 the state induced a "terror famine" to destroy peasant independence once and for all. Altogether, some 6 million to 11 million people perished in the course of collectivization, and as glasnost proceeds the higher figure seems increasingly to be the more probable.[20] At the same time, some 30 million peasants were forced to migrate to the new industrial cities then being created under the plan—the largest and most rapid rush, or more accurately push, to urbanization in world history.

Economically the result for those who remained in the countryside was the greatest man-made disaster of the twentieth century. The rural standard of living sank far below that of 1929, indeed below that of 1913, and has never reached those levels since. Russia, which before 1914 had been a grain-exporting country, has for the past decade been obliged to import food (whereas both India and China now export it). The Russian peasantry became, and has remained, a demoralized, listless, and often alcoholic work force, suspicious of state power and unwilling to take any initiative on its own. Moreover, the cost of this operation in human lives, in slaughtered livestock, and in material loss has been exorbitant beyond calculation.

What, then, was the rationale behind the whole enterprise? Initially the Party genuinely expected that large-scale, mechanized, and collective agriculture would be more productive than small, family, or "capitalist" farming. When this proved not to be the case, the Party settled for the political advantage of state control over the peasantry: with collectivization, the last fortress of Soviet civil society was destroyed. At the same time, economically the regime was guaranteed a food supply independent of the caprices of the market, a supply for which the regime therefore did not have to pay. With this assured, they could then advance on the second, and more important, front—the Promethean development of heavy industry. Thus, the net advantage of collectivization for the regime was, as in all things, political and not economic.

On the industrial front operations were conducted with the voluntaristic conviction that "there are no fortresses that Bolsheviks cannot storm." And here the results were genuinely spectacular, at least up to a point. In such grandiose projects as the steel manufacturing city of Magnitogorsk (erected for the man of steel himself), the Dnieprostroi dam and electrification project, the Turksib railroad, and the Moscow metro, the Soviet Union gave itself the basis for a modern industrial economy that was also autarkic, depending on international capitalism for nothing but the prototypes, blueprints, and imported specialists necessary to get things started. And growth rates for the 1930s overall were quite good, but nowhere nearly so good as has long been assumed. At the time, the Soviet government gave out the figures of some 20 percent, while Western specialists generally accepted a figure of from 12 to 14 percent and these figures have been repeated in countless textbooks and journalistic accounts ever since. But later calculations by Western economists, recently confirmed by the revelations of glasnost, yield a much more modest 4 to 6 percent. And a comparable lowering of growth rates from some 15 to around 5 percent is now generally accepted for the first postwar decade. Witte in the 1890s, with far milder market methods, did much better at 8 percent, as did Meiji Japan at 6 percent, not to mention postwar Japan at 16 to 18 percent—or even Deng Xiaoping's China at 10 to 12 percent.[21]

Moreover, Stalinist growth was extremely one-sided: all that grew was heavy industry to produce capital goods, to produce more capital goods, to produce more heavy industry, to produce, after 1937,

equipment for the military. The primary sector, agriculture, as we
have seen, was blasted and blighted; and the tertiary, or service,
sector was barely developed, as was that part of the secondary, or
industrial, sector devoted to consumer goods. So Soviet modernization meant essentially a hypertrophied secondary sector producing
neither for an internal market nor for export, but for itself and for the
all-encompassing state, with just enough in the way of consumer
goods and services to keep the population alive.

Even when, under Khrushchev, the Soviet Union became the
world's "second largest economy," just behind the United States,
indeed outstripping it in output of the sinews of modern industry—steel—this number two status was true only in quantitative, not
qualitative, terms. Almost all Soviet products were imitative, archaic,
crude, or outright defective. Almost nothing the Soviet Union produced, outside of military hardware, was competitive on the international market; and it could sell its products on the internal market
only because it had a monopoly that excluded more efficient foreign
competition. Even in its most successful decades, therefore, under
Stalin and in the early years of Khrushchev, the Soviet Union was
never a great industrial power, and still less a "modern" society. The
belief that it was such a power is among the great illusions of the
century, shared until recently not just by the editorialists of our major
newspapers, but by economists of the prominence of John Kenneth
Galbraith, and even Wassily Leontiev.[22] In reality, however, the
Soviet Union in its prime was never more than a great military-
industrial complex and a Party-state superpower.

VI

In still another domain Sovietism at its height represents a deviant
form of modernity: the indispensable underpinning of its power by
terror. A minuscule underground organization before 1917, the Party
inevitably developed a conspiratorial mentality, and after it seized
power as a minority of some 115,000 in a largely hostile country of
170 million, surrounded moreover by a hostile world, it added to this
a state-of-siege mentality. Barely 600,000 at the end of the Civil War,
and hardly more than a million at the time of the Great Break, it is
this small and ever-beleaguered army that carried out the titanic
"revolution from above" of the 1930s. And the enormous risks of

this task enhanced the Party's sense of the precariousness of its power. Indeed, by 1932, at the worst of the collectivization drive and before the new industrial plant had begun to function, it looked as though the whole enterprise might well collapse. The sole reassurance, therefore, was a return to the terror of the Civil War period; so the political police shifted its efforts to combating "crypto-Menshevik" and "bourgeois specialist wreckers."

Matters did not stop there, however, because of another imperative of Sovietism. It is in the logic of a system where everything is nationalized, with a single, omnicompetent bureaucracy accountable to no one but itself, to secrete permanently the phenomenon of apparat ossification. The problem first appeared when the Civil War was won and the dying Lenin, misdiagnosing it as a tsarist holdover, sought a cure in the inefficacious, indeed utterly self-defeating, solution of creating parallel monitoring bureaucracies: the Workers and Peasants Inspectorate for the soviet, or state, administration and the Central Control Commission for the Party. Then Stalin, in response to the extraordinary social tensions generated by the building of socialism, developed this control mechanism on a scale commensurate with the rest of his enterprise. Beginning in the early 1930s he used periodic administrative purges of Party membership rosters to remove the incompetent or those lukewarm toward the General Line. After the great crisis of 1932–1933 had finally passed, however, he decided on a complete renewal of Party-state personnel in order to give himself the human base of the socialism he had built. And this led to the Great Terror of 1936–1938.

It would be too much to say that this was a rational political undertaking in the usual sense of that term. It did, nonetheless, have its rationale in the nature of the system and the circumstances of the day. And this rationale lay in the transition from utopia *in potentia* to its realization *in actu*. Until the mid-1930s, socialism existed only in the "radiant future," and belief in its supreme beneficence was thus easy. But after the Party's "Congress of the Victors" in 1934 socialism had been declared built, and it turned out to be nothing more than a system of inefficient state-driven industrial expansion as an end in itself, achieved, moreover, at appalling cost. In short, the instrumental program of integral socialism had been carried out, but the expected moral results had not followed; quite to the contrary, a moral disaster of unprecedented proportions had ensued, and this fact had somehow to be negated and denied. As Pasternak put the matter in *Doctor Zhivago*, "Collectivization was an erroneous and unsuccessful measure and it was impossible to admit the error. To conceal the failure people had to be cured, by every means of terrorism, of the habit of thinking and judging for themselves, and forced to see what didn't exist, to assert the very opposite of what their eyes told them."[23] So the great bloodletting of collectivization led "naturally" to the bloodletting of the Great Purges.

But there were other, more political reasons for this connection as well. Stalin and the Party leadership were clearly responsible for the perverse outcome and the costs of the First Five-Year Plan; hence, doubts about the new system, and with them opposition to its author, were only to be expected. Stalin, therefore, decided to make a preemptive strike against all the forces that might menace him and the socialism he had wrought. His person and his work as "the Lenin of today" had become one, both in his mind and in the regime's relentless propaganda.

So in 1936 he carried out a gigantic coup d'état against the personnel of the system over which he himself presided (somewhat as Mao would later wage the "cultural revolution" against his own Party). Stalin reorganized the political police descended from the old Cheka into a spanking new People's Commissariat of Internal Affairs, or the NKVD, and brought it under his personal control by placing at its head his creature Yezhev. With this refurbished instrument he made a clean sweep of all potential opponents, indeed of all simple doubters, waverers, and critics, and not just at the top, among such has-beens as Zinoviev and Bukharin, but at every level of the Party and the state administration. Thus by 1939 he had given himself a Party membership, a staff of industrial managers, and a corps of military officers that was 80 percent new, all of them products of the system built since 1929 who owed everything to it and to him personally—and who indeed would grow old together as "the Brezhnev generation."[24]

This course was no doubt not the wisest policy on what turned out to be the eve of total war; and the potential for Party disloyalty in a crisis was nowhere near so great as Stalin imagined. Still, this course does make sense as an extreme effort to render irreversible the fruits of the Great Break. And it was Leninist in its basic principle, although Leninism of a greatly intensified variety; for splitting the Party to purge deviant groups and then recruiting new loyalist cadres was a constant tactic of the founder from his break, in 1903, with the Mensheviks onward. Moreover, Stalin's action did solve the problem of bureaucratic petrification for many years. After the end of the frenetic terror of Yezhev years, 1937–1938, the repression of "enemies of the people" was routinized into a system of periodic purge and the pervasive fear of purge, backed up by the Gulag, to keep everyone constantly on his toes, a system which continued right through the war and until the leader's death in 1953. So approximately another 10 million victims were added to Stalin's score, to yield a grand total of 20 million, the conservative estimate of the American historian Robert Conquest now generally accepted, indeed amplified, by such Soviet scholars of Stalinism as Roy Medvedev.[25]

One final, momentous consequence of these extraordinary transformations was that their source, the Myth, was now transformed into the Lie, to use a term first brought to public attention by Solzhenitsyn but long current throughout Eastern Europe; for Soviet socialism as actually realized was a fraud in terms of the Myth's own standards. This Lie could be made to appear to be the truth, and the fraud concealed for a time, indeed for quite a long time, by a combination of terror and drumbeat indoctrination. Until Khrushchev's "secret speech" of 1956, millions, both within the Soviet Union and in the outside world, believed that the Myth had in fact been realized and that Stalin was its Coryphaeus. But eventually the truth would out and the fraud be exposed, and then the regime would be confronted with a terrible dilemma: namely, that Sovietism has a criminal past which is at the same time the centerpiece of Soviet achievement. But when this moment came, could the regime admit to the truth and at the same time preserve the results of the achievement? This moment has now arrived and constitutes one of the great unresolved contradictions of perestroika today. The collapse of the Lie under glasnost is destroying acceptance of the system itself, especially among the young, just as Gorbachev is trying to save it by restructuring.

Nor is this all: decades of living under the Lie have had a morally debilitating effect on the national culture and the population, among ruled and rulers alike. As de Tocqueville once put the problem, "Men are not corrupted by the exercise of power, or debased by the habit of obedience; but by the exercise of a power which they believe to be illegitimate, and by obedience to a rule they consider to be usurped and oppressive."[26] And this degradation of the "human factor," a factor Gorbachev puts at the center of his reform effort, must be contended with, both in himself and in his people, if perestroika is to succeed.

VII

The system completed by Stalin in 1939 would have four long decades of success before the bill came due for living high on the Lie for so long. To be sure, the Soviet edifice as of 1939 was still very much a jerry-built, shaky affair, and Stalin knew it, which is why he tried so desperately to avoid submitting it to the test of war by his pact with Hitler. But when, in spite of all, the test did come, the Soviet Union survived, yet not through a win on the merits of the system, at least in the first phase. Rather, survival came because the country was so huge it could afford (though not through conscious design) to lose space long enough to permit Hitler to make mistakes enough to set himself up for defeat. And at that point, the essentially military command structure of the Party-state indeed proved effective in relocating factories, mobilizing the economy, and mounting its counterattack for victory.

It was this belated victory that at last made the Soviet system impregnable. It transformed what had been since 1929, indeed since 1917, an extravagant gamble into a world-class success. This success, moreover, was attributed by the regime to the superiority of socialism and endlessly extolled as the justification for all the suffering and sacrifices of the 1930s. Thus the "Great Fatherland War" at last conferred on Soviet power a measure of the legitimacy that had hitherto eluded it. As Solzhenitsyn has argued, the victory of 1945 was a tragedy in triumph for the Russian people, for it fixed on them for decades more a regime that otherwise lacked the inner resources to endure.

The Party was now no longer a small army of occupation, molding by force from above a recalcitrant population, but instead the structural ribbing of a new Soviet imperial nation; and the Party's ranks swelled to almost 7 million at the end of the war and then upward to 19 million under Brezhnev. When to all this was added the security zone of an empire in Eastern Europe and the grandeur of great power status, Marshal Stalin towered to world-historical stature. At home he was the Father of his people, and abroad he was either the hero of the Left as the foe of American imperialism or to the Right the object of awe of such a hard-headed *realpolitiker* as Henry Kissinger, and of such an anti-Communist economist as Joseph Schumpeter. Stalin's "rational terror," in Camus's phrase, created power, and power compels universal respect.[27]

Soviet success followed Soviet success seemingly without end. Stalin acquired the atom bomb with stunning rapidity in 1949. Then Khrushchev triumphed with Sputnik and the first man in space, and frightened the world with his rockets. Brezhnev intervened at will throughout the Third World, ringed the continents with his submarines, and at last attained nuclear parity with the United States. Russia bestrode the world as a superpower. And after 1968, as the West reeled under the impact of the Vietnam disaster, Watergate, two oil shocks, and the collapse of the shah's Iran, it seemed that the "correlation of forces," as the Soviets were wont to put it, was shifting definitively "in favor of socialism."

In reality, however, the high opinion held in the West of Soviet achievement was quite wide of the modest truth. For if there was always enough accomplishment to make the world avoid looking squarely at Soviet reality, the world in fact was being hoodwinked by the assertion of efficacy and power in just one domain. This was the domain of "extensive" economic development, which operates effectively only by using great quantities of men and capital in large-scale projects (and in the Soviet case, without regard for costs). But this technique is adequate only for the simpler modern tasks such as launching heavy industry or concentrating resources for winning a war. But once institutionalized, the apparatus for extensive development becomes an impediment to the next state of economic development, the intensive growth necessary for the refined and skilled tasks of a more complex modernity.

To put the matter another way, in the 1930s the Soviets had built a crude, but serviceable imitation of a Pittsburgh-Detroit or a Rhur-Lorraine economy; then they rebuilt it after the war, when it was already becoming obsolete, or at least was no longer at the cutting edge of economic practices in the West; finally, after Stalin's death, they multiplied the same model seven or eight times over when genuinely advanced countries were phasing out their Garys, Birminghams, and Essens. At the same time, the West and East Asia passed them by, first with an electronic, and then with a computer, revolution. And so, by the end of the 1970s, as Russia reached the peak of her international standing, domestically she was becoming a gigantic Soviet socialist rust belt.

At the same moment the country encountered still another limit to easy economic expansion: the depletion of cheap natural resources and a decline of available labor. The great expansion from the 1930s onward had been possible only because the vast Eurasian heartland offered, or seemed to offer, inexhaustible resources of raw materials; and they were used up wantonly, without regard for cost, by extravagant engineering projects, waste, and mismanagement. By 1980 these reserves were no longer abundant, and in their place ecological disaster zones had appeared, such as the shrinking Aral Sea and the dying Lake Baikal. At the same time the demographic trend turned too. The great population explosion of the late nineteenth and early twentieth centuries, which had made Russia by far the most populous nation of Europe, had offered to the Soviet experiment a demographic reservoir on which Stalin's extensive development, as well as the Gulag, had drawn without counting. The poor housing of Soviet urbanization made this reservoir shrink further still, especially in the Slavic heartland, and by Brezhnev's demise that labor reserve was gone.

A similar impasse appeared in the method of managing the Soviet economic mastodon, the Plan. It is in the logic of a system where everything is nationalized, and where the market and real prices are eschewed as "capitalist," that all production decisions should be taken by administrative fiat and implemented in a quasi-military manner through what Western analysts have come to call a command economy. In other words, economic decisions are taken for political and not economic reasons, in accordance with the policy priorities of the Party-state, and not in response to social demand (except from the military) or for reasons of production efficiency. The inevitable result is that the Plan operates through what the reform economist Gavriil Popov has recently baptized the *kommandno-administrativnaia systema*, or "command-administrative system," where everything is run by imperious order from above and blind submission from below, a system that operates not only in industry, but in all social relationships.[28]

This method, like the strategy of extensive development, worked effectively, if not efficiently, during the early, crash phase of Soviet industrialization and the war. It still worked effectively after the war when Stalin and Khrushchev crash-programmed their way to nuclear weapons and ballistic missiles, and then when Brezhnev ploughed on to global superpower parity. But it was a method developed by, and only suitable for, such economic and technological semiliterates as Sergo Orjonikidze, the Civil War commissar who became Stalin's industrializer-in-chief during most of the 1930s; it could not be successfully adapted to the high-technological world symbolized, say, by Andrei Sakharov. In that world it became only a stultifying hindrance, an institutionalized damper on inventive initiative and entrepreneurial innovation.

Thus, on every front the "storm and conquer" methods of bolshevism's Homeric age that had worked to build socialism eventually became a brake on the system's further development and modernization. The techniques of extensive economic growth became institutionalized and ossified in Gosplan, "Gossnab," and the specialized economic ministries, which grew in number from a handful during the 1930s to some seventy by the time Brezhnev died. By the same period the kolkhoz system had acquired hundreds of thousands of nonproductive bureaucrats. And all of this constituted a network of entrenched vested interests, comprising, according to Gorbachev, some 18 million functionaries. The command-administrative ways of the nomenklatura society, also created by Stalin's "storm" tactics, had turned against their own purpose and become a source of "stagnation," to use Gorbachev's term for the Brezhnev era. The result was that by 1979—the same year as the great Afghan miscalculation—the growth rate of the once Promethean Soviet Union was down to about zero, and there it has stubbornly remained for the past decade.[29]

This outcome will be all the more difficult to remedy because in the mature Soviet system the economy is in fact at bottom a polity, a projection of the purposes of the Party-state and at the same time the chief means of the regime's hold over the population. This interlocking of the economy with a political structure—and of both with culture—in one overarching unity is the institutional essence of totalitarianism.

VIII

It is with this unitary and increasingly petrified socialism that all of Stalin's successors have had to contend. And they have done so in a pattern of alternating reform and retreat, for the hope of soft communism never wholly died after 1929 and would revive every time hard communism, by its very rigidity, provoked system-threatening problems.

First, Khrushchev liquidated Stalin's last chief of terror, Beria, and greatly reduced the power of the political police and the size of the Gulag, in part as a measure of self-defense by the Party against its monitors, and in part to humanize the system and make it more efficient. Khrushchev was perhaps the last ideological Leninist among Soviet leaders; he was convinced that the system, if properly managed, could produce not just power for the state, but the realization of utopia for the masses.

Even more daring than his crushing of Beria, in his secret speech at the Twentieth Party Congress of 1956, Khrushchev attacked Stalin himself for his crimes against the Party. But Khrushchev soon discovered that de-Stalinization had a logic he could not control. It delegitimized the system per se and released a flood of pent-up grievances throughout the empire; this process in turn provoked a conservative reaction among the apparat, and so Khrushchev was compelled to fight back by unleashing the creative intelligentsia against the conservatives, most notably by publishing Solzhenitsyn's *One Day in the Life of Ivan Denisovich*, which unmasked not just Stalin's person, but his camp system as well.

The ideological crisis produced by this "thaw" was compounded as Khrushchev simultaneously tampered with the institutional basis of the regime. In order to limber up the economy, he decentralized it by establishing Regional Economic Councils, or *Sovnarkhozes*. More disturbingly still, he tried to split the Party in two, making one part responsible for industry and the other for agriculture, a brutal change of role for the political and ideological functionaries of the apparat. Moreover, to break their resistance to this institutional attack on the "little Stalins," in Yevtushenko's phrase, he sought to limit all important Party mandates to fixed terms. It is this presumption even more than his foreign policy misadventures in Cuba that provoked his fall.

In October 1964 Khrushchev was deposed for "voluntarism" by the very colleagues he had made safe against the political police, by then called the KGB. And their safety was indeed the source of his vulnerability. By bringing Stalin's terror to a halt, he gave away his only leverage against the apparat and thus his own safeguard. By the same token he gave the *apparatchiki* not only security of their persons; he inadvertently gave them life tenure in their positions as well. It was to preserve this status that the Politburo decided that he and what they considered his "hare-brained" innovations had to go.[30]

The result of Khrushchev's failed reform, therefore, was the triumph of the nomenklatura rather than the Leader as the fulcrum of the system; and it is only in the late 1970s that the world learned of this new term and the privileged caste it designated.[31] Brezhnev and his allies prudently drew from Khrushchev's fate the lesson that this group's privileges must forever remain inviolate. This policy was the origin of the extraordinary gerontocracy, led by Brezhnev himself, Suslov, Andropov, and Chernenko, who dominated the Soviet scene in the last decade before Gorbachev and whose longevity compounded the arteriosclerosis of all other aspects of Soviet life.

Under their direction the Soviet Union experienced eighteen years of "stagnation," as the period after Khrushchev is now officially designated. First of all, de-Stalinization was halted as too dangerous to the system's stability. The late leader was never formally rehabilitated, but attacks on "the cult of personality" ceased. As for the economy, the moderate decentralizing reforms of Prime Minister Kosygin, developed from the Lieberman incentive experiments of the Khrushchev era, were smothered at birth by the noncooperation of the industrial ministries. Concurrently, the working class, secure with a minimal but universal welfare safety net and comforted by the socialist ethos of egalitarian leveling, or *uravnilovka*, developed a mentality of minimum effort for minimum reward. At a higher social level, the officially stigmatized entrepreneurial ethos expressed itself in a growing "second," or "black," economy, which was indispensable to the functioning of the official "first" economy, a phenomenon that led to the "Mafiaization" of the police, industrial management, and portions of the Party, especially in the southern border republics where these Mafias also had an ethnic base.[32] Finally, Andropov's reinvigorated KGB exiled or repressed Russia's best talent, such as Solzhenitsyn, Sakharov, and Brodsky, to mention only the Nobel Prize winners among them; Russian culture was either driven underground into *samizdat* (clandestine self-publication) or abroad into *tamizdat* (publication in the West). In consequence, sometime around the mid-1970s the Myth faded away almost completely among the people, and left only a repressed awareness of the Lie, which as yet no one dared speak of publicly.

By the turn of the 1980s, therefore, as one gerontocrat after another was laid to rest in the Kremlin wall, a pall of gloom and despair descended over the nation. And so, at the zenith of Soviet power internationally, internally the system became a Eurasian-sized Stalin mausoleum.

IX

Against the background of such a history and the highly constraining structural logic underlying it, the task of reform can only be Herculean. But do the system's constraints permit the emergence of the people, and of the vision, necessary for such a staggering task? In this question lies the whole drama, and the dilemma, of the Gorbachev era.

Awareness that something was seriously amiss with Sovietism first came to the surface in 1983 under Andropov. As head of the KGB, he knew far better than his colleagues the true state of affairs; and he took the novel step of calling on intelligentsia specialists, especially economists and sociologists from the Academy of Sciences, to consult on possible remedies, an enterprise in which his protégé Gorbachev was involved. This endeavor produced the *Novosibirsk Report* by the sociologist Tatania Zaslavskaia, who argued that the Soviet system of centralized planning had become obsolete, a fetter on production, and that Soviet society, far from being a harmonious unity, was riven by the conflicting interests of both the ruling and the ruled—an analysis that implied the necessity of radical restructuring for sheer survival. This document, leaked to the Western press in the once putatively fatal year of 1984, first alerted the world to the impending end of Soviet stability.[33]

At the beginning of his general secretaryship, Gorbachev may be considered as Andropov redux, though the younger leader was driven by a much more acute sense of crisis and a correspondingly bolder willingness to experiment. His initial program of perestroika as controlled economic reform from above therefore quickly branched out in new directions under the pressure of events. *Perestroika* soon came to stand for "radical reform," then "revolutionary change"; and further policies were added to it: "new thinking," or retrenchment, in foreign relations, and "acceleration," "glasnost," and "democratization" domestically. It is in this historical sequence that its course will be examined here.

When Gorbachev first launched perestroika in April 1985, it had the relatively limited purpose of producing a rapid acceleration, or *uskorenie,* of national economic performance; and his method was similar to Andropov's: reliance on administrative action from above in consultation with intelligentsia experts and operation within the existing structures of the Plan and its attendant ministries. For *perestroika* means, literally and simply, refashioning an existing edifice, or *stroika,* the root also of the Russian term for the "building" of socialism. Thus, while he summoned Zaslavskaia and the Novosibirsk economist Abel Aganbegyan to Moscow and positions in Academy of Science think tanks, his basic approach was to jump-start the stalled Soviet productive mechanism by the classic administrative methods of exhortation and bureaucratic reorganization.

An example of the first tack was his 1986 anti-alcohol campaign. This measure backfired, however, by increasing the budget deficit through loss of sizable vodka sales, which now went to the "black" economy. An example of the second tack was the "quality control" of industrial products by state inspectors, whose power to refuse substandard goods, and hence also to lower enterprise revenues, generated insecurity among both managers and workers. In addition, Gorbachev regrouped ministries and replaced cadres on a scale not seen since Stalin. As a result of this, by the fall of 1986 strong resistance emerged among the apparat to further changes, whether of policy or of personnel.[34]

Gorbachev therefore embarked on a second policy, glasnost. In this he was advised by his chief theoretician, Alexander Yakovlev, who had become a connoisseur of modern, Western ways during a decade as ambassador to Canada, an experience that both sharpened his appreciation of Russia's backwardness and acquainted him with the contemporary television techniques required to stimulate innovation. In choosing this new course, Gorbachev was guided by two considerations. As a question of conviction, he recognized that a dynamic economy could not be built with a passive population, isolated from knowledge of the modern world, ignorant even of real conditions within the Soviet Union—a state of affairs that produced Chernobyl, for example. Glasnost was thus intended to energize the nation. Also, as a matter of political tactics, he now made an all-out wager on the "creative intelligentsia" to bring pressure for reform on the recalcitrant apparat.

To signal this change, and to give the intelligentsia assurance that they could speak up without fear, he made a dramatic telephone call to Sakharov in Gorki in December 1986 to summon him back from exile. During the next eighteen months the liberal intelligentsia, in the press and on television, began to criticize society's ills, and to fill in the "blank spots," in Gorbachev's expression, of the Soviet past, with a fervor born of the twenty years of frustration that had built up since the previous thaw under Khrushchev. They did this with all the more passion since it was only by owning up to the errors of the past that they could attack the problems it had created for the present.[35]

In the course of this glasnost explosion, both Gorbachev and his supporters radicalized as they encountered resistance from "conservative" (or more accurately, old socialist) forces under Ligachev. A note of desperation crept into the debate, and on both sides. Ligachev and his allies asserted that the liberal intelligentsia's criticism was leading the country to ruin by undermining the institutions and values that had built socialism and won the Fatherland War. Gorbachev and his supporters answered that the situation was so far gone that there was "no alternative to perestroika": to continue the policies of stagnation would lead to the rapid obsolescence of the economy, loss of superpower status, and ultimately the death of the system. As Yakovlev, in early 1989, put it more bluntly than Gorbachev himself would have dared, "We probably have no more than two to three years to prove that Leninist socialism can work."[36] Thus in 1987 and 1988, the initially self-confident campaign for perestroika of 1985 took on the air of an increasingly desperate gamble, an ever more urgent race against time; and by 1989 matters had acquired the aura of a crisis of survival, which recalled, though in different form, the disaster years of 1921, 1932, and 1941.

The flood of candor under glasnost did indeed produce the consequences of which the conservatives complained, and in a form more radical than during Khrushchev's thaw. For each new revelation about past crimes and disasters did less to stimulate the people to new effort than to desacralize the system in their eyes; it did so all the more thoroughly since the Myth was long since dead, especially among the young. Repressed awareness of the Lie poured forth in a flood progressing from the publication of Anatoli Rybakov's mild novel *Children of the Arbat* in 1986 to that of Solzhenitsyn's outright anti-Soviet *Gulag Archipelago* in 1989. In the process, not only were the long decades of Stalin and Brezhnev swept away, but the very foundations of Sovietism, the economic theories of Marx and the political practices of Lenin, were touched. By 1988 Marxism-Leninism was a shambles; and by 1989 it could be openly denounced by leading intellectuals, such as the historian Iuri Afanasiev, as a dead weight on the mind of the nation.[37]

In the midst of the turmoil unleashed by glasnost, the system was threatened by still another danger: the nationalities crisis and the beginning of the breakup of the empire. The leadership had known from the start of perestroika that it faced an economic problem, but in its Russocentric naiveté was quite unaware it had an equally grave nationalities problem. So the mass strikes of February 1988 in Armenia over the issue of Nagorny-Karabakh came as a total surprise, a "moral Chernobyl," as one Soviet leader put it. But soon autonomist, even separatist, agitation spread to the Baltic states, then to Georgia and Azerbaijan, and by 1989 to the vital Ukraine.

These movements, moreover, everywhere assumed the form of "popular fronts," grouping all classes of the population against the Party apparat (or in the Baltic virtually taking the Party over), a pattern reminiscent of the "dual power" that existed between the original "soviets," or workers' councils, and the Provisional Government in 1917. The cause of this sudden explosion lay in the same process of desacralization that was undermining all Soviet institutions. The fiction that the Party-state was a federal "union" was perhaps the most egregious form of the Lie, for all the border "republics" had in fact been conquered by the Great Russian central region beginning in 1920, with the Baltic states and the Western Ukraine added only as recently as 1939–1944, and then only after a deal with Hitler. When the freedom to criticize released these border populations from fear, the result was a national as well as an anti-Party upsurge; for them *perestroika* came to signify "sovereignty," by which they really meant independence.

With this danger added to the other strains produced by glasnost, the old-line socialists, or conservatives, redoubled their efforts to retain control of the apparat, where the general secretary still lacked an unquestioned majority, from the Politburo down to the base. Given the constraints of Party discipline, this resistance could express itself in public only obliquely, but behind the scenes, what liberals called a bloodless civil war in fact was raging. Its most open expressions were the firing of Boris Yeltsin as Moscow Party chief in the fall of 1987 and the national-Communist, anti-Gorbachev manifesto, known as the "Nina Andreeva Letter," published in much of the press in the spring of 1988.

In response to these pressures, the general secretary moved to a third and still more revolutionary policy: democratization. First bruited in early 1987, this meant double or multiple candidacies in elections and fixed terms of office for all Party and state, or Soviet, posts. This policy was first applied to the Party by convening a Special Party Conference (in effect, a mini-Congress) in June 1988 in an effort to gain at last the majority necessary for a renewed attempt at economic reform. Yet this device, like glasnost, overshot the mark assigned to it, while at the same time it fell short of achieving its intended positive function. The conference turned out to lack the necessary majority of proreform delegates for a purge of apparat deadwood yet began the politicization of the hitherto quiescent Russian lower classes, since the partially televised proceedings revealed the once monolithic and mysterious Party to be a fallible and quarrelsome body of self-seeking interests.

Failing to revitalize the Party, Gorbachev then upped the ante of democratization by using it the following year to reanimate the hierarchy of state administrative bodies, the soviets. Taking up the 1917 slogan "all power to the soviets," he sought to give real political life to both halves of the system of dual administration, in which all power, since Lenin, had belonged to the Party. Again his motives were mixed. There was first his Leninism—by no means a mere ritual invocation—which he vaunted as the "pragmatic" capacity to adapt policy rapidly to changing circumstance and the constant willingness to risk a gamble. Then, too, democracy, like glasnost, was necessary to galvanize the population for perestroika. But above all, Gorbachev sought to give himself a structure of power parallel to the regular apparat. He sought this in part so that he could not be deposed by a Central Committee coup as Khrushchev had been in 1964—a precedent on everyone's mind in the perestroika era—and in part to give himself an independent instrument for putting through his stalled economic programs.[38] And, as some Soviets noted, this effort to outflank the old guard by a parallel power was reminiscent, *mutatis mutandis*, of the way Stalin had used the NKVD against the mainline Party.

This second round of democratization overshot its intended mark far more widely than the first. This became apparent during the elections in March 1989 to a Congress of People's Deputies, whose function was to create a strong executive presidency for Gorbachev and to elect a Supreme Soviet, or national parliament, with some measure of legislative power, unlike its rubber-stamp predecessor. An unintended result of these elections, however, was to produce a resounding defeat not just for the apparat, as Gorbachev wished, but for the Party as an institution. For the first time in seventy years, the population had the possibility of saying no to official candidates, and did so, at least in the large cities, on a major scale. As a result, the "correlation of forces" within the country changed radically: the Party which had hitherto inspired fear in the people suddenly came to fear the population, and demoralization spread throughout its ranks.

This effect was compounded at the Congress meetings, televised live for two weeks during May and June. To be sure, Gorbachev got himself elected president and thus secured a buffer against a coup by the Party. He also obtained the selection of a new Supreme Soviet—in effect, a consultative assembly, rather than a genuine legislature—which he felt confident would do his bidding. But the authoritarian way he pushed these elections through the Congress caused his popularity, already low because of the economic and ethnic problems engendered by perestroika, to reach its nadir; he, too, was desacralized and made to appear as just a bigger apparatchik. Moreover, the liberal delegates, though a minority, dominated the proceedings with a barrage of exposés of all the ills with which the country is afflicted: the poverty, the abominable health service, the rising crime rate, the ecological disasters, the economic disintegration, the KGB's "secret empire," as one deputy dared call it, and the Party corruption. The net result of the Congress was, in the words of another deputy, "the demystification of power."

As a result, Gorbachev's initially demagogic slogan "all power to the people" began to acquire some real content. The Congress first of all produced an organized Left opposition to Gorbachev in the form of the Interregional Group, led by such figures as Sakharov, Yeltsin, Afanasiev, and the economist Popov, a loyal opposition to be sure, yet one that nonetheless insisted that real perestroika was still in the future. Even more boldly, this group broke the supreme taboo of communism and demanded an end to the leading role of the Party.[39] Simultaneously, the Congress debates produced a politicalization of the Great Russian and Ukrainian populations almost as intense as that of the border nationalities. And since the Congress had come up with no concrete remedies for the ills its debates had exposed, by July the population began to take matters into its own hands. The country was swept with a wave of self-organization from below; popular fronts and embryonic trade union associations appeared in the cities of Russia and the Ukraine. Thus "civil society", as the opposition called these new formations, began to emerge for the first time since it had been suppressed in 1918; and in some areas this movement edged off into a form of "dual power," as some radicals asserted, a phenomenon of which the Kuzbas and Donbas miners' strikes in July 1989 were only the most visible and spectacular manifestations.

X

While all this was going on, what had been accomplished in the economic sphere to produce the hoped-for "acceleration" that had been perestroika's starting point? The short answer is: nothing much. Or more accurately still, those measures that were taken led to an outright deterioration of the situation.

Gorbachev's economic program has thus far consisted of two main components, both formulated in 1987.[40] The first of these is the creation of small "cooperatives," in reality private ventures, in the service sector. But the impact of this cooperative sector has been derisory, since its services are priced far above the purchasing power of the 200-rouble-per-month average wage of the majority of the population. These enterprises have therefore become the focus of popular hostility to economic reform in general, since any form of marketization is perceived by "the people"—as the miners made clear during their strike—to benefit only "speculators" and the privileged—a reaction quite in conformity with the socialist egalitarianism the regime inculcated in the population for decades. Moreover, the cooperatives are harassed by the state bureaucracy, whose monopoly they threaten, and are often either taken over by, or made to pay protection money to, various Mafias from the "black" economy.

The second component of Gorbachev's economic reform is the Law on State Enterprises, providing for "self-management" and "self-financing." If actually applied, these provisions would significantly reduce the role of Gosplan and the central ministries by using self-interest to correct the predominance of administrative directives. This reform is thus an effort to return to the spirit, if not the precise institutions, of the NEP, and to its policy of *khozraschyot*, or businesslike management and accountability under a regime of state enterprise. In other words, it is a variant of the half-measures of soft communism, put forth periodically in Soviet history from Bukharin to Eugene Varga just after World War II to Kosygin, but never really implemented because they threaten the Party apparat's "leading role." And, indeed, this time too, the Law on State Enterprises has remained a dead letter ever since it took effect in January 1988, because the silent resistance of legions of apparatchiki has kept industry operating at 90 percent on "state orders"—that is, on the old Plan.[41]

In still other domains, Gorbachev's economic perestroika has met with failure, but this time without his having really tried to produce a program. In agriculture Gorbachev has spoken repeatedly of long-term leases of land, indeed up to fifty years, for the peasantry. But this proposal has gone nowhere, in part because of the resistance of the huge kolkhoz bureaucracy, in part because the peasantry has seen so many different agrarian reforms imposed from above that it will not trust the regime to respect leases of any duration and hence will not take up the government's half-offer.

Thus, Gorbachev is in a far more difficult position than his predecessors in communist economic reform. He no longer has the option of Lenin in 1921 at the beginning of the NEP, or of Deng Xiaoping in 1979 of reviving agricultural and artisan production rapidly by granting the 80 percent of the population that is peasant a free market. The Russian peasantry, now disproportionately aged and only 35 percent of the population, is too decimated and demoralized by over sixty years of collectivization to respond to any NEP-type initiatives. In consequence, Gorbachev has been obliged to begin his perestroika with industry, where the transition to marketization is far more difficult than in agriculture. Here the very success of Stalin in urbanizing Russia has created a cast-iron block to progress.

Another such block is financial and monetary policy. Heavy state subsidies to hold retail prices low, to keep unprofitable factories running, to maintain full employment, and to secure the safety net in place—what some Western specialists call the social contract between regime and people—cannot be abolished without unleashing inflation and thus igniting a social explosion. But unless these subsidies are abolished, or at least reduced, the economy cannot move to real prices; and without real prices there can be no dilution of the Plan by marketization or privatization; nor can there be convertibility of the rouble to reintegrate Russia into the international order. And without movement in these directions, there can be no revival of the economy. So the alternative before Gorbachev is either economic stagnation through subsidies or social upheaval through real prices.

And perestroika faces other problems as well: the infrastructure and the capital stock created by decades of extensive development are now approaching exhaustion. In a nationally televised address in October 1989, Prime Minister Ryzhkov warned that the overburdened railway system (Russia still lives basically in the railroad age) was on the verge of collapse. The country's enormous metallurgical plant is outmoded and unprofitable. Housing and administrative buildings are in a state of disrepair often bordering on disintegration. The extraordinary number of industrial "accidents," from Chernobyl to the gas-line and train explosions of June 1989 are usually due to functional breakdown or criminal neglect. All this exhausted equipment must be restored or replaced, and much of the work force retrained and remotivated.

Then, too, the stores must be filled again. Under the present conditions of collapse and penury, available goods are either siphoned off legally by state enterprises to supply their workers, or they disappear illegally into the black economy. But short of massive imports of foreign goods, stocking the shelves is an impossible task, since decades of wasteful investments and subsidies, and of printing money to finance both, have now created an enormous budget deficit and rapid inflation—both "discovered," or admitted, by the government only in late 1988. As a result of this, a movement away from the rouble to the dollar or to barter is well under way, a phenomenon that presages the collapse of the consumer market.

Under such conditions of near breakdown, any transition to real prices, self-management, and self-financing are quite out of the question for the foreseeable future; and the old reflexes of the command-administrative system are sure to persist, if only to ensure a modicum of order. Thus, active consideration of real market reform has been postponed time and again and is now slated, more or less, for the mid-1990s. Indeed, economic perestroika of any type has been stalled since early 1988.

Overall, then, the balance sheet of more than four years of perestroika has been that the half-reforms introduced so far have unsettled the old economic structures without putting new ones in their place. And in this, perestroika resembles earlier failed halfway-house reforms in Central Europe: General Jaruzelski's reforms of self-management in 1982 and of self-financing in 1987 in Poland, and earlier still the failed, halfway New Economic Mechanism in Hungary. Yet, despite this accumulated evidence of failure, Gorbachev intends to stick to the unnatural hybrid of "market socialism," as his chief economic advisor, Leonid Abalkin, made clear in November 1989 in launching an updated plan of alleged "transition" away from statism.[42]

The current impasse of perestroika, furthermore, resembles the Soviet NEP, but in reverse. The NEP saw the progressive stifling of the surviving prerevolutionary market economy by the nascent ambitions of Party-state power. Gorbachev's perestroika has witnessed the tenacious resistance of an ailing but still massive Party-state structure to a fledgling yet corrosive market. Whereas it proved easy to move brutally from a market to a command economy, it is turning out to be inordinately difficult to make the more delicate reverse transition. Between Gorbachev and a neo-NEP stands the mountainous mass of decaying Stalinist success, whereas between Lenin and the first NEP there stood only the failed wreckage of War Communism. So Gorbachev is left with the worst of two possible worlds: an old one that refuses to die and a new one without the strength to be born.

At the same time, this failure of economic perestroika coincides with the runaway success of glasnost and the progress of democratization and popular politicalization. The result is a new kind of "scissors crisis," to appropriate a metaphor used by Trotsky during the unstable NEP to describe the upward curve of industrial prices when charted against the downward curve of agricultural prices. Similarly, under the unstable neo-NEP of perestroika, the curve of glasnost and political-ization is running alarmingly high, and that of economic restructuring is sinking catastrophically low.[43] So perestroika, like its predecessor, risks being destroyed by the widening gap of the scissors unless energetic emergency measures are taken soon.

By late fall 1989, Moscow began to hear rumors of a coup. Other rumors, more plausibly, offered speculation about an imminent state of emergency or of a mitigated form of martial law (*osoboe polo-zhenie*). To everyone, society seemed to be adrift in disorder. Fear of state authority had almost vanished during the summer after the Congress, and with it, so it seemed, the regime's ability to govern. When the emigré Andrei Amalrik twenty years ago published his *Will the Soviet Union Survive until 1984?* his question was met with incredulity, even derision.[44] Now it may well turn out that he was only a few years off.

In the midst of all this, what of Gorbachev, on whose person the West concentrates its attention and hopes? To the outside world, he passes for a bold and decisive leader, a mover and a shaker of major stature, especially in international affairs. When seen from Moscow, however, after his first initiative in unleashing the perestroika deluge, he has come to look more like a reactive than an active figure, a man increasingly incapable of staking out strong policy positions on the two make-or-break domestic issues of his reign, the economy and the nationalities. Instead, he appears essentially as a political tactician, fully at home only in Party maneuvering, now pruning the Politburo of conservative foes such as the former KGB chief, Chebrikov, or the Ukrainian Party boss, Shcherbitsky, as in the fall of 1989, now tacking from left to right and back again in the debates of the new Supreme Soviet. Indeed, by giving way totally and immediately to the miners' demands in July 1989, he appeared downright weak. And in all things he acts as if his economic problems could be solved by political means. Yet, since the direct road to economic perestroika is closed to him by structural blockage, this easier political route of glasnost and democratization is the only one left open to him.

Nor does he seem to be able to make up his mind whether he is head of state or head of the opposition. As one Soviet commentator put it, he is trying to be both Luther and the pope at the same time.[45] But in such a contradictory situation, for all his political prowess, he may yet turn out to be no more than the ultimate sorcerer's apprentice of Sovietism.

XI

As 1989 draws to a close, it is clear that it will enter history as the beginning of communism's terminal crisis, the year of the Second Great Break, but in the descending, not the ascending, phase of utopia in power; and this not just in Russia, but from the Baltic to the China Sea, and from Berlin to Beijing. It is also clear that perestroika and glasnost, welcome as they are in their intention, have in their application only aggravated the systemic crisis they were intended to alleviate. And they have done so because like all forms of soft communism, they go against the logic of the system they are trying to save. The internal contradiction of perestroika is that Gorbachev has been trying to promote soft communism through structures and a population programmed for hard communism. But the latter is the only variety of Sovietism that is the genuine article, for the essence of all varieties of Sovietism is Party supremacy. Thus, the instrument of Gorbachev's reform—the Party—is at the same time the basic cause of Sovietism's troubles. To adapt a diagnosis of Alexander Herzen regarding earlier revolutionaries, the Party is not the doctor; it is the disease.

And the way out of this contradiction then? As one Soviet reformer put it after the June Congress, "The country now stands at a cross-roads. From here we either go the Chinese way or the Polish-Hungarian way." Although the speaker obviously wished for the latter course, the alternative he posed may well be a Hobson's choice. The Chinese way since June 1989 means relative, though declining, market prosperity under a regime of political and military repression. Repression is certainly a possibility in Russia, but market prosperity is out of the question for the foreseeable future. Conversely, the Polish-Hungarian way means genuine democracy, but this is being attempted in the midst of economic ruin so severe as to constitute a real danger to the success of the new constitutional order. In Russia the economic ruin is even worse than in Poland and Hungary, but real democracy, as opposed to mere democratization, is not yet on the agenda. Thus, the Russian way could well contribute the worst of the Chinese and the

Central European scenarios: economic failure in conjunction with the Party and military repression.

Indeed, all paths of communist reform seem to end in one or another type of impasse. In this way Leninist totalitarianism shows another facet of its difference from ordinary authoritarianism. As Polish radicals discovered in the early 1980s in looking for possible models of liberation, post-Franco Spain and post-Pinochet Chile could not serve as examples. For those countries were able to make the transition to democracy because they had only been political authoritarianisms, not economic, social, and ideological monoliths. And, of course, they possessed market economies, so when political tyranny was ended, civil society, which had never been destroyed, could emerge fully into the light of day. But Leninist regimes, when they enter their final decline, seem able only either to implode, as in Poland, Hungary, East Germany, Czechoslovakia, and Romania, or to dig in their heels militarily to stave off implosion, as under Deng Xiaoping in 1989, or his favorite model, the General Jaruzelski of 1981.

Yet whether they implode or hang on for a last desperate stand, all that they leave behind is economic and social rubble—hardly the foundation for building a "normal" society, as the Poles call their hoped-for post-Leninist order. And the leaders of Solidarity are acutely aware of the enormous risk they are taking in assuming power under such parlous conditions. Yet they have no choice but to try, since after eight years of Jaruzelski's failed attempt at being a Polish Kádár—that is, repression followed by liberalizing economic reform—the Party was as bankrupt as the country.

XII

This grim impasse at the end of utopia in power is the logical outcome of the structures which that power had built. The whole impossible enterprise of Lenin and Stalin was sustainable only as long as the human and material resources on which the system fed retained the vitality to endure the burden of the regime, and as long as some modicum of material success undergirded the Party's monopolistic position. But when these conditions ceased to hold, beginning with Deng Xiaoping's marketization of 1979 and Solidarity's revolt of 1980, the Communist parties' will to power began to flag and their people's habit of fear began to fade. This soon made necessary, for the Soviet Party-state's survival, the recourse to the expedients of perestroika and glasnost. But these are only pale substitutes for the market and democracy, halfway measures designed to square the circle of making the vivifying forces of a resurrected civil society compatible with the Party's leading role.

But this circle cannot be squared. If marketization and privatization are the economic goals of reform in communist countries, then Party planning becomes superfluous, indeed downright parasitical. If multiple parties, elections, and the rule of law are the political goals of reform in communist countries, then the dual administration of the Party-state becomes supernumerary, indeed positively noxious.

The Party is not a party, in the normal sense of an association for contesting elections and alternating in government under the rule of law. The Party is, rather, a self-appointed society for the monopoly of power. It can tolerate normal parties only as temporary expedients, satellites, or fronts when the political weather is stormy. Likewise, the dual administrative body of the Party-state is not a normal state, but a special instrument created by the Party to act as a transmission belt of its policies to the population through the nomenklatura. Such a state cannot therefore be turned into a normal polity simply by legalizing other parties, since they will not have equal access with the Party to the monopolistic facilities of the state apparatus, from its police to its press. Nor is socialist planning an alternative way to organize the economy; it is the negation of the economy, its death as a separate sphere of human activity through its subordination to politics and ideological imperatives. It is this total amalgam, this whole surreal world, that is summed up by the sacrosanct tenet of the leading role.

This role is in its essence inimical to all the professed goals of reform now echoing throughout the Soviet Union and Central Europe, whether glasnost, democratization, or multiparty elections. All these reforms imply that there is a third way, a halfway house between what the ideological call socialism and capitalism, or what the inhabitants of the East think of as Sovietism and a "normal society." But there is no third way between Leninism and the market, between bolshevism and constitutional government. Marketization and democratization lead to the revival of civil society, and such a society requires the rule of law. But civil society under the rule of law is incompatible with the preservation of the lawless leading role.

At some point, therefore, the redline will be reached where reform crosses over into the liquidation of the leading role and all the structures it has created. And both Russia and Central Europe are now reaching that critical line. The false problem of how to restructure Leninism is now giving way to the real problem of how to dismantle the system, how to effect at last an exit from communism. Perestroika is not a solution, but a transition to this exit. As Milovan Djilas foresaw early in perestroika: communism is not reforming itself, it is disintegrating.[46]

XIII

As yet, the only country that has posed the problem of the exit from communism openly and as a matter of practical policy is Poland. (We may leave aside the special case of East Germany, where this exit will be effected via the unique path of absorbtion into the Federal Republic.) But Poland has already crossed the red line with a Solidarity-led government proclaiming a goal of full marketization, the phasing out of the nomenklatura, and the decommunization of the army, the police, and the public adminstration—in short, the end in fact, not just in law, of the leading role, indeed of the whole communist system.

But even in Poland all the structures and coercive power still remain in the Party's hands, and the Solidarity ministry is proceeding very cautiously with de-Sovietization for fear of provoking a "Kabul reaction," a bunker defense, among the 2-million-member Party. Simultaneously, the official trade union, larger than worker Solidarity, can demagogically exploit the socialist reflexes inbred by forty years of Sovietism to "defend the rights of workers" against the free-market policies of the Solidarity ministry. Under such unstable conditions, the oldest and most lucid critic of Polish communism, Stefan Kisielewski, concludes that it will take twenty years to de-Sovietize the Polish mentality and Polish institutions.[47]

So as we rub our eyes in astonishment at the most stunning communist implosions of all, the November collapse of the Berlin Wall and the ensuing Prague revolt, we should not conclude that the structures it shielded for so long can be transformed by a few reform decrees. The revolutionary rapidity of events in 1989 should not breed the illusion that the exit from communism these events presage will itself be a rapid process.

And the most difficult case of all will be the Soviet Union. There, unlike Central Europe, the real problem of dismantling, not reforming, communism is not yet openly posed, not even by the democratic opposition, the Interregional Group of People's Deputies: Russia, after all, has had seventy, not forty-five, years of Sovietism. Also, the Soviet Party is a national institution, not an alien imposition, with deep roots in the patriotic success of World War II. Finally, this national-imperial Party has the military apparatus of a superpower. And these circumstances give to the Soviet Party's leading role vertebrae that its little brothers lack.

XIV

Let us return now to the questions with which this inquiry began: Can Gorbachev succeed? Should we help him? It is now the official United States position, to quote President Bush, that Gorbachev is a "genuine reformer" and that we all "wish perestroika to succeed," a stance that implies at least moral help. But to answer these questions meaningfully, we must, as with the questions of Stalin's necessity, rephrase them first. Succeed at what? Help him to do what?

If by perestroika's success we mean producing a communist system that is economically effective and politically democratic, then the answer must be no: the empirical record of seventy years shows that the fundamental structures of the Leninist system reached an inextricable impasse at the end of the 1970s; and the mounting contradictions of perestroika indicate that the system cannot be restructured or reformed, but can only either stagnate or be dismantled and replaced by market institutions over a long period of time. In this case, any aid the West might render to the Soviet state to save or improve the existing system would be futile: on this score, Gorbachev is beyond our help. Such aid would also work against the real interests of the restive Soviet peoples and thus of international stability. Like Western credits to Eduard Gierek and the Polish Party-state in the 1970s, aid to the Soviet government would simply prolong the agony of everyone concerned.

Yet if by perestroika's success we mean effecting a transition from a Party-state and a command economy to democracy and the market, then the answer, unfortunately, must still be no. First of all, such a transition is not the aim of Gorbachev's perestroika; its aim, rather, is to salvage what can be saved of the existing system by halfway-house concessions to economic and human reality, concessions moreover that are constantly being revised as new sections of the system give way and as the regime improvises frantically in the hope that something might turn the situation around. Second, and even more important, such a transition would bring the end of the cardinal leading role and hence would amount to the self-liquidation of communism, something Gorbachev clearly does not intend to do.

Still, events are pressing toward the eventual dwindling away of the system, whatever the Soviet leadership's intentions and whoever that leader might be in the future. And here Western help could play a constructive role. First, reducing the mutual burden of armaments, if carried out with due attention to legitimate security concerns, would ease the severity of the Soviet crisis (though it would not alter its structural causes). And Gorbachev has clearly indicated his willingness to engage in arms reductions, while at the same time taking care that the Soviets' international retreat does not turn into a rout.

Second, although Western aid should not go to shoring up Soviet economic institutions in the state sector, it could be usefully applied to the piecemeal development of parallel structures in a private sector operating on market principles so as to promote economic and eventually, political pluralism. This could take the form, say, of free economic zones operating under IMF conditions in such places as the Baltic states, Armenia, or the Soviet Far East. In this case, the expectation would be that such a parallel sector, perhaps with its own convertible currency, would eventually spread across the Soviet Union.

Such a policy is, indeed, the approach that the Mazowiecki government and its finance minister, Leszek Balcerowicz, are now attempting to inaugurate in Poland. But what Gorbachev is prepared to accept for his outer empire in Central Europe (where he effectively lost control over events sometime in 1988) would be much more difficult for him to accept for the inner empire of the Soviet Union itself, since foreign investment would imperil national sovereignty. So Western investment, in joint or other enterprises in Russia, would have to be handled without triumphalism about capitalism's superiority, and with due sensitivity to Soviet national pride. The West's aim should be to encourage the change of Soviet realities, while leaving the old labels intact—in a kind of socialist-emperor-of-Japan arrangement.

Yet, however the Soviet Union edges toward its particular exit from communism, this unchartered process can only be a long and painful one. Nor will it be a unilinear or an incremental progress toward integration in some "common European house." Instead, further crises will most likely be necessary to produce further, and more real, reforms. And a last-ditch attempt to stave off ruin by curtailing destabilizing reform altogether could lead to that military reaction so feared by Moscow liberals. And who knows, in this scenario Gorbachev might be agile enough to become his own successor, or if perestroika ends in another eighteenth of Brumaire, to be his own Bonaparte. Gorbachev would be hard to replace because his international reputation is now the Soviet Union's chief capital asset; yet he could not afford to be a very tough Bonaparte, since he has become the prisoner of his foreign policy successes.

Obviously, none of these prospects is a cheering one, and none would be easy for the West to live alongside. But it is better to look realistically at the genuine options in the East as they have been molded by seventy years of failed utopia than to engage in fantasies about Gorbachev as a demiurge of instant democracy or about the end of conflict in history. Nor should we forget that communism, though a disaster in almost every creative domain, has always been supremely successful at one thing: resourcefulness and tenacity in holding on to its monopoly of power. So the Soviet world's transition to normality will be a long time coming, for the Party, though now dyed with the hues of glasnost and democratization, will cling to the bitter end, like some poisoned tunic of Nessus, around the bodies of nations it has enfolded in its embrace for so many decades.

ENDNOTES

[1] Francis Fukuyama, "The End of History?" *The National Interest* (Summer 1988).

[2] See, for example, Judy Stone, *The Coming Soviet Crash: Gorbachev's Desperate Pursuit of Credit in Western Financial Markets* (New York: The Free Press, 1989)—a bad title for an otherwise good book. The threat of financial crash is

quite real, but until now Gorbachev has steadfastly refused to use foreign credit extensively for fear of compromising national independence.

[3] See, for example, Frederic J. Fleron, Jr., ed., *Communist Studies and the Social Sciences: Essays on Methodology and Empirical Theory* (Chicago: Rand McNally, 1969); and Susan Gross Solomon, *Pluralism in the Soviet Union* (New York: St. Martin's Press, 1983). See also the social-science-oriented essays in Erik P. Hoffman and Robin F. Laird, eds., *The Soviet Polity in the Modern Era* (New York: Aldine Publishing Company, 1984). For the thesis of "stability" as the great common characteristic of the Soviet Union and the United States, see Samuel P. Huntington, *Political Order in Changing Societies* (New Haven: Yale University Press, 1968).

[4] See notably *Stalinism, Essays in Historical Interpretation*, ed. Robert C. Tucker (New York: Norton, 1977), especially the Introduction and contributions by S. Cohen and R. Tucker.

[5] The theme of a seminal, and for the most part penetrating, essay by Richard Lowenthal, "Development versus Utopia in Communist Policy," in Chalmers Johnson, ed., *Change in Communist Systems* (Stanford, Calif.: Stanford University Press, 1970). A revised version of this essay, entitled "Beyond Totalitarianism?" in Irving Howe, ed., *1984 Revisited* (New York: Harper and Row, 1983) could still be presented as the last word on Sovietism on the eve of Gorbachev's accession to power. In the same volume see also Michael Walzer's more categorical rejection of the relevance of the totalitarian concept, in "On 'Failed Totalitarianism.' "

[6] Jerry F. Hough and Merle Fainsod, *How the Soviet Union is Governed* (Cambridge: Harvard University Press, 1979). The book in fact has kept virtually nothing of Fainsod's original *How Russia Is Ruled* (Cambridge: Harvard University Press, 1963), which offered the classic statement of the totalitarian model. For urbanization as the supposed key to Sovietism, see Moshe Lewin, *The Gorbachev Phenomenon: A Historical Interpretation* (Berkeley and Los Angeles: University of California Press, 1988).

[7] See *Cultural Revolution in Russia, 1928–1931*, ed. Sheila Fitzpatrick (Bloomington, Ind.: University of Indiana Press, 1978), especially the essays by S. Fitzpatrick and J. Hough; and Sheila Fitzpatrick, *The Russian Revolution* (New York: Oxford University Press, 1982), especially 8, 157, and 159.

[8] *Politics, Society and Nationality Inside Gorbachev's Russia*, ed. Seweryn Bialer (Boulder and London: Western Press, 1989).

[9] The theme of Mikhail Heller and Alexander Nekrich, *Utopia in Power*, transl. Phillis B. Carlos (New York: Simon and Schuster, 1985). First published in Russian (London: Overseas Press, 1982).

[10] Adam Michnik, "Towards a Civil Society: Hopes for Polish Democracy," *Times Literary Supplement* (4, 429) 19–25 February 1988: 188, 198–99.

[11] See especially the essays of Pierre Hassner, Jacques Rupnik, and Aleksander Smolar in *Totalitarismes*, ed. Guy Hermet (Paris: Economica, 1984).

[12] Paul Thibaud, "Réflexions sur la décomposition des communismes," *Notes de la Fondation Saint-Simon* (July 1989).

[13]Leszek Kołakowski, *Main Currents of Marxism*, transl. P. S. Falla, vol. 3 (Oxford: Clarendon Press, 1978), 523.

[14]For a convenient short course in revisionist history on 1917 as a proletarian revolution, see Ronald Suny, "Toward a Social History of the October Revolution," *American Historical Review* 88 (1) (February 1983).

[15]See Thomas Remmington, *Building Socialism in Bolshevik Russia: Ideology and Industrial Organization, 1917–1921* (Pittsburgh: University of Pittsburgh Press, 1984); and Silvana Malle, *The Economic Organization of War Communism, 1918–1921* (New York: Cambridge University Press, 1985).

[16]See Laszlo Szamuely, *First Models of the Socialist Economic Systems* (Budapest: Akademiai Kiado, 1974).

[17]Alec Nove, *Was Stalin Really Necessary?* (New York: Praeger, 1965).

[18]The classic statement of this position is Stephen Cohen, *Bukharin and the Bolshevik Revolution* (New York: Oxford University Press, 1980[1971]). See also Moshe Lewin, *Lenin's Last Struggle*, transl. A. M. Sheridan Smith (New York: Random House, 1970). The most sophisticated elaboration of this position is Lewin's *Russian Peasants and Soviet Power*, transl. Irene Nove and John Biggard (Evanston, Ill.: Northwestern University Press, 1968).

[19]For the essentially political nature of the Great Break, see especially Alexander Gerschenkron, *Economic Backwardness in Historical Perspective* (Cambridge: Harvard University Press, 1962), passim. See also Alexander Erlich, *The Soviet Industrialization Debate, 1924–1918* (Cambridge: Harvard University Press, 1960).

[20]Robert Conquest, *The Harvest of Sorrow* (New York: Oxford University Press, 1986). The best general work on the Stalin period as a whole remains Adam B. Ulam, *Stalin: the Man and his Era* (Boston: Beacon Press, 1987).

[21]For the revision of Soviet growth statistics, see Abram Bergson, *The Real National Income of the Soviet Union since 1928* (Cambridge: Harvard University Press, 1961). For the comparison with Russia under Witte, see Gerschenkron, chaps. 6 and 10.

[22]For example, John Kenneth Galbraith, *The New Industrial State* (Boston: Houghton Mifflin, 1967), and Wassily Leontiev, "The Decline and Rise of Soviet Economic Science," *Foreign Affairs* 38 (January 1960): 261–72.

[23]Boris Pasternak, *Doctor Zhivago*, transl. Max Hayward and Manya Harari (London: Collins and Harvil Press, 1958), 422.

[24]Interpretive literature on the Great Purges is both sparse and shallow. The view expressed here draws on Heller and Nekrich; Ulam; Nicholas Werth, *Les Procès de Moscou* (Brussels: Editions Complexe, 1987); and Jonathan Haslam, "Political Opposition to Stalin and the Origins of the Terror in Russia, 1932–1936," *The Historical Journal* 29 (2) (1986): 395–418.

[25]Robert Conquest, *The Great Terror* (New York: Macmillan, 1968), now being published legally in the Soviet Union. For Medvedev's most recent estimate of Purge victims, see *Argumenti i Facty* (September 1989).

[26]Alexis de Tocqueville, "Introduction," in vol. 1, *De la démocratie en Amérique, Oeuvres Complètes*, 6.

[27] For example, the last sections of Joseph Schumpeter, *Capitalism, Socialism and Democracy*, 3d ed. (New York: Harper and Row, 1950).

[28] Gavriil Popov, *Puti perestroiki: mnenie ekonomista* (Moscow: Ekonomika, 1989) is the most recent statement of this influential critic of the Soviet economy and society.

[29] The most relevant items are: *CIA Handbook of Economic Statistics* for 1987 and 1988; Robert Gates, *Revisiting Soviet Economic Performance Under Glasnost: Implications for CIA Estimates* (1988), a critique of the preceding item. On the Soviet side see especially the relatively optimistic early item of Abel Aganbegyan, *The Economic Challenge of Perestroika*, transl. Pauline M. Tifflin (Bloomington, Ind.: Indiana University Press, 1988) and his more recent and rather alarmist *Inside Perestroika, The Future of the Soviet Economy* (New York: Harper and Row, 1989). Recent Soviet estimates of their economy's performance tend to be lower than Western ones, and the most recent are the lowest of all. It is these estimates that have been followed here. For a statement of the misleading character of attempting to measure the Soviet economy at all in Western terms, see Alain Besançon, *Anatomie d'un Spectre* (Paris: Calmann-Levy, 1981). This work also effectively brings out the "surreal" nature of the Soviet world in general, a factor the dominant Western social science approach quite misses.

[30] Pierre Daix, *L'Avènement de la nomenklatura: La Chute de Khrouchtchev* (Brussels: Editions Complexe, 1982).

[31] Mikhail Voslensky, *Nomenklatura: the Soviet Ruling Class*, transl. Eric Mosbacher (Garden City, N.Y.: Doubleday, 1984). Published several years earlier in Russian and German, this work brought the nomenklatura's role to world attention.

[32] See, for example, Konstantin Simes, *U.S.S.R.: The Corrupt Society, The Secret World of Soviet Capitalism* (New York: Simon and Schuster, 1982).

[33] Tatiana Zaslavskaia, "The Novosibirsk Report," *Survey* 28 (1) (1984): 88–108. An early and perceptive Western statement of the growing contradictions of Sovietism is Seweryn Bialer's *The Soviet Paradox: External Expansion, Internal Decline* (New York: Knopf, 1986).

[34] The best treatment of the beginnings of perestroika is Michel Tatu's *Gorbachev: L'U.R.S.S., va-t-elle changer?* (Paris: Le Centurion-Le Monde, 1987).

[35] The most comprehensive collection of reformist intelligentsia writings was issued for the June 1988 Special Party Conference. See *Inogo ne dano*, ed. Iuri Afanasiev (Moscow: Izdatel'stvo Progress, 1988). A partial translation exists in French under the title *La Seule Issue* (Paris: Alban Michel, 1989). For the geneology of the submerged tradition of soft communism from the 1920s on, see Moshe Lewin, *Political Undercurrents in Soviet Economic Debates: From Bukharin to the Modern Reformers* (Princeton, N.J.: Princeton University Press, 1974).

[36] Quoted in *Le Monde*, 20 December 1988.

[37] Quoted in *Russkaia Mysl' (La pensée russe)* (Paris), 4 August 1989.

[38] Igor Kliamkin, *Moscow News*, 15 April 1989.

[39] Sakharov's speech at the Congress launching his idea was reproduced in *The New York Review of Books*, 17 August 1989, 25–26.

[40]The best discussion of the background to Gorbachev's economic reforms and the development of his early programs is Ed. H. Hewett, *Reforming the Soviet Economy* (Washington, D.C.: The Brookings Institution, 1987). On the Soviet side see Tatiana Zaslavskaia, in *A Voice of Reform: Essays by Tatiana Zaslavskaia*, ed. Murray Yanovitch (Armonk, N.Y.: M. E. Sharpe, 1989) and especially Nikolai Shmelyov and Vladimir Popov's *Na perelome* (*At the Breaking Point*) (Moscow: Ekonomika, 1989).

[41]The most informed, penetrating, and realistic study of economic perestroika's record to date is Anders Åslund, *Gorbachev's Struggle for Economic Reform* (Ithaca, N.Y.: Cornell University Press, 1989).

[42]The best general treatments to date of the Gorbachev era overall are: Alec Nove, *Glasnost in Action: Cultural Renaissance in Russia* (Boston: Unwin Hyman, 1989), which is moderately pessimistic; and Walter Laqueur, *The Long Road to Freedom: Russia and Glasnost* (New York: Scribners, 1989), which is distinctly pessimistic. A strong statement of the internal contradictions of Gorbachevism is Vladimir Bukovsky's "Who Resists Gorbachev?" *Washington Quarterly* (Winter 1989).

[43]The scissors metaphor was applied to Gorbachev by the historian Sergio Romano, Italian ambassador to Moscow during the last four years. It will be the theme of his forthcoming book, in Italian, on perestroika.

[44]Andrei Amalrik, *Will the Soviet Union Survive Until 1984?* (New York: Harper and Row, 1970).

[45]Andranik Migranyan, *Literaturnaia Gazeta*, 16 August 1989.

[46]Milovan Djilas and George Urban, "Djilas on Gorbachev," *Encounter* 71 (September-October 1987): 3–19.

[47]For an example of his thought, see Stefan Kisielewski, *Polen-Oder die Herrschaft der Dilletanten: Sozialismus und Wirtschaftspraxis* (Zurich: Edition Interform, 1978).

December 1989

POSTSCRIPT

A minor mystery began in the Winter 1990 issue of *Dædalus* with an article entitled "To the Stalin Mausoleum" and signed "Z," which was simultaneously excerpted on the *New York Times* Op-Ed page. After another visit to the Soviet Union this past summer, I feel that the time has come to explain this anonymity. More important still, in the wake of the XVIII (and no doubt last) Soviet Party Congress, and especially of Boris Yeltsin's

This Postscript is by Martin Malia. An earlier version of this text was published in *The Bulletin of the American Academy of Arts and Sciences,* 44 (November 1990).

rise as parallel Soviet leader, it is pertinent to assess the article's relevance to the continuing communist drama.

In the August heat of our first post–Cold War year it became manifest that the Soviet Union, modestly aligning itself with the United States and the United Nations, was no longer a superpower. Less obviously, this is so because "the Soviet Union no longer exists" (as one now hears in Moscow), either as a coherent polity or as a functioning economy. And this stunning fact will weigh on world affairs for years after the Gulf crisis has ended.

WHY "Z"?

But first the "mystery." In scholarship or journalism the only justification for anonymity is protection of the author, his associates, or sources. In the remote period of October 1989 when I was writing, this concern was germane, for the fall of the Berlin Wall and the collapse of Central European communism had not yet demonstrated that Leninist regimes are mortal.

The "leading role of the Party" had been openly challenged by Andrei Sakharov at the June 1989 Congress of People's Deputies; he also challenged the "secret empire" of the KGB; conversion to the market was still a taboo topic. Thus Solidarity visitors to Moscow, though already heading the Warsaw government, anxiously inquired where the "red line" of the Kremlin's tolerance might lie.

In this context, my article could appear in Moscow as provocatively anti-perestroika. For its thrust was that, because of structural reasons going back to 1917, communism was irreformable; it could only be wholly dismantled if the nations it had ruined were to survive. Gorbachev's half-measures thus encouraged the illusion of reformability and put off the moment of truth for the system. I took this hard line because of the inveterate overestimation by mainline Western sovietology of communism's achievement and of its potential for "within-system reform." Even more, I wished to give urgent expression to analyses, long axiomatic in Warsaw and Budapest, but only then becoming current among Soviet liberals.

It is ironic that these views, considered "left" in the East, were interpreted as "Cold War" or "neocon" by some U.S. commentators on "To the Stalin Mausoleum." In fact, the article advanced a hard analysis coupled with a soft policy conclusion, advocating arms control and aid to the Soviet private sector.

This assessment was confirmed by my return visit to Moscow during the summer of 1990. Members of the Moscow intelligentsia who had read the *Times* excerpt from the article by "Z" in the *Moscow News* thought it was by a disabused Soviet. Persons with good connections in the Central Committee Secretariat told me that the whole article had been translated into Russian for restricted, governmental circulation and that it had had a sobering impact on thinking during the January-February Plenum of the Central Committee.

But in Moscow in 1989, as I was told at that time, such sober views were "ten months ahead of what could prudently be said openly." My experience during the Khrushchev thaw also inclined me to caution—for example, friends to whom I had loaned *Doctor Zhivago* were later interrogated by the "Organs" and severely penalized. Because *Dædalus* was agreeable to anonymity to forestall compromising my friends, I signed "N. Perestroikin" in imitation of Vladimir Ulianov's practice of signing "N. Lenin" ("N" is the letter of anonymity in Russian).

When *Dædalus* editor Stephen Graubard showed proofs of the article to persons in New York, including eventually Leslie Gelb and William Safire of the *New York Times*, no one understood my pedantic allusion; all thought Perestroikin was a real person. So to make the fact of anonymity clear, someone suggested "Z." I was of course consulted (through *Dædalus*) and agreed to the change, though I did so reluctantly because it seemed pretentious. But there was no time to come up with an alternative before an excerpt, chosen by the *Times*, was printed. This solution, of course, was unfair to the Western sovietologists I had criticized; however, they now know their target.

CREEPING COLLAPSE
OF THE SOVIET UNION

But just as this precaution was taken, it became superfluous; for the unraveling of communism, begun in Berlin in November, crossed the Soviet border in January with Lithuania's move to independence and the Baku revolt. Matters cascaded in February when Gorbachev, under the impact of his own economic failures and of Poland's "shock therapy" liberalization, accepted the principle, at least, of marketization, while in politics he had to give way on the sacrosanct leading role of the Party. In March local elections brought to power in the major centers of Russia and the Ukraine the "democratic opposition" led by Gavriil Popov in Moscow, Anatoly Sobchak in Leningrad, and Yeltsin in Sverdlovsk, all soon to resign from the Party.

The program of this democratic movement was no mere restructuring of communism, but a genuine transition from totalitarianism to the sovereignty of civil society, through the phased liquidation of all the pillars of the system: Party, plan, police, and monolithic Union. Their positive goals were pluralistic democracy, private property, the market, and a negotiated federation, even republic independence.

This movement culminated at the end of May with Yeltsin's election, in direct defiance of Gorbachev, as president of the Russian Republic. This shock event catalyzed all the post-communist forces emerging from the rubble of Leninism. It led, first, to Russia's declaration of sovereignty, which broke the stalemate on federal reform, where Gorbachev had stalled since the Nagrony-Karabakh crisis broke out in 1988. This act, in effect, dissolved the Soviet Union by triggering thus far thirteen successive republican declarations of sovereignty or independence, together with movements for autonomy within Russia, notably in Siberia. Second, Russia's assertion of control over its natural resources and banking system at last forced the issue of privatization and the market, against which Gorbachev and Prime Minister Ryzhkov had stonewalled since 1988. This declaration led to Yeltsin's "500 day" program of transition to the market, which Gorbachev was soon compelled, at least verbally, to accept.

Moreover, Yeltsin has put together a large, young, and highly competent team of experts and won the support of the country's leading liberal figures. Long dismissed in the West as a demagogic populist, he has turned out to be an imaginative and constructive leader and the recognized spokesman for all reform movements from below.

In short, in six months in 1990 the Soviet Union went about half the distance covered by Central Europe during six weeks in 1989—halfway, because the husk of the old Party-state remains in place. What occurred was in fact a creeping collapse, a slow-motion implosion, of Soviet socialism, less spectacular than the fall of the Berlin Wall but just as portentous.

Clearly there is peril in this process because the Soviet Union is now dissolving into local political and economic units and is functioning increasingly through barter. But there is also promise because the real problems have at least been named and the population is being mobilized to meet them.

CAUSES FOR DISINTEGRATION

The first cause of this transformation was the boomerang effect of communism's mortality in Central Europe: The fact that the "conquests of socialism" could be reversed in so huge an area—and that the Kremlin could not prevent it—showed that socialism could be undone anywhere, even under the Kremlin's walls.

The second cause of this disintegration lay in the working out of the internal contradictions of Gorbachev's perestroika (as, I believe, they are described in "Z"'s analysis): a predominant emphasis on the politics of glasnost and democratization and a paralyzing timidity in facing up to economic reconversion.

This combination delegitimized and disrupted the old system, killing fear of central authority while generalizing penury. This conjunction of circumstances emboldened the democratic movement to take matters into its own hands, dismantling from below what Gorbachev had failed in five years to transform from above. Indeed, the experience of Central Europe indicates that it is only in this way, from outside the system, that the Party-state can ever be phased out.

"To the Stalin Mausoleum" proved less accurate in overestimating the staying power of the Party in the final crunch. On the one hand I argued that the terminal crisis was nigh, and on the other hand that the Party would fight to the bitter end for its hegemonic role. It turned out that the Party had far less fight left in it than I—or the Poles, or Gorbachev and Ligachev for that matter—ever imagined. The poisoned tunic of Nessus, after one stitch gave way, unraveled nonstop. At the same time, again unexpectedly, there had been no sharp breakdown and no answering crackdown, as many in Russia and the West (including myself) feared last January.

Nevertheless, the Party is by no means dead. The *apparat*, with its millions of members, is still in place and will fight (as in Romania) if directly assaulted. But its morale is shattered because the members know it has no future as an institution. The problem for the democratic opposition, then, is to roll it back gradually, so as not to panic it into overt resistance.

BALANCING GOVERNMENT
AFTER THE TRANSFORMATION

Thus, the situation in the Soviet Union is now extraordinary. The country is governed (if that is the right word) by an unstable and, no doubt, transitional triarchy. On the left there is the democratic movement based in the large cities and the more dynamic republics and regions. On the right there is the *apparat*, which controls the more backward provinces, the industrial ministries, the larger factories, much of the army, and the KGB. Soviet politics is now basically concerned with a struggle for power between these two factions, centering on control of Party real estate, state banks, the media, natural resources, and a declining economic product. In the center there is President Gorbachev and the Soviet government, more or less suspended in mid-air and increasingly irrelevant to the real political struggle at the local level.

Gorbachev and the official government wound up in this position for two reasons. First, Prime Minister Nikolai Ryzhkov failed, in three tries during the past six months, even to begin the transition to a market economy. This failure alienated the liberal left. Second, Gorbachev characteristically concerned himself too much with political tactics. This concern resulted in his efforts last winter to build a power base independent of the Party: an "executive presidency" equipped with decree power. This action also alienated the left. Then last summer he was wholly absorbed in keeping the Party Congress—initially called to give himself, at last, a perestroika majority in a new Central Committee—from falling into the hands of the disgruntled apparatchik right.

In a virtuoso performance Gorbachev kept control of the Congress and made its conservative majority reelect him general secretary; he defeated Ligachev, dismantled the Politburo, and emasculated the Central Committee, and then made the pliant Vladimir Ivashko his deputy secretary—in effect his overseer for a now side-lined Party. Simultaneously Gorbachev and his principal aides, such as Aleksandr Iakovlev and Eduard Shevarnadze, retired to an expanded "presidential council," apparently intended as a surrogate Politburo, but which in fact commands no administration to implement whatever policies it might develop or the decrees that Gorbachev might issue. This brilliant political performance was thus a hollow victory, for it left Gorbachev somewhat in the position of the Empress Dowager of China amid rival local warlords.

Thus, the era of perestroika, in its fifth year, came to an end. But to Gorbachev belongs the historical merit of having demonstrated, though no doubt in spite of himself, that communism is in fact irreformable. He also deserves credit for having prepared, again probably inadvertently, a new political class of post-communist leaders in the form of the democratic movement.

CONTINUED INVOLVEMENT

Since the economic summit meeting in Houston in July 1990, the West is on record in support of some type of Soviet transformation. And Soviet liberals warn that we must indeed support this effort, if only in self-defense; if a nuclear-armed Soviet Union collapses in anarchy, it could well take us with it. But what and whom should we support in the present fluid situation? Clearly not the failed structures of Party and plan; the democratic movement explicitly advocates such a boycott as well. Still, so long as those structures are partially in place—and they will be for some time—we will have to deal with them. And this necessitates a dual approach.

First, in international and central economic affairs, we must deal with President Gorbachev, even at the cost of some wasted aid. Because his main constituency is now in the West, he represents an international asset the democratic opposition cannot do without. But increasingly we must deal directly, and over Moscow's head, with the forces seeking to phase out communism at the local level, from Leningrad and the Baltic to Vladivostok and Sakhalin; and the leaders of these forces, from Yeltsin on down, are actively seeking such foreign contact.

At the same time we should realize that, at any level in the Soviet Union, we are dealing with a morass—as the hopeless obsolescence of the most successful communist state, East Germany, has recently revealed. So our phase-out support to the East will be an involvement of decades—as was the burden of containment that made possible the East's present exit from communism.

September 1990

About the Book and Editor

At a time of tremendous flux throughout Europe, this book provides solid analyses of the events and trends that are rapidly reshaping the region. Originally published as an edition of *Dædalus*, this updated volume brings together leading scholars to examine such issues as the major paradigmatic shifts occurring in Eastern Europe, the long-term role of Gorbachev, and the effects of glasnost and perestroika on the future of Europe.

Stephen R. Graubard is editor of *Dædalus* and professor of history at Brown University.

339

About the Contributors

Timothy Garton Ash is a Fellow at St. Antony's College, Oxford University.

Ivo Banac is professor of history and Master of Pierson College at Yale University.

Ernest Gellner is professor of social anthropology at Cambridge University.

Bronisław Geremek serves as Solidarity's floor leader in both houses of the Polish parliament and is a historian of medieval France.

Elemér Hankiss, president of Hungarian Television, is on leave as director of the Center for the Sociology of Values at the Institute of Sociology of the Hungarian Academy of Sciences in Budapest.

Tony Judt is professor of history in the Institute of French Studies at New York University.

János Mátyás Kovács is a Research Fellow of the Institute of Economics at the Hungarian Academy of Sciences in Budapest and Visiting Scholar at the Institute for Human Sciences in Vienna.

Jacques Rupnik is Senior Fellow at Fondation Nationale des Sciences Politiques (C.E.R.I.) in Paris.

George Schöpflin is lecturer in East European politics at the London School of Economics and at the School of Slavonic and East European Studies.

Josef Škvorecký is professor of English at the University of Toronto.

Z is **Martin Malia,** professor of Russian history at the University of California at Berkeley.

Index

Abalkin, Leonid, 319
Abkazians, 274
Absolutism, 147, 166, 174
Academic exchange, 11, 33
Adenauer, Konrad, 6, 246
Administrative market, 173, 179, 186
Afanasiev, Iuri, 313, 315
Afghanistan, Soviet invasion of (1979), 35, 44, 255
Aganbegyan, Abel, 311
Agriculture, 86, 88, 89. *See also* Peasantry; *under* Eastern Europe; *individual countries*
Air pollution, 247, 248
Albania, 146, 150, 163
  minorities, 153
  and Ottoman Empire, 152
  and Soviet Union, 151
  tribal society, 75
  and World War II, 149
Albanians, 148, 154, 157, 159, 160, 211
Albertz, Heinrich, 3
Ali Pashë Tepelena (Albanian ruler), 151
Almond, Gabriel, 172
Alpen-Adria group, 4
Alternative (journal), 32, 52(n9)
Amalrik, Andrei, 320
American uncle. *See* Exiles, return visits
Amerongen, Otto Wolff von, 9, 10
Anatolia, 274
"Anatomy of a Reticence, The" (Havel), 256
Andrássy, Gyula, 147
Andropov, Yuri, 309, 310, 311
Anti-alcohol campaign (1986) (Soviet Union), 311

Anti-Americanism, 121, 246. *See also under* Western Europe
Anticommunism, 27, 29, 31, 55, 77, 151, 305. *See also* Czechoslovakia, anti-Communists
Antifascist uprising (1923) (Bulgaria), 153
Anti-intellectualism, 57
Antikulak campaigns, 82
Antimaterialism, 39
Antipolitics, 4, 257
Anti-Semitism, 57, 77. *See also under* Poland
Anti-Stalinism, 156, 157. *See also* De-Stalinization
Aral Sea, 306
Arato, Andrew, 167
Arcimboldi, Josef, 138
Arendt, Hannah, 288, 289
Armenia, strikes (1988), 313
Armenians, 87, 273
Arms control, 333
Arms race, 256
Arms reduction, 3, 326. *See also* Disarmament
Aron, Raymond, 31, 34, 171
Assimilation, 147, 279
Association of Young Democrats (FIDESZ) (Hungary), 188(table)
Aufhebung, 156
Austria, 6, 24, 25, 40, 41, 42–43, 44, 60, 118, 122, 123, 146, 184
  environmental issues, 247, 248
  pre-1914, 66, 70, 238, 240
  See also under Central Europe
Austria-Hungary, 2, 25, 47, 75
Austro-Hungarian Empire, 25, 247
Austromarxists, 43

341

Eastern Europe, 1, 2, 8, 30, 43, 232, 255
 agriculture, 147, 203
 Communist parties, 17, 102, 163, 199
 concept, 146
 diversity in, 145–146, 147, 279
 economies, 147, 165–166, 181–182, 198, 200, 223, 225, 231
 and European Community, 41
 medieval, 147
 and military service, 39
 and national identity, 146
 nationalism, 149–150, 151–153, 164, 279
 and Nazi Germany, 28
 organizational principles, 167, 173, 175, 176, 195(n42)
 political traditions, 59–60, 65–91
 post–World War I, 148
 revolutionary change in (1989), 225, 230, 233
 rural, 92, 147
 Sovietization of, 28, 150
 and Soviet Union, 27–28, 29, 30, 41, 60, 91, 150, 233, 246, 253
 and the West, 27
 and World War II, 148–149, 150
 See also Soviet bloc; *individual countries*
Eastern front (1944–1945), 5
East European Reporter (journal), 32
East Germany, 3, 6, 41, 146, 247, 263, 338
 anti-*perestroika,* 251
 Communist party. *See* Socialist Union party
 economy, 8, 11, 15, 111
 environmental issues, 247
 labor force, 8, 11
 Left, 90
 nationalism, 152
 "October Revolution" (1989), 21, 233, 322
 peace movement, 38, 249, 255, 256
 and Poland, 252, 253–254, 264
 political prisoners, 15, 16
 politics, 90, 91

riots (1953), 102
 and Soviet Union, 14–15, 110, 249–250, 252
 working class, 89, 90, 91
 See also Central Europe, East German view; German unification; *under* West Germany
East-West relations, 6, 10, 13, 256, 284–285
Ebert, Friedrich, Foundation, 4, 246
"Ecolo-pacifism," 253
Economic cycle, 111
Edelman, Murray, 172
Education, 81, 85, 117, 186
Egalitarianism, 191, 309, 316
Eisenstadt, S. N., 168, 169, 174
Eliade, Mircea, 33, 34, 45
Elites, 67, 68, 69, 70, 71, 72, 73–74, 76, 79, 80, 84, 85, 86, 88, 92, 150–151, 174, 175, 179, 181, 182, 195(n42)
 consumption, 89
 values, 87
Emigrants, 115–116, 118, 121–122, 123, 132
Emigré journals, 32, 52(n9), 126, 127, 131–132
END. *See* European Nuclear Disarmament
Energy, 6, 248
Enlightenment, 65, 67
Enterprise autonomy, 202
Entrepreneurial agriculturist, 81–82
Entrepreneurial class, 69, 70, 71, 75, 87. *See also* Bourgeoisie
Entrepreneurship, 191, 214
Environmental issue, 11, 247–249
Estonia, 25, 247, 269, 278, 281–282
 Communist party, 276, 277
 economy, 277, 282
 Germans in, 278, 281
 nationalism, 275–277, 313
 and Soviet Union, 150, 246
 Swedes in, 278
Etatism, 66, 92, 173–174, 177, 179, 186, 216

Oligarchy, 166, 174, 175,
178(table), 179, 180, 184, 186,
187, 198
One Day in the Life of Ivan Denisovich
(Solzhenitsyn), 308
One-party system, 166, 173, 174,
177, 178(table), 179, 180, 186,
212, 225, 292, 323
Opposition parties, 76, 187,
188(table), 225
Organizational principles, 166–168
structural non-correspondence,
169–172, 174–176, 178(table),
179–180
Western, 169–173
See also Reform economics; *under*
Eastern Europe; Hungary
Orjonikidze, Sergo, 292, 307
Orthodox Church, 148, 160, 163,
268, 273, 278
Ossetians, 274
Osteuropapolitik. See West Germany,
and Eastern Europe
Osthandel, 9–10
Ostpolitik, 2, 3, 6–7, 8–11, 17, 42,
250, 251, 252, 253
defined, 8–9
Ottoman Empire, 60, 66, 72, 75,
148, 152
Oxenstierna, Axel G., 121
Oxford University, 33, 46, 63

Palacky, Frantisek, 243
Pale of Settlement, 87
Pannonia group, 4, 207
Pannonius, Janus, 147
Pan-Slavic tradition, 99
Parenti, M., 172
Paris Peace Settlement (1919), 78
Parliamentary democracy, 55, 187,
263
Partisan movement (Yugoslavia),
155, 156, 157, 158
Party-state. *See* One-party system
Pasternak, Boris, 302
Pastoralism, 270
Paternalism, 178(table)
Patočka, Jan, 99
Patrician-military-mercantile elite,
70

PCI. *See* Italy, Communist party
Peace initiative (1979), 31
Peace movement. *See under* East
Germany; West Germany
Peasant insurrection (13th century
Bulgaria), 152–153
Peasantry, 74, 76, 79, 80–84, 89,
92, 147, 267–268, 270, 271,
286, 294, 295–296, 298, 317
political parties, 76, 80, 83–84,
98
production strike (1918), 296
socioeconomic categories, 81–83
values, 81, 82, 84
and World War I, 83. *See also*
War Communism
Peasant War (1525), 152
People's party (Austria), 43
Perestroika (1985), 15, 49, 110, 251,
252, 270, 277, 280, 284, 285,
286, 287, 294, 304, 310, 311,
312, 314, 315, 316–317, 323,
324, 325–326, 327
aim of, 326
contradictions of, 303, 321, 325
crisis of, 290, 312, 318, 319–320,
321, 337
Perestroika and New Thinking
(Gorbachev), 287
Perle, Richard, 6
Pershing missiles, 31
Persia, 272–273
Personal politics, 76–77
Peter the Great (tsar of Russia),
277
Pětka, 71
Petöfi Club (Budapest), 105
Phillipse, Frederick, 117
Pilsudski, Jósef, 244
Pinochet, Augusto, 289, 322
Pirenne, Henri, 96
Plan and market (PM), 201, 202–
203, 204, 205, 206, 208, 210,
211, 212, 224, 225
Planned economy, 178(table), 179,
181–182, 210, 214, 291, 310,
323
Planometrics, 207